STUDIES IN THE HISTORY
OF CHRISTIAN MISSIONS

R. E. Frykenberg
Brian Stanley
General Editors

STUDIES IN THE HISTORY OF CHRISTIAN MISSIONS

Opening China

Karl F. A. Gützlaff and
Sino-Western Relations, 1827-1852

Jessie Gregory Lutz

WILLIAM B. EERDMANS PUBLISHING COMPANY
GRAND RAPIDS, MICHIGAN / CAMBRIDGE, U.K.

Published 2008 by
Wm. B. Eerdmans Publishing Co.
2140 Oak Industrial Drive N.E., Grand Rapids, Michigan 49505 /
P.O. Box 163, Cambridge CB3 9PU U.K.

Printed in the United States of America

14 13 12 11 10 09 08   7 6 5 4 3 2 1

Library of Congress Cataloging-in-Publication Data

Lutz, Jessie Gregory, 1925-
Opening China: Karl F. A. Gützlaff and Sino-Western relations, 1827-1852 /
Jessie Gregory Lutz.
p.   cm.   — (Studies in the history of Christian missions)
Includes bibliographical references.
ISBN 978-0-8028-3180-4 (pbk.: alk. paper)
1. Gützlaff, Karl Friedrich August, 1803-1851.
2. Missions — China.   3. Missionaries — China — Biography.
4. Missionaries — Germany — Biography.   I. Title.

BV3427.G8L88   2008
266.0092 — dc22
[B]

2007042551

www.eerdmans.com

In Memory of Ray

Contents

Contents

Foreword

What Jessie Lutz has accomplished in her work can perhaps be more fully appreciated by contextualizing the career of Karl Gützlaff, both in geographical and historical and in cultural and sociological terms. Without a wider perspective of this kind, his arrival in Macau and Guangzhou (Canton), following in the wake of missionary arrivals that had began half a millennium earlier, cannot be adequately understood. Indeed, without reference to processes stretching back to the earliest beginnings of Christianity, insights become blurred.

Throughout this longer history, two features characterized such processes. One is that Christianity has always been migratory, but its presence almost everywhere has been transitory, so that from its beginnings Christianity has never found any single or permanent abiding place. The other is that Christianity has never been fully captured, contained, or encapsulated within any single culture or language. Taken together with several parallel yet intermingled processes, these features provide a matrix for understanding Christian movements in modern China.

James Kurth labelled the imperative of the gospel "one of the most profound revolutions the world has ever known."[1] The spreading of this gospel

1. "Religion and Globalization," *Foreign Policy Research Institute WIRE* (28 May 1999), 7:7 [The 1998 Templeton Lecture on Religion and World Affairs]. Email address: fpri@aol.com [*Orbis* 42:2 (Spring 1998)].

I am deeply grateful to my colleague, co-editor, and friend, Brian Stanley, for critical comments and useful suggestions, in helping me to write this Foreword. Over the years, I have continued to benefit from his sharp eye and shrewd insights.

was never, even from its very earliest beginnings, supposed to be optional. For all followers of Jesus,[2] this was an ideology that was by its very nature expansive, transcultural, and globalizing. Yet its universalizing claims also required localizing incarnation in flesh and blood, ethnic or indigenous expression, and in particularities of each local culture. It could never function as a mere abstraction, but had to be realized in concrete earthly manifestations, not merely as a disembodied or spiritual reality (as the Gnostics tried to assert). Thus, with each new wave of expansion, the very nature of the gospel itself was refashioned in the light of what each people knew and were able to comprehend of eternal truth.

What was refashioned, in other words, was something that, in each instance, sank roots deep into local cultural soil — within each particular people that was touched during some one specific time. Thus, within a mere half-century of its beginnings, the initial milieu in Jerusalem had already been profoundly altered and shifted, if not buried, when the city was destroyed in 70 A.D. Subsequent interactions in the Greco-Roman world, in Celtic, Germanic, and Slavic cultures, and within the cultures of Mesopotamia, Armenia, Ethiopia, India, Persia, and China, led to amazing metamorphosing manifestations of the gospel. Each expansion generated its own distinctive ceremonies, creeds and doctrines, institutions and ideals, qualities and styles of life. Consequent variations brought localized forms of expression, as Christian truths found reincarnation within new languages. Changes developed in new and even unpredictable ways. Many such transformations have yet to be fully studied or understood. Some, quite probably, are beyond historical recovery.

It is all too easy to forget that the westward movements of the Christian message and mission from Antioch into Latin, Celtic, Nordic, and Slavic lands were paralleled and indeed preceded by eastward movements that took the gospel down the valley of the Euphrates and then beyond Babylon, steadily further and further eastward to Arabs of the sea, to Persians in Zoroastrian domains, to Turko-Mongols of the steppes, and onward, to peoples of India and China.[3] Beyond the eastern frontier of the Roman Empire, Christianity became the official religion of Armenia well before it became official

---

2. "Go forth to every part of the world and proclaim the Good News [gospel] to the whole of creation" (Mark 16:15); ". . . Bear witness of me in . . . to the ends of the earth" (Acts 1:8).

3. H. J. W. Drijvers, *East of Antioch: Studies in Early Syriac Christianity* (London: 1984). Robin E. Waterfield, *Christians in Persia: Assyrians, Armenians, Roman Catholics and Protestants* (London: 1973).

in Rome; and Syriac rather than Greek writings addressed cosmic struggles between Darkness and Light, rather than categories of Greek philosophy.[4]

One of the anomalies of historical contextualization is that the tensions between faith and force, between things belonging to God and belonging to Caesar — in short, between claims of Christianity and claims of Christendom — never ceased. Christendoms as "kingdoms on earth" laying claim to the whole of Christianity invariably proved to be delusory. The idea that faith can be forced upon hearts and minds, or imposed by coercion and violence, has flown in the face of history. Thus the writer who penned the canonical Letter to the Hebrews (11:13) could declare: "These all died in faith, not having received the promises, but having seen them afar off, and embraced them, confessing that they were strangers and pilgrims upon the earth."

Before modern missionaries came to Canton (Guangzhou), Christianity had already come to China at least three times. First, in the seventh century, missionaries sent from the Church of the East in Edessa, Nisibis, Seleucia-Ctesiphon, and outposts of Sassanian Persia brought the faith into T'ang China. The importance of the political position it once seems to have enjoyed was spectacularly revealed when, in 1625, a great stone-slab, dating from 781, was unearthed. This monument, cut on orders of the Emperor, celebrated the place of Christian truth within his realm. Second, during the thirteenth century, Christian tribes from the high steppes and Catholic missionaries both sought to influence the Yuan (Mongol) Empire of Kublai Khan in Beijing. And third, during the seventeenth century, due to learned Jesuit missionaries such as Matteo Ricci, highly placed Mandarin Christians of the late Ming realm exercised astounding authority as ministerial Keepers of the Imperial Calendar. The number of Chinese Christians may have swelled to over three hundred thousand. Yet influence in the highest seats of power waned and Catholic Christians struggled for survival, such that, from 1724 onward, they suffered from official hostility and persecution. Thus, prior to the nineteenth century, Christianity in China had already been present, in some form, for some 1200 years.

The fourth, or modern, movement of Christian entry into China that began with Karl Gützlaff and other pioneers such as Robert Morrison, was not a "top-down" attempt to impose Christendom. In the face of official opposition, the Christianity brought to China in the nineteenth century was more pietistic in nature. Missionaries concentrated on translation, literacy, and learning, rather than establishing a Chinese Christendom. Good thing, too,

---

4. For more on this perspective, see Andrew F. Walls, "Eusebius Tries Again: Reconceiving the Study of Christian History," *International Bulletin of Missionary Research* 24:3 (July 2000): 105-11.

because the breaking of East India Company's commercial privileges by inter-lopers, pirates, and smugglers, along with the Opium War, the Taiping Rebel-lion, and the "Open Door" intrusions that undermined the Middle Kingdom, brought anything but the kingdom of God on earth. Rather, in the face of vio-lence and war, the modern forms of Christianity that gradually spread would have to take root as localized, indigenous movements.

A two-way process of mutual appropriation entered China two centuries ago. This has continued down to this day, and is still going on. The intricacy of this double process, this two-way flow of information, lies at the heart of this study of Karl Gützlaff. Jessie Lutz shows us that that role of missionaries, how-ever crucial, was secondary in the dynamic of Christian dissemination. Like al-chemists, they strove to transform the gospel into golden idioms that might then be appropriated by the peoples of China. Yet, as "double agents," or two-way conduits, their role was almost invariably, even inescapably, also ambigu-ous and controversial. In pursuit of success, they could be perceived as betray-ers of hallowed verities. Thus the fact that Gützlaff became a highly controver-sial figure seems hardly surprising. His association with the opium trade further complicated matters; it gave him and his gospel message unusual ac-cess to remote areas, but often at a substantial cost to the very credibility of that message. One of the virtues of Lutz's treatment of her subject lies in her way of placing such ambiguity and controversy into a judicious perspective.

Gützlaff and other nineteenth-century missionaries seeded and nurtured Christianity in China with high hopes for dramatic results. They were disap-pointed far more often than not. Gützlaff had grander dreams than most, and such grandiosity fuelled his support, and his celebrity, in Europe. But in his lifetime his dreams for China never came true, and his bold vision may have been, at least in part, his undoing. Yet the story doesn't end there. While zeal for Christianity in Europe has waned since Gützlaff's day, it has only grown in China, where some estimates now place the number of Christians at 65 to 70 million, if not more.[5] Such dramatic growth of Christianity in China makes re-examination of Gützlaff's life and legacy all the more needful. The editors of this series hope you will agree that this volume admirably meets that need.

ROBERT ERIC FRYKENBERG
The University of Wisconsin–Madison
Missionskonferenz in Herrnhut
October 2007

5. Simon Elegant, "The War for China's Soul," *Time*, August 20, 2006; "O Come All Ye Faithful," *The Economist*, November 1, 2007.

Preface

First, I should like to express my appreciation to Suzanne W. Barnett and John K. Fairbank for introducing me to Karl Gützlaff (1803-1851). After writing a paper for their seminar, "Karl F. A. Gützlaff, Missionary Entrepreneur,"[1] I wanted to know more about this fascinating, conflicted man. How could one be so arrogant, insecure, linguistically talented, pious, and yet willing to assist the opium trade; impatient with authority and yet able to hold an office with the Hong Kong administration for a decade; an ardent Protestant evangelist and yet willing to act as a scout for British troops during the Opium War? I still am not able to give a definitive answer to these questions, but I do think that I now understand Gützlaff better. He was in many ways a product of his time, a time when a self-confident, ethnocentric West was expanding to all parts of the earth and when the Second Great Awakening was rejuvenating evangelical missions. Gützlaff was not so much unique among pioneer Protestant missionaries to China of the second quarter of the nineteenth century as an exaggerated expression of their strengths and failings. On several occasions during the 1830s and 1840s, his hyperbole about the glorious opportunities to evangelize all China was followed by deep disappointment about the reality of an open China. Such experiences became background to the "love-hate" attitude that has ever since characterized relations between China and the West, particularly the United States. Gützlaff's dream of evangelizing all China by employing Chinese catechists collapsed in shambles. He died in disgrace, his missionary career considered a failure.

1. Lutz, in *Christianity in China: Early Protestant Missionary Writings,* ed. Suzanne W. Barnett and John K. Fairbank (Cambridge, MA: Harvard University Press, 1985), pp. 61-88.

As I learned more about Gützlaff's career, I realized that for a quarter of a century he had been at the center of Western activities relating to China in numerous spheres. He had participated in the knowledge transfer east and west, and in myth-making. Adept at propagandizing, he had stimulated Western interest in China and Christian missions. As Chinese interpreter for the Hong Kong government, he had sometimes pled the cause of the Chinese; on the other hand, he believed in free trade, open international relations between sovereign states, and religious tolerance, specifically tolerance of Christianity. On these matters he pled the British cause. He could, I decided, serve as a lens through which to reexamine Sino-Western relations during the crucial years from 1827 to 1852. I discovered, in addition, that his proselytizing efforts had a legacy in the Hakka Christian church and in a number of early Chinese evangelists who began "Sinifying" Christianity. He preached an evangelical Protestantism which continues to have echoes in the independent Chinese churches of the twentieth century and in the Chinese church today, especially the "house churches."

When a book had been this long in gestation, one incurs innumerable debts. I should like first to thank all those archive librarians who were so patient and helpful, particularly Martha Smalley of Yale Divinity School Special Collections, Paul Jenkins and Waltrud Haas of the Basel Mission Society Archive, Rosemary Seton of the London School of Asian Studies, J. M. Walpole of the Selly Oak Colleges Library, John Wells of the Jardine Matheson Archives, Cambridge University, and Barbara Faulenbach of the United Evangelical Mission, Wuppertal, Germany. How would scholars work without such wonderful librarians!

I am grateful for permission to draw material from the following previously published items:

Lutz, Jessie. "The Grand Illusion: Karl Gützlaff and Popularization of China Missions in the United States during the 1830s," in *United States Attitudes and Policies toward China: The Impact of American Missionaries.* Ed. Patricia Neils. Armonk, NY: M. E. Sharpe, 1990. Pp. 46-77.

———. "Karl Gützlaff and Changing Chinese Perceptions of the World during the 1840s," in *Jidujiao yu Zhongguo wenhua congkan* (Christianity and cultural communication). Ed. Ma Min. Hubei: Hubei Jiaoyu chubanshe, 2003. Pp. 354-392.

———. "Karl F. A. Gützlaff: Missionary Entrepreneur," in *Christianity in China.* Eds. Barnett & Fairbank. Pp. 61-85.

———. "The Missionary-Diplomat Karl Gützlaff and the Opium War," in *Zhongguo jindai zhengjiao guanxi guoji xueshu yantaohui lunwenji*

(Proceedings of the first international symposium on church and state in China). Ed. Li Chifang. Taipei: Danjiang daxue, 1987.

———. "A Profile of Chinese Protestant Evangelists in the Mid-Nineteenth Century," in *Authentic Chinese Christianity.* Eds. Ku Wei-ying and Koen De Ridder. Leuven: Leuven University Press, 2001. Pp. 67-86.

Lutz, Jessie G., and R. R. Lutz. *Hakka Chinese Confront Protestant Christianity, 1850-1900.* Armonk, NY: M. E. Sharpe, 1998.

———. "Karl Gützlaff's Approach to Indigenization: The Chinese Union," in *Christianity in China.* Ed. D. Bays. Stanford: Stanford University Press, 1996. Pp. 269-291.

I am deeply indebted to Gary Tiedemann of the University of London, who furnished information about Gützlaff's family background and alerted me to new source materials. He also read the entire manuscript and offered numerous suggestions for improvement as well as corrections; for this I am most grateful. Thanks also to Bob Frykenberg and Brian Stanley for their support and help.

My greatest debt is to Ray, who translated all the sources in nineteenth-century German *handschrift,* who read and corrected numerous drafts, and who contributed much of the background material on nineteenth-century Germany. He was essential to the production of the work, and I am sure that if he were here, he would be pleased to see the manuscript finally in print. Of course, none of the above are responsible for any errors, which are mine alone.

In the text I have used pinyin transliteration except for the names for a few places and people better known in the West in their Westernized form. For Chinese authors I have retained the transliteration they employ. In footnote references to Barmen (Rhenish) and Basel holdings, the German transliteration of the archive has been kept as an aid to scholars.

JESSIE G. LUTZ

Abbreviations

ABCFM	American Board of Commissioners for Foreign Missions
ABS	American Bible Society
AJMR	*Asiatic Journal and Monthly Register*
ATM	*American Tract Magazine*
ATS	American Tract Society
BFBS	British and Foreign Bible Society
BMG	Basel Missions Gesellschaft, Archives of
BMM	*Baptist Missionary Magazine*
CMS	Church Missionary Society
CRep	*Chinese Repository*
CWM	Church World Mission Society
Dong-Xi	*Dong-Xi yang kao meiye tongzhizhuan*
EIC	British East India Company
EMM	*Evangelisches Missions-Magazin*
EMMC	*Evangelical Magazine and Missionary Chronicle*
ER	*Evangelischer Reishsbote*
FMC	*Foreign Missionary Chronicle*
HJAS	*Harvard Journal of Asiatic Studies*
International Bulletin	*International Bulletin of Missionary Research*
J-M	Jardine Matheson
Journal of the RAS	*Journal of the Royal Asiatic Society*
LMS	London Missionary Society
MH	*Missionary Herald*
MissReg	*Missionary Register*

Abbreviations

NAM	National Army Museum, Department of Records
NYO	*New York Observer*
NZG	Nederlandsch Zendeling Genootschap
SDUK	Society for the Diffusion of Useful Knowledge
VEM	Vereinte Evanglische Mission, Archives of Rheinische Missionsgesellschaft

The Changing Context of Sino-Western Relations and Protestant Missions, 1807-1851

Sino-Western exchange has a long history despite earlier theories about the autonomous development of Chinese civilization, beginning in the Wei and Yellow river basins and spreading southward. Many of the early exchanges were mediated through Arabs and peoples of inner Asia, but there were also direct contacts. The stories of the popularity of silk among the wealthy of the Roman Empire and the transmission of Buddhism from India to China are well known. But scholars are currently discovering evidence of Western imports on artifacts found in China: motifs and weaponry from early Middle Eastern cultures as well as designs from classical Rome. Later came famous travelers, some of whom settled in China. During the openness of the great Tang dynasty (618-907), Muslims, Jews, Zoroastrians, and Nestorian Christians came. Then there were Marco Polo of the thirteenth century and Zheng He, who voyaged to India, Ceylon, Africa, and even Aden in the fifteenth century. Except in the case of Buddhism, however, little is known about the exchange of ideas, values, and beliefs. Contacts were intermittent, and apparently there was little residue.

Only with the Jesuits and other Roman Catholic missionaries of the seventeenth and eighteenth centuries did significant cultural interchanges occur between China and Europe. Along with Christianity, the Jesuits brought information about mathematics (especially geometry), cartography, astronomy, and technology, particularly weaponry. Ideas about philosopher kings, religious tolerance, and a bureaucracy selected on the basis of merit and knowledge flowed westward. As trade grew, goods also traveled across the ocean in both directions, but most Western businessmen lived in their own enclaves, and both Chinese and European businessmen concentrated on profits. The Jesuit order was disbanded by the pope in 1773, not to be reestablished until 1814, and Christian proselytism was banned in 1724. Not until well into the nineteenth century did cultural contacts achieve the density and continuity conducive to significant change. Missionaries had a unique role in the interchange, for they dealt in the realm of faith and values, and their personal contacts reached into interior China.

The era of Protestant missionaries in China was actually quite short: only 150 years. In 1807 Robert Morrison, LMS, was the lone Protestant missionary on the China scene. He had gained legitimacy as a resident by serving as an interpreter for the British East India Company (EIC), and he could work only on the fringes of China in Macao and Canton. Within a century and a half, missionaries, both Protestant and Roman Catholic, had been ousted from the People's Republic of China. The period of legal evangelism in China was even briefer, only a little over a hundred years, from the mid-1840s to the mid-1950s. Under the shadow of gunboats, Westerners had gained the right in the 1840s to reside in five cities dubbed "treaty ports," and both Christianity and Christian evangelism were tolerated. Ten additional treaty ports were opened by the Treaty of Tianjin in 1858, and Westerners with passports could travel throughout the empire. Still, in 1860 only 168 Protestant missionaries were operating in China. Thereafter the number increased rapidly. By the turn of the century, over 700 Roman Catholic missionaries, 500,000 Chinese Roman Catholics, 1,300 Protestant missionaries, and more than 37,000 Protestant communicants were claimed.[1] Western trade and traders, military and foreign service personnel, tourists, and eventually scholars made their way to China.

During the nineteenth century the West was the seeker, motivated by some combination of the Faustian spirit and individual curiosity, Christ's commission to carry the gospel to all people, the lack of self-sufficiency of the European states, and a tradition of seafaring trade. The Chinese became convinced that the West needed China, but that China had no need for the West. As the Qianlong emperor wrote in his famous letter to King George III in 1793:

> As a matter of fact, the virtue and prestige of the Celestial dynasty having spread far and wide, the kings of the myriad nations come by land and sea with all sorts of precious things. Consequently, there is nothing we lack, as your principal envoy and others have themselves observed.

1. K. S. Latourette, *A History of Christian Missions in China* (London: Society for Promoting Christian Knowledge, 1929), pp. 328-29, 405-6, 479; Daniel H. Bays, "Missions and Christians in Modern China, 1850-1950" (paper delivered at the Symposium on American Missionaries and Social Change in China, Linfield College, McMinneville, OR, 14-17 July 1994). The figures would be higher if missionary wives had been included in the total.

We have never set much store on strange or ingenious objects, nor do we need any more of your country's manufactures. . . .[2]

As economic and cultural exchanges expanded, personal contacts inevitably increased. Thousands of Chinese encountered Westerners on a regular basis, whether as compradors, merchants, servants, translators, language tutors, laborers, transporters, converts, or teachers and pupils in parochial schools. A crucial period of gestation had begun as China slowly moved toward dramatic changes, even revolution in the twentieth century.

Karl Friedrich August Gützlaff (1803-1851) was one of the pioneer Protestant missionaries in daily contact with Chinese during the second quarter of the nineteenth century. Of German origin, he, like most of the English and American evangelists, was individualistic, ambitious, and adventurous. Like them, he was also deeply committed to the cause of bringing the gospel to all non-Christians of the world. China, as the most populous nation of all, was the focus of their efforts. The call to open China pervaded Gützlaff's writings. Despite the illegality of proselytizing in China and the prohibition against Chinese converting to Christianity in the 1830s, Gützlaff declared China open to Protestant evangelists. The masses, moreover, were receptive to the Christian message. But Gützlaff wore other hats as well. A prolific writer, he published Chinese-language works to introduce Chinese to Western civilization. Works in Western languages pled the cause of China missions while also introducing Westerners to Chinese civilization, and his two-volume work, *China Opened* (1838), was designed to serve these dual goals. It was subtitled: *A Display of the Topography, History, Customs, Manners, Arts, Manufactures, Commerce, Literature, Religion, Jurisprudence, etc. of the Chinese Empire.*

For Gützlaff, opening China also included opening China to Western trade and diplomatic relations as well as Christianity. The three were complementary. For over two years he was employed as an interpreter for the leading exporter of opium to China, the Jardine-Matheson Company. And for over sixteen years he served with the British administration, first in Canton-Macao and then in Hong Kong. In these several capacities, he participated in the Western expansion that became so closely identified with imperialism. He strongly supported British demands for access to China, even acting as scout for British troops during the Opium War, 1839-1842. According to Chang Hsi-pao, he was, between 1826 and 1851, an actor in most of the important aspects

2. Quoted in numerous places. See Teng Ssu-yü and John K. Fairbank, *China's Response to the West: A Documentary Survey, 1839-1923* (Cambridge, MA: Harvard University Press, 1954), p. 19.

of Sino-Western relations: evangelism, opium trading, the Opium War, negotiating the Treaty of Nanjing (1842), and knowledge exchange.[3] Gützlaff, however, also became a controversial figure in both the Protestant mission community and the British civil community in Hong Kong. It is not always easy to discover the reality that was Karl Gützlaff. Perhaps his use of four different names — Karl Gützlaff, Charles Gutzlaff, Philosinensis, and Gaihan — is indicative of his complexity.

The Changing Context of Sino-Western Relations during the Nineteenth Century

To understand the changing and diverse nature of Sino-Western relations during this crucial quarter-century, we must first look at some of the assumptions of the two cultures. The inhabitants of most great empires, whether Roman, Muslim, Greek, or Mughal, have considered themselves civilized compared to the rest of humankind. The same was true of Chinese and Westerners when they came into frequent and direct contact during the early nineteenth century. Not until a comparatively late stage did the idea emerge that there are different and valid civilizations, and that these civilizations normally meet and interact.[4] In China, religiosity centered on a diffuse folk religion infused with Buddhism and Daoism. The orthodox ideology was Neo-Confucianism, which was regulated by the state. In the West, despite theories of separation of church and state, the concept of Christendom was very much alive. The church was central to village culture and a venue for recreation and social life as well as worship. Moral standards were the province of the church, and the Genesis story of creation was widely accepted. God continued to be active in history, and the progress and prosperity of the West could ultimately be traced to God's favor and adherence to Protestant Christianity. In many ways Christianity did not seem any more separable from Western civilization than Confucianism was separable from Chinese civilization.

Significant differences existed nevertheless. Christianity was a proselytizing religion, whereas neither Confucianism nor Daoism sought to convert others, and Buddhism had long since given up active evangelism. Christianity

3. I have made more specific the statement of Chang Hsi-pao that Gützlaff played "a part in almost every major event on the China coast" during the second quarter of the nineteenth century. See Chang Hsi-pao, *Commissioner Lin and the Opium War* (Cambridge, MA: Harvard University Press, 1964), p. 26.

4. Bernard Lewis, "I'm Right, You're Wrong, Go to Hell," *Atlantic Monthly*, May 2003, pp. 36-42.

was exclusivist and had a strong sense of heresy, while most Eastern religions were inclusive and generally characterized by a sense of relativism or heterodoxy. The Great Awakening in the West, moreover, had brought a new impetus to evangelism as the duty of all Christian believers. Pietists like Gützlaff and the Basel missionaries might sail for China with the sole intent of spreading the Christian promise of salvation and making converts, but they found it difficult to separate nineteenth-century Protestantism from the essential gospel message. Neither abstinence from gambling, smoking, and alcohol, nor churches with steeples and Christian hymns, nor even strictures against prostitution and concubinage could be considered part of the original Christian doctrine. They were, however, practices that Protestant missionaries expected of their Chinese converts. As a rule, Protestants of the nineteenth century believed in the reality of Christendom and the universality of Christianity. How could the missionaries carry out Christ's commission if China remained closed to foreign intercourse? How could they transform China into a Christian nation if the dynasty forbade conversion to Christianity and even preaching the gospel? Missionaries joined in the demand for an open China and for religious tolerance. Mission activities spilled over into the realms of foreign relations, education, and the role of church and state. Karl Gützlaff, in his dual capacity as missionary and civil servant, did not hesitate to propagandize for a China open to trade and foreign relations along with evangelism. For him, the three were interdependent.

Strains of Protestantism

Since the 1980s the number of Chinese Christians has grown with surprising rapidity, so that Christians now form a significant, though still small, minority in the Chinese religious landscape. Christianity is, however, even more fragmented than in the nineteenth century. There are the official churches, the Roman Catholic Patriotic Church and the Three Self Patriotic movement, which are recognized and regulated by the government. In addition there are registered and unregistered "house churches," underground Catholic churches, and Catholic congregations that are tolerated by the government but outside the official Catholic church. New sects have arisen, based mostly in rural China and characterized by speaking in tongues, faith healing, lay leadership, and fundamentalism. Other sects are amalgams of Christian and folk traditions, whose status as Christian churches is questionable. Many are focused on the end times. Both the growth and the diversity of Christianity in China can be traced in part to the repressive policies of the Communist Party during the Cultural

Revolution and the subsequent discrediting of Maoism among many Chinese. Even so, scholars are searching for the roots of current Chinese Christianity and are asking whether there are continuities with nineteenth-century versions.

The Protestantism of the pioneer missionaries of the early nineteenth century, despite a shared worldview, was not uniform. Protestantism lacked the unifying structure and leadership of the Roman Catholic Church. Protestants found it difficult to limit variants, so that differences in the strains of Protestantism were even greater than those in Catholicism. To simplify a complex picture, one can contrast the confessional approach of the highly institutionalized denominations with the strong experiential emphasis of evangelicals, including Gützlaff. The ramifications of the divergence, especially as Gützlaff interpreted his role, could be extensive: disagreements over the definition of Christian conversion and the meaning of the baptismal rite, rejection of denominationalism, the degree of autonomy given to Chinese evangelists, and the amount of leeway they had in interpreting Christianity for their audiences, just to name a few. The Taiping Christians were, of course, closer to the evangelical wing; they used Gützlaff's translation of the Bible, and several of his converts joined the Taipings in Nanjing. Their goals, however, soon became as much political as religious, and after over a decade of turmoil, they went down to defeat. Their identification with Christianity reinforced widespread antagonism toward Christianity, especially among the gentry.

As the number of denominational missionaries grew and faster ships enabled the home boards to maintain closer supervision during the second half of the nineteenth century, the confessional strain became dominant. The mission establishment became highly institutionalized, with schools, social services, and hospitals drawing increasing attention and personnel. Urban centers were the principal locale of their central stations. Gützlaff and other evangelicals such as August Hanspach of the Berlin mission, William C. Burns of the English Presbyterian Church, and early Basel and Barmen missionaries had successors nevertheless. These successors and their Chinese assistants in the latter half of the nineteenth century modified Gützlaff's methods, but they still worked primarily in the rural interior and retained the experiential approach and non-denominationalism. They depended heavily on Chinese to make the initial contacts and to nurture the congregations at the substations. Much the same was true of the China Inland Mission, whose leader, Hudson Taylor, drew inspiration and influence from Gützlaff.[5] Many Hakka Christians converted by Gützlaff and his successors emigrated overseas, where they

5. A. J. Broomhall, *Hudson Taylor and China's Open Century* (London: Hodder and Stoughton, 1981-1982), 1:291-92, 324-25.

founded branch churches that still retain ties with churches at home and with organizations such as the Chong Zhen [Tsung Tsin] Mission, associated with Basel.[6] Several independent Chinese churches that sprang up during the early twentieth century represent continuities with both nineteenth-century Protestantism and Chinese Protestantism of the twenty-first century. Some sectors of these early independent churches function even today and contribute much to the dynamism of Christianity in China.[7]

Conversion: Its Significance and Meaning

Conversion in a society hostile to Christianity carries different consequences than does conversion in a Christian society such as the nineteenth-century West. In Europe and America, most Christians were reared in a Christian family. They attended church in their childhood; often they were baptized as infants or youths of twelve years or so. Confirmation or joining the church followed as a natural course of events, and even if one had a conversionary experience, it often meant an emotional reaffirmation of a faith already held. Certainly, there were always new converts lacking a Christian background, but for them as well as other Christians, society offered numerous support mechanisms. Conversion in a non-Christian environment could be much more stressful. Some Chinese who came to accept Christian teachings long hesitated to ask for baptism, a public rite with implications for familial and social relations. Christians could not participate in traditional ancestral and burial ceremonies, and they were forbidden to attend festivals for the local deities. They were required to adopt a new lifestyle, to practice monogamy, and to keep the Sabbath holy. All of these set them apart. Perhaps this explains why baptism assumed such importance for Chinese converts. As one missionary commented, they seemed to expect that a miraculous transformation would occur following baptism.[8] For

---

6. Jessie G. Lutz and Rolland R. Lutz, *Hakka Chinese Confront Protestant Christianity, 1850-1900* (Armonk, NY: M. E. Sharpe, 1998), pp. 258-61.

7. Daniel H. Bays, "The Growth of Independent Christianity in China, 1900-1937," in *Christianity in China, from the Eighteenth Century to the Present*, ed. Daniel H. Bays (Stanford: Stanford University Press, 1996), pp. 307-16. See also Lian Xi, "No Earthly Salvation: Wang Mingdao, John Sung, Watchman Nee, and the Rise of Indigenous Christianity in China" (paper presented at the annual meeting of the Association for Asian Studies, Boston, March 1999).

8. Phillip Winnes, "Sieben Sonntagen in Tschong-lok. Predikt. Taufunterricht Taufen" (Lilong, 1863), Basler Missionsgesellschaft Archives, China (BMG), A-1.5, no. 17.

them, it had implications similar to those of initiation into a Chinese religious sect.

Today in China, Christianity has found enough acceptance as a minority religion that conversion is less stressful. Some Chinese, as in the West, are reared in Christian families, and baptism with entrance into the church is expected. Nevertheless, one is a Christian within a religiously pluralistic society that is formally committed to atheism. Risks and penalties remain. Christianity is not normative, as it is for many in the West — even those Westerners who do not affiliate with a church. The term "cultural Christian" has different meanings in China and the West.

To complicate the issue further, missionaries themselves did not agree on the meaning of baptism. In the confessional tradition, a declaration of conversion was generally followed by doctrinal instruction and a trial period proving one's determination to lead a new life; only then would baptism be granted. Only ordained ministers could administer baptism, and this meant at first that baptism was the monopoly of Westerners. The timeframe from conversion to baptism could vary with the individual missionary, but after numerous cases of apostasy, many ministers were inclined to extend the period of probation. Gützlaff, his Chinese evangelists, and other evangelicals who emphasized the experiential nature of religion, on the other hand, were willing to baptize after the candidate accepted the minimal essentials of Christian doctrine and expressed a willingness to reform. In these cases Chinese evangelists as well as Westerners were permitted to baptize. Instruction in Christian doctrine and guidance in church practices would follow baptism. But many declared converts had economic rather than religious reasons for attesting to their conversion, and the majority of these fell away when church membership ceased to bring economic benefits. A minority, however, did internalize their faith as they assumed the role of evangelists, colporteurs, or church members. A few became successful evangelists and prominent church leaders. The pietist missionary might conceive of conversion as a specific and datable experience, but for numerous Chinese, gaining a new identity as a Christian was a process.

Mission boards in the West were eager for statistics on the number of converts, so that they could publicize the successes in their appeals for support. Thus missionaries in the field felt a compulsion to offer concrete proof of their accomplishments. By the late 1840s Gützlaff and his Chinese evangelists were reporting tens, even hundreds, of converts. Meanwhile most missionaries were able to report only perhaps a dozen or so conversions. Their efforts were being cast in an unfavorable light by Gützlaff's claims, and the pressures from the home board increased. This was one source of a growing antagonism toward Gützlaff among the missionary community. His critics insisted, with some justice, that Gützlaff's reports of multitudes of converts were greatly exaggerated and in many instances false. Gützlaff died during the controversy, and there have been few attempts to reevaluate Gützlaff and his accomplishments from a longer perspective.

During the twentieth century many independent churches, house churches, and new sects would reach definitions of baptism and church membership closer to the evangelical approach than the confessional one. Undoubtedly, this was related to the fact that there were resonances with traditional folk religion. Also, many rural semiliterate villagers found that a simplified, emotional religion with promises of aid in both this life and the next best met their needs. The extent to which there were direct links with evangelicals of the nineteenth century awaits further research.

A Note on Sources

Historical accounts of Christian missions and Christianity in China during the second quarter of the nineteenth century thus far have depended primarily on Western-language sources. There were only a small number of converts, and few of these left written records during these early years. One exception is the work of the first Protestant Chinese evangelist, Liang Fa. He wrote *Chuanshi liangyan (Good Words to Admonish the Age)*, which consists of quotations from the Bible with his commentaries, homiletic essays, and an account of his conversion. A few other short tracts by Liang Fa are also extant. In addition, there are biographies, autobiographies, and reports of Chinese assistants and evangelists, but Western missionaries are frequently the intermediaries. Insofar as I have been able to discover, these items are available only in translations by Western missionaries, who did some editing. Of necessity, one must rely on the voluminous correspondence and reports of the pioneer missionaries. These provide graphic and specific details of value, though the biases and outlook of the missionaries are pervasive. Missionaries were writing for a Western audience from whence came their support; they needed to assure their donors of the merits of the mission cause. Frequently the frustrating reality was masked in pious hopes.

Karl Gützlaff was an astute and effective publicist for China missions, but he relied heavily on drama and exaggeration, and he tailored his reports to his audience. An eternal optimist, he sometimes let his imagination override the truth, and he naively accepted the claims of his evangelists, some of whom were writing to please him and receive their stipend. Insofar as possible

Gützlaff's reports should be corroborated by other sources, and I have tried to do so.

Unfortunately, writings by women are rare. There are a few diaries and accounts of daily life by missionary wives and almost nothing from Chinese Bible women during the period. This account is perforce incomplete.

Happily, Chinese scholars on the mainland and in Hong Kong and Taiwan have become interested in the history of Christianity and Christian missions in China. Stimulated in part by the recent growth of Chinese Christianity, they are reassessing the Christian missionary movement, formerly viewed as an instrument of Western imperialism. They no longer have to adhere to a strict Marxist line and can present a more nuanced assessment. Whether they can locate many Chinese sources on Christianity in China during the second quarter of the nineteenth century is questionable. But they can at least tell the story from a Chinese perspective. International cooperation in research and writing is now feasible and is occurring with increasing frequency. Meanwhile, we can hope only to approach the truth.

CHAPTER TWO

Youth in a Turbulent Germany
and an Expanding West

Gützlaff's Germany in Transition, Politics, Protestantism

Karl Friedrich August Gützlaff, the first German Protestant missionary to China, was born in 1803 into a Europe in ferment. Central Europe was being restructured politically and territorially. Romanticism was gaining ascendance over the rationalism of the Enlightenment, while in the field of religion, pietism contended with latitudinarianism. Soon the Second Great Awakening would reach Europe. This evangelical revival, along with the broadening horizons that accompanied the expansion of Europe into Africa, Asia, and the Americas, was the inspiration for the era of Christian missions. What Andrew Walls has called "the cross-cultural transplantation of Christianity" had begun.[1] And Christian missions carried a lot of baggage.

Between 1801 and 1803, the Holy Roman Empire of the German Nation was forced by Napoleonic France to accept a drastic territorial reorganization. Of the over 300 sovereign member states, some 112 cities and principalities lost their independence and were incorporated into other states. In 1804 the Holy Roman Emperor, Francis II, was crowned as Emperor of Austria and, two years later, resigned his German imperial title. Thus after eight hundred years the curtain came down on the first German empire. Treaties accompanying the fall of Napoleonic France in 1814-1815 continued Germany's realignment. It now consisted of thirty-five sovereign principalities and four free cities loosely bound together in The German Confederation. At the time of this

---

1. Andrew F. Walls, *The Missionary Movement in Christian History: Studies in the Transmission of Faith* (Maryknoll, NY: Orbis Books, 1996), p. 21.

peace settlement, Karl Gützlaff was about twelve years old, an adolescent attending a classical middle school in the Prussian province of Pomerania.

The vast changes — territorial, religious, and otherwise — that occurred in the late eighteenth and early nineteenth centuries greatly influenced Gützlaff's career. His native state of Prussia had greatly expanded. With the settlement of 1814-1815, Prussia gained almost half of Saxony, the Rhenish provinces of Rhineland and Westphalia, and also Swedish Pomerania, which included the adjacent large Baltic island of Rügen. Suddenly Prussia was no longer a small insular principality, but a state with great-power potentialities. Its monarch and its citizens soon began to look toward the larger world beyond Germany.

At this juncture the Prussian king, Frederick William III, was presented with a letter written by a Prussian missionary, Karl Ewald Rhenius (1790-1838). The missionary, who was a graduate of the Berlin Mission Institute and currently serving in India, urged his monarch to support the effort to bring salvation to the millions of "heathens" in the non-Western parts of the world.[2] Surprised to learn that Berlin, his capital city, contained an institute that prepared students for service as missionaries, the king resolved not only to discover and support a mission student but also to subsidize the Berlin Mission Institute. He had earlier promised to support Karl Gützlaff's education in Halle; in response to Rhenius's plea, he recalled his commitment to Gützlaff and determined to send Gützlaff to the Berlin Mission Institute.

The institute was headed by Pastor Johann Jänicke (1748-1827) and was affiliated with Berlin's ethnically Czech community of Protestants who had fled persecution in Bohemia and Moravia. The community was known as "the Bohemian-Lutheran community," and Jänicke was its chief leader in his capacity as pastor of the Bethlehem Church, the official church of the community. Jänicke himself was an ethnic Czech whose parents had fled from Bohemia to Berlin.[3] Their family name of Jenik had been Germanized as Jänicke.

This change in name was more than a mere concession to a German environment. Jänicke was fluent in German and held services in Bethlehem Church in the German language as well as the Czech language.[4] Ethnic Germans could feel at home in Bethlehem Church not only because their lan-

2. Cited in Karl Friedrich August Gützlaff, "Kurzgefaszte Lebensbeschreibung," typescript, p. 2, Nederlandsch Zendeling Genootschap (hereafter NZG) Archives, Kast. 19, No. 1, Doss. G; J. C. Reichardt, "Gützlaff's Eintritt in die Missionslaufbahn und seine Erweckung," *Evangelisches Missions-Magazin*, 1859, p. 451.

3. Karl Friedrich Ledderhose, *Johann Jänicke der evangelisch-lutherische Prediger an der böhmischen oder Bethlehems-Kirche zu Berlin. Nach seinem Leben und Wirken dargestellt.* (Berlin: G. Knak Selbstverlag, 1863), p. 32.

4. Ledderhose, *Johann Jänicke,* p. 104.

guage was employed but also because the church bore the designation "Lutheran" and had been built for the Bohemian refugees in 1737 in response to King Frederick William I's orders.[5]

Whatever the designation of the churches founded by the Protestant refugees from the Bohemian crownlands, their churches were especially attractive to the pietists, those German Protestants who were born-again Christians. This was because of the starkly biblical and revivalist character of the Protestantism practiced by these Czech religious heirs of the Bohemian reformer Jan Hus (1369?-1415). Known variously as "the Bohemian Brethren," "the Moravian Brethren," "the Herrnhutters," and "the United Brethren," the Moravians originated in the early fifteenth century as followers of Hus, who was burned at the stake as a heretic in 1415. They made the Bible the sole authority on all matters relating to Christianity, and they rejected all aspects of Christianity that could not be justified on the basis of scripture. Thus they were close in spirit to the young Martin Luther of 1520, the year in which he wrote three early Protestant treatises. In these works, Luther judged the contemporary Catholic church against the text of the Bible and found it lacking. Luther wrote, "[I]f we are all priests, . . . and all one faith, one Gospel, one Sacrament, why should we not also have the power to test and judge what is correct in matters of faith?"[6] Here and elsewhere in the three treatises of 1820, Luther seemed to embrace the doctrine of "every man his own priest," a doctrine propounded earlier by John Wycliffe and Hus. Luther did, however, delineate a valid role for the clergy as persons chosen by their fellow Christians to preach the gospel.

Once the Protestant Reformation got underway, the Moravians, in turn, were influenced by Luther and John Calvin. By the early eighteenth century, when the Moravians fled from the Bohemian crownlands into Germany, they were perceived as fellow Protestants. Indeed, they exercised a strong influence on evangelical Protestantism, reinforcing the biblical and Christocentric character of evangelical Protestantism, as well as its emphasis on the experience of conversion. As was true in Berlin, the Moravians sometimes resided as religious minorities in towns and cities, but they also established self-contained communities like the Herrnhutter in Germany and The Netherlands. The Moravians were also forerunners of the great missionary impulse of Protestants in the nineteenth century. One Herrnhut community under

5. Ledderhose, *Johann Jänicke*, pp. 22-23.
6. Martin Luther, *Three Treatises* (Philadelphia: Muhlenberg Press, 1947), p. 22. The quotation is from Luther's "An Open Letter to the Christian Nobility of the German Nation concerning the Reform of the Christian Church."

Count Nicholas von Zinzendorf founded several Moravian settlements in the American colonies during the first half of the eighteenth century. They also sent Moravian missionaries to Greenland, the West Indies, Ethiopia, South America, and elsewhere. As of 1800, the Moravians had 161 missionaries in service.[7] Thus the Moravians had a tradition of mission activity almost a century before most of the European Protestant churches became interested in overseas missions.

Pietism, the German version of evangelical Protestantism, achieved popularity during the Great Awakening of the first half of the eighteenth century, but by in the second half of that century pietism was largely displaced by rationalistic Protestantism. This was the heyday of the Enlightenment, the era of the enlightened Prussian king, Frederick the Great, and of his friend and house guest Voltaire. After Frederick ascended the throne in 1740, pietism lost its strong influence in the state-controlled schools and universities.[8] The University of Halle, Prussia's largest university, became thoroughly rationalistic in all its faculties, including the theological faculty.[9] Since this university provided the bulk of Prussia's pastors and many classical school rectors, a rationalistic attitude prevailed among these graduates well into the nineteenth century.[10] Pietism lost its influence on the popular culture in northern Germany, and pietist laymen and pietist clergymen became "isolated quiet voices in the rationalist sea."[11]

During this period when pietism was in recession, the churches of the emigrés from Bohemia and Moravia provided a refuge for pietists. This was particularly true in the case of the United Brethren, popularly known as the Moravians. Their schools were attractive to Protestants who did not want their children exposed to a rationalistic education. The Moravian sect played a key role in keeping German pietism alive during the second half of the eighteenth century.[12]

The changes that began in the second decade of the nineteenth century

7. John Dillenberger and Claude Welch, *Protestant Christianity Interpreted thru Its Development* (New York: Scribners, 1954), p. 167; David A. Schattschneider, "William Cary, Modern Missions, and the Moravian Influence," *International Bulletin of Missionary Research* 22.1 (January 1998): 10.

8. Hajo Holborn, *A History of Modern Germany, 1648-1840* (New York: Knopf, 1964), p. 141.

9. Holborn, *A History of Modern Germany*, p. 138; Ledderhose, *Johann Jänicke*, p. 39.

10. Robert M. Bigler, *The Politics of German Protestantism: The Rise of the Protestant Church Elite in Prussia, 1815-1848* (Berkeley: University of California Press, 1975), pp. 14, 65.

11. Bigler, *The Politics of German Protestantism*, pp. 14-15; Holborn, *A History of Modern Germany*, p. 141.

12. Holborn, *A History of Modern Germany*, p. 141.

were not confined to Germany; they extended to the Protestant areas of Europe, Great Britain, and North America. With the arrival of the Second Great Awakening, revivalistic, born-again Protestantism experienced a new period of vitality. In Berlin, Pastor Johann Jänicke became a key figure in this upsurge of evangelical Protestantism. His Bethlehem Church gained popularity among neo-pietistic Prussian officials, army officers, and other aristocrats.[13] Simultaneously, Jänicke was instrumental in the founding of Bible societies and in the distribution of Bibles in the Czech and German languages.[14] His Mission Institute in Berlin had been supplying missionaries to mission societies since 1800 and continued to do so, though it did so quietly.[15]

If missions had been a modest and little-known part of Protestantism in the eighteenth and early nineteenth centuries, the Second Great Awakening soon brought dynamism and popularity to the Protestant mission effort. Unlike the First Great Awakening of the eighteenth century, however, the Second Great Awakening coincided with a "sea change" in Western society. Fueled by technological progress, the power available to new nation-states, and the growth of global commerce, the Western world was on the threshold of expansion into Asia and Africa. The Protestant missionaries who were sent out by mission societies in the first half of the nineteenth century were forerunners and participants in that expansion.

The great majority of the Protestant missionaries of the early and mid-nineteenth century were products of the Second Great Awakening. Most of the German missionary pioneers were from the lower middle classes, primarily artisan, merchant, and clerical families in small cities and towns. Since few were university graduates and many had not completed their secondary education, the mission schools were obliged to include remedial courses in their curricula. The volunteers, however, tended to be ambitious, eager for an education, quite articulate, and autodidactic. A missionary career seemed to offer a means of upward mobility.[16] From a sociological standpoint, therefore, Gützlaff was a fairly typical recruit.

The new Protestant mission societies of the early nineteenth century aspired to nothing less than the conversion of the whole world to Protestant Christianity. Many of their early volunteers were heroic, dynamic men who ventured into life-threatening situations, and who sometimes paid with their

---

13. Bigler, *The Politics of German Protestantism*, p. 130.

14. Ledderhose, *Johann Jänicke*, pp. 70-73.

15. Ledderhose, *Johann Jänicke*, pp. 99, 102.

16. Thoralf Klein, "Die Anfänge der deutschen protestantischen Mission in China, 1846-1880: Kulturelle Missverständnisse und kulturelle Konflikte" (M.A. thesis, Freiburg University, 1995), esp. pp. 13-15.

lives for their temerity. They were generally enterprising, independent, and resourceful. They were an expression of that spiritual assertion of selfhood and individualism which had emerged in the Italian Renaissance. Yet pietist evangelism contained contradictory impulses, for its stated ideals were self-effacement, humility, pacifism, quietism, mystical communion with God, and total surrender to God's purpose. In their mission publicity, they denied credit for their accomplishments, for they saw themselves as the instruments of God, obliged to answer God's call and carry out God's purpose. God told them where to go and what to do, and if there were successes, these were God's accomplishments. But pietism was a dynamic, explosive force; during the nineteenth century, Western evangelical circles launched the Protestant world missionary movement. All these contradictions were embodied in the person and career of Karl Gützlaff. In comparison with other "awakened" missionaries, he was in many ways the epitome of evangelical contradictions.

What differentiated pietists from most of their German Protestant con-temporaries? Among other things, pietists disliked state control and state reg-ulations, an arrangement that prevailed in the German states. When the pietist circles of southern Germany decided in 1815, therefore, to establish a mission society, they located it in Basel, Switzerland, just outside the borders of the German Confederation.[17] There it would be relatively insulated from the power of the monarchs, their ecclesiastical officials, and university theolo-gians. Pietists had little appreciation for ecclesiastical bureaucrats or denominationalism.[18]

The conversionary experience or "atonement struggle" *(Busskampf)* was central for pietists. Since most of the "awakened" were already Protestants, "conversion" usually referred to a dramatic renewal of faith. For the German pietist, the prelude to seeing oneself as sinful and unworthy was an awareness of the inherent corruption of humanity and a thorough hatred of sin.[19] From that stage, one moved to a full recognition of one's own sinfulness and a re-jection of one's self, a crisis that could only be resolved through receiving God's grace, the actual gift of faith. Finally came peace, in which one saw one-self as a servant of the Lord. This was the pattern to which Gützlaff was ex-posed in the course of his missionary education, and he personally would go through these stages in compressed form. As a missionary, however, he took

17. Paul Eppler, *Geschichte des Basler Mission, 1815-1899* (Basel: Verlag der Missions-buchhandlung, 1900), pp. 1-50, 107.

18. Dillenberger and Welch, *Protestant Christianity,* p. 126.

19. Anthony La Vopa, *Grace, Talent, and Merit: Poor Students, Clerical Careers, and Pro-fessional Ideology in Eighteenth-Century Germany* (Cambridge: Cambridge University Press, 1988), p. 146.

liberties with it and was consequently criticized by the young German missionaries whom he recruited to assist him.

Beyond their emphasis on the conversionary experience, pietists upheld the ideal of a highly personalized religion nourished by prayer, introspection, and Bible reading. They were not, however, fundamentalists in the modern sense, for they rejected both a heavy emphasis on doctrine and the rigidly literal interpretation of the Bible characteristic of Protestant orthodoxy.[20] Though they insisted on thorough acquaintance with the text of the Bible, what they sought in the Bible were the spirit and the mystery behind the words. Viewed from this vantage point, the Bible was seen as the only tool of salvation, and it was to be studied on a daily basis by groups, the family, and individuals. It was against this background that the young German missionaries reacted in dismay when they discovered that their Chinese converts seemed only capable of understanding the literal, surface features of Christianity; the inner meaning and mystery escaped them. The comment of Basel missionary Philipp Winnes (1824-1874) in 1862 is typical: "Among them, these truths remain for the most part an external knowledge and are not intrinsically comprehended in their hearts and do not constitute a real element of their inner lives."[21]

If the pietist emphasis on the role of the Bible was to be a shaping force in the faith and the mission methodology of Karl Gützlaff, this was also true of the doctrine of "the calling" and the related work ethic. In discussing German pietism, historian Anthony La Vopa offers a description ideally suited to the character of Karl Gützlaff: "The doctrine of calling . . . incorporated a work ethic that bore close resemblance to the Puritan ideal of 'continuous labor in the calling.'" It was "'the self-affirming activity of the Godly' and promised a similar 'utopia of men without leisure.' The calling no longer was limited to duty in the traditional sense; it required an intensively self-disciplined, never-waste-a-minute, almost feverish activity in a lifelong occupation or office, maximizing use of time and effort in the service of 'the common welfare.'"[22] These features of pietism, so strongly embedded in Gützlaff, point up an incongruity that was widespread among pietists. On the one hand there was an abhorrence for regimentation, formality, and structure, while on the other hand there was an almost frantic passion for work perceived as a calling. The same person who was averse to a disciplined environment could be a highly

20. Holborn, *A History of Modern Germany,* p. 139.

21. Philipp Winnes, "Geschichte der Entstehung und Ausbreitung der Gemeinde in Tschong-lok," Archiv der Basler Missionsgesellschaft, China (hereafter BMG): Berichte und Korrespondenz, November 1862, A-1.4, no. 19, p. 18.

22. La Vopa, *Grace, Talent, and Merit,* p. 143.

disciplined person in relation to his "calling." The discipline that Gützlaff and other pietists disliked was an *imposed* discipline, a discipline coming from without; they readily imposed self-discipline. Whatever the task, Gützlaff functioned at breakneck speed with an almost pathological frenzy that allowed a minimum of sleep.

The Berlin to which Gützlaff was assigned for his missionary education in 1821 was a major center of the Second Great Awakening. Gützlaff was already eighteen years old when he arrived in Berlin. Though he would be profoundly affected by his experiences in that city, he had spent his early youth in the sleepy Pomeranian city of Pyritz, located some twenty-seven miles southeast of the provincial capital of Stettin.

Gützlaff's Early Years, 1803-1821

Gützlaff was born into an artisan family in Pyritz in 1803.[23] In the Pyritz church records his father, Johann Jacob Gützlaff (ca. 1767-1825), was classified as a citizen *(Burger)* and master tailor *(Schneider)*. Karl's mother, née Maria Elisabeth Behncke, died in 1807, four years after Karl's birth.[24] A year after her death, Johann Jacob married Carolina Louisa Ockert Schultz, widow of another master tailor and mother of eight children. In Gützlaff's autobiographical sketch, he declared that his mother's death left him grief stricken and desolate: "In my fifth year, I received a stepmother who treated me barbarically for eight years. This was for me a time of tribulation and trial. My cheerful nature became transformed into one that was gloomy and melancholy."[25] These problems were offset somewhat by a warm relationship he developed with one of his new siblings: "The eighth of my stepsisters reared me with motherly care and taught me my letters."[26] These experiences did not permanently change Gützlaff's disposition from cheerful to melancholy, for his vo-

---

23. The best biography of Gützlaff is Herman Schlyter, *Karl Gützlaff als Missionar in China* (Lund: C. W. K. Gleerup, 1946), but see also Thoralf Klein and Reinhard Zöllner, eds., *Karl F. A. Gützlaff (1803-1851) und das Christentum in Ostasien. Ein Missionar zwischen den Kulturen* (Nettetal: Steyler Verlag, 2005), and Gu Changsheng, "Guo Lishi (Charles Gutzlaff, 1803-1851)," in *Cong Malixun dao Situ Leideng — Lai hua xinjiao chuanjiaoshi pingzhuan* [From Morrison to Stuart — Critical Biographies of Protestant missionaries to China] (Shanghai: Shanghai renmin chubanshe, 1985), pp. 50-61.

24. Elizabeth Behncke, according to some records, was the second wife of Johann Jacob. I wish to thank Dr. R. G. Tiedemann of the School of Oriental and African Studies, University of London for this and other data that he obtained from the Pyritz church records.

25. Gützlaff, "Kurzgefaszte Lebensbeschreibung," p. 1.

26. Gützlaff, "Kurzgefaszte Lebensbeschreibung," p. 1.

luminous writings reveal a personality that is basically optimistic and cheerful. What they may have contributed to was a sense of insecurity. After his father's remarriage, Gützlaff felt rejected and unwanted. Thereafter he had difficulty in establishing warm and enduring relationships.

When Gützlaff was eight years old, his father enrolled him in the Pyritz Latin school, where the ancient languages, history, mathematics, and other subjects were taught. It was here that he began to acquire the language facility that later assisted him in his biblical translations. In addition to other subjects, Gützlaff mentions geography, which greatly interested him.[27] Gützlaff remained at the Latin school for five years, that is, until his confirmation, which was identified as 7 July 1816 on the margin of the typed transliteration of his *"Lebensbeschreibung."*

Gützlaff's description of the intellectual influence to which he was exposed in this period, 1811-1816, was written seven years later, that is, after he had studied for two years at the Berlin mission school and had undergone a conversion experience. Thus he was inclined to stand in judgment on his preconversion past and on the "unawakened" associates of those years:

> The rector of the school was a capable man who could convey to the others what he knew in an agreeable fashion. He did well in all fields in which he gave instruction except the field of religion, in which his instruction was the most miserable in the world. In religion, he sought to transfer to his students the neo-logical poison he had absorbed at the university. After being his student for a few years, all good emotions within me had been smothered. I developed contempt for the Bible and became indifferent to religion. By the time I began catechism instruction with the two local preachers, I had become a free thinker. Unfortunately, this was not remedied here because the instruction was based on principles similar to those of the rector. The unsavory company of my fellow catechumen stifled all my feelings for things that are holy. My confession of faith, instilled in me by the preachers, consisted of an oath to be ever virtuous and to accept God as my father. I soon learned how powerless such an oath is without the might of the Holy Spirit to enable a person to resist sin.[28]

This evangelical religious outlook is surely retrospective. The only reference in his autobiographical sketch to the religious orientation of his family is

27. Gützlaff, "Kurzgefaszte Lebensbeschreibung," p. 1.
28. Gützlaff, "Kurzgefaszte Lebensbeschreibung," p. 1.

his statement that he had undergone instruction in catechism followed by confirmation in the Lutheran church.[29] In 1839, in an article entitled "Early Life of Charles Gützlaff, Missionary in China," Issachar Roberts, Gützlaff's colleague and house guest in Canton, took issue with writers who tended to project Gützlaff's pietism into his infancy and childhood:

> He received no pious instructions but was educated in the doctrines of Deism and Socinianism; enjoyed no prayer-meetings, nor intercourse with pious Christians; nor did he feel any natural inclination for such exercises. Hankering after vain philosophy, engaged in frivolous occupations, and a determined enemy of Godliness, which he dared deride, he was systematically taught to reject the word of God as fabulous, and too antiquated for these enlightened times. He had a love for adventure and often pictured to himself the leisures of a traveller. . . .[30]

It does seem likely that during Gützlaff's school years he was under the influence of the Enlightenment outlook which then prevailed among the Protestant clergy. On the other hand, the hostility toward the Enlightenment that characterized resurgent pietism focused on the exponents of rationalism. The contemptuous tone of Gützlaff's description of his encounter with religious rationalism reflects general pietistic hostility as well as his personal experiences. In his later writings he would lose no opportunity to denigrate Enlightenment spokesmen.

Upon completing his confirmation in the Lutheran church, Gützlaff was offered the possibility of continuing his education at the expense of the city. Instead, he chose the life of a craftsman and was promptly apprenticed by his father to a master artisan in the provincial capital of Stettin.[31] Gützlaff, therefore, interrupted his formal education in 1816 at the age of thirteen. Despite having opted for the life of an artisan, Gützlaff soon realized that such an existence was too limited for him. His five years of classical education had instilled a lifelong delight in learning. He had brought from Pyritz a small collection of books, and he continued to read them. In his Stettin rooming house, furthermore, he became acquainted with the widow of a Pastor Heydenreich and her son. Young Heydenreich and Gützlaff became friends, and they spent time reading and discussing the poems of "very famous Ger-

29. Gützlaff, "Kurzgefaszte Lebensbeschreibung," p. 2.

30. Issachar J. Roberts, "Early Life of Charles Gutzlaff, Missionary in China," *The China Mission Advocate*, January 1839, pp. 30-31.

31. No explanation is given for this uncharacteristic choice, but economic difficulties on the part of his father may have dictated the decision.

man poets," probably such popular romantics and pre-romantics as Ludwig Tieck (1773-1853), August von Schlegel (1769-1845), Fredrich Hölderlin (1770-1845), and Gotthold Lessing (1729-1781).[32] Gützlaff's stepbrother testified that Gützlaff, during his Stettin years, used every hour of leisure for his continuing education. After he had completed his work as an apprentice at 10:00 P.M., he used a lamp he had purchased to study the books he had borrowed from Heydenreich. He studied these deep into the night.[33]

Gützlaff became acquainted as well with a merchant who was avidly interested in Protestant foreign missions. Gützlaff's curiosity about missions had actually been aroused even earlier during geography instruction, when his Pyritz teacher had pointed to the locations of mission stations in faraway places. Thus when the merchant shared with Gützlaff issues of the *Evangelisches Missions-Magazin,* the Basel mission periodical, he read the articles and news dispatches with great interest. Upon hearing a rousing sermon on foreign missions, Gützlaff decided that he wanted to be educated as a missionary.[34]

Surely Gützlaff's decision can be attributed at least as much, if not more, to a romantic spirit of adventure than to religious motivation, but in any case, he lacked the funds necessary to follow through. Appeals to his father and his Latin school rector came to naught. The elder Gützlaff was in no position to aid his son, and the teacher replied contemptuously that the whole mission enterprise was only *"Schwärmerei,"* a euphemism for fanaticism.[35] Gützlaff was consequently obliged to give up, for a time, his plan of becoming a missionary.

Meanwhile Gützlaff continued to enjoy the company of young Heydenreich. When the two learned that Frederick William III was to pay a visit to Stettin, Heydenreich proposed that they compose a poem of welcome and present it to the king upon his arrival. They did so, and Gützlaff credits Heydenreich with taking the initiative and handing the poem to the king, who graciously accepted it.[36] Then, appalled by their presumption and fearful of punishment, they ran into the city and hid. Only after the king had sent three successive messengers to search for them did the third one find them at home. He led them to the king's residence, but the king had already retired for the night — not, however, before leaving instructions with his ad-

32. Gützlaff, "Kurzgefaszte Lebensbeschreibung," p. 2.

33. Anonymous, "Der Missionär Gützlaff," *Allgemeine Kirchen-Zeitung* 135 (26 August 1832), col. 1098.

34. "Der Missionär Gützlaff," col. 1098.

35. "Der Missionär Gützlaff," col. 1098.

36. "Der Missionär Gützlaff," col. 1098.

jutant to pay each youth four ducats and record information respecting their circumstances.[37]

As a consequence of the incident, Heydenreich was rewarded with a royally financed education at a university of his choice. Since Heydenreich was in the final year of his secondary education, his university education could start following graduation from the Latin school. Gützlaff, however, was something of a problem for the king. The boy had dropped out of a classical preparatory school at age thirteen to become an artisan's apprentice. He did not have the proper preparation for matriculation into a university. How, then, could the king reward him? The king finally decided to have an official test Gützlaff to ascertain the level of his intellectual development. Gützlaff passed the test with ease, so that Frederick William decided to send him to the Halle orphanage, where he could reside while continuing his education in one of the schools of the Francke Foundation.

Training at Berlin Mission Institute and Conversion

In 1821, while Gützlaff impatiently awaited instructions from the king, Frederick William received the letter from Rhenius describing his work in India and informing the king of Jänicke's Mission Institute in Berlin. The institute had been founded in 1800 by Jänicke with the financial support of a pietist nobleman named Schirnding.[38] Designed to train Protestant missionaries rather than send them out under its own auspices, it had been supplying workers to English and Dutch mission societies for twenty years; these societies, in turn, helped support the institute. Rhenius urged the king to patronize the institute so that it could expand its training program.[39] Subsequently Jänicke was informed that the king had decided to contribute to the support of the mission institute. Moreover, Frederick William had selected Karl Gützlaff as a candidate for education in Jänicke's school and was allocating five hundred Prussian dollars annually for his education. The sum would thereafter be continued indefinitely to support the institute.

J. C. Reichardt, Gützlaff's future Berlin roommate, shared the religious orientation of Jänicke and understood what this meant to the pastor. Though Jänicke had doubtless enjoyed his newfound influence and popularity among

37. J. C. Reichardt, "Gützlaff's Entritt in die Missionslaufbahn und seine Erwecklund," *Evangelisches Missions-Magazin,* 1859, pp. 452-53.
38. Ledderhose, *Johann Jänicke,* pp. 95-96.
39. Ledderhose, *Johann Jänicke,* pp. 95-96; Reichardt, "Gützlaff's Entritt," p. 453.

courtiers, army officers, and bureaucrats as pastor of Bethlehem Church, it was quite another thing to have the royal limelight turned on his mission institute. The latter had been something of an in-group project for the Bohemian community and pietists, and Jänicke had quietly recruited persons imbued with what he considered the proper religious attitude. Now, however, the king had become aware of the institute and had selected a religious outsider for enrollment. Moreover, the institute would henceforth be beholden to the king of Prussia for his continuing support. Indeed, in 1823 the king bestowed a written constitution on the Berlin Mission Institute.[40]

When Gützlaff presented himself at the Mission Institute in April 1821, Jänicke had no option but to waive the preliminary examination ordinarily used to screen candidates and to accept him. According to Gützlaff's Berlin roommate, the pastor asked Gützlaff what he hoped to become after his education at the institute, and Gützlaff replied, *Kanzelredner* ("an eloquent preacher"). Jänicke thereupon responded that such an ambition was not compatible with the character of his institute.[41] Though the roommate's direct quotations must have been based on hearsay, since he arrived at the Mission Institute some weeks later than Gützlaff, the comments probably did reflect the attitudes of the two parties. Hope of social mobility, an appetite for adventure, the ideal of the romantic hero, as well as the desire to bring the gospel to the heathen motivated Gützlaff.

Jänicke was concerned enough about his new student's spiritual condition to place him, as a roomer, with a Bohemian family living near the institute. The head of the family, Mr. Ebner, had a brother who was a missionary stationed in Africa.[42] Six weeks after Gützlaff's arrival, he was joined by J. C. Reichardt, who was a recent graduate of a classical preparatory school. Doubtless with Gützlaff's spiritual condition in mind, Jänicke had arranged for Reichardt to room with the Pomeranian. Gützlaff was impressed by both Reichardt's educational background and his studiousness. The two young men studied together late into the night. Though Gützlaff viewed his fellow students as too lax, too inclined to waste time discussing religious and spiritual matters,[43] he could not say this about Reichardt, who yielded nothing to Gützlaff in diligence.

Gützlaff soon became a favorite topic of conversation among his schoolmates. They marveled at his industriousness and his scholarly capabilities,

---

40. Ledderhose, *Johann Jänicke,* p. 101.
41. Reichardt, "Gützlaff's Entritt," p. 459.
42. Reichardt, "Gützlaff's Entritt," p. 455; 3 February 1823 in NZG Archives, *Extract-Acten, 1823,* p. 6.
43. Reichardt, "Gützlaff's Entritt," p. 456.

but were critical of his pride, his conceit, and his lack of a true mission sense. "No one," wrote Reichardt, "felt this more strongly than the companion who lived with him and who, on this account and in love, often sought to influence him."[44] Reichardt reasoned with Gützlaff that education ought to be a means to a higher, exalted end and should not be seen as an end in itself. The goal of education should be to live for others, not to promote one's own advancement. This line of approach was, for the time being, lost on Gützlaff. The attempts of young pietists to reshape a stubborn outsider were reinforced in early July 1821 by two fellow students who had recently arrived. One of these was simultaneously a degree candidate in the University of Berlin's theological school, a status that was likely to impress young Gützlaff. The newcomers pointed out to Gützlaff that he was in danger of raising education to the status of a false god. He was here in Berlin to prepare to serve others, not for self-cultivation.

Gützlaff initially showed no sign of responding to the arguments of his schoolmates. Later, while the two roommates were engaged in their studies, Reichardt pursued the argument, telling Gützlaff,

"If a person were preparing to become a missionary who would proclaim the Gospel to others, he would first have to be permeated by the spirit of the Gospel. He must first experience what he hopes to convey to others. Without this experience, he can neither love the Savior nor serve Him. Moreover, he cannot endure the hardships that attend the life of a missionary. Without his change of heart, he remains spiritually dead and, in the end, all his zeal and all his knowledge will serve only to please himself and enhance his honor. It will not promote service to the Lord and His honor." This was approximately the content of my conversation with Gützlaff, who listened, for the most part, in silence. Eventually, however, he became completely silent. That was around 10:00 P.M., still very early for us. He put down his pen and said, "I'm going to bed; I can no longer study." For some time, I had been aware of a certain restlessness in him and I had seen how his studying had not been progressing very smoothly. At the point where he stood up and said he was going to bed, I asked him if, perhaps, he was not feeling very well. "I don't feel completely well," he replied, and he lay down to rest in the same room.

Reichardt then describes what is an almost classic conversion experience in the pietist tradition:

44. Reichardt, "Gützlaff's Entritt," p. 456.

I was awakened . . . by the restlessness of my neighbor, who groaned and tossed about in bed, apparently unable to go to sleep. I asked him: "What is it with you, Brother Gützlaff? Are you not well?" Suddenly, he called out, "Oh, I am lost! I am lost!" By now, I was fully awake and I said: "Dear Brother Gützlaff, what do you want? What is this all about?" Gützlaff, however, took no note of these questions and continued to express his innermost thoughts and to bewail his sinfulness. He enumerated his sins, beginning with his adolescence, and cried: "Yes, Satan, you have captured me in your net. I now stand on the brink of the abyss, on the verge of falling into damnation. You have filled me with pride and vanity and have so misled me that I have misused holy things and have centered my attention on my own needs and my vain honor. Oh, how sly you are. And now you have succeeded in causing me to fall into eternal damnation." After listening to him carry on in this fashion for a long time, I sought to reassure him and to call his attention to the promises of the Gospel. Then, in response, he cried out: "Yes, but that is not for me. No, I have forfeited my salvation. For me there can be no grace! I have sinned and engaged in hypocrisy too much! I have deluded myself! Satan has me completely ensnared! I am lost, lost! Hell now opens its jaws and I shall soon become its prey."

I waited till he had quieted down somewhat and there was a short pause. Then I tried to make him aware of God's Word. He responded in such instances with comments as: "That is certainly true and it is a dear worthy teaching that Jesus Christ came into the world to save sinners, among whom I am one of the foremost." In all such instances, he took the position that this did not apply to him because he was doomed to be dragged away to the hell which awaited him. I did not desert my friend, however, and continued to cite passages of the Gospel which offered words of consolation. Finally, his deeply shattered and depressed spirit showed a slight sign of grace. "Oh, Brother Reichardt," he said in a humble childish voice, "Do you really think that salvation would be possible for a poor sinner such as me?" "Yes, dear brother," I replied, highly pleased with his change of spirit and with the signs of grace which followed the fearful battle. "Yes, even you may dare to believe that the Lord Jesus came to forgive your sins and to receive you in grace. And that is why he spoke those reassuring words: 'Come unto me, all ye that travail and are heavily laden and I will give you rest' [Matthew, 11:28]. Go now to the Savior; he will accept you and refresh you." At this, Gützlaff remarked, "Oh, would this really be possible for me, a sinner worthy of damnation, a person who has failed to seek grace and has lived accordingly." And whereas earlier he had been in a condition of doubt . . . he now spoke once again loudly to himself but in a manner which showed the first signs of the path of grace and the emergence from the deepest doubt. He gradually pursued this path and his spirit became ever clearer. . . . Finally he said a childish, animated prayer which simultaneously was a compact with his Savior and which brought him inner peace. Now the heated struggle over atonement and faith, a struggle which had lasted over three hours, had been fought through, and both Gützlaff and his sympathetic and instrumental friend soon fell fast asleep.[45]

In the morning Reichardt waited impatiently for Gützlaff to awaken, for Reichardt was eager to discover how authentic the previous night's experiences had been.

Finally, he did awaken and he stood up. What a thrill this was for me! For the first time, I saw him kneel beside his bed and pray, something he had never found time to do before. That was the second sign that the night's experience had been no illusion. Then came a third sign. Gützlaff rose from his prayers with an earnest demeanor and then seated himself in silence at his desk in order to begin work. I was so filled with inner joy and with thankfulness to the Lord that I could not resist breaking the silence. "Dear, dear Brother Gützlaff, how goes it with you now?" In response to this question, tears came to Gützlaff's eyes. He laid his book down, suddenly stood up, and then threw himself to his knees in the middle of the room and poured out his impassioned heart through a loud prayer of thanks that flowed mightily out of his innermost depths. Now there could not longer be any doubt. Gützlaff had been transformed from a proud, conceited youth into a converted Christian. Following his prayer of thanks, he grasped my hand and greeted me as a brother in Christ through whose grace both hoped to become blessed and in whose service both were willing to sacrifice their powers in order to lead immortal souls to Him.

From this day forward, Gützlaff was a completely different man. Although he remained as industrious in his studies as before, he now regarded these as subordinate. . . . The other brethren, also Pastor Jänicke and other Christian friends, soon became aware of Gützlaff's change of spirit. Every one took great pleasure in this transformation, especially

45. Reichardt, "Gützlaff's Entritt," pp. 457-58.

the dear Christian landlord [Ebner], who was initially informed of it in secret and whose experiences in Christianity and rich knowledge of the Word of God later became of great value to both mission students. Thereafter, Gützlaff stood much closer to his brethren and lived with them in a Christian community of love [*Liebesgemeinschaft*].[46]

Reichardt and the other pietists of the Berlin Mission Institute seem to have been convinced that Gützlaff had taken the values of the Great Awakening into his innermost being. The values that Gützlaff thereafter explicitly expressed would apparently bear them out.

Several features of Gützlaff's autobiography and of Reichardt's account of Gützlaff's conversion and the events preceding it are worthy of note. Reichardt had never seen his roommate pray until after his conversion. Indeed, Reichardt remarked that young Gützlaff "lacked any real Christian knowledge and experience."[47] Until Gützlaff's emotional rebirth that night in early July 1821, his intellectual and emotional world had been shaped more by the Enlightenment than the Great Awakening. Gützlaff stood out above his classmates in his scholarly and intellectual capabilities. Despite the fact that they were in awe of him in this respect, they were highly critical of what they considered his ambition, pride, and arrogance. Gützlaff seemed to feel sufficient unto himself, rarely if at all seeking divine assistance and support in private prayer. His conversion, though it apparently mitigated his pride and arrogance, had little effect on his ambition or his keen interest in learning. Reichardt notes that Gützlaff was just as zealous and hard-working a student after his conversion as before.[48] Now, however, he no longer viewed education either as an end or as a means for exalting and advancing himself, but rather as a means for serving God.

Perhaps so, but how intrinsically his sudden conversion changed the patterns of his personality and value system is a matter open to question. Throughout his career, he eagerly amassed information on a remarkable variety of subjects, both secular and religious: irrigation techniques to help China; folk religions, including festivals, institutionalized religion, and Confucian and Daoist philosophy; Chinese secret societies, tea culture, medicine, literature, history, geography, and economics. He sought out challenges and relished describing how he overcame them with God's help.

When in 1859 the Basel Mission's *Evangelisches Missions-Magazin* re-

---

46. Reichardt, "Gützlaff's Entritt," p. 459.
47. Reichardt, "Gützlaff's Entritt," p. 455.
48. Reichardt, "Gützlaff's Entritt," p. 459.

printed the Reichardt article, the editor commented on its importance for understanding Gützlaff's career: "Our reprint of this article reveals something unusual: First, the entrance into the mission career and then the conversion. Though there have been individual unusual cases in which this sequence has been followed, they have been very rare. . . . There can be no doubt that Gützlaff was fundamentally awakened before undertaking his mission work and that this was the beginning of the godly life which later ran its course . . . but we should take note of the stormy, sudden, powerful character of his awakening and the haste with which he resumed his ambitious studies. He did not leave sufficient room and time to permit a quiet and harmonious transition to the new life. Thus, there must have been left in his spirit a remnant of the overwhelming ambition which had characterized his old makeup, and this must necessarily have helped to shape the later course of his career. Certainly Gützlaff fought throughout his life with great earnestness against this remnant of his natural makeup, but the remnant nevertheless introduced a foreign element into his extensive work."[49]

Such an assessment is borne out by Gützlaff's activities in Berlin. The limited curriculum at the institute did not satisfy Gützlaff's craving for knowledge. Since the students were being prepared for service with English or Dutch missions, they were instructed in English and Dutch. Biblical studies, however, had pride of place. Jänicke had, after all, received his preparation for the ministry at the United Brethren's seminary in Barby, a small town located near Magdeburg; he had, moreover, taught there for a number of years. According to his biographer, Jänicke was often heard to say, "The Bible is itself sufficient. Missionaries should bring the Bible to the heathen and, beyond this, nothing more. The teaching of the pure Scriptures is all that is necessary."[50] There is little doubt that the theological instruction at the Berlin Missionary Institute was minimalist, Christocentric, biblical, and non-sectarian, qualities that were to characterize Gützlaff's religious orientation throughout his career.

Yet despite his sympathy with this orientation, Gützlaff decided in 1822 to supplement his education by study with *Dozent* August Tholuck, a linguist at the University of Berlin. Tholuck was a member of Berlin's pietist circle and would later become a full professor at the University of Halle, where he began a successful effort to deflect the theological faculty away from its rationalist orientation.[51] Like Gützlaff, Tholuck was the son of an artisan. And like

49. *Evangelisches Missions-Magazin*, 1859, pp. 450-51. The Basel magazine reprinted the essay from a recent issue of the *Evangelischer Reichsbote*.

50. Ledderhose, *Johann Jänicke*, pp. 41, 101.

51. Bigler, *The Politics of German Protestantism*, pp. 86-87. Bigler devotes a substantial coverage to Tholuck; see his index.

Gützlaff, Tholuck combined evangelistic zeal with emotional restlessness and ambition. Tholuck owed his rapid promotion in the field of theology to his contacts with the pietist group around Crown Prince Frederick William. Gützlaff attended Tholuck's classes in Persian and simultaneously studied English, Dutch, and the classical languages.[52] Despite his career as a missionary, Gützlaff coveted recognition as a scholar and took pride in his linguistic abilities.

Two major aspects of Gützlaff's experience at the Jänicke institute marked his mission career: the emphasis on the centrality of the Bible and the informal, personal nature of training at the school. According to Protestants and most especially pietists, the Bible should be accessible to all. To further the distribution of the Scriptures and religious tracts, Jänicke had worked with the Prussian Central Bible Society *(Die Preussische Hauptbibelgesellschaft)* and had fostered the establishment of the Berlin Central Society for Christian Edifying Writings *(Der Berliner Hauptverein für christliche Erbauungs- schriften)* in 1816.[53] Mission graduates of Jänicke's school, including Gützlaff, were expected to devote themselves to Bible translation and distribution. The anti-institutional outlook of Jänicke prompted them to minimize structure and to dislike regimentation. The result was an informal approach to education that encouraged each student to proceed at his own pace and to emphasize those studies which he found most interesting. Thus, the precocious Gützlaff was allowed to move like a whirlwind through the mission school's curriculum and to supplement it with outside reading and outside courses, while his fellow students and his teacher observed his remarkable progress with astonishment and mixed feelings.[54]

If Gützlaff's ambition and drive survived his conversion, pietism nevertheless influenced the development of his character. Pietism helped to shape a Gützlaff who was averse, in educational and religious affairs, to regimentation, structure, bureaucracy, sectarian doctrine — indeed, to institutionalization and all it entailed. This orientation was doubtless reinforced by his childhood experiences with a stepmother whom he perceived as tyrannical, as was his lifelong sense of insecurity. As a stepchild in the midst of several new siblings headed by a stepmother who apparently did not welcome his presence, he saw himself as an outsider in his own home. Later, when he entered the Berlin Mission Institute, he was perceived by his teacher and his fellow

---

52. L. Hoff, who like Reichardt was a former schoolmate of Gützlaff's at the Mission Institute, is quoted in the *Evangelisches Missions-Magazin*, 1859, p. 461, in relation to Tholuck; see also Schlyter, *Karl Gützlaff,* pp. 19-20.

53. Schlyter, *Karl Gützlaff*, p. 19.

54. Schlyter, *Karl Gützlaff,* pp. 14-16.

students as an outsider, and he reacted to this reception by assuming an aloof, superior attitude and by striving to excel in his studies over all his fellow students. After he had undergone conversion, his teacher and fellow students accepted him as one of them, and his relations with his colleagues improved considerably. That did not prevent him from continuing his efforts to stand out from his colleagues. He never became a "team player" who could interact freely as an equal with his associates.

Some, at least, of the inconsistencies in Gützlaff and other pietists of his times may perhaps be traceable to a conflict between the values of pietism and Romanticism. Both Romanticism and pietism focused on the individual, and both turned the individual's attention toward his or her own psyche or soul. The two, however, differed radically in what they expected of the individual. According to pietism, the individual should be low key and self-effacing. The egoistic pursuit of fame and fortune was severely frowned upon, and deliberate heroism met with disapproval. The United Brethren refused military service, not merely out of pacifism, but also because of rejection of the military code of honor, which expected heroic behavior on the battlefield. The Romantics, on the other hand, admired the ambitious, daring person, one who triumphed over all obstacles — in other words, the hero, the unique individual. Nature was often identified with the divine, and notable human action was viewed as a reflection of the sublime.

The two traditions coexisted incongruously and often in a state of tension within many German intellectuals of the early nineteenth century. They helped to produce the inconsistencies so conspicuous in Gützlaff and other pietists. On the one hand, Gützlaff saw himself as the insignificant tool of God, but on the other hand, he aspired to convert, not merely China, but all of East Asia in his own lifetime. Yet he managed to reconcile the two in his own thinking. God, he believed, had called upon him to convert the East Asian peoples. On Gützlaff's tombstone in Hong Kong, he is characterized as simply "Apostle to China." This was in accord with his wish, though sometimes it seems that he considered himself *the* apostle to China. He perceived this as his divinely ordained calling; he had no choice but to carry it out. In the final analysis, however, its accomplishment depended upon the will of God and the operation of the Holy Spirit.

Certainly, Jänicke had detected the Romantic impulses in Gützlaff upon his arrival in Berlin in 1821, but Jänicke's initial dismay turned to approval following Gützlaff's conversion. The pastor was so impressed by Gützlaff's intellectual abilities that in January 1823 he decided to support Gützlaff as a matriculated student at the University of Berlin preparatory to becoming a teacher in the Berlin Mission Institute.[55] Gützlaff was ordered, therefore, to prepare himself for the necessary qualifying examination, in lieu of the secondary school diploma, which he lacked. If he passed, he would be expected to begin full-time university study at Easter 1823. Shortly after being informed of this decision, Gützlaff fell seriously ill; his powers and his concentration waned, and he even feared death. Faced with this turn of events, Jänicke contacted the Dutch Missionary Society (*Nederlandsch Zendeling Genootschap*, hereafter NZG) in Rotterdam and also Frederick William III.[56] The pastor subsequently announced to Gützlaff that with the permission of the king, he was being sent to Rotterdam. "Upon hearing this," Gützlaff wrote, "my heart was filled with heavenly joy. . . . In several days I was restored and could renew my studies."[57] Though there is no reason to doubt that Gützlaff had been truly ill, the turn of events suggests that Gützlaff had little desire to spend the rest of his career teaching at the Berlin Mission Institute under the authority of a superior mission official. The prospect of traveling to a distant part of the world to become a missionary was doubtless more appealing.

Rotterdam: Completion of Formal Mission Training and Ordination

On June 5, 1823, Karl Gützlaff arrived at the Dutch Missionary Society in Rotterdam, where he studied at the seminary for three years. In contrast to the Jänicke Institute, the Dutch seminary was designed not only to offer ministerial instruction but also to provide the future missionary with the specific training necessary for work in the field. Included was minimal information on how to prescribe for common ailments, which Gützlaff supplemented with extensive reading in medical works. Gützlaff improved his command of English and Dutch while also studying the Malay language, on the assumption that he would be serving in the Dutch possessions or in regions where the Dutch had trading interests. He learned about the history of the Netherlands missions in East Asia, a study which made Gützlaff aware of two outstanding problems that would prove difficult to resolve: devising an effective mission methodology and agreeing on an exact definition and locale for his labors.

The Dutch mission field was inherently a difficult one, because the Dutch

---

55. Gützlaff, "Kurzgefaszte Lebensbeschreibung," p. 3.

56. NZG Archives, *Extract-Acten*, 1823, E129, p. 6. The relevant entry, dated 3 February 1823, reports that "Brother Jänicke" had called their attention to three of his promising students. One of those listed was Gützlaff.

57. Gützlaff, "Kurzgefaszte Lebensbeschreibung," p. 3.

East Indies (now Indonesia) consisted of some 3,000 islands inhabited by a multitude of peoples who spoke different dialects, belonged to diverse religious sects, and were often at war with one another. Much about conditions in the region remained unknown. Often, the missionaries were not welcomed by the colonial administrators, who feared that evangelists would stir up unrest and reduce business profits. Plagued by a perennial shortage of missionaries, missionaries had previously concentrated on preaching tours, in which they declaimed the promise of salvation offered to true believers, distributed Christian literature, and baptized those who gave evidence of conversion. Competition with the well-entrenched Muslim faith and with Roman Catholicism (a legacy of sixteenth-century Portuguese activities) encouraged a policy of quick baptism.[58] After a few weeks the missionary moved on to spread the word, while months might elapse before he returned to nurture the flock. The hope was that in the meantime native evangelists would follow through with further instruction and guidance of the incipient congregation. Though the Dutch missionaries relied per force on local workers, they had little success in producing a qualified and dedicated corps of native evangelists. The result had been weak and often ephemeral Christian communities.

The NZG, despite the fact that it was cognizant of these problems, had not succeeded in formulating an alternative, partly because of the nature of the field and partly because of the desire to disseminate the Christian message to "heathens" throughout the world as quickly as possible. Gützlaff, made aware of the problem, would seek to ensure adequate instruction and training of local evangelists early in his career. Eventually, however, his ambition and his dream of Christianizing all East Asia led to his being considered the embodiment of this weakness in the Protestant mission effort in East Asia.

Gützlaff's penchant for independence did not facilitate the determination of his mission field. During his first year at Rotterdam he had written Rhenius that he hoped to work in the Far East. Later, he had befriended a Greek Orthodox priest whom he hoped to convert to pietist Protestantism. Enamored of the Balkans and the Near East, and doubtless also drawn by the romance and heroism of the current Greek fight for independence from the Turks, Gützlaff journeyed to Paris. Here he spent the spring of 1824 studying the Turkish and Arabic languages while making the acquaintance of French evangelicals. The Dutch society's contact with Robert Morrison, however, opened up even more enticing opportunities.

In October 1825, the NZG sent Gützlaff to the headquarters of the London Missionary Society to continue discussions regarding cooperation in the East

58. Schlyter, *Karl Gützlaff*, pp. 24-26.

Indies. They explored the possibility of Gützlaff's visiting the Anglo-Chinese College in Malacca in preparation for his founding a similar institution in the East Indies.[59] During that trip he made the acquaintance of Morrison and several other English missionaries. Morrison had brought to England his library of 10,000 Chinese books, his Chinese-English, English-Chinese dictionary, and his Chinese translation of the Bible. During his leave in 1824-1826 he co-founded an Institute of Oriental Languages, donated his Chinese library to it, and taught Chinese language there.[60] Among his students, whom Gützlaff may have met, were Mary Ann Aldersley (1797-1868), Jacob Tomlin (1793-1880), and Maria Newell (ca. 1800-1831). Tomlin and Newell were later associated with Gützlaff in his Thailand mission; Newell would become Gützlaff's wife and fellow missionary. Mary Ann Aldersley would later found one of the first Protestant schools for girls in China. She was the first single Protestant woman missionary working in mainland China and was praised by Gützlaff for her courage and dedication on more than one occasion.[61] Gützlaff's London trip influenced him decisively, for henceforth his sights would be set on the Chinese in Southeast Asia — and on China itself.

During the three years in Holland, Gützlaff was also busily engaged in other activities. He cultivated influential persons and organizations that might be of assistance in facilitating his missionary career. Though he did not sustain direct personal relations well, he could be very impressive in short-term personal contacts. Even while en route from Berlin to Rotterdam, he had stopped off in the Wupper valley to visit Rhenish mission associations in Barmen.[62] There he initiated a relationship which would, in 1846, influence Barmen's decision to send two missionaries to assist Gützlaff in his China mission. In the Netherlands he made the acquaintance of eminent Dutch evangelicals and also contacted communities of the United Brethren and their headquarters in Zeist. Such contacts he would continue to foster, especially after he became an independent missionary and had to solicit his own financial support from many individuals and societies.

Simultaneously, he worked on a history of missions in Dutch. Though he handed the manuscript to a Dutch publisher in September 1826, shortly before

59. Suzanne W. Barnett, "Practical Evangelism: Protestant Missions and the Introduction of Western Civilization to China, 1820-1850" (Ph.D. diss., Harvard University, 1973), p. 84.

60. A. J. Broomhall, *Hudson Taylor and China's Open Century* (London: Hodder and Stoughton, 1981-1982), 1:161-62. The language institute lasted only a few years, and the Chinese library was eventually transferred to University College, London.

61. Broomhall, *Hudson Taylor and China's Open Century,* 1:165.

62. Schlyter, *Karl Gützlaff,* p. 22.

his departure for the Indies, the work was probably not published until 1828.[63] The title, in translation, reads, "History of the Expansion of God's Kingdom on Earth since the Days of the Founding of the Church until the Present Time with Particular Reference to Missionaries and Mission Societies."[64] Certain features of the work reveal much about Gützlaff's abiding interests and his career as a Protestant missionary. The title is pretentious and promises more than the book delivers. Ten pages are devoted to "heathen" religions, four to Islam, two to primitive Christianity, four to the early spread and development of Christianity, and twenty-five to the development of Christianity in Europe. Three hundred pages narrate the history of Christian missions in Asia, with 130 of these pages focused on the East Indies, where Dutch interests were paramount. The last part deals with the work of the London Missionary Society in the East Indies, Singapore, the Malay peninsula, and China, with fifteen pages devoted to Robert Morrison, who looms large as a heroic figure.

The main emphasis in the book is on the training and sending out of missionaries, on their achievements, and on the nobility and worth of the missionary cause. Its purpose in part was to elicit Dutch support of the missionary effort in the East Indies, where Gützlaff expected to work. In the final paragraph of the introduction, he wrote, "It is hoped that this presentation will foster a general participation on the part of Christians in the Netherlands in this all-important cause."[65]

Gützlaff's preoccupation with languages and with making the Bible accessible to all people informs the work. What made Morrison especially admirable, according to Gützlaff, was Morrison's pioneering work in translating and publishing the Old and the New Testaments and, as a corollary, producing a Chinese-English, English-Chinese dictionary. After mentioning the various works which Morrison had written and published in the Chinese language, Gützlaff wrote, "It is a cause for wonder that it took Morrison barely four years to put the apostolic gospels into print. Thereby many of us are obliged to say: 'You have served the Lord!' This worthy missionary had given himself so thoroughly to the study of the Chinese language, that he had an impact on that language itself and through it, he contributed to the salvation of this great people."[66]

63. Schlyter, *Karl Gützlaff*, p. 31.

64. Karel Gützlaff, *Geschiedenis der uitbriding van Christus koningrijke op aarde Sedert de Dagen der Kerkhervorming tot op den tegenwoordigen Tijd inbezonderheid met betrekking tot de Zendelingen en Zendeling-Genootschappen* [History of the extension of Christ's kingdom on earth from the days of the founding of the church, to present time, with special attention to the missionaries and missionary societies], 2 vols. (Rotterdam, 1928).

65. Gützlaff, *Geschiedenis der uitbriding*, p. xvi.

66. Gützlaff, *Geschiedenis der uitbriding*, p. 367.

Among the unusual features of Gützlaff's work are two large centerfolds, each measuring about twenty-one by fifteen inches. The first is a chart divided into columns, with Matthew 4:16 printed in various languages. Looking across the columns, one can see how the same biblical verse looks in Arabic, Aramaic, Malay, Turkish, Kashmiri, Hindustani, Burmese, Senegalese, Javanese, modern Greek, Kalmuk, and Bengali. Centerfold No. 2 is entitled, "World Map: Assignment Places of the Missionaries of the Protestant Church." Actually, the map covers, in designated colors, the areas of activity by the Protestant, Roman Catholic, and Eastern Orthodox churches as well as Islam. Clearly, the map was designed to arouse a competitive reaction by Protestants in the face of the challenge from non-Protestants.

Like virtually all of Gützlaff's published works in Western languages, this book was an instrument of propaganda. It was intended not only to stimulate interest in Protestant missions, but also to get Gützlaff's name before the Dutch public as a Dutch missionary. He dedicated his book to six Dutch missionaries who had set an inspiring example for him with their bravery, sacrifices, and achievements.

Gützlaff also published in 1826 a hortatory Dutch-language pamphlet entitled "Pamphlet on Behalf of the Heathens and Mohammedans Addressed to all Christians in Holland."[67] Already, Gützlaff was showing promise as a prolific writer of books, journal articles, biblical translations, and religious tracts, all designed to inspire material and moral support for foreign missions in general and for his own mission enterprise in particular.

As Gützlaff approached graduation and ordination, the NZG finally resolved to assign him to work among the Bataks of northwest Sumatra. Dutch colonial interests had prevailed. On the eve of Gützlaff's departure, the NZG received a letter indicating that two hundred Prussian dollars were being transferred from the treasury of the Prussian Ministry of Education to the society for the use of missionary Karl Gützlaff.[68] The king of Prussia was now facilitating the start of Gützlaff's career. On September 11, 1826, Gützlaff sailed for the East Indies. He arrived in Djakarta four months later and began his long career in East Asia. More than two decades would elapse before Gützlaff returned home, and then only on a tour to build support for his China mission.

---

67. *Smeekschrift, ten behoeve der Heidenen en Mahomedanen, gerigt aan all Christenen van Nederland* [Plea on behalf of heathens and Muhammadans addressed to the Christians of Holland] (Amsterdam: H. Hoveker 1826; German edition published in 1833).

68. "Preussen, Unterrichts-Abteilung des Ministerium der Geistlichen Unterrichts- und-Medicinal Angelegenheiten, an Bernhard Ledeboer, Sekretär," Berlin, 6 September 1826, NZG Archives, Kast. 19, No. 1, Doss. G.

CHAPTER 3

Independent Missionary

The Great Challenge

For almost a century, China represented the great challenge for Protestant missions. At the same time, its huge population inspired dreams of an almost limitless market for Western manufactured goods. Yet the dreams never became a reality. Most Chinese proved singularly indifferent or even hostile to the foreign religion propagated by Westerners. Only in the late twentieth century, after the Chinese had attained a "three-self" church — self-governed, self-supported, and self-propagated — did Christianity gain a degree of popularity in China. However correct the British manufacturers were in estimating the tremendous market if only every Chinese bought two cotton garments, most Chinese were too poor to buy even one, much less two foreign manufactured shirts; even today, when a middle class is emerging in China, internal producers are filling much of the demand for goods.

Disappointments fostered misunderstandings and even bred antagonism. Until the unequal treaties of the mid-nineteenth century forced China to make Christian proselytism and conversion by Chinese legal, missionaries often pointed to the imperial restrictions on their activities in explaining their meager achievements in gaining converts. Likewise, merchants chafed over being confined to only one trading port, Canton. Western businessmen and clerics would join forces in seeking to open China to the "benefits" of Western civilization. Karl Gützlaff was at the forefront in advocating change in both realms.

Despite hardships and dashed hopes, China remained the great magnet in Asia well into the twentieth century. Civil war, international defeats, and economic stagnation could not obliterate the fact that China was the major Asian power in terms of population, territory, cultural heritage, and political weight. The myth of 350,000,000 customers remained very much alive, and even the drive to open Japan was motivated, at least in part, by the desire for coaling stations en route to the China market. The millions of Chinese "heathens" ignorant of the gospel posed to Protestant missionaries their greatest challenge. Western expansionism, fueled by industrialization and nation-state building, found expression in merchants, missionaries, soldiers, and diplomats. The field beckoned adventurous entrepreneurs, especially since communications were slow enough to give them considerable leeway on the China scene. Because of shortages of experienced personnel, more than a few old China hands filled multiple roles. For an individual as ambitious and free-wheeling as Karl Gützlaff, the lure of China was irresistible.

One element of continuity throughout the nineteenth century (and beyond) was the conviction of Christians that theirs was the one true religion and that all peoples stood in need of the gospel. Such a viewpoint was especially pronounced among Protestant evangelicals, from whose ranks came officials of the home mission societies, overseas missionaries, and their supporters. For them, all "heathens" were destined for hell unless they could be converted. This concept of the "heathen" robbed the targeted convert of individuality and minimized cultural differences among non-Europeans. Furthermore, many missionaries initially found it much easier to love the "heathens" in the abstract than to relate to individual Chinese. They were convinced of the superiority of Western civilization and they considered Christianity to be the ultimate source of Western progress, wealth, and knowledge.

In China, on the other hand, Westerners met equally ethnocentric Chinese, aware of their great cultural heritage and certain of its superiority. The Middle Kingdom was equated with civilization. Villagers, whether or not they were acquainted with the Confucian classics, were ordinarily wary of outsiders, suspecting them of no good. Despite the diversity of China, despite the differences between the seaward-looking southeast Chinese and the landward-looking north Chinese, the Chinese shared a culture that valued family and especially sons, a hierarchical society that culminated in the imperial Son of heaven, rituals for the ancestors, and an agrarian orientation.[1] Only gradually would a few Westerners and Chinese develop friendships and an appreciation of the other's outlook and values. Only hesitantly would cultural exchanges begin.

However limited the achievements of the pioneer missionaries were, how-

---

1. See the essays in James L. Watson and Evelyn S. Rawski, eds., *Death Ritual in Late Imperial and Modern China* (Berkeley: University of California Press, 1988).

ever small the demand for Western manufactures, the first half of the nine-teenth century was crucial for future Sino-Western relations. Information, however distorted, flowed back and forth, producing images, myths, and atti-tudes among both Chinese and Westerners about "the other." In the search for marketable products, Western traders relied ever more heavily on opium, creating a serious trade imbalance for China and contributing to two wars be-tween China and Great Britain, in both of which China was defeated. Imple-mentation of the unequal treaties concluding the conflicts led to Christian missions being inextricably linked with imperialism in the minds of most Chinese.

Economic and political imperialism not only oppressed China; it also stimulated the growth of Chinese nationalism, and sometimes, at least, it was used as an all-sufficient explanation for China's failures in the modernizing process. Missionaries developed their strategies in response to being confined to the fringes of China. They evangelized in Southeast Asia; they translated the Bible into Chinese and composed religious tracts, even publishing some secular works in the hope of undermining the Middle Kingdom concept among Chinese. In addition, a home support base for China missions ex-panded. Serendipitous effects were the revitalization of church congregations and new public roles for women as they organized their own mission societies and raised their own funds for mission workers.

Gützlaff and Medhurst's Methodology in Java

Initially, Java, not China, was Gützlaff's assigned destination when he de-parted Rotterdam in the fall of 1826, and Gützlaff's experiences in Southeast Asia were crucial both to the evolution of his mission methodology and to his preparation for the China mission. After a four-month sea journey, Gützlaff was welcomed in Djakarta (Batavia) on 6 January 1827 by LMS missionary Walter Medhurst (1796-1857). Though the NZG had assigned Gützlaff to work with another Rotterdam graduate, H. Wentink, in developing a mission among the Bataks in northwest Sumatra, local warfare delayed Gützlaff's tak-ing up the post. He therefore spent his first four months in Asia working in association with Medhurst on Java.

Medhurst, with only a modest education, had originally been sent to Malacca in 1817 as a printer for the mission press there, but he was intelligent and quick to learn; like Gützlaff, he was one of those activist pioneers who thrived on adventure, challenge, and travel to foreign lands. He had by 1821 been ordained and had taken charge of the LMS Java station at Djakarta.

From this base, he worked for twenty years, evangelizing in Java, venturing on a half-dozen tours in Southeast Asia, and traveling up the China coast in 1835. In 1843, after the Treaty of Nanjing opened new cities, he joined the flow of missionaries to China, and he remained a prominent figure in the China mission community until his death in 1857.

Medhurst combined itinerant preaching with tract distribution among the Malays and Chinese in Southeast Asia. One of a handful of early Protestant missionaries who acquired facility in both spoken Chinese dialects and the written characters, he often used the technique of drawing a few bystanders into discussion, reading a short selection from the Bible and explaining the Christian doctrine as illustrated in the Bible verses. In conclusion, he might present his listeners with a pamphlet explicating the topic discussed.[2] Sometimes he attracted an audience by singing a hymn before he read from a religious tract, paraphrasing and interpreting sections of the tract as he progressed. Or, he began by referring favorably to Confucian moral precepts and then, when individuals admitted transgressions against these teachings, he declared that only the Christian God can forgive and enable one to overcome evil. In the tracts that he wrote himself, he favored devoting an entire brochure to explanation of only one Christian tenet stripped to its essentials. His converts, nevertheless, were few, and only faith in the sanctity of the work compensated for the frustration.

Gützlaff, in working with Medhurst, was impressed by Medhurst's methodology, and especially by his ability to communicate with the people. He determined to acquire such skill as rapidly as possible:

> Oh, if I could only open my mouth in order to make known the grace of our Lord Jesus Christ. Whenever Medhurst spoke, I listened as attentively as possible, even though I was not at all capable of speaking either Malay or Chinese. This morning a priest came to me with the intention of teaching me to speak Arabic. In order to gain respect and receptivity among the inhabitants, it is absolutely necessary to be somewhat acquainted with Arabic. As long as I am here, I shall apply myself to this purpose in order to contribute to God's grace.[3]

2. "Religious Intelligence, Java," *Chinese Repository* (hereafter *CRep*) 2 (March 1834): 519-21; Jane K. Leonard, "W. H. Medhurst: Rewriting the Missionary Message," in *Christianity in China: Early Protestant Missionary Writings*, ed. Suzanne W. Barnett and John K. Fairbank (Cambridge, MA: Harvard University Press, 1985), pp. 48-55.

3. "Reisverhaal van Zendeling Gützlaff, 11 Sept 1826–12 Feb 1827," entry for 6 January 1827, Nederlandsch Zendeling Genootschap (hereafter NZG) Archives, Kast. 19, No. 1, Doss. G.

Gützlaff also studied Chinese with a Fujian tutor who "obliges me to converse with him in his mother tongue." After only two months of intensive study, he felt ready to try out his Chinese on the children in Medhurst's school. Though Gützlaff apparently had a natural linguistic talent, he combined this with a single-minded concentration on language study and a readiness to employ his Chinese on any and all occasions. A missionary colleague described one of Gützlaff's early attempts to converse with Chinese:

> It is delightful and amusing to see him conversing with the people. His simplicity, frankness, and benevolence, win their hearts, and fix their attention. Though yet a novice in the language, he presses onward regardless of difficulties. The people laugh at his blunders, and he, good humouredly, laughs with them. And when they observe him in straits, they kindly help him out, by supplying the words.[4]

The results were notable; he eventually acquired facility in spoken Fujianese, Cantonese, Hakka, and Malay, along with some knowledge of Thai, Japanese, and the language of the Cambodians. He also studied classical Chinese [*wen yen*], reading the Confucian canon with a Chinese scholar and learning to write a straightforward Chinese, though not the high classical style with its many allusions and special syntax. While he acknowledged the importance of translating and composing religious literature in the local language, and he himself would publish many such works, he never forsook his belief that an evangelist should not confine himself to the study and pulpit, but should work regularly among the populace. He would follow in the footsteps of Medhurst rather than less venturesome missionaries such as Robert Morrison and William Milne (1785-1822).

Gützlaff Becomes an Independent Missionary

Within a week after landing in Batavia, Gützlaff had sent an appeal to Europe for greater support for work among the Chinese, and by April he had obtained the permission of the Batavia Missionary Society, an autonomous branch of the NZG, to transfer to the Dutch-controlled island of Bintan off Singapore. Here Chinese comprised the largest segment of the population. Without waiting for authorization from Rotterdam, he made a brief excur-

4. Jacob Tomlin, *Missionary Journals and Letters, Written during Eleven Years' Residence and Travels among the Chinese, Siamese, Javanese, Khassias, and Other Eastern Nations* (London: James Nisbet & Co., 1844), pp. 108-9.

sion to Singapore, which he characterized as an international bridge between China and Europe. Expressing the hope that one day he would be able to devote himself entirely to the China mission, he relayed to the NZG his desire for a Dutch ship to travel throughout the area so that he could win Siam (Thailand) and Cochin China (South Vietnam) for Christ. Wentink had also moved to Bintan, and the two of them decided that Gützlaff should concentrate on the Chinese while Wentink worked among the Malays.

Even so, Gützlaff soon felt confined by the small island of Bintan, and he wrote in August 1827:

> Lord, send me wherever thou wilst. If the answer shall be . . . that I must remain on Bintan, this will sorely oppress my heart. I could have access to millions of Chinese who live only five to eight days removed from me and to whom I could bring the bread of life. God formed my mouth so that I could speak the wonderful Chinese language, and I look on this as His gift of grace. . . . Various China missionaries . . . have produced a host of Christian writings which command our highest respect. . . . We have, therefore writings in abundance, but as for preachers of the word, we are completely wanting.[5]

Gützlaff had taken a Fujianese clan name by this time, and he signed his appeal "Koet Sit-lap" (Guo Shilie or Guo Shila). He explained, "The entirety of the great Chinese nation is divided into one hundred family lineages. Each of these lineages bears a particular name. As soon as I had begun to work among this people, I was obliged to affiliate with a lineage in order to overcome many disadvantages. . . . Those who bear the same name also share the same lineage and are my kindred. We are obliged, generally, to help one another, I as their cousin and they as my relatives."[6] Despite Gützlaff's oversimplification, he had quickly perceived the crucial function of kinship in Chinese social relations and he had begun to identify himself with the Chinese people.

The NZG director Baron A. Mackay responded that Gützlaff was too preoccupied with China, which was beyond the power and resources of the NZG; it would be much better to concentrate on smaller, more realizable objectives — that is, the Dutch possessions in Southeast Asia.[7] Despite the

5. Gützlaff, "Dagverhaal van Februari tot Augustus 1827," entry for 12 August 1827, NZG Archives, Kast. 19, No. 1, Doss. G.

6. Gützlaff, "Dagverhaal van verblijf of het eiland Bintan van 24 Augustus 1827 tot 9 Maart 1828," entry for 9 December 1827, NZG Archives, Kast. 19, No. 1, Doss. G, typescript.

7. Mackay to Gützlaff, Rotterdam, 3 March 1828, NZG Archives, Kast. 33, No. 8, Copy Book, pp. 252-54.

Dutch society's repeated requests that Gützlaff take up his originally assigned post in Sumatra, he was by June 1828 preparing for a trip to Siam and Cochin China with or without the sanction of the NZG. The plan was for Gützlaff, Medhurst, the LMS missionary Jacob Tomlin (1793-1880), and three Chinese assistants to take a supply of medicines and twenty-seven cases of Chinese Bibles and tracts to Bangkok, and to evangelize among the Chinese and Thais. Since Medhurst was delayed, the group departed without him in August. Tomlin was forced by ill health to return to Singapore the following May, but Gützlaff worked in Thailand for three years, his residency interrupted only by voyages to Bintan, Cochin China, Malacca, and Singapore to coincide with the seasonal arrival of the Chinese trading junks. He had for all intents and purposes become an independent missionary, beholden to no society. Even so, he continued, for some years, to identify himself as a NZG missionary[8] and to receive grants from the NZG, the Batavia Society, the Dutch Tract Society [Traktaat Genootschap], and other support groups.

Work among the Chinese and Thai
in Southeast Asia, 1828-1831

In Southeast Asia Gützlaff worked in close association with a small number of pioneering Protestant missionaries. Though their ranks were frequently depleted by illness or death, new recruits came to begin their language studies and take up the cause. All were searching for effective ways to convey their message while they struggled to adjust to a difficult climate and a foreign culture. Ecumenism prevailed, for denominational differences receded before the contrast between Christian and non-Christian. After spending weeks or months among the unresponsive "heathens," missionaries derived comfort and support in the familiar company of fellow evangelists. They shared lodging, religious tracts, and even funds and supplies if necessary. They also went on joint preaching tours. The Singapore missionaries furnished Gützlaff with a chest of religious pamphlets, and the LMS sent a shipment of medical supplies. Gützlaff filled in for absent or ill LMS missionaries and on one occasion worked at the LMS Anglo-Chinese College in Malacca.

These Protestant pioneers also shared a belief that God was active in his-

---

8. See, for example, his letter to the British and Foreign Bible Society (BFBS), 24 September 1832, where he introduces himself as Charles Gützlaff, missionary of the Netherlands Missionary Society; BFBS Archive, Cambridge University, Monthly Extracts, No. 188, 30 March 1833, p. 704.

tory, and that they had been called by God to save the heathen living in darkness. They were evangelicals and adventurers, willing to sacrifice all for the sacred cause. One advantage of the British workers over Gützlaff and the NZG missionaries was that the former had been assigned to the Ultra-Ganges mission field: all of Asia east of India. Thus circulation throughout Southeast Asia was legitimate. The Dutch societies tried to limit their recruits to the Dutch colonies, but even here there were problems, because the Dutch government disapproved of evangelism among Muslims as disruptive of its rule.[9] Dutch mission societies were expected to locate their personnel among minority groups outside the cities — for example, among the Bataks in northwest Sumatra, where Gützlaff had originally been assigned.

Missionaries were often left to formulate policy and make decisions on their own initiative, for their sending societies in the West had such scanty knowledge about the region and peoples that they could offer only general guidance. An exchange of letters between Europe and Southeast Asia in the 1820s required eight months or more, so that responses to opportunities or to events on the field had already been taken by the time the missionaries received instructions. Proselytism among the Malays was the province of some missionaries who expected to spend their career in Southeast Asia, but for others, work in Southeast Asia was considered preparatory to the evangelism of China, once it had been opened. Gützlaff definitely placed himself in the latter category.

The Chinese of Southeast Asia in the 1820s might be divided into three principal categories: (1) partially assimilated males who had emigrated earlier and had taken local wives, (2) recent immigrant laborers and traders who dreamed of acquiring enough wealth to enable them to return to their families in China, and (3) great numbers of Chinese seamen from Fujian and northeastern Guangdong [Shantou and Chaozhou] who came for the trading season. Depending on the monsoon, the thousands of junks bringing bullion and articles for Chinese consumption ordinarily arrived in early spring and departed by mid-summer with their cargoes of sugar, rice, sandalwood, indigo, ivory, and other luxuries.

Gützlaff was cognizant of China's rich historical and cultural heritage, and in his mission appeals he repeatedly asserted that the Chinese were the most civilized of the heathen peoples of Asia. He even argued that the morality of the Chinese sages was superior to that of the Greek and Roman philosophers, though both could only be imperfect since they lacked the truth of

9. David Abeel, *Journal of a Residence in China and the Neighboring Countries,* 2nd ed. (New York: J. Abeel Williamson, 1836), pp. 164-65.

Christianity.[10] All aspects of Chinese society interested him. His writings are interspersed with descriptions of New Year's celebrations, funerals and weddings, the educational system, diet, opium smoking and gambling, worship at temples, and other customs.

Like other early nineteenth-century Protestant missionaries, Gützlaff formed his opinions regarding Chinese character and lifestyle on the basis of his experiences with Chinese merchants, artisans and laborers, Buddhist monks, and seamen, none of them members of the educated elite. The portraits he painted contained more darkness than light despite his professions of love for the Chinese. He did compare Chinese industry and efficiency favorably with the easygoing ways of the Siamese, which in his pietist view equated to indolence and slovenliness. The Chinese devotion to the work ethic explained their dominance of trade and commerce in Southeast Asia, he concluded. He praised Chinese appreciation of education, though he was critical of the emphasis on rote memorization and he lamented the reliance on non-Christian texts.[11]

On the other hand, the raucousness of Chinese festivities, the food offerings and burning of incense on the altars, and the multiplicity of deities, some of them depicted as fierce and ugly in order to ward off evil spirits, offended him.[12] The Buddhist rituals with rosaries, chanting, candles, and appeals to intermediaries reminded him of Roman Catholicism, which for Protestant evangelicals in the early nineteenth century was not true Christianity, but "Papism." Like the Moravians, Gützlaff had been schooled in an unadorned Christianity in which the didactic sermon was the focus of the church service. In one instance, he seized a temple statue and threw it out the window in an attempt to demonstrate the powerless of the people's gods.[13] The gambling, drinking, and feasting that accompanied holiday celebrations distressed him; furthermore, he found it impossible to gain an audience amidst such festivities. He, along with many Westerners, deplored the lack of cleanliness and of civic concern beyond the family. The image of China conveyed in his writings for the Western public was, therefore, at considerable variance with that presented by the Jesuits two centuries earlier.

10. Gützlaff, "Dagverhaal van Februari tot Augustus 1827," entry for 1 August 1827.

11. Gützlaff, "Riouw op Bintang: Uittreksel uit het Dagboek van Broeder Gutzlaff van 1 April tot 8 Juli 1828," *Maandberigt van het Nederlandsch Zendeling Genootschap* [Monthly report of the Dutch Missionary Society] 8 (1828), NZG Archives, Kast. 1, No. 63, entry for 20 May 1828.

12. Gützlaff, "Reisverhaal," entry for 7 February 1827; "Dagverhaal van verblijf," entries for 13 November 1827, 11 February 1828.

13. Gützlaff, "Dagverhaal van Februari tot Augustus 1827," entry for 1 August 1827.

Gützlaff adopted Medhurst's techniques of public exposition, prayer, and tract distribution; later, when he recruited young German missionaries, this was the model he expected them to follow. He insisted on their rapid acquisition of the local dialect so that they could live among and mingle freely with the populace. Gützlaff's forceful personality and his conviction of the exclusive truth of Christianity, on the other hand, must have impeded attempts at real give-and-take discussion. During Gützlaff and Tomlin's journey to Thailand, Tomlin described an evening service of thanksgiving after the first sighting of land. "The captain, and several others, joined us in reading the 106th Psalm. Gutzlaff suddenly rose at the end of this spirited and energetic song of praise, and with peculiar vehemence of manner, commanded every one to kneel down, and praise the God of heaven for His mercies; instantly, as if moved by a sudden and irresistible impulse, one and all were down on their knees, and Gutzlaff poured forth a strain of impassioned praise to the Most High."[14]

It was Gützlaff rather than Tomlin who took the initiative in most of their activities, protesting to the Thai foreign minister about attempts to restrict their work, for example. Tomlin told of one occasion in which they were pestered by visitors whose only motive was curiosity. "One man, of some authority with the Chinese, came in a rude manner and was intrusive. At first, Gutzlaff spoke rather sharply to him, but afterwards brought him into our private room, and *made* him sit down to dinner with us. He evidently wished to alarm us; but we spoke to him plainly and boldly, showing that we had no fear in a righteous cause. He left us apparently in a very different spirit from what he manifested on coming."[15]

Gützlaff was initially impressed by the readiness of Buddhist priests to acknowledge the merits of Christian doctrines and their failure to counter with arguments from Buddhist texts.[16] He even concluded that Chinese religious tolerance made them more susceptible to the gospel than other Asians. In his reports he described numerous instances when he was almost mobbed by individuals trying to get their hands on the free printed texts. He soon learned that seeming agreement without public confrontation did not imply a willingness to substitute Christianity for their own religious beliefs and practices. He also discovered that the possession of books brought social prestige, whether one read them or not; also, the paper itself could be put to all manner of uses.

14. Tomlin, *Missionary Journals,* pp. 108-9.
15. Tomlin, *Missionary Journals,* pp. 128-29.
16. Gützlaff, "Reiseverhaal," entry for 11 January 1827; Gützlaff, quoted by Tomlin, *Missionary Journals,* pp. 49-50.

An illustration of Gützlaff's residence in Bangkok
from his *Journal of Three Voyages*, 1834

Such information did not deter Gützlaff or most Protestant missionaries of this era from continuing to itinerate and distribute tracts even when the possibility for follow-up instruction was limited. During the trading season Gützlaff and Tomlin met the Chinese junks and handed out Christian pamphlets to Chinese sailors in the hope that they might read them or at least carry them home and thereby be a means for conveying Christian literature into China. Despite the wastage, missionaries pointed to the occasional individual who read the work given him and returned for discussion and further instruction.[17] There was the additional consideration that until the Chinese emperor's toleration edicts of the 1840s, the possibility of direct evangelism in China was limited. The translation, compilation, and distribution of Bibles and other religious literature remained a major facet of Protestant work in East Asia during this preparatory period. Missionaries also sought to convert Chinese working overseas in the hope that the converted, upon returning home, would proselytize among their kinfolk and form Christian nodes within China.

Medicine proved a valuable asset in creating a favorable climate for evangelism and attracting an audience. Gützlaff regularly engaged in doling out quinine for malarial fever and ointments for skin diseases, treatment of eye infections, and the prescription of other simple remedies; he even engaged in minor surgery when needed. He also prescribed a potion composed of opium and a strong emetic in efforts to cure opium addition.[18] These services were

17. Tomlin, *Missionary Journals,* pp. 139, 187.
18. Tomlin, *Missionary Journals,* pp. 127-28, 132, 198.

accompanied by proselytism, and though few were converted, they did provide protection against opponents of Christianity and its propagators. On the basis of his reputation as a physician, he gained access to the foreign minister of Thailand and even to the inner quarters of a prince seeking treatment for his wife and children. He stimulated a growing curiosity about the West and the sources of its power and wealth.

At this point in his career, Gützlaff was slow to baptize inquirers; in fact, he baptized only one individual during his four and a half years in Southeast Asia.[19] Among his assistants, he had observed their uneasiness over being associated with Western Christians, and he had noted the resistance of inquirers to accepting the exclusiveness of Christianity and their difficulty in abiding by the strictures placed on converts. The Chinese converts who accompanied Tomlin and Gützlaff to Thailand, for instance, had been most reluctant to have fellow countrymen observe them attending the regular evening services held on ship.[20] One of the principal Thai translators quit because the missionaries insisted on his observing the Sabbath and reprimanded him for gambling and prostitution. Tomlin wrote, "The good hopes we had of the old man, Hing, for awhile, were latterly much blighted. . . . At times, he was apparently much impressed with the truth, and has often struggled with the convictions of an awakened conscience. He would gladly have made a partial covenant with the Lord, but the *whole law* was too hard for him. He thought it sufficient to keep six or seven of the commandments!"[21]

Hing was one of many disappointments; over and over again, Gützlaff and Tomlin reported discussions of Christian doctrines with inquirers for an extended period only to have the individuals vanish. Doctrines relating to the Trinity, the crucifixion of the Son of God, and the sacrament of Holy Communion were incomprehensible to most, and they were not yet able to accept them on faith. How could Jesus be both God and the Son of God? The power of Jesus to forgive sins based on his righteousness and merit they could accept, for it was compatible with Buddhist teachings, but that Jesus derived such power as a consequence of his being the Son of God they found implausible. Metaphors based on a herding-vineyard culture conveyed little meaning to individuals from a settled rice economy. Misunderstandings arose as a result of different customs. Once, a man rushed into Tomlin and Gützlaff's room with a handful of burning incense sticks, whereupon Gützlaff seized

---

19. Gützlaff to MacKay, Bangkok, 2 February 1831, NZG Archives, Kast. 19, No. 1, Doss. G, Correspondence, typescript; Abeel, *Journal of a Residence in China*, p. 291.

20. Tomlin, *Missionary Journals*, p. 104.

21. Tomlin, *Missionary Journals*, pp. 188-89.

them and threw them into the river. Tomlin recorded in his journal: the man "was quite taken by surprise at this rebuke, having come, probably in simplicity and ignorance, like the foolish Lycaonians, who wished to do sacrifice to the apostles."[22]

For the local Chinese and Thai assistants and inquirers, the possibility of recrimination by fellow countrymen was real. The Thai ruling elite were well aware of England's expansion into India, Burma, and Malacca. Tomlin and Gützlaff were once accused of being spies for the English, who had designs on Thailand. The religious tracts they had distributed were confiscated and burned, and they were ordered out of the country. Only by citing their treaty rights and presenting their Christian literature for inspection did they manage to get the ruling rescinded. To protect those associated with them, they ceased public preaching and tract distribution and remained in their quarters until the furor died down.[23] Those desiring books, medicine, or instruction would have to seek them out. On another occasion, they were accused of smuggling opium, and their residence was sacked.

In the fall of 1829 Gützlaff went to Malacca to assist at the Anglo-Chinese College of the LMS mission, whose ranks had been depleted by death and sickness. There, he met and married Maria Newell. Newell, the first single woman to be sent to Asia by the LMS, had been orphaned at an early age and had found a home with the family of Rev. Andrew Reed, a non-conformist minister and philanthropist. While Robert Morrison was on furlough in England during the 1820s, she had studied with him and had also become acquainted with Mary Ann Aldersley, fellow student and future China missionary. It was the latter who provided the financial support for the LMS to send Newell to Malacca in 1827. By 1829 she had already founded five girls' schools and had acquired some knowledge of the Chinese and Malay languages.[24]

After marriage in December 1829, she accompanied Gützlaff back to Bangkok, where the two engaged in linguistic and translation work. Maria Gützlaff began to compile a Thai-English, English-Thai dictionary, while Tomlin and Karl Gützlaff embarked on a translation of the New Testament and the Book of Psalms into Thai. Throughout his stay in Southeast Asia, however, Gützlaff continued to be drawn by the challenge of China's unconverted millions. Even marriage did not dampen his restlessness and ambition; rather, he began to anticipate a journey along the China coast with his wife.

22. Tomlin, *Missionary Journals*, p. 148.

23. Gützlaff, *Acht Maanden te Bankok*, NZG Archives, A15c. 311.40.

24. See biography of Maria Newell by Jocelyn Murray in *Biographical Dictionary of Christian Missions*, ed. Gerald H. Anderson (Grand Rapids: Eerdmans, 1999), p. 492.

When Maria became pregnant, thoughts of a joint trip to China were replaced by plans for a journey by Tomlin and Gützlaff. But then Tomlin's poor health closed off this possibility. Even Gützlaff suffered a bout of malarial fever, which depleted his energies and frustrated his ambitions. In July 1830, Maria Gützlaff wrote to her mentor in England: "My dear Charles is very poorly just now with a fever, and I cannot get him to rest. . . . Today he has made attempts to work at many things, but is too weak and has to throw himself on the floor repeatedly."[25] Gützlaff's aspirations were therefore held in abeyance while he continued his linguistic activities and proselytism among the Thais and local Chinese. Again in October 1830, Maria Gützlaff wrote that Gützlaff would probably go to China in May; most likely, he would go alone to ascertain the possibilities for their continuing work there and also finding a means of subsistence.[26]

In February 1831 Maria Gützlaff died while giving birth to twins, one of whom also died. Gützlaff, always insecure and in need of approbation, was devastated by the death of his admiring partner. As in previous crises, he interpreted the loss as a signal from God: "After having seen my beloved wife sink into the grave, there is nothing left for me to do but wander through the world alone. I have lost my only sister, a wife rich in love, and an industrious co-worker." "My work in Siam is almost at an end. As the hand of the Lord is just now stretched out over China by the most dreadful wonders of nature, I trust the Lord will also reveal his glorious Gospel. If my unworthy life can serve the great cause, Lord here am I; let thy will be done."[27] To compound his troubles, he suffered another bout of ill health and became convinced that he would die without a change of climate. Providence was dictating that he go to China. Whatever formal links with the NZG remained, he now severed. He made arrangements for the surviving twin daughter to be cared for until she reached the age of two, whereupon she would be sent to England, and he began seeking passage on a junk bound for China.[28] After several disappoint-

25. Extracts of letters from Mrs. Gützlaff to Rev. Mr. Reed, July 1830, NZG Archives, Kast. 19, No. 1, Doss. G.

26. Extracts of letters from Mrs. Gützlaff to Rev. Mr. Reed, 14 October 1830, NZG Archives, Kast. 19, No. 1, Doss. G.

27. Gützlaff to Pastor van den Ham, "Übersetzung eines Briefes von demselben an Herrn Prediger van den Ham in Rotterdam," 11 May 1832, Vereinte Evangelische Mission, Archives of Rheinische Missionsgesellschaft (hereafter VEM), Gützlaff Correspondence; extracts of letter of Gützlaff to Mrs. Reed, Bangkok, 22 February 1831, NZG Archives, Kast. 19, No. 1, Doss. G.

28. The second twin died while Gützlaff was on a junk waiting to leave port. There were persistent rumors that Mary N. Gützlaff's legacy helped finance Gützlaff's coastal trip. I have been unable to find documentation confirming these rumors. Karl Gützlaff

ments, a Chinese friend from Guangdong offered to take him in the capacity of navigator and physician. Gützlaff, dressed in the garb of a Fujian sailor, boarded a ship traveling to Tianxin in June 1831.

Gützlaff's Legacy in Southeast Asia

Klaus Fiedler, in his study of German Protestant missionaries in Tanzania, classifies missionaries according to their methodology and their attitude toward the local culture.[29] Those who had a positive attitude toward the cultural heritage and tried to accommodate both tradition and Christianity he calls conservatives. Those who hoped to reconstruct African culture on the modern Western model he labels progressives. Fiedler argues that German romanticism with its concepts of *Volk* and the authenticity of the non-rational influenced the conservatives' approach to cultural traditions. According to Johann von Herder (1744-1803), philosopher, poet, and court preacher at Weimar, each *Volk* has its own history and cultural heritage, and these are the source of its cultural identity. All these find expression in its "mother tongue." Whether or not missionaries were consciously or subconsciously influenced by such Romantic themes is difficult to determine. Perhaps the dichotomy between the two categories is not so sharp as Fiedler seems to indicate, since many missionaries, over the years of their residence in a foreign land, grew to understand and even appreciate aspects of the local heritage. Certainly Gützlaff had become acquainted with the Romantic poets during his youth, but their long-term influence is uncertain. Gützlaff, at any rate, operated according to many of the tenets of the conservatives: his emphasis on the use of Chinese catechists, who could employ the vernacular dialect, his contention that conversion was the work of the Holy Spirit, his goal of establishing native Christian communities in village China, and, of course, his spirit of independence, adventure, and individualism.

Herman Schlyter, in his biography of Gützlaff, offers a different categorization of missionaries that is also useful in understanding Gützlaff and his China career. He distinguishes among three types of Protestant missions according to affiliation and structure:(1) the church mission, wherein a specific denomination recruits missionaries and solicits funds primarily from among

---

gives the impression that the Chinese captain of the junk provided transportation in return for his services.

29. Klaus Fiedler, *Christianity and African Culture: Conservative German Protestant Missionaries in Tanzania, 1900-1940* (Leiden: E. J. Brill, 1996), pp. 1-27.

its own members; it ordinarily seeks to establish branch churches in the mission field; (2) the society mission, frequently characterized by ecumenism and public fundraising campaigns; examples are the China Inland Mission (CIM) of Hudson Taylor and the YMCA; and (3) the free mission, of which Gützlaff was the first modern Protestant model.[30] Free or independent missionaries can choose their own field and methodology and guide their work from the field. Emancipated from human authority, they are responsible only to God. They must, however, find their own support, either by employment or by building a home base, or both. Individual personality obviously is central to the nature of the free mission, and because a strong personality is typical of independent missionaries, their careers are often marked by controversy. To the long line of independent missionaries belong such figures as David Livingstone, who was inspired by Gützlaff's call for medical missionaries but was sent by the LMS to Africa because of the Opium War and subsequently severed connection with the LMS; Issachar J. Roberts, who became famous because of his Taiping connections;[31] the multitalented Albert Schweitzer, and hundreds of workers of pietist, Pentecostal, or charismatic persuasion currently residing throughout the world.

NZG officials had repeatedly reprimanded Gützlaff for not going where he had been assigned and for seeking funds from other sources to enable him to follow his own wishes.[32] After Gützlaff embarked for China, he was criticized for his restlessness and ambition, and particularly for his abandonment of the Thai mission when it was only in the preparatory stages. In a lengthy critique, Otto von Gerlach, Prussian court preacher and conservative spokesman for pietism, objected to Gützlaff's methodology as superficial. The establishment of Christian congregations, not the writing and distribution of tracts, was the principal goal of missions, he asserted in a series of essays published in the *Evangelische Kirchen-Zeitung* in 1834-1835. Those following the apostolic way would not have embarked on an adventurous "voyage of discovery" unless they could leave behind a viable Christian community. The tie between missionaries and their denomination was more than a financial one, wrote von Gerlach; it protected preachers "from the dangers that inhere in the purely subjective aspects of their office."[33] Robert Morrison, while appre-

30. Herman Schlyter, *Karl Gützlaff als Missionar in China* (Lund: C. W. K. Gleerup, 1946), pp. 9-10 (paraphrased).

31. Roberts was on occasion associated with Baptist mission societies, but in times of disfavor he gained support from Gützlaff and other Western residents in Hong Kong.

32. *Extract Acten,* January 1830, pp. 1-2; 2 May 1831, p. 91; *Handlungen der Directeuren,* 19 July 1831, NZG Archives, 165.

33. Quoted in Schlyter, *Karl Gützlaff,* pp. 57-58.

ciating Gützlaff's enterprise and his contribution to the China mission cause, reported to the LMS in 1832: "He would not work well, I fear, with others. Secondly, he would be insubordinate and, at first, domineering. He is unaccustomed to the yoke of social intercourse, but seems since he came [to Macao] to improve."[34]

In May 1831 Tomlin and the American missionary David Abeel (1804-1846) had made a hurried trip to Bangkok in the hope of detaining Gützlaff in Thailand until he had completed the revision of the Thai version of the New Testament, but they missed him by a week and a half.[35] Tomlin, however, was not critical of Gützlaff, at least not in his published journal. Gützlaff's medical and evangelistic work, he wrote, had helped create a friendly attitude toward Protestant missionaries and had given them access to the Thai ruling nobility. He had also left behind several earnest inquirers plus a baptized assistant named Boon Tee (Koë Bun Tai), originally from Chaozhou. Boon Tee had accepted Christianity after three years and was apparently an effective evangelist. Sent to Annam to preach, he later returned to Thailand, where he was rebaptized by immersion by the Baptist missionary John T. Jones (1802-1851) and served as the mainstay of the Bangkok Baptist community. In 1836, though, he left the church because of differences with his supervisor, William Dean (1807-1895).[36] When in 1844 Gützlaff founded the Chinese Union to recruit Chinese evangelists to work in the Chinese interior, a number of members were Chaozhou Christians. While still in Southeast Asia, Gützlaff had sent urgent appeals to the American Board (ABCFM) and the American Baptists for workers in Thailand. The ABCFM responded to the pleas of Gützlaff and others by transferring Abeel from Canton to Bangkok, and in 1833 the Baptists relocated Mr. and Mrs. John T. Jones from Burma to Thailand. Jones would be followed by William Dean, later a pioneer for the Baptists in Hong Kong and Shantou.[37]

Gützlaff admitted that Protestant work in Thailand was still in the prepa-

34. Morrison to W. A. Hankey, treasurer, LMS, Macao, 10 February 1832, Council for World Mission (CWM), School of Oriental and African Studies, London, Archives of LMS, Box 3, So. China, Incoming, 1830-1839, Fol. 1C, Jacket e. Gützlaff was at the time a house guest of Morrison, having recently arrived in Macao after his first China coastal trip.

35. Tomlin, *Missionary Journals*, pp. 301, 306-7; Abeel, *Journal of a Residence in China*, p. 208.

36. "Religious Intelligence: Rev. [John Taylor] Jones from Bangkok, 22 Sept, 1833," *CRep* 2 (February 1834): 478-79; Joseph Tse-Hei Lee, *The Bible and the Gun: Christianity in South China, 1860-1900* (New York: Routledge, 2003), pp. 22-24.

37. Lee, *The Bible and the Gun*, pp. 23-25; A. J. Broomhall, *Hudson Taylor and China's Open Century* (London: Hodder and Stoughton, 1981-1982), 1:186-87.

ratory stage at the time of his departure, but he justified his action by citing the will of Providence as manifested in his illness, the death of his wife, the fickleness of the Thais, and the power of state Buddhism.[38] In summarizing his career in Thailand, he particularly emphasized his literary and linguistic work.[39] Many of his writings, however, were still in draft. He had translated church hymns and prayers into Thai and had published two tracts with the aid of the Dutch Tract Society. The English-Thai, Thai-English dictionary he and his wife had been compiling was not yet complete, but he had written an article on the Thai language for the Royal Asiatic Society.[40] He and Tomlin had made a Thai translation of the New Testament.[41] In the process, they had benefited from manuscripts containing sections of the New Testament translated by Roman Catholic missionaries. They had also depended heavily on their Thai assistants to put their oral translations into acceptable form, eliminating foreignisms and correcting syntax. They relied particularly on Boon Tee, who was said to be "peevish" initially and contemptuous of Christian works, but was a master of the Thai language. Boon Tee wrote out the whole New Testament for them and also corrected the entries for the Thai dictionary.[42] (Such reliance on native linguists, though typical of all translation work by the pioneer missionaries, has received inadequate recognition and awaits further research.[43])

Whereas the Thais preferred an elegant style, Gützlaff desired a Bible accessible to the general public, and he once expressed delight upon discovering several Siamese works almost in the language of the people; these he hoped to use as models.[44] Such an approach accorded with the Protestant belief that all Christians should be able to read the Bible, as the Bible alone conveyed the

38. Gützlaff, *Journal of Three Voyages along the Coast of China in 1831, 1832, and 1833* (1834; Taipei: Ch'eng-wen Publishing Co., 1968), pp. 24-25, 65-66.

39. Gützlaff to Mackay, February 1831, NZG Archives, Kast. 19, No. 1, Doss. G.

40. Gützlaff, "Remarks on the Siamese Language," *Journal of the Royal Asiatic Society* 3 (1835): 291-304; Gützlaff to W. A. Hankey, Treasurer, LMS, Bangkok, 1 April 1831, CWM, LMS Box 3, So. China, 1830-1839, Folder 1 B; extracts of letters from Mrs. Gützlaff to Rev. Mr. Reed, July 1830.

41. Abeel, *Journal of a Residence in China*, pp. 226-27; extracts of letters from Mrs. Gützlaff, July 1830, 14 October 1830; 31 October 1830.

42. Tomlin, *Missionary Journals*, pp. 328-30.

43. See, however, Jost Zetzsche, *The Bible in China: History of the Union Version; or: The Culmination of Protestant Missionary Bible Translation in China*. Monumenta Serica Monograph Series 45 (Nettal: Monumenta Serica, 1999) and Jessie G. Lutz, "Western Nationalism, Chinese Assistants, and Translations of the Chinese Bible." Paper delivered at conference on "A Bridge between Cultures: Commemorating the 200th Anniversary of Robert Morrison's Arrival in China," University of Maryland, March 15-16, 2007.

44. Letter of Gützlaff to Tomlin, Bangkok, 26 June 1829, quoted in Tomlin, *Missionary Journals*, p. 215; see also p. 161.

Word of God. It did not, however, accord with Thai prototypes of sacred literature, and the translation left much to be desired, as was pointed out by the Thai king, to whom he sent a copy.

In July 1830 Gützlaff had sent the New Testament translation to the Netherlands Bible Society with an appeal for funds to print it in Thai, Laotian, and Cambodian. The Bible Society, uncertain about its quality, delayed allocating monies until 1833, and then it provided for the printing and distribution of only the Gospel of St. Luke.[45] The British Foreign and Bible Society in the same year assisted with the publication of part of the Thai New Testament after it had been proofed by a competent Thai scholar. By 1835 J. T. Jones had arranged for the printing of the Gospel of St. Matthew and had begun a revision of Gützlaff's draft New Testament; Jones's version, published in 1850, helped standardize Christian theological vocabulary in Thai. Mrs. Jones also prepared a Thai dictionary based on the Gützlaff manuscript. All of these preliminary works would be superseded, but Tomlin and Gützlaff were correct in stating that the foundations of the Thai mission had been laid down. Gützlaff's contribution to this phase was vital.

Juggling Coastal Evangelism and Secular Employment

From mid-June to mid-December 1831, Gützlaff served as navigator and physician on the Chinese junk, traveling from Bangkok north to Liaoning in Manchuria and back down to Guangdong. The trader stopped to exchange goods at ports all along the China coast, while Gützlaff joyously took the opportunity to distribute medicines, hand out scriptures and religious tracts, and proclaim the gospel of salvation. He even tried to convert his fellow sailors; he reported that he was able to shame them into admitting the correctness of the gospel. On the other hand, after he had prayed to God for protection during a tornado and "God had sent the sun to shine," the sailors went on shore to thank Ma Zu despite Gützlaff's reprimands.[46] In December an exhilarated Gützlaff landed in Macao, where he was welcomed by Robert Morrison and provided with lodging. The Chinese populace, he had discovered, eagerly accepted the Christian writings; they were friendly and would gladly trade with Westerners. Only the throne and high officials were antagonistic and adamant in maintaining a closed China. At least this was the message that he immediately began to convey to Christians throughout Europe and Amer-

---

45. *Extract-Acten*, NZG, Session 5, August 1833, pp. 264-65, NZG Archives, E 12.1.
46. Gützlaff, *Journal of Three Voyages*, pp. 94-100.

ica. He gloried in the challenge of China as his dream of converting the most populous nation on earth to Christianity began to seem a possibility.

Though Gützlaff was quite successful in securing funds for medicines, publication of tracts, and other specific ventures, as an independent missionary he did not receive a regular salary from a mission society. This is perhaps one reason why Gützlaff was by February 1832 already on another coastal journey, this time in the employ of the East India Company. Between 1831 and 1837 he would make almost a dozen such tours. He would for the rest of his career try to juggle dual roles: apostle to the Chinese and Chinese interpreter for secular agencies, initially with the British trading company Jardine-Matheson, and later with the British government.

Even with his boundless energy and drive, he had to tailor his evangelistic activities to accommodate his civil responsibilities. Not that he acknowledged the compromises to his Christian constituencies in the West, or possibly even to himself. Reports to mission societies and supporters rarely mentioned his secular activities, but rather described his itinerations, the welcome accorded him by villagers (in contrast to the arrogance and hostility of bureaucrats), the cheerfulness of the populace even amidst poverty, and so forth. Even while he was with the British military in Ningbo during the Opium War and was serving as a civil magistrate on British-occupied Zhoushan, he wrote about visiting the inhabitants' homes in order to tell them of the one true Christian God and of His son Jesus, who was the means of salvation. He hoped to organize Christian communities and establish a school; he had set up a printing press and was publishing the New Testament, he reported.[47]

During the 1830s Gützlaff devoted especial attention to the written word. He composed Chinese religious tracts, publishing over two dozen between 1833 and 1838.[48] In collaboration with Walter Medhurst, he worked through several revisions of the Chinese Bible, and he also wrote histories, geogra-

47. Gützlaff to NZG, Herr B. Ledeboer, Secretary, Nanking [Nanjing], 30 August 1842, NZG Archives, Kast. 19, No. 1, Doss. G, Correspondence no. 23; Gützlaff to NZG, Chusan [Zhoushan], 2 October 1842, no. 24; Gützlaff to NZG, Tinghai [Dinghai], 8 January 1843, no. 25.

48. See the record in Alexander Wylie, *Memorials of Protestant Missionaries to the Chinese: Giving a List of Their Publications, and Obituary Notices of the Deceased, with Copious Indexes* (1867; Taipei: Ch'eng-wen Publishing Co., 1967), pp. 56-63, and the more complete bibliography by Hartmut Walravens, *Karl Friedrich Neumann (1793-1870) und Karl Friedrich August Gützlaff (1803-1851): Zwei deutsche Chinakundige im 19. Jahrhundert* (Wiesbaden: Harrassowitz Verlag, 2001). In Gützlaff's report to NZG on 7 September 1836, he listed thirteen tracts that had been printed with the aid of American societies. Extracted in *Extract-Acten*, 1837, pp. 144-48.

phies, and other secular works, both in Chinese and in English.[49] He studied Japanese and Korean with the goal of translating the Scriptures into these languages, while he also embarked on a reading program of Chinese novels, dynastic histories, classical philosophy, Buddhist literature, and folk tales. Almost every issue of the *Chinese Repository* during this period contained a Gützlaff commentary on one or more Chinese literary works. Even though he could dash off letters at lightning speed, a voluminous correspondence with potential supporters and the publicizing of China missions occupied considerable time. All of these literary pursuits could be carried on during odd moments and after hours.

As for more direct evangelistic activities, they were ordinarily divided between preaching and tract distribution during his travels and his labors among the populace of the Canton-Macao region. Gützlaff's reliance on the distribution of tracts and scriptures was derived partly from the restrictions of his civil duties, but he had implicit faith in the power of the Word and the working of the Holy Spirit.

To critics like Gerlach, Gützlaff responded:

> I am fully aware that I shall be stigmatized as a headstrong enthusiast, an unprincipled rambler, who rashly sallies forth, without waiting for any indication of divine providence, without first seeing the door opened by the hand of the Lord; as one fond of novelty, anxious to have a name, . . . [as one] who leaves a promising field, and restlessly hurries away to another; all of whose endeavours will not only prove useless, but will actually impede the progress of the Saviour's cause. I shall not be very anxious to vindicate myself against such charges. . . . I have weighed the arguments for and against the course I am endeavouring to pursue and have formed the resolution to publish the gospel to the inhabitants of China Proper, in all the ways, and by all the means, which the Lord our God appoints.[50]

Gützlaff sometimes even acknowledged that the motives of Chinese in clamoring for Christian books might be questioned, and that few Chinese could understand the foreignized texts without further explanation, but he answered in terms difficult to gainsay: the analogy of sowing seeds that might sprout who knows when and where, the contention that God worked in His

---

49. For discussions of Gützlaff's English-language works, see chapter 5; for his Chinese-language works, see chapters 6 and 7.

50. *Extract-Acten*, 1837, pp. 124-25.

own wondrous ways. When an occasional inquirer came seeking instruction, he pointed out that if one soul were saved from perdition, the efforts had not been in vain. For a time the British, Dutch, and American Bible and tract societies as well as numerous mission organizations operated on these assumptions. Donations for the printing and distribution of tracts poured in; societies contributed toward the development of a set of movable metallic Chinese type in order to facilitate and expedite the production of tracts — more specifically so that Gützlaff might have tens of thousands of tracts to distribute.[51]

Those whom Gützlaff treated for various medical conditions seldom left without having heard a brief disquisition on the truth of Christianity and receiving a Christian tract. With some success, he publicized the need for a few trained physicians to join the China mission. When Peter Parker, first American medical missionary to China, delivered his farewell address before embarking for China in June 1834, he expressed his admiration of the pioneering spirit of both Robert Morrison and Gützlaff: "I would commend to you [the example] of Morrison and Gutzlaff. To these I might refer you for illustrations of what *individual enterprise* united with *faith,* and *humble dependence* on God may accomplish."[52] But for Gützlaff, the purpose of medical missions was evangelism, not social service. Providing medicine to gain access to the populace and to demonstrate the benevolent spirit of the gospel was only preliminary to evangelism.

Gützlaff soon decided that Chinese could communicate more effectively with their fellows than the Western missionaries, and so during his first decade in the Canton–Macao–Hong Kong region he devoted much of his time to training assistants and inquirers. Often he combined instruction with apprenticeship. Before sending Chinese evangelists out on their own, he had them attend Bible classes and prayer sessions, after which he had them accompany him on preaching tours. Sometimes a new candidate joined an experienced Chinese evangelist on visits to nearby villages. According to a colleague in 1847, a typical weekday schedule for Gützlaff, would be:

Early morning to 10:00 A.M., the reading and explanation of Scriptures, then prayer, and biblical instruction with Chinese inquirers and assistants in various dialects and classes;

10:00 A.M. to 4:00 P.M., British office;

4:00 to 7:00 P.M., itineration, with two or three Chinese aides to nearby villages and workplaces, Gützlaff giving a short introduction, the Chinese preacher offering a sermon ordinarily in the form of a Bible story, and a con-

---

51. American Tract Society, *Tenth Annual Report,* 1835, pp. 87-95.
52. "Mr. Parker's Farewell Address," *New York Observer* 12.24 (14 June 1834): 93.

cluding prayer by Gützlaff, ending with the distribution of tracts.[53] Gützlaff, unlike many of his colleagues, could speak local dialects fluently enough so that he frequently did much of the preaching himself. Often he visited the nearby islands where Hakka stonecutters were quarrying granite. George Smith of the Church Missionary Society (CMS) described accompanying Gützlaff on one such occasion:

> On Dec. 22d, about nine o'clock, A.M., we embarked in a Chinese boat, accompanied by two native preachers. . . . We first landed at a stone quarry, where the Chinese workmen were induced to leave their labour, and, without any difficulty or delay, about twenty natives were assembled around us, and formed a little congregation of attentive listeners. Mr. Gutzlaff commenced addressing them in their own language, on the truths of the Gospel, with much energy, adapting himself in tone, gesture, and manner to the assemblage before him. They listened with apparent pleasure, frequently responding and offering observations. . . . They seemed to recognise in Mr. Gutzlaff and his native assistants, old acquaintances, and the authoritative tone and manner with which he compelled any hesitating or inattentive individual to give his presence and attention was sometimes amusing. . . . The dialect which they spoke was Hok-ka [Hakka], which differs considerably from the Canton dialect generally spoken in these parts.[54]

In contrast, Smith described another preaching tour: "Not long after the former excursion, some other Missionaries formed a little party to accompany Agong [Wat Ngong], a Chinese Christian . . . on a visit to the villages on the mainland opposite Victoria. I went in the company; and, as no one present could speak the local dialect fluently, Agong was the chief speaker."[55] On Sundays Gützlaff devoted himself entirely to religious duties: three services in Chinese, one or two in Japanese, and one in English, plus home visits to Chinese converts.[56] Congregations were small, generally ten to twenty.

Other colleagues also attested to Gützlaff's effectiveness as a speaker.

53. *Maandberigt van het Nederlandsch Zendeling Genootschap* [Monthly report of the Dutch Missionary Society], August 1847.

54. George Smith, *A Narrative of an Exploratory Visit to Each of the Consular Cities of China and to the Islands of Hong Kong and Chusan in Behalf of the Church Missionary Society in the Years, 1844, 1845, 1846* (New York: Harper & Bros., 1847), pp. 73-75.

55. Smith, *A Narrative of an Exploratory Visit*, p. 77.

56. Gützlaff to NZG, Macao, 7 September 1836, extracted in *Extract-Acten*, 1837, pp. 144-48.

Ferdinand Genähr of the Rhenish Mission reported that Gützlaff talked with his whole body. He was lively and interesting, and he could preach fluently in four different dialects.[57]

Gützlaff's goal was to spread the word of God, and he believed that Chinese would be the primary agents in accomplishing his goal. He would, like many preachers of the Second Great Awakening and also many evangelicals of today, leave to others the building of church congregations. He thought that denominations were irrelevant in China, for the differences between Christianity and Chinese religions were so great that it was difficult for Chinese to perceive the differences among denominational teachings and practices. Chinese need accept only the most basic Christian doctrines: God the Father and Creator, Jesus the Savior through his sacrifice on the cross, and Holy Spirit, guide and comforter. They must, however, accept these to the exclusion of all non-Christian doctrines. It has been argued that Gützlaff's primary contribution lay in awakening interest in China and China missions in Europe and America; certainly this was a major legacy. Yet in the Canton–Hong Kong region where he could work with his inquirers, he did make quite a number of converts. As with most missionaries, he saw many of them apostatize. A few of his converts, however, after receiving further instruction from Gützlaff's missionary recruits, proved crucial to the founding of Christian congregations in interior China, particularly among the Hakka.

Gützlaff engaged in a certain amount of educational work, though he quickly perceived the difficulties of education as a branch of missions in China.[58] Yet, unlike many Westerners, he argued against fundamental alteration of the curriculum and methodology. Respect and prestige were closely associated with literacy, and he saw no way to acquire a decent Chinese style without knowledge of the classics and commentaries. Since funds were limited, he recommended concentration on middle or higher education, with attention to the training of Chinese assistants. Facility in English would be an asset, since it would open up a whole new realm of knowledge, but it had the disadvantage that it often led to the pupil's leaving school early for a business position. The essential task was to provide, in the Chinese language, information that could combat prejudice — namely, science and the history and geography of the West. All would be presented as illustrations of the working of God's will in the universe. Reforming Chinese civilization, however necessary,

---

57. Genähr to Inspector, Hong Kong, 25 March 1847, VEM, Genähr Korrespondenz und Tagebücher, 1846-1864.

58. Philosinensis [Gützlaff], "Christian Missions in China," *CRep* 3.12 (April 1835): 546-65.

was the province of Chinese awakened by the missionaries, but not of the missionaries themselves.

The one branch of education about which Gützlaff expressed few reservations was basic schooling for females. Here he apparently accepted the familiar aphorism: educate a mother and you educate a nation. Even so, he viewed female education as the province of missionary wives and single women. Both his first and his second wives organized small girls' schools, and he gave support insofar as his other duties permitted.

Mary Wanstall Gützlaff and Parochial Education

Missionary wives are almost as invisible as Chinese evangelists in mission records. They did not ordinarily send reports to the home board, and they did not participate in general assemblies of missionaries or in the formal deliberations of the ruling bodies of denominations or congregations. Though caches of personal letters to relatives are available, and the memoirs of certain wives such as Henrietta Shuck and Helen Nevius were published,[59] most early missionary wives remain in the shadows. To bring these women into focus is often difficult. Caught up in the duties of bearing and rearing children, running a household in a foreign environment, and tending family members during their frequent illnesses, many wives, no matter how dedicated to the mission cause, found themselves cutting back on their evangelistic and educational activities.[60] There were, nevertheless, a few who gained recognition in their own right: Julia B. Mateer and Eliza J. Bridgman, who were childless, and Mary Ann Aldersley, Lottie Moon, and Harriet N. Noyes, who were single.[61] The three wives of such a forceful personality as Karl Gützlaff remain

59. Henrietta Shuck, *Scenes in China: or Sketches of the Country, Religion, and Customs of the Chinese* (Philadelphia: American Baptist Publication Society, 1852); Helen S. C. Nevius, *Our Life in China* (New York: R. Carter, 1869).

60. For a perceptive discussion, see Jane Hunter, *The Gospel of Gentility: American Women Missionaries in Turn-of-the-Century China* (New Haven: Yale University Press, 1984).

61. Information on these workers is available in Irwin T. Hyatt Jr., *Our Ordered Lives Confess: Three Nineteenth-Century American Missionaries in East Shantung* (Cambridge, MA: Harvard University Press, 1976); Samuel H. Chao, *Practical Missiology: The Life and Mission Methods of John Livingston Nevius, 1829-1893* (New York: P. Lang, 1996); Helen S. C. Nevius, *The Life of John Livingston Nevius, for Forty Years a Missionary in China* (New York: Fleming H. Revell, 1895); E. Aldersey White, *A Woman Pioneer in China: The Life of Mary Ann Aldersey* (London: Livingston Press, 1932); Harriet N. Noyes, *A Light in the Land of Sinim and History of the South China Mission of the American Presbyterian Church, 1845-*

hazy figures, even though Maria Newell and Mary Wanstall seem themselves to have been women of determination and character.

In the spring of 1834, Gützlaff had journeyed to Malacca and Singapore to make arrangements for publication of several of his religious works by the LMS press. He was also to pick up ten thousand copies of the New Testament translated by Medhurst and himself and financed by the British Bible Society.[62] While in Malacca, he met and married Mary Wanstall, an independent missionary partially supported by an East India Company resident there. She joined Gützlaff in Macao in November 1834, and shortly thereafter opened a girls' school in their home. Partial support came from the Morrison Education Society, founded in honor of Robert Morrison. Pending the establishment of a school for boys, Mary Gützlaff's school enrolled a few boys in her classes. Yung Wing [Rung Hong], who was one of Mary Gützlaff's first pupils, later became organizer of the First Educational Mission to the United States. He provides perhaps the best picture of her, along with his reaction to his first encounter with a Western woman:

> If my memory serves me right, she was somewhat tall and well-built. She had prominent features which were strong and assertive; her eyes were of clear blue lustre, somewhat deep set. She had thin lips, supported by a square chin, — both indicative of firmness and authority. She had flaxen hair and eyebrows somewhat heavy. Her features taken collectively indicated great determination and will power.
>
> As she came forward to welcome me in her long and flowing white dress . . . , surmounted by two large globe sleeves . . . , I remember most vividly I was no less puzzled than stunned. I actually trembled all over with fear at her imposing proportions. . . . Her kindly expression and sympathetic smiles found little appreciative response at the outset, as I stood half dazed. . . . [W]hen my homesickness was over and the novelty of my surroundings began gradually to wear away, she completely won me over through her kindness and sympathy. I began to look upon her more like a mother. She seemed to take a special interest in me; I suppose, because I was young and helpless, and away from my parents.[63]

1920 (Shanghai: Presbyterian Mission Press, 1927); Eliza Bridgman, *Daughters of China; or Sketches of Domestic Life in the Celestial Kingdom* (New York: Robert Carter and Bros., 1853).

62. Gützlaff to NZG, 13 April 1834, NZG Archives, Kast. 19, No. 1, Doss. G, no. 11, typescript.

63. Yung Wing (Rong Hong), *My Life in China and America* (New York: Henry Holt & Co., 1909), pp. 3-4.

Like most of the first Protestant educational efforts, the school was a small affair and its continued existence depended on the health and availability of its founder. Most of the pupils were abandoned infants, beggars, or excess daughters whose parents were willing to risk conversion to Christianity in return for the free food, clothing, and lodging. Funds had to be pieced together from various sources; in Mary Gützlaff's case, the Morrison Education Society, the Society for Promoting Female Education in India and the East (SPFE), the merchant William Jardine (Gützlaff's employer), and Gützlaff's personal income. Mary herself solicited support from a wealthy American family prominent in the American Tract Society.[64] Maintaining continuity in the student body was difficult, since parents generally withdrew daughters as soon as they were able to help at home and sons as soon as they had learned enough English to secure employment as shop clerks; few stayed longer than two years.[65] In the fall of 1836 Gützlaff reported that there were thirteen boys and four girls enrolled.[66] Then, upon the opening of the Morrison Society school in 1839, the boys' department was disbanded, while the number of girls increased. The pupils studied Chinese under a traditional Chinese tutor, while Gützlaff, when in residence, examined them twice a week on the Chinese classics and his Chinese translation of the Gospel of St. Mark. Bible study and catechism classes loomed large. Otherwise, the curriculum was similar to that of a girls' primary school in the West: the three R's, along with English.

Having become increasingly troubled regarding the plight of blind Chinese girls, Mary Gützlaff enrolled several in her school and tried to develop techniques for teaching them Chinese. The fate of most blind Chinese girls was indeed heart-rending; many were sold into prostitution or beggary. Remaining childless despite the birth of a stillborn baby in January 1842, Mary focused her compassion and love on these unfortunate girls and even adopted a half-dozen or more: Lucy, Agnes, Jessie, Laura, Mary, and Fanny. Apparently without securing prior permission, she sent two of these girls to the SPFE for training in England in 1839. While expressing irritation over the presumption of Mary Gützlaff, the society also used the occasion to call attention to the importance of its work:

> Two little blind girls, of the ages of six and seven, have been sent to this country by Mrs. Gutzlaff. It was impossible for the Committee to receive

64. Letter of Mary Gützlaff to Mrs. Perit, 15 June 1836, printed in *Foreign Missionary Chronicle*, February 1837, pp. 29-30.
65. "Second Annual Report of the Morrison Education Society," *CRep* 7 (October 1838): 306-7.
66. Gützlaff to NZG, Macao, 7 September 1836, extracted in *Extract-Acten*, 1837.

them, or to appropriate the funds of the Society to their support . . . still, as they are here, they must not be suffered to want. Several friends have united to take charge of them, and they have been placed at the Blind School in Gloucester Street, Queen Square. They are remarkably intelligent; and have learned to read with raised letters, to work, and even to write. Their religious knowledge is also very satisfactory. They were rescued from those who had blinded them to make them objects of charity, a practice too common in China. They are thus living witnesses of the necessity there is, for bringing the humanizing influences of Christianity to bear on this barbarous and degraded race.[67]

Despite the fact that the SPFE severed its ties with Mary Gützlaff, her efforts on behalf of blind girls were not without long-term benefits. Agnes, after training in Braille, returned to teach blind pupils in Mary Ann Aldersley's school in Ningbo. Moreover, Harry Parkes of the British Consular Service, who had studied Chinese with Gützlaff and had married one of Mary Gützlaff's cousins, established an Agnes Gützlaff Fund to perpetuate Mary Gützlaff's work for the blind. Agnes, in her will, bequeathed her property for the relief and education of the blind, and the monies were used to establish the Gützlaff Hospital in Shanghai.[68] On a health furlough to the United States in 1842, Mary Gützlaff took several of her adopted blind daughters, two of whom were placed in the Pennsylvania Institution for the Blind in Philadelphia, where they lived out their lives as "thoroughly Americanized" Chinese.[69]

Yet another sequel to Mary Gützlaff's work with the blind was a small pamphlet for children, entitled "Little Mary Gutzlaff" and published in both English and Dutch.[70] It tells the story of Mary Gützlaff's adopted namesake, "little Mary Gützlaff," and the frontispiece shows two blind girls in Chinese dress reading Braille Bibles. Mary was said to have been deliberately blinded and wounded by her master for use as a beggar. Upon being brought to Mrs.

---

67. "Proceedings and Intelligence," *Missionary Register,* January 1840, p. 47.

68. Suzanne Hoe, *The Private Life of Old Hong Kong: Western Women in the British Colony, 1841-1941* (Hong Kong: Oxford University Press, 1991), pp. 108-9, 172, 289; Carl Smith, *A Sense of History: Studies in the Social and Urban History of Hong Kong* (Hong Kong: Hong Kong Educational Publishing Co., 1995), p. 292. The Gützlaff Hospital was later incorporated into St. Luke's Hospital.

69. Hoe, *Private Life of Old Hong Kong,* p. 292.

70. Two pamphlets on the oppression of Chinese girls and women were published together under the title *China en deszelfs inwoners, en de Geschiedenis van de Kleine Mary Gutzlaff* [China and its inhabitants and the history of little Mary Gutzlaff] (Rotterdam: M. Wijt & Zonan, 1850).

Gützlaff, she was clothed, treated by a local doctor, taught to speak English and to read the Bible, and then sent to England for further training. Under "the influence of the Holy Spirit," she was transformed into a "model of piety and humility." Becoming ill while in England, she died in the faith, to be rewarded in heaven.[71] Though bordering on the maudlin, the story had a basis in fact, and it was effective in eliciting the sympathy of European women for their "oppressed sisters" in China. Designed to arouse European interest in missions to Chinese women and girls, the pamphlet was a part of Gützlaff's publicity campaign of 1850-1851 that led to the establishment of the Berlin Foundling Home in Hong Kong under the auspices of the Berlin Women's Missionary Society for China. German Sunday School children "adopted" and supported their individual Chinese girls in the Foundling Home and other parochial schools. A Hildesheim Mission for the Blind and a Blindheim Industrial School were later established; in 1904 the Hildesheim had forty inhabitants and was fully supported by the local Hong Kong community.

Not a great deal more can be related about Mary Gützlaff and her work. In Macao she helped set up a Poor Fund to assist destitute Chinese and Portuguese, especially the sick, who came to her house.[72] The Gützlaffs provided temporary lodging to numerous newly-arrived missionaries as well as to those in transit or financial difficulty. Issachar Roberts, for example, lived with them for several months and was given subsidies when in need.

During the Opium War (1840-1842) political events impinged on Mary Gützlaff's life as on that of other missionaries; furthermore, her husband, as a British civil servant, was deeply involved in the military campaigns and British occupation.[73] In the fall of 1839 the Portuguese government ousted British citizens from Macao; Mary Gützlaff was one of those who spent six weeks on board ship in the Hong Kong harbor. For a brief time in 1840, she, her two cousins, and five adopted blind daughters found refuge in Manila. In October 1840 she and her entourage joined Karl Gützlaff on occupied Zhoushan, where she immediately began to make plans for opening a school.

There are hints of depression and social withdrawal on the part of Mary Gützlaff, especially after the loss of her only natural child. Even so, personal letters by Karl Gützlaff to the merchants William Jardine and John Matheson indicate a loving relationship. When Gützlaff was arranging a trip to interior Fujian to obtain tea plants and information on tea processing in 1835, for ex-

71. *China en deszelfs inwoners*, p. 172.

72. Gützlaff to NZG, Macao, 7 September 1836, extracted in *Extract-Acten*, 1837.

73. Peter W. Fay, *The Opium War, 1840-1842* (Chapel Hill: University of North Carolina Press, 1975), pp. 255-57, 267, 278, 305, 341; Hoe, *Private Life of Old Hong Kong*, pp. 28-29.

ample, he petitioned Jardine to allow Mary Gützlaff to accompany him on the boat as far as the entrance to the Min River, a request that Jardine refused even though Mary Gützlaff expressed willingness to incur the risk.[74] In 1840 Karl Gützlaff sent numerous pleas to Matheson for assistance in arranging passage for Mary Gützlaff so that she could join him in Zhoushan. Ill health eventually took its toll, and though she traveled abroad in the hope that a change of climate would enable her to recover, Mary Gützlaff died in April 1849. The life of a missionary wife in nineteenth-century China was, more often than not, short.[75]

74. Jardine-Matheson Archive, Reel 31, Pvt. Macao, 1834-1836, entries for 3/5/35 and 3/12/35, Cambridge University Library.

75. According to an 1851 survey, of the hundred missionaries who were married, twenty-four had lost their wives, "a far greater percentage of deaths among females than males." "List of Protestant Missionaries to the Chinese with the Present Position of Those Now among Them," *CRep* 20 (1851): 520. Depression and even mental instability were not uncommon among both male and female missionaries. The subject of attrition among missionaries awaits study.

CHAPTER 4

The Multiple Roles of
Nineteenth-Century Missionaries

In accounts of China during the nineteenth century, Karl Gützlaff is sometimes characterized as the "parson who handed out Bibles from one side of ships cruising the coast of China and opium from the other side." Though such a portrayal is neither kindly nor completely accurate, it does indicate Gützlaff's dual careers. During most of his years in East Asia, Gützlaff held a full-time lay appointment along with his missionary position. Details concerning evangelistic activities might dominate his reports and correspondence, but from 1832 on Gützlaff was employed first as an interpreter by representatives of the British East India Company and then by the first superintendents of British trade with China; subsequently he served as interpreter and administrator for British civil and military officials during the Opium War. His last position was Chinese Secretary for the Hong Kong government, which he held from September 1843 until his death in August 1851. In his multiple roles, Gützlaff managed to take part in almost every major event on the China coast during the second quarter of the nineteenth century.

A man of remarkable energy and zeal, Gützlaff never let up on his evangelistic activities before and after office hours, during his lunch break, and on weekends. He managed to engage in almost as much mission work as many missionaries without other responsibilities, a fact remarked on by several colleagues. His civil employment did, however, influence his mission methodology, and after 1840 it limited his personal evangelistic efforts to the Hong Kong environs or other areas where he was stationed. This was one impetus to the founding of the Chinese Union, designed to rely primarily on Chinese converts to carry the gospel to interior China. His secular writings and activities also informed British perceptions of China and Chinese perceptions of British goals in China. Themes that ran through Gützlaff's reports on his coastal journeys were: (1) the eagerness of the general Chinese populace for trade and religious tracts, (2) Chinese arrogance in the face of humility, but acquiescence to force, and (3) the military weakness of China. Chinese leaders, meanwhile, worried that the coastal probes were preparation for an invasion of China.

In undertaking lay work, Gützlaff was not, of course, unique among missionaries. The Western community on the fringes of China during the second quarter of the nineteenth century was small; interactions and interdependence were customary. The shortage of Westerners with a knowledge of Chinese language and society during much of the nineteenth century meant that missionaries were frequently pressed into service as interpreters and consultants. For twenty-five years Robert Morrison protected his position as a missionary by working for the British East India Company. Elijah C. Bridgman and Peter Parker on the ABCFM served as interpreters and advisors in negotiating the treaties concluding the two opium wars. Other than Morrison and Gützlaff, however, missionaries generally served secular authorities only briefly or resigned from their mission society upon accepting a diplomatic position. Gützlaff, furthermore, was never one for half measures. He not only performed his civil duties with enthusiasm, but he publicized his findings in every conceivable outlet: mission magazines, newspapers, learned periodicals, books issued in several languages and numerous editions, the Blue Book of the British Parliament, reports and correspondence with mission societies, tract associations, and through influential individuals in Europe, England, and America. In addition, he participated in the opium trade more directly than most missionaries.

Some advocates of Christian missions have expressed regret over this union of church and state and argued that it contributed to the linkage of imperialism and Christian evangelism in the minds of Chinese. They may well be correct in thinking that most Chinese thought of missions as simply one facet of Western expansionism. As Westerners and Western culture spread to every continent, missionaries in China and elsewhere played multifarious roles as educators, doctors, publicists, government advisers, and historians. Anti-Christian movements of the 1920s condemned Western "cultural aggression" and placed it on a par with economic and political aggression.[1] Traditional

1. For detail, see Ka-che Yip, *Religion, Nationalism and Chinese Students: The Anti-Christian Movement of 1922-1927* (Bellingham: Western Washington University, 1980), and Jessie G. Lutz, *Chinese Politics and Christian Missions: The Anti-Christian Movements of 1920-1928* (Notre Dame, IN: Cross Cultural Publications, 1988). See also Yang Tiankeng, "Jidujiao yu xindai zhongguo" [A study of the Anti-Christian Movement in China], and Zhao Qing, "Cong fan 'Kongjiao yundong' dao 'Fei zongjiao datongneng yundong'" [From

China, however, neither advocated nor practiced separation of church and state. Ethics and Confucian orthodoxy were intertwined with politics, while the government tried to regulate institutionalized Buddhism and Taoism. Even today, Chinese leaders expect religious groups to support government policies and goals and to accept the guidance of Beijing. When the Chinese condemned Christian missions as an arm of imperialism, they were not necessarily implying that the relationship was abnormal; indeed, it was what they expected.

British commercial demands, diplomacy, and missionary activities became, however, intertwined with the humiliation of China and the importation of opium. The union of missionary and official did not make acceptable the collusion of opium traders, British officials, and evangelists, or the growing infringements on Chinese sovereignty. Many Chinese found such cooperation indefensible even if Chinese were an essential link in the smuggling operation. Reverend George Smith, though he had condemned the opium trade, took passage on a ship delivering opium when he surveyed the treaty ports on behalf of the Church Missionary Society in 1844-1846. He reported, "My Chinese boy more than once on the voyage asked me . . . what I should say in reply to the Chinese, if after hearing me speak about Yay-soo taolu le (Jesus' doctrine), they should ask why I had come in a ship that brought opium, of which so many of his countrymen ate and perished."[2]

Perhaps no one gave clearer expression to the linkage of evangelism, opium, and Western infringement on China than Karl Gützlaff. After his 1831 journey up the China coast distributing religious tracts and preaching the gospel to all comers, Gützlaff wrote, "We will hope and pray, that God in his mercy may, very soon, open a wider door of access; and we will work as long as the Lord grants health, strength, and opportunity. I sincerely wish that something more efficient might be done for opening *a free intercourse with China,* and would feel myself highly favoured, if I could be subservient, in a small degree, in hastening forward such an event. In the merciful providence of our God and Saviour, it may be confidently hoped that the doors to China will be thrown open."[3] Gützlaff, along with other Protestant missionaries of

---

the "anti-Confucian movement" to the "anti-religious league movement"], both in *Zhong-Xi wenhua yu jiaohui daxue* [Christian universities and Chinese-Western cultures], ed. Zhang Kaiyuan and Arthur Waldron (Wuhan: Hubei jiaoyu chubanshe, 1991), pp. 61-83.

2. George Smith, *A Narrative of an Exploratory Visit to Each of the Consular Cities of China and to the Islands of Hong Kong and Chusan in Behalf of the Church Missionary Society in the Years, 1844, 1845, 1846* (New York: Harper & Bros., 1847), pp. 115-16.

3. Gützlaff, *Journal of Three Voyages along the Coast of China in 1831, 1832, and 1833* (1834; Taipei: Ch'eng-wen Publishing Co., 1968), p. 151.

the early nineteenth century, viewed the opening of China to trade and inter-course and the opening of China to Christian proselytism as part of the same process designed to bring the blessings of Western Christendom to the hea-then East. It is to be hoped, he wrote, that while Protestant missionaries preach the glorious gospel of Christ, they will also "show that the spread of the divine truth opens the door for every useful art and science; that unshack-led commercial relations will be of mutual benefit, and that foreigners and Chinese, as inhabitants of the same globe, and children of the same Creator, have an equal claim to an amicable intercourse, and a free reciprocal commu-nication."[4] To prevent open exchange was to deter progress based on the spread of knowledge and truth throughout the world, according to Gützlaff. It was to dispute the legitimacy of commercial activities and to reveal a lack of concern for the people's welfare. When England demanded the right of free intercourse among all nations, it was not merely seeking material benefits; it was acting in accord with natural law. Those who denied people access to truth and to Western manufactures were infringing on an inherent human right. Chinese resistance to international trade amounted to defiance of God, who had decreed the brotherhood of all men. Even Confucius had taught that all people were of one family.[5]

Gützlaff's Coastal Journeys: *Lord Amherst*

A job offer with the possibility of implementing Gützlaff's dream came less than three months after he returned in December 1831 from his initial journey on a Chinese junk. Gützlaff's first secular position in East Asia was as inter-preter aboard the *Lord Amherst,* which sailed from Macao on 20 February 1832 northward up the China coast to Korea, returning on 5 September 1832. Charles Marjoribanks, president of the East India Company (EIC) Select Committee, had suggested a journey "to ascertain how far the northern ports of this Empire may gradually be opened to British commerce, which would be most eligible, and to what extent, the disposition of the natives and local

---

4. Gützlaff, "Journal of a Residence in Siam and of a Voyage along the Coast to Mantchou Tartary," *Chinese Repository* (hereafter *CRep*) 1 (June 1932): 51-52.

5. This was a frequent theme with Gützlaff. See "Mouyi" (Trade), *Dong-Xi yangkao meiyue tongji zhuan* (East-West monthly magazine; hereafter *Dong-Xi*) 1 (1838): 8-11; "Tongshang" (Commerce), *Dong-Xi* 12 (1837): 160-62; Gützlaff, *Da Yingguo tongji* [Short account of England] (Malacca: LMS, 1834), 5:22; Gützlaff, *A Sketch of Chinese History, An-cient and Modern: Comprising a Retrospect of the Foreign Intercourse and Trade with China,* 2 vols. (London: Smith, Elder, & Co., 1834; reprinted, New York: John P. Haven, 1834), 2:291.

governments would be favorable to it."[6] The trip was, of course, in defiance of Chinese regulations restricting Chinese trade to the Canton-Macao area.[7] It was sponsored by the EIC in part as a response to the contention of Manchester cotton manufacturers that the company was so well satisfied with its monopoly of British trade with China and its profits from tea that it made little effort to expand the China market. An additional incentive was dissatisfaction over the restrictions and numerous fees imposed at Canton. Carrying two hundred bales of cotton goods for sale, but no opium, the *Lord Amherst* was under orders not to employ military force.

H. H. Lindsay of the EIC was officer in charge, and Captain Thomas Rees was commander. Gützlaff signed on as interpreter and ship's physician. Not only did Gützlaff embrace an opportunity to preach the gospel and distribute religious tracts along coastal China, but he needed income now that he was an independent missionary without the regular support of a missionary society. Since the journey was illegal according to Chinese statutes, Lindsay and Gützlaff operated under assumed Chinese names and concealed their connection with the EIC. When entering a Chinese port, Lindsay would issue a formal Chinese statement which represented the ship as a private English vessel from Bengal on its way to Japan. Lindsay often justified his stopover to local officials by citing the need for provisions.

Accounts of the journey by both Lindsay and Gützlaff were published in *Report of Proceedings on a Voyage to the Northern Ports of China*, while Gützlaff also incorporated his report in *A Journal of Three Voyages along the Coast of China in 1831, 1832 & 1833*. The latter went through many editions and was translated into a half-dozen languages. Extensive excerpts from the journals were published by the *Chinese Repository* and numerous Western publications and were also inserted in the *British Parliamentary Papers*.[8]

The *Lord Amherst* called at Xiamen (Amoy), Fuzhou, Ningbo, and Shanghai to trade, and then went on to Weihai on the Shandong peninsula, Korea, and the Ryukyu islands. Xiamen, according to Lindsay and Gützlaff,

6. "Experimental Voyage to the Northeast Coast of China," Parliamentary reprint, 19 June 1833, *Asiatic Journal and Monthly Review* (hereafter *AJMR*) 12 (September 1833): 94-107; (October 1833): 157-73.

7. Hosea B. Morse, *The Chronicles of the East India Trading Co. Trading to China, 1635-1834*, 5 vols. (Oxford: Clarendon Press, 1922), 4:278ff.

8. The following account is largely based on these reports. H. H. Lindsay and C. Gutzlaff, *Report of Proceedings on a Voyage to the Northern Ports of China in the Ship Lord Amherst* (London: B. Fellowes, 1833). Reports by the two authors are separate, but are bound in one volume under one title. In contrast to Lindsay, Gützlaff included observations on Chinese character, customs, society, and so forth. See chapter 4.

was a city of wealth, had an excellent harbor, and was the base for enterprising Chinese merchants who controlled much of China's coastal shipping. Fuzhou and Ningbo they recommended as closer than Canton to the sources of tea, porcelain, and silk; transportation costs could be reduced by opening them to trade. Shanghai's significance as a trading and transportation hub was a revelation; it ranked only after Canton in importance, according to Gützlaff. It was a bustling port with a good harbor, was nearer to the market for British woolens than Canton, and provided avenues to communication with all China. Already British goods were to be found in the markets of these cities.

At all ports, they reported, the defenses were in ill repair; the fortresses were understaffed; the soldiers were poorly trained and even more poorly fed and clothed; many either lacked guns or had only rusty, untrustworthy flintlocks. Fifty resolute and well-disciplined men could rout the Chinese troops at Wusong, guarding the entrance to the Yangtze, according to Lindsay.[9] Gützlaff concurred: "Had we come here as enemies, the whole army would not have resisted half an hour, for they were all dispirited."[10] Captain Rees and Gützlaff, with the aid of a draughtsman, surveyed the ports' harbors and rivers, correcting navigational charts previously available to Westerners. From a Chinese naval official, Gützlaff even managed to obtain a Chinese maritime chart of the Min River on which Fuzhou is situated.[11] It was not happenstance that Ningbo, Fuzhou, Xiamen, and Shanghai were the four cities, along with Canton, that Britain demanded be opened to Western trade and residence in the Treaty of Nanking, 1842.[12] They had been made a known quantity and, according to Lindsay and Gützlaff's widely publicized opinion, they presented great possibilities for profitable trade.

Gützlaff's presence on the journey was valuable because he was able to prescribe medications. He was also familiar with the vocabulary of the Fujian working class, could sprinkle his conversations with Confucian aphorisms, and could translate imperial edicts and communications from Chinese administrators. All these contributed to a friendly reception by the general pop-

9. Lindsay and Gutzlaff, *Report*, pp. 190-91.

10. Gützlaff, *Journal of Three Voyages*, p. 310.

11. Arthur Waley, *The Opium War through Chinese Eyes* (New York: Macmillan, 1958), p. 234.

12. See Samuel Ball, "Observations on the Expediency of Opening a Second Port in China," *Journal of the Royal Asiatic Society* (hereafter *Journal of the RAS*) 6 (1841): 182-221. This consisted of a memorial by Lord Amherst, 2 July 1816, with numerous emendations by Ball, quoting Lindsay's observations regarding the most desirable ports as well as a possible permanent base.

ulace. On more than one occasion, Gützlaff's fluency in the Fujian dialect and his general appearance led to his being mistaken for a Chinese. Though Lindsay knew Chinese, he lacked skill in spoken dialects and read Chinese with difficulty, so the party relied on Gützlaff when quick repartee or accurate renditions were required. Lindsay had Gützlaff accompany him on all visits so that Gützlaff could help him when he was at a loss for an appropriate expression or was unsure of the exact meaning of what was said.

After curiosity about the foreigners had attracted crowds, Gützlaff would explain a few Christian concepts in the local dialect and distribute books and pamphlets to eagerly outstretched hands: Morrison's translation of the Bible, William Milne's tracts against gambling and lying, various Christian pamphlets, and issues of Milne's *Cha shisu meiyu tongji zhuan* (World examiner and monthly record).[13] The works were desired by the populace for diverse reasons, yet on subsequent visits missionaries did come across an occasional individual who had read their gifts and desired further information about Christianity. Some of the mandarins, in contrast to the masses, became uneasy upon discovering that foreigners were adept in Chinese and informed about Chinese geography and civilization; it was, after all, illegal for a Chinese to teach a Westerner the language. What was the intent of these brash intruders who defied imperial edicts? One official even accused Gützlaff of being a Chinese traitor in the employ of barbarians until Gützlaff took off his hat and revealed the absence of a queue. Often the magistrates tried to prevent contact between the Westerners and the people by employing lashers and threatening punishment by the cangue or bamboo.

Particularly controversial was the pamphlet written by Charles Marjoribanks and translated into Chinese by Robert Morrison, *Da Yingjiliguo renpin guoshi lüeshuo* (A brief account of the people and affairs of the Great English nation). Its thesis was that China and England should be friendly nations dealing with each other on a free and equal basis. This theme composed the content of Lindsay and Gützlaff's message, and it was reiterated many times in communications with the Chinese. Lindsay decided to distribute the work after his contacts with Chinese magistrates revealed their ignorance concerning the world beyond China. In a packet of literature to be sent the emperor, Gützlaff included a copy along with religious tracts. Once word of the pamphlet had spread, many Chinese officials eagerly requested it as a source of information; one administrator expressed gratification upon learning that England desired only trade, not territory. Others, however, were incensed by the attempt to place England on an equal plane with China. A memorial by a

13. For the themes of *Cha shisu meiyu,* see chapter 6.

Zhejiang provincial official, extracted in the *Peking Gazette*, stated, "I have carefully examined the barbarian book. . . . Some parts of it are highly rebellious and full of falsehoods, many other parts are perfectly unintelligible. The general purport of it is complaining that commerce was not conducted with justice at Canton; and on this pretext they desired to abandon that place and come to this [province], thus manifesting a highly perverse and crafty disposition. But since the reign of Kien Sung these barbarians have not been permitted to come and trade in Che-keang. . . . How could I in the smallest degree permit any change in opposition to the fixed laws?"[14]

Citations of imperial edicts limiting Western trade to Canton were the common response of Chinese officials to Lindsay's attempts to sell cotton goods. Whether some mandarins and merchants desired legal changes to permit trade, as Lindsay and Gützlaff claimed, is hard to say. Certain officials did offer to allow sales if the *Lord Amherst* would only depart the port for the high seas. Negotiations with minor officials and merchants for exchange of goods outside the port were conducted even while edicts threatening punishment for dealing with foreigners were being promulgated. The price offered for calicoes and broadcloth, however, was not always a favorable one. Although the general populace seemed willing to sell provisions and merchandise, Lindsay and Gützlaff undoubtedly overestimated the ability of the Chinese to buy foreign goods. Opium was the item most frequently requested, and it appeared that obstacles to its sale offshore could be overcome by tendering the requisite bribes. Concerning Fuzhou, for example, Lindsay reported: "I therefore believe, that even in opposition to the expressed permission and authority of the Chinese government, a sort of forced trade, both in opium and all descriptions of British manufactures . . . may be established and maintained at Fuh Chow-foo, and that in a short time it would be connived at, and form a source of revenue to the local government on the same footing as the trade at Linting [opium receiving station for Canton and Macao]."[15] Concerning Ningbo, Gützlaff wrote, "The highest officers did not scruple to acknowledge openly their regret that we had not been allowed to prosecute a trade which would have been so mutually advantageous. All articles of European imports are much dearer here than at Canton; and had we been permitted to trade, . . . we might have realized a considerable profit."[16]

Pointing to the amount of goods unsold by the *Lord Amherst* and the low prices offered for the cottons, the directors of the EIC were unimpressed by

14. Lindsay and Gutzlaff, *Report,* pp. 157-58.
15. Lindsay and Gutzlaff, *Report,* pp. 85-86; also, on Ningbo, pp. 160-62.
16. Gützlaff, *Journal of Three Voyages,* p. 270.

Lindsay and Gützlaff's optimism and even somewhat apprehensive about Chinese reaction to their tactics and their misrepresentation of their identity and purpose. British manufacturers and private traders, however, foresaw possibilities for a growing Chinese market, while Jardine-Matheson and Company, Dent and Company, and other opium traders promptly intensified efforts to exploit the opium market beyond Canton and Macao. Within a few years, a line of a half-dozen offshore opium receiving stations extended as far north as the Yangtze River. Some of the captains of the opium smugglers had learned about navigating the China coast while on the *Lord Amherst* journey, and they would later pilot British warships during the Opium War. The exchange of other manufactures along the illegal route also expanded, though in a limited way. China's losses in the export of silver for opium and in customs dues for goods grew, as did the desire of Britons for a more open market. Data regarding poor defenses, navigational information and charts, the inability of officials to enforce government trading restrictions in view of the willingness of Chinese to cooperate in illegal trade, and the expanding opium market all became background to the Opium War.

From the perspective of the early twenty-first century, the conduct of Lindsay and Gützlaff in their contacts with educated Chinese officials seems insensitive and condescending, though ritual, hierarchy, and the authority of the powerful were and still today remain potent forces in Chinese society. At any rate, many "old China hands" in the mid-nineteenth century were convinced that aggressiveness paid off in Chinese compliance, while acquiescence to the low status Chinese accorded merchants and foreigners resulted only in humiliation. Lindsay and Gützlaff portrayed numerous incidents that fed into this opinion.[17] After Xiamen, where Lindsay stood to deliver his request to trade while the Chinese officials remained seated, he concluded that he had lowered himself in Chinese esteem and gained nothing. He would, henceforth, refuse to be treated as an inferior foreign merchant, but would insist on being treated as a British citizen for whom any indignity was an insult to the British nation. He would object to any document employing the term "yi" (usually translated as barbarian).

At Fuzhou therefore, Lindsay, Gützlaff, and their party proceeded directly to the mandarin's office without seeking permission, and when inferior accommodations were offered they went to a large public office, where, despite remonstrances, they declared they would stay. A heated discussion with two military officers occurred after the Chinese naval commander accused them

17. Gützlaff, *Journal of Three Voyages,* pp. 265-67, 281-85, 288-89, 302-3; Lindsay and Gutzlaff, *Report,* pp. 26, 48-51, 122-23, 172-73.

of hiding sinister purposes behind a plea for provisions. Gützlaff replied in high dudgeon, and the outcome was that the Chinese agreed to sell supplies to the *Lord Amherst* and to allow it to remain in port temporarily.[18] At Ningbo, Lindsay and Gützlaff walked out of an audience with the governor when, despite previous agreement on protocol, no chairs were provided for them while the Chinese officials were seated. Employing the pretext that they must be English officials since they were educated, the governor then allowed chairs to be brought for them. And at Shanghai, the Westerners walked through the crowds directly to the daodai's yamen, pushed their way past lictors who tried to shut the outer gates, and broke down the closed doors to the hall of justice, where they were politely served tea.

The reaction of Chinese officials to the uninvited entry of their coastal ports and the insistence on trade ranged from friendliness and expressions of regret over trade restrictions to anger, humiliation, and fear. In the case of a few officials, curiosity about Western technology and geography was aroused. They inspected the *Lord Amherst,* its telescope and equipment, as well as Lindsay's pistol; they inquired about the English warships; and they revealed an interest in the information on England supplied in the Marjoribanks pamphlet. A few even dared to hope for trade in the future. Negative reactions, however, were more common. The Chinese military were humiliated by the inability of their warships to deter the *Lord Amherst.* Revelations of the inadequacy and unpreparedness of Chinese defenses, in combination with persistent rumors that the *Lord Amherst* was to be followed by a British armed fleet, evoked fears of invasion. Fortresses and city walls began to be repaired. At Xiamen, the commander in chief of military forces ordered officials to acquaint the barbarians with the fixed laws of the dynasty, to demand that the vessel depart immediately, and to direct soldiers along the coast to prevent any communication with the intruders.

As the *Lord Amherst* proceeded up the coast despite condemnations and Lindsay adopted more aggressive tactics, the tone of Chinese edicts became sharper and military resistance more frequent. The emperor and high officials, having received information of the *Lord Amherst*'s incursion, demoted both military and civil executives who had been unable to prevent port entry by the ship. In Shanghai, Gützlaff and Lindsay observed an official, his cap with gold button carried before him, being marched through the streets between two executioners, blindfolded and having a small flag on a bamboo stick pierced through each ear. His crime was that he had allowed the *Lord Amherst* to pass his fort without reporting it. Chinese who approached the

18. Lindsay and Gutzlaff, *Report,* p. 25.

ship or engaged in secret trade were threatened with punishment "to the utmost rigor of the law."[19]

By this stage in the journey, numerous edicts had been issued venting outrage and dismay over the fact that a barbarian ship had been "rambling about the inner seas" and that the crafty barbarians "search about like rats" so that it was difficult to protect against them.[20] Since it was impossible to predict where the ship would next appear, all harbor soldiers and police were placed on alert. Shanghai administrators refused to enter into any official negotiations with Lindsay and Gützlaff, returning their communications and recommending that the *Lord Amherst* return to Canton if they wished to trade. Even so, Lindsay and Gützlaff were able to find lesser officials who were willing, for a price, to connive in the trade and merchants who were willing to take the risks of participation. The emperor, meanwhile, received official reports of Chinese ships having driven *the Lord Amherst* out of one port after another. This pattern of reporting only favorable information was a source of weakness and frustration, as it became increasingly difficult for the court to obtain accurate data about events in the provinces.

Returning to Macao via Korea and the Ryukyu, Lindsay discounted the hostile environment of Shanghai in his conclusion that the journey had established "that the natives of China in general wish for a more extended intercourse with foreigners; and . . . that the local governments, though opposed to such a wish, yet are powerless to enforce their prohibitory edicts."[21] Gützlaff reported, "We have sailed the whole coast of China and have visited Korea and the Loeshoe Islands. Everywhere I have spread the teachings of the Gospel. . . . Also, the first steps for the establishment of commerce have been taken . . . thus a great door will have been opened to the Gospels."[22] Despite the unenthusiastic response of the EIC, these views found acceptance among many Westerners.

19. Lindsay and Gutzlaff, *Report*, p. 196.

20. Lindsay and Gutzlaff, *Report*, pp. 72, 115-16, 155-60, 179-81; for the correspondence of Chinese officials regarding the voyage, see John K. Fairbank, *Trade and Diplomacy on the China Coast: The Opening of the Treaty Ports, 1842-1854*, 2 vols. (Cambridge, MA: Harvard University Press, 1953-1956), 2:5 n. 31, citing *Shiliao xukan*, 13:471-475, 15:547-549, and passim.

21. Lindsay and Gutzlaff, *Report*, p. 212.

22. Gützlaff to Nederlandsch Zendeling Genootschap (hereafter NZG), Macao, 9 October 1832, NZG Archives, Kast. 19, No. 1, Doss. G.

Gützlaff's Coastal Journeys: Opium Ships

Gützlaff's next several coastal journeys were as interpreter aboard the fast, armed opium vessels ("smugs") that William Jardine and James Matheson engaged to expand opium distribution northward. Opium trading had become big business with international ramifications. The best-quality opium was grown and processed in India under an EIC monopoly. Though the EIC did not engage directly in the sale of opium abroad, it permitted its employees to sell opium on their own, and after the abolition of the EIC monopoly of English trade with China in December 1833, numerous private British and American merchants entered the competition. Despite the fact that Chinese law forbade the importation and smoking of opium, the cooperation of armed British vessels, little Chinese "crabs" that delivered the opium to Chinese intermediaries, and Chinese officials who looked the other way for a price fed the growing appetite of addicts. By 1830 the cost of imported opium so far outweighed the value of China's exports that she was exporting silver to rectify her trade imbalance.

Missionaries condemned opium as an addictive drug, destructive of life, morality, and family. With their Protestant work ethic, they found something inherently disturbing in the indolent pose of a reclining opium smoker. The *Chinese Repository,* edited by the American missionary Elijah Bridgman, ran numerous essays deploring opium smoking in China. Some British citizens, including a few members of Parliament, joined the chorus. Walter Medhurst of the LMS wrote: "Not only are the wretched victims of the indulgence, themselves, impervious to remonstrance . . . but the difficulty of convincing others of the truth of Christianity, and of the sincere intentions of Christians, is greater, in proportion, to the extent of the opium trade to China. Almost the first word uttered by a native, when urged to believe in Christ is, 'Why do Christians bring us opium, and bring it, directly in defiance of our own laws? . . . Surely, those who import such a deleterious substance, and injure me, for the sake of gain, cannot wish me well, or be in possession of a religion that is better than my own.'"[23] Most missionaries, however, did not simply blame Westerners for importing the drug to China; they were equally critical of Chinese officials for accepting bribes instead of enforcing the ban on opium. They believed it was the responsibility of the Chinese government to stop opium smoking by Chinese. Often, they emphasized their own obligation to bring China the blessings of Christianity to offset the evils of the opium trade.

23. W. H. Medhurst, *China: Its State and Prospects, with especial reference to the spread of the Gospel* (Boston: Crocker & Brewster, 1838), p. 82.

No proposal to end the EIC production of opium in India stood a chance of passage in the British Parliament. Rather, committees of both the House of Lords and the House of Commons investigated the opium question and concluded that growth of opium should not only be continued but should be expanded. Why? The income in silver from opium was crucial to the financing of the Indian administration in India and to the whole fiscal exchange system of the tripartite trade among Britain, China, and India; during the 1830s the opium monopoly was bringing in almost one million pounds per annum.[24] British nationals might have no desire to colonize China, as stated in the Marjoribanks pamphlet, but neither did they show any disposition to disband British rule in India or tax English citizens to cover its cost.

Not unlike the hardening of attitudes against tobacco in the West during the second half of the twentieth century, sentiment against opium would harden during the second half of the nineteenth century. Until chloroform became the preferred anesthetic at mid-century, however, opium was extensively used as a medicine for relieving pain. As one author put it, "Opium was the Victorian's aspirin, Lomotil, Valium, and Nyquil, which could be bought at the local chemists for as little as a penny."[25] The contention that opium smoking was a pleasant relaxant for many while only addictive to a minority was widely accepted. Sustained campaigns against opium were launched only late in the century, and it was 1906 before a Chinese edict ordering the eradication of opium had a real prospect of implementation.[26] Opium, furthermore, had become the major source of bullion for Westerners in the China region.[27]

Missionaries, like all Westerners in the Canton area before the Opium War, were dependent on the opium trade and could hardly avoid participating in it, at least passively. Opium clippers transported salaries, mail, and reports for missionaries, merchants, and foreign service personnel. Religious

24. "Opium: Revenue Derived from It by the British Government in India," *CRep* 6.4 (August 1837): 193 (based on an 1832 report to the British House of Commons).

25. Terry Parssinen, *Secret Passions, Secret Remedies,* quoted in Joyce Madancy, *The Troublesome Legacy of Commissioner Lin: The Opium Trade and the Opium Suppression in Fujian Province, 1820s to 1920s* (Cambridge, MA: Harvard University Press, 2003), p. 276.

26. See Kathleen L. Lodwick, *Crusaders against Opium: Protestant Missions in China, 1874-1917* (Louisville: University Press of Kentucky, 1996).

27. For further detail, see Peter W. Fay, *The Opium War, 1840-1842: Barbarians in the Celestial Empire in the Early Part of the Nineteenth Century and the War By Which They Forced Her Gates Ajar* (Chapel Hill: University of North Carolina Press, 1975), pp. 41-52, 110-27; Michael Greenberg, *British Trade and the Opening of China, 1800-1842* (Cambridge: Cambridge University Press, 1951), pp. 104-42; Jonathan Spence, "Opium," in his *Chinese Roundabout* (New York: W. W. Norton & Co., 1992), pp. 228-56.

tracts awaiting distribution were stored at the opium depot of Lintin. The dominant opium dealer, Jardine-Matheson, served as banker and money changer for missionary and trader alike. Salary checks were translated into cash derived from opium credits, and opium often displaced silver bullion as a medium of exchange in the interior as well as in the maritime provinces. During the Opium War, opium clippers and sailors provided pilots, supplied data on harbors, furnished troop transport, and even backed up warships with armed smugs. The comptroller general of the British forces regularly bought the silver of the opium trade to finance the campaigns. Roman Catholic priests seeking surreptitious entry into interior China took passage on opium clippers, and Protestant missionaries frequently traveled on vessels carrying opium. While attempting to secure a residence at Shantou despite gentry opposition, Rudolf Lechler of the Basel mission accepted the hospitality of an opium captain on Nan'ao island holding station, and the first Protestant missionary to Fuzhou, Stephen Johnson, arrived on an opium clipper in 1847.[28] Jusus Doolittle, ABCFM, became so frustrated and disillusioned by the parsimonious support of his mission society, lack of progress in gaining and retaining converts, and poor relations with his Fuzhou colleagues that he resigned his missionary post in 1868 and worked for three years as interpreter for Augustine Heard Jr., whose firm was deeply involved in opium smuggling. He then returned to mission employ with the Presbyterian Board.[29] One missionary who had published articles condemning the opium trade experienced problems in delivery of his salary and correspondence. Among the most generous contributors to mission publications such as the *Chinese Repository*, to hospitals, poor relief, schools, and other philanthropies were those companies most heavily involved in the opium trade.[30] Even works such as James Legge's translation of the Chinese classics were subsidized by Jardine.

Gützlaff, however, participated in the opium trade in a more active fashion than most other missionaries. Because of the damage to the evangelist

28. Rudolf Lechler, quoted in William Gauld, "History of the Swatow Mission" (M.A. thesis, unfinished and unpublished, University of London, School of Oriental and African Studies, London, England), pp. 5-6; Ellsworth Carlson, *The Fooshow Missionaries, 1847-1880* (Cambridge: Harvard University Press, 1974), p. 7.

29. Marilyn Blatt, "Problems of a China Missionary — Justus Doolittle," *Papers on China* (Harvard University Center for East Asian Studies) 12 (1958): 42-45.

30. A. Coates, *Prelude to Hong Kong* (London: Routledge & Kegan Paul, 1966), p. 151; "First Report of the Society for the Diffusion of Useful Knowledge in China," *CRep* 4.8 (1835): 354-61; "First Annual Report of the Morrison Educational Society," *CRep* 6.1 (1837): 229-33; "A Letter from Dr. Parker to Dr. Reed, Dec. 25, 1836," *EMMC* 15 (1837): 437.

cause, many missionaries privately regretted Gützlaff's deep involvement even if few publicly condemned him for it. As one twentieth-century author commented, Gützlaff is "remembered as the person in whom the contradictions of humanitarianism and the opium traffic reached their most astonishing embroilment."[31] In a tactfully worded bribe during the fall of 1832, William Jardine requested Gützlaff to serve as interpreter and physician on the journey of the opium clipper *Sylph* to Shanghai and Tianjin: "Tho it is our earnest wish that you should not in any way injure the grand object you have in view by appearing interested in what by many is considered an immoral traffic, yet such a traffic is absolutely necessary to give any vessel a reasonable chance [of gain] . . . and the more profitable the expedition the better we shall be able to place at your disposal a sum that may hereafter be usefully employed in furthering the grand object you have in view, and for your success in which we feel deeply interested."[32] Jardine, in addition, promised six months' support for the Chinese-language periodical, *Dong-Xiyang kuo meiye tongzhizhuan (Dong-Xi)*, that Gützlaff was just founding. Gützlaff hesitated. He had written essays condemning opium as addictive and debilitative; he had distributed emetics to help addicts break the habit; and he had worked with individuals who turned to Christianity in the hope that it would provide the strength to forsake the drug. But "after much consultation with others, and a conflict in my own mind," he accepted.[33] He found irresistible another chance to preach the gospel and distribute literature among villagers along China's coast, and furthermore, he would be provided with three times as many religious tracts as he had taken on the *Lord Amherst*. Besides, he needed the income.

Gützlaff's account of his trip on the *Sylph* was much shorter than for his previous two journeys; only rarely did he mention opium. He evidently had compartmented his evangelistic and mercantile activities and had pushed the true nature of the latter in the recesses of his consciousness. Even in his private reports to William Jardine, he wrote of disposing of all of the "cargo," of the excellent price received for the "current shipment," and so forth. Specific details about the sale of calico, long cloth, and woolens were included, but references to the principal trade item were veiled.[34]

Though Gützlaff did reveal in his journal that he was aboard the *Sylph*, "a fast sailing vessel, well manned and armed" — that is, an opium clipper — his

31. Coates, *Prelude to Hong Kong*, p. 150.
32. Quoted in Greenberg, *British Trade*, pp. 139-40.
33. Gützlaff, *Journal*, p. 413.
34. See Gützlaff's correspondence with Jardine in Jardine Matheson Archive (J-M Archive), Cambridge University Library.

Karl Friedrich August Gützlaff, 1834

account emphasized his evangelistic activities and the hardships of the winter trip amidst boisterous weather. On more than one occasion, he wrote, God's protection alone brought them through their perils. Graphic details reiterated the themes of earlier reports: the friendliness of the populace and the inability of mandarins to enforce restrictive edicts, the ability of Westerners to bluff their way into ports and villages in view of China's military weakness and of official acquiescence, and the almost overwhelming demand for religious tracts. Near Shanghai, where he returned to villages that he had visited earlier, inhabitants welcomed him with tea and invitations to dine in their homes; they almost mobbed him in their demand for new books. At the Buddhist center of Putuo, Gützlaff reported, monks "begged, almost with tears, that he would give them a few tracts," though he admitted that they were motivated more by curiosity and desire to learn about a new doctrine than by a desire for the Word of God.[35]

35. Gützlaff, *Journal*, pp. 439, 445.

Gützlaff's letters to Jardine along with information from others, however, confirm that Gützlaff carried out his secular duties on this and subsequent trips conscientiously and even with enthusiasm. Perhaps the sense of adventure appealed to him. Considerable risk accompanied the trade, not so much because importing opium was illegal as because of typhoons that could suddenly blow in with great ferocity, uncharted waters, and armed pirates who harassed coastal shipping. Ordinarily, supply ships brought the opium up the coast for deposit at a depot such as Nanao or for transfer to a small opium clipper; the supply ship also collected funds from sales for transport south to company headquarters. The clippers made contact with Chinese buyers and, if necessary, paid off the officials. Chinese themselves generally conveyed the opium to the mainland to be purchased by opium smokers. In August 1834, Gützlaff's vessel failed to make contact off Xiamen with the supply ship *Fairy;* after waiting two days they moved on to another harbor, only to miss the *Fairy* by two hours. With seventeen thousand dollars on board, they anxiously tracked the *Fairy* before finally making contact.[36] When Gützlaff began to fear that he might not be in William Jardine's good graces, Jardine reassured him, "I really begin now to have a lively interest in your affairs."[37] One captain reported,

Shortly after we arrived a fleet of six [vessels with Chinese officials] anchored near us. Dr. Gutzlaff (dressed in his best, which on such occasions is his custom) paid them a visit accompanied by two boats made to appear rather imposing. He demanded their instant departure and threatened them with destruction if they ever in future anchored in our neighborhood. They went away immediately, saying that they had anchored there in the dark by mistake, and we have seen nothing more of them.[38]

Jardine was so impressed with Gützlaff's knowledge and performance that he instructed one captain: "You will be pleased to consult with Doctor Gützlaff on all points, connected with your change of destination, and avail yourself of his extensive knowledge of the language, and the character of the Chinese, in forming your plans; and in carrying them into effect."[39] Another smuggler

36. Pvt. Namoa, 585, #1, J-M Archive.

37. Hwuylai, 19 September 1834, 495, P18, Hwuylai, J-M Archive; also quoted in George A. Hood, *Mission Accomplished? The English Presbyterian Mission in Lingtung, South China* (Frankfurt am Main: Verlag Peter Lang, 1986), pp. 329-30 n. 52.

38. Quoted in Fairbank, *Trade and Diplomacy,* 1:70.

39. Quoted in Chang, *Commissioner Lin,* p. 27.

considered the services of Gützlaff invaluable: "I would give a thousand dollars for three days of Gützlaff," he wrote.[40]

Following the lapse of the EIC monopoly over English trade in East Asia at the end of 1833, control over the activities of merchants declined, and competition, especially in opium, became keen. Threats, price cutting to drive out small sellers, and occasionally military confrontations occurred. Jardine-Matheson, determined to retain dominance, employed Gützlaff in at least four more coastal journeys between 1833 and 1835, some to establish new receiving stations, some simply to deliver opium and other goods. Jardine and Matheson, in turn, continued to contribute to Gützlaff's evangelistic work. Gützlaff also managed to fit in a trip to Singapore and Malacca during the spring of 1834 to make arrangements for publication of his Siamese New Testament and other religious works.

Gützlaff's Tea Explorations

Two of Gützlaff's last trips were unique in that their purpose was to obtain tea seed and plants along with information about tea cultivation and processing. Such information was sparse because the Chinese kept it a closely guarded secret. In hopes of establishing tea plantations and curing shops in India, and thereby breaking the Chinese monopoly, the Calcutta Tea Company in 1834 sent its secretary, G. J. Gordon, to enlist Gützlaff on a trip into the Chinese tea-growing district.[41] Gordon and Gützlaff, with a small armed escort, departed on the *Fairy* in July 1834. While the ship disposed of its opium, Gützlaff, Gordon, and their escort attempted to make their way to the tea-producing hills of Fujian.[42] On both this and a subsequent trip they lacked adequate maps and guides, so that they repeatedly lost their way and ran aground. On the 1834 excursion the party entered Weitou Bay and went upriver, avoiding the port of Xiamen to the southwest and the likelihood of meeting opposition by Chinese officials and naval forces. The populace were generally friendly and eagerly sought the religious tracts they handed out; except for the fact that the Chinese wanted payment in silver rather than the

---

40. Quoted in Greenberg, *British Trade*, p. 140.

41. J. Forbes Royle, "Report on the Progress of the Culture of the China Tea Plant in the Himalayas, from 1835 to 1847," *Journal of the RAS* 12 (1850): 125-52.

42. G. J. Gordon, "Visit to the Ankoy Tea District," *AJMR* 17 (February 1835): 281-89, and *AJMR* 20 (July 1836): 130-37; Rev. Edwin Stevens, "Expedition to the Bohea (Wooe) Hills," *CRep* 4 (June 1835): 82-96; "Attempts to Penetrate the Eastern Provinces of China," *Missionary Herald* 22 (February 1836): 75-80.

gold that Gordon had brought, the party met with little difficulty in obtaining provisions and accommodation at inns. Their chair carriers and boatmen did try to fleece them, and they were besieged by villagers so curious about these exotic human beings that the inhabitants even offered the Chinese transporters a fee to halt and allow examination. Gordon and Gützlaff observed the growing conditions of tea plants and the curing process; they obtained seeds and a few seedlings to be sent to India; and they eventually arranged for several Chinese processors to come to India as instructors.

The prime quality tea in which they were interested, however, was grown in the hills northwest of Fuzhou. So in May 1835 Gützlaff, Gordon, and a small support party attempted to sail up the Min River. Joining them was Edwin Stevens of the American Seaman's Friend Society, who wanted to test the feasibility of evangelizing in interior China. Without a Chinese pilot and using an old map by the French scholar Jean-Baptiste Du Halde, they took the wrong branch of the river in their efforts to avoid Fuzhou. Grounded and lost, they had to accept a military official's offer to tow them to Fuzhou. Word of the foreign incursion had by this time reached government offices; villagers refused to communicate with them or sell provisions, and soon warships began to track them. Attempts to escape the military escort were defeated by sandbars, storms, rapids, and unnavigable river channels. They were fired on, one bullet narrowly missing Gützlaff's head. Under orders not to return fire, they turned back, having gone upriver about seventy miles and obtained some Bohea tea seeds. Gützlaff's threats of reprisal by the English government were ignored as the Chinese refused negotiation and their warships victoriously escorted the intruders toward the coast where the opium runner was waiting. In his report on the trip, Gützlaff reiterated the theme that failure to insist that the Chinese treat Westerners as equals could only be injurious, and he warned that without a change in policy "the celestial government will so irritate other nations as to become sooner or later the victim of their vengeance."[43] Stevens concluded on the basis of his experiences, "The result of this expedition . . . will go to prove that the interior of China cannot be traversed with impunity by foreigners. The erection of new, and the repairing of old, forts, and the garrisoning of deserted military stations, all indicate a sort of indefinite apprehension of danger from abroad. The vigilance of the imperial officers in the interior forbids the hope that a foreigner can penetrate far

---

43. "Gutzlaff Letter on Bohea Tea Expedition," Macao, 20 December 1834, *New York Observer* 13 (9 May 1835): 73; *New York Observer* 13 (23 May 1835): 84; *New York Observer* 14 (12 March 1836): 46; *New York Observer* 14 (2 June 1836): 41. Medhurst, Abeel, and Bridgman held similar views, though the latter two were not as aggressive in their actions. See "Speech by Abeel to ABCFM," *New York Observer* 13 (6 June 1835): 89.

without detection."[44] Stevens did end on an optimistic note with the observation that millions of coastal Chinese were accessible for brief visits by Christian evangelists.

The tea seeds were sent to Calcutta and then the sprouted seedlings distributed to various nurseries in the India highlands. Though most died en route, the remainder were propagated so that within a decade several tens of thousands of plants were producing small amounts of creditable tea. Also, information about Chinese techniques for processing green and black teas had been obtained. In the long run, however, the experiment lost much of its importance when native tea plants were discovered growing in Assam; these became the main progenitors for the Indian tea production that in time largely displaced Chinese exports to the West.[45]

Repercussions for Sino-Western Relations

Certainly Gützlaff facilitated the expansion of opium smuggling beyond Canton during the 1830s and thereby participated in the undermining of the Canton trading system. He had, in the process, distributed tens of thousands of copies of the New Testament and religious tracts. But Gützlaff was far from alone. In addition to the hundreds of Western merchants and seamen exerting pressure on the Canton system, at least nine Protestant missionaries were preaching, translating Christian writings into Chinese, and dispersing Christian literature in the Macao–Hong Kong–Canton nexus by 1836. A handful of Christian converts were also evangelizing and disseminating the Word; best known was Liang Fa, who proselytized in Guangdong, had once made a 250-mile interior tour in the entourage of a public examiner, and, with Edwin Stevens, had dispensed tracts to examination candidates at Canton. Catholic priests and Chinese seminary students had long made the hazardous trek between Macao and the interior.

In August 1835 Walter H. Medhurst of the LMS and Edwin Stevens had embarked on a two-month coastal trip to test Gützlaff's assertion that China was "open" for proclamation of the gospel.[46] Unwilling to travel on an opium

---

44. Stevens, "Expedition to the Bohea (Wooe) Hills," p. 93.

45. Royle, "Report on Progress," pp. 125-52; "The Tea of Assam," *AJMR* 28 (January 1839): 31-35; "Cultivation of Tea in British India," *AJMR* 29 (May 1839): 53-60.

46. W. H. Medhurst, *China: Its State and Prospects, with especial reference to the spread of the Gospel* (Boston: Crocker & Brewster, 1838), pp. 291-422; "Voyage to the East Coast of China," *AJMR* 19 (April 1836): 286-87; Edwin Stevens, "Voyage of the Huron," *CRep* 4 (November 1835): 308-35.

ship, they were fortunate to secure from the merchant-philanthropist D. W. C. Olyphant the brig *Huron* for their journey up to Shandong; they did, however, rely on navigational maps by Gützlaff and smug captains. Their reception was not unlike that of Gützlaff in his forays: friendliness, curiosity, and eagerness for books among the populace when in the absence of officials; resistance by mandarins when the Westerners tried to penetrate the interior. Inhabitants frequently inquired about Lindsay and Gützlaff, while they discovered that in one village in the Zhoushan region almost every shopkeeper had a tract previously obtained from Gützlaff.[47] They also met increasing opposition as word of their activities reached Beijing and pressure on administrators to block the intruders intensified.

In encounters with officials, Medhurst also proved the equal of Gützlaff in bluster and bluff. At Weihai, Shandong, for example, their way was blocked by a mandarin who inquired as to their business. Medhurst replied that their object was to do good by distributing books and dispensing medicines, then moved forward. "They then placed themselves between us and the town and said that we could not be permitted to proceed in that direction. The ground on which we trod was the celestial empire, and the emperor who commanded all under heaven, had given strict orders that no foreigners should be allowed to go a single step into the interior. We said, if this were the celestial empire, and comprised all under heaven, then we, as dwelling under heaven, were subjects of the emperor, and entitled to his protection; we should therefore proceed but a little way and return."[48] Medhurst also acted on the assumption, commonly held by Westerners in China, that the Chinese respected only those who insisted on ritual denoting authority while they humiliated those who conformed to their demands. At Shanghai a controversy erupted over whether they would kneel, stand, or sit in an interview with the chief magistrate. Medhurst insisted on sitting if the official sat: "'[I] will not submit to stand as a culprit, before any mandarin in the empire. Messrs. Lindsay and Gutzlaff,' I continued, 'were allowed to sit at the conference to which they were admitted, and the same privilege was now expected.'" Upon the officials denying that such had occurred, Medhurst referred to the journals of Lindsay and Gützlaff. When Medhurst argued that he had been allowed to sit in the presence of Shandong magistrates and military officials, he was told that "the chief magistrate was the greatest Chinese in Shang-hae. 'Well then,' said I, 'and the individual who now addresses you, is the greatest Englishman in

47. A. Broomhall, *Hudson Taylor and China's Open Century* (London: Hodder and Stoughton, 1981-1982), 1:233.

48. Medhurst, *China*, p. 315.

Shang-hae, and does not choose to compromise the honor of his country, or risk the success of his enterprise, by submitting to be treated as a barbarian, or contemplated as an offender.'"[49] After handing out tracts to the negotiators, Medhurst and company departed. By this time officials were ready to use force to deter intrusions, and they directed that the tracts be publicly burned. Medhurst and Stevens were henceforth obliged to avoid ports and major cities if they were to make individual contacts.

Relations had been exacerbated as well by the "Napier Fizzle" in 1834.[50] To replace the EIC Select Committee as the negotiating and regulating agency for trade, the British Parliament had created the post of chief superintendent of trade. The position and the instructions of the first occupant, Lord Napier, William John, could not have been more ambiguous and contradictory. His primary responsibility as well as his title related to commerce, but he was a representative of the British government, not of a trading company; he was to announce his arrival in Canton to the governor-general and to inquire about opening other ports to trade and even about the possibility of establishing diplomatic relations with Beijing, but he was to conform to Chinese usage — which meant, of course, that he would negotiate with the co-hong merchants, not Chinese officials. Finally, he was not to employ force unless in dire danger. Well might Governor-general Lu Kun pronounce: "Whether . . . Lord Napier be an officer or a merchant, there are no means of ascertaining. But having come for affairs of commerce to the celestial empire, it is incumbent on him to obey and keep the laws and statues." He added: "The barbarians of the said nation, coming to or leaving Canton, have beyond their trade, not any public business; and the commissioned officers of the Celestial Empire never take cognizance of the trivial affairs of trade."[51]

Seeking to carry out his orders, Lord Napier had landed in Canton in July 1834 without obtaining a pass and had attempted to have a letter requesting a personal interview delivered to the governor-general at the "Petition Gate." The letter, not coming through the co-hong, lacking a petition superscription, and presented as between equals, was refused, though Napier's emissaries, including R. M. Morrison and Gützlaff, spent three hours of negotiation with lesser officials and endured jostling and derision by bystanders. Lu Kun issued edicts ordering Napier back to Macao, and Napier returned in kind by refusing to receive the edicts. Napier had his version of events translated into

---

49. Medhurst, *China*, p. 372.

50. "A Sketch of Lord Napier's Negotiations with Authorities at Canton," *AJMR* 23 (April 1837): 262-79; for the viewpoint of the EIC, see "The Dispute with China," *AJMR* 16 (March 1835): 145-52. Fay, *The Opium War*, pp. 67-79, provides a good chronological summary.

51. "Journal of Occurrences," *CRep* 3.5 (September 1834): 235-36.

Chinese and posted for public view. It concluded: "the viceroy will find it as easy to stop the current of the Canton river, as to carry into effect the insane determinations of the hong."[52] In the Chinese and Western declarations, arrogance met arrogance and ethnocentrism met ethnocentrism. Lu ordered all trade halted, all Chinese staff to leave the factories on pain of being branded traitors, and soldiers to surround the foreign enclave. Lu reported to the emperor: "The foreign ships clandestinely selling opium in the outer seas were daily increasing; it was requisite that the commercial barbarians be severely brought to order and discretion."[53]

Napier was, in effect, under house arrest; furthermore, his health was declining. Though he ordered up frigates, the river had been blocked and they got no farther than Whampoa. By mid-September, Napier was seriously ill and was under pressure from Parsee and English merchants to accede so that trade could be resumed. When Napier finally requested a permit to return to Macao, however, the governor-general replied that the frigates must depart first. Napier gave the order on September 21, and a feverish superintendent of trade departed that evening on a small chop boat escorted by Chinese armed vessels. The journey from Canton to Macao required four and a half days as the boat idled until the frigates were out of the passage. On 11 October Napier died in Macao and was buried with all due honors. His successors initially followed the line of least resistance, communicating through the co-hong and labeling their letters with the word for petition.

Government edicts followed hard upon the heels of one another as traders and missionaries continued their coastal journeys and the mission press poured forth tracts and Bibles for circulation. Imperial anger over the intrusions and the inability of officials to stop them mounted. In response to Lindsay and Gützlaff's complaints to the emperor about Canton trading restrictions, the emperor expressed indignation at the governor's remissness in allowing the *Lord Amherst* to enter port, and ordered that the ship be driven off wherever it appeared and that any foreigners who ventured on land be imprisoned. When a governor reported that if such a ship came within his jurisdiction, he would search it for prohibited goods and, if any were found, he would send the vessel away, the emperor replied, "This view of the case is utterly erroneous. *Foreign ships are neither allowed to anchor, nor to sell any goods there. They are restricted to the port of Canton.*"[54] The *Sylph* journey of

52. "Journal of Occurrences," p. 238.

53. "Memorial from the Canton Government to the Emperor, Forwarded Sept. 8, 1834," *CRep* 3.7 (November 1834): 330.

54. "Attempt to Open Trade," *AJMR* 10 (April 1833): 145-46; "China," *AJMR* 11 (July 1833): 124.

1832-1833 elicited edicts ordering officials to ensure that foreign ships secured no provisions and be driven away by military force if necessary. The co-hong merchants and the "foreign chief" were to be held responsible for enforcing the regulations of the Middle Kingdom.

Other edicts expressed alarm over the dissemination of heterodox doctrines that undermined Chinese order and morality while propagating "the absurd fables of Western nations."[55] Chinese who cooperated in the composition, printing, and circulation of such heretical writings were traitors of their countrymen. The new literature apparently expounded the same faith as that propagated during the time of the Qian Long emperor, when Christian evangelism and conversion to Christianity had been forbidden. This flagrant defiance of imperial rule was intolerable. Having received a copy of Gützlaff's Chinese-language magazine, *Dong-Xi*, distributed during the Fujian tea expedition, the emperor expressed disbelief that it could have been written by a foreigner and ordered an investigation of those who prepared the work, cut the blocks, and printed it, with severe punishment of all involved and destruction of the wood blocks.[56] Ten Chinese linguists accused of assisting Napier in composition and printing of his broadsides and of printing evil and obscene literature under the pretext of "admonishing the age" were arrested in 1834. Among them were Liang Fa and two of his assistants. Two were bambooed and imprisoned; Liang was ransomed by Elijah Bridgman and escaped to Singapore, but police raided Liang's home village, confiscating his property, seizing three kinsmen, and sealing up his house.[57]

After the *Huron* explorations, an imperial edict in October 1834 reviewed transgressions by the foreigners beginning with the *Lord Amherst* journey of 1832. The English barbarians are "violent and turbulent, crafty and deceitful." "Their wish to distribute foreign books designed to seduce men with lies [was] a most strange and astonishing proceeding!" Also cited were riding in sedan chairs with four carriers, bringing foreign females to Canton, and sending petitions and statements to local authorities rather than through the co-hong merchants. "These repeated instances of contempt towards the laws, are indeed highly inconsistent with what [the kingdom's] dignity requires." Con-

55. Quoted in E. C. Bridgman to J. C. Brigham, Secretary of American Bible Society, Canton, 18 March 1836, American Bible Society (ABS) Archives.

56. "China," *AJMR* 20 (May 1836): 37-38.

57. S. Wells Williams, *The Middle Kingdom*, 2 vols. (New York: Charles Scribner's Sons, 1883), 2:328; "China Mission, Letter of E. C. Bridgman and J. R. Morrison, 30 January 1835," *New York Observer* 13 (16 May 1835): 80; "Review of Public Occurrences," *CRep* 11 (1842): 131; "China: State and Prospects of the Mission in China," *EMMC* 13 (1835): 337-39. It was John Morrison who had actually translated Napier's broadside.

sciousness of Britain's threat to China as a political entity was appearing. All foreign books were to be turned over to the government within six months, on pain of punishment.[58] No new strategy was set forth, however. Chinese officials, the co-hong merchants, and the "foreign chief" were enjoined to enforce the rules of the empire under threat of halting commercial intercourse. Tens of Chinese cooperating in illegal trade were apprehended and punished, so that foreign vessels began conveying opium directly to shore. A search for printers of the pernicious literature, however, unearthed only material published in Malacca; Liang's son and his assistant, nevertheless, sought temporary safety in Singapore.

Even so, the information of the central government regarding the foreigners' activities was impressive; fortifications were being reinforced and soldiers stationed at formerly deserted military posts. During the Opium War the British discovered at Xiamen a nearly completed replica of a British man-of-war with thirty guns and more ships under construction. At Wusong they found five new Chinese paddlewheel boats with newly cast brass guns, and at Shanghai they captured six new eighteen-pound ship's guns.[59] The beleaguered provincial officials had made it clear that missionary residence or tours in the interior carried great risk, even if they could not deter brief forays into villages of the maritime provinces or stop the smuggling trade off the coast. In the West, the voyages heightened interest in East Asia, while the imperial reaction stirred up debate over China's closure policy. On both sides, aggravation and frustration intensified.

Gützlaff as Chinese Interpreter for the British Superintendent of Trade

Despite the gusto with which Gützlaff carried out his responsibilities, he was apparently never comfortable in his role as interpreter on the opium clippers. At one point, he wrote, with not a little disingenuousness, "I hate the idea of the most nefarious opium, but I could never banish it out of a ship where I was by mere sufferance. I had nothing to do with it except restoring habitual smokers from their evil habit."[60] In December 1834, he welcomed the offer of appointment as second Chinese interpreter to the British superintendent of

58. "Journal of Occurrences," *CRep* 4 (November 1835): 343-44.

59. J. Spence, *The Search for Modern China* (New York: W. W. Norton & Co., 1991), p. 158.

60. Gützlaff to CMS Committee, Macao, 13 October 1835, Church World Mission Society (hereafter CWM), CMS Correspondence, CH C CH/047.

trade after J. R. Morrison succeeded his father as first interpreter. He would have an assured income without direct involvement in the opium trade, even if much of his time would be occupied with secular duties rather than evangelism. To one of his English supporters, Gützlaff wrote justifying his acceptance: "You will hear that I am for the present a King's officer in the Chinese department. It was a matter of necessity, but my hands are not tied and I shall have in this capacity an ample opportunity of cooperation for the propagation of the Gospel, by procuring permission for the heralds of salvation to settle in China."[61] To William Jardine, he apologized for leaving his employ and promised to help him if he needed translations of documents or other assistance. His sole reason for accepting the position was "to cooperate for the extension of our trade to the northeast"; also, he hoped for the improvement of relations with China.[62] Jardine continued his financial support of Gützlaff's evangelistic activities.

As interpreter, Gützlaff spent much of his time translating government documents, co-hong communications, and other materials regarding Sino-British relations. He acted as interpreter in direct negotiations, which frequently related to the opium smuggling trade. Even if British superintendents of trade professed to have nothing to do with the illegal commerce, coastal ships were often attacked by pirates. If shipwrecked, their crew members might be held for ransom by the local populace. The captain would then appeal to the British representative for aid in securing release or redress, and he was rarely refused.

In January 1835, for example, the *Argyle* was forced by high winds to take refuge on a coastal island. When Captain Macdonald sent a dozen men to shore to request a pilot to guide the ship to safety, the pilot was dispatched, but the sailors were seized and five hundred dollars in ransom was demanded. Hoping to obtain aid from Chinese officials in securing release of the sailors, the superintendent sent Captain Charles Elliot, R.N., Gützlaff, and Captain Macdonald directly to the Canton petition gate with a narrative of the events. The letter was not labeled "petition," and the Western party had not made prior arrangements for receipt of the communication, so the document was refused and insults were hurled at the Westerners.[63] Among the merchants in the factories, some concluded that the superintendent should have backed up

---

61. Gützlaff to Rev. Reed, Macao, 20 January 1835, included in letter of Thomas Fisher to John R. Morrison, London, 3 July 1835, CWM, China Personal, Morrison, Box 2.

62. Pvt. Macao, #96, 19 December 1834, J-M Archive.

63. James B. Eames, *The English in China, Being an Account of the Intercourse and Relations between England and China from the Year 1600 to the Year 1843* (London: Sir Isaac Pitman & Sons, 1909), p. 220.

his emissaries with force, while others regretted that normal protocol had been ignored. The sailors were released soon thereafter, but even so, irritation among both parties mounted a notch. In an essay commissioned by the British Foreign Office, Gützlaff wrote, "The moment the Chinese government is persuaded that Great Britain will take no notice of the late, most lamentable occurrences, it will grow bolder, glory in the impunity with which it can carry it's [sic] measures into effect and become more troublesome than before."[64] On another occasion a Chinese seaman was seized near Quanzhou, a receiving station for distribution of opium in the Xiamen region, and Gützlaff was sent to secure his liberation. Gützlaff took advantage of the assignment to tour Xiamen and over a dozen villages, proselytizing and dispensing Christian literature. It is hardly surprising that the Chinese, unlike many Westerners, had difficulty discerning differences in British policy toward legitimate commerce, the opium trade, and evangelism.

The *Morrison* Expedition to Japan, July-August 1837

An attempt to defy Japan's policy of isolation from Western contact illustrated once again that many Westerners during the mid-nineteenth century believed in the reality of a universal Christendom characterized by material progress, an entrepreneurial spirit, and a Christian God active in history. In order to test the possibility of opening Japan to commerce, Christian evangelism, and diplomatic relations, C. W. King of Olyphant and Company proposed to send the ship *Morrison* for the ostensible purpose of returning seven shipwrecked Japanese sailors to their homeland. Benefiting would be not only Japan, but also Western business, national interests, and the cause of Christianity. Adventure was promised, along with an opportunity to learn more about this closed country. Gützlaff had no intention of being left out of such an expedition. Besides, he was one of the few Westerners in Macao who had studied Japanese, and he was needed as an interpreter.

The remarkable story of the shipwrecked Japanese sailors to be repatriated provides further insight into Gützlaff's insatiable curiosity and ambition, all put to the service of evangelizing the world. Three of the sailors had been part of a crew that had left Owari Bay near Nagoya in 1834 on a rice junk

64. Gützlaff, "Present state of our relations with China," separate enclosure, Robinson to Palmerston, 26 March 1835, FO 17/9/131, quoted in Glenn Melancon, *Britain's China Policy and the Opium Crisis: Balancing Drugs, Violence, and National Honour, 1833-1840* (Hampshire, England: Ashgate Publishing, 2003), p. 42.

92

bound for Tokyo. Blown off course in a typhoon and adrift for fourteen months (during which eleven of their members died), the three came to land on an island off the coast of Oregon. Here they were taken into custody by native Americans, then transported to London by a Hudson Bay Company trader, and finally provided with passage to Macao. The other four had been driven to the Philippines in a storm and had also made their way to Macao. They were taken under the care of Gützlaff and S. Wells Williams, a printer for the ABCFM. Gützlaff immediately began studying Japanese with two of them, and with their aid he translated his "Life of the Savior" and the Gospel of St. John into Japanese. The latter was published in Singapore with the aid of the American Bible Society. Gützlaff began holding weekly services in Japanese for local Japanese residents in the hope that a convert might carry the Word to Japan; he also began to envision a visit to Japan to carry the gospel to this closed country.[65]

The *Morrison,* with David Ingersoll as captain, carried Dr. Peter Parker as physician, S. Wells Williams as naturalist, Gützlaff, Mr. and Mrs. King, the seven Japanese sailors, and crew members. The ship was unarmed and took medicines and a small assortment of cotton and woolen goods for sale, but, to Gützlaff's disappointment, no religious tracts. Several documents, translated into Chinese by John R. Morrison and Elijah Bridgman, illustrated the collusion of interests. One, addressed to His Imperial Majesty from the American merchant, King, set forth the object of the visit. After introducing the seven Japanese seamen and relating their travails, it concluded, "Now I, seeing the distressed condition of these men, have brought them back to their own country, that they may again behold their aged parents. Respectfully submitting this statement, I request that an officer may be sent on board to receive them — to hear the foreign news — to inspect the register of my vessel — to grant supplies and permission to trade."[66] The second introduced America, settled by the English and the Dutch, governed by a president, and worshipping the God of Peace. "[I]ts people have never attacked other countries, nor possess themselves of foreign territory. . . . Our countrymen have not yet vis-

---

65. "Letter of Rev. Mr. Gutzlaff, Macao, 16 May 1836," *Foreign Missionary Chronicle* 5 (February 1837): 30-31; "Extracts from Letter from Mrs. Gutzlaff, 15 June 1836," *Foreign Missionary Chronicle* 5 (February 1837): 29-30; "Survey of Missionary Stations," *Missionary Register,* April 1838, p. 185; Robert M. Martin, *China: Political, Commercial, and Social; in an Official Report to Her Majesty's Government,* 2 vols. (London: James Madden, 1847), 1:328; Charles King, *The Claims of Japan and Malaysia upon Christendom exhibited in notes of voyages made in 1837 from Canton in the ship* Morrison *and Brig.* Himmaleh, 2 vols. (New York: E. French, 1839), 1:ix-xxi, 116-19.

66. Martin, *China,* 1:328.

ited your honorable country, but only know that in old times the merchants of all nations were admitted to your harbours. Afterwards, having transgressed the laws, they were restricted or expelled. Now, coming for the first time, and, not having done wrong, they request permission to carry on friendly intercourse on the ancient footing. . . . If permitted to have intercourse with Japan, *they* will *communicate* always the latest intelligence."[67] They offered as gifts a telescope and a barometer, a picture of George Washington and some American coins, two globes, a collection of American treaties, a history of America, and the possibility of one of the party remaining in Japan for a year to teach English. The third document described the medical skills of Dr. Peter Parker and the "wonderful efficacy" of his medicines.[68]

After stopping at Naha, Okinawa, to pick up Gützlaff, the *Morrison* sailed for Japan, sighting Tokyo Bay in July 1837. Cannon fire immediately greeted them, but ceased after King furled his sails. Fishermen came on board, some soliciting medical treatment by Dr. Parker. Though the intruders requested that water and provisions be supplied and that an officer be sent aboard to receive their communications, the Japanese instead brought cannon to the shore and began close fire. King hastily retreated, pursued by gunboats. Next, they tried Kagoshima Bay in the Satsuma domain, where they sent ashore two of the Japanese sailors along with ship's officers and crewmen. This time, they were gratified by having a Japanese officer and a pilot come aboard to guide them to anchorage and receive their documents for conveyance to the emperor. The next day a messenger promised that a high officer would be sent to negotiate; unbeknownst to King, he returned the packet of documents unopened. Though the request was made known to the authorities, the local official was unwilling to take responsibility for receiving the papers without permission. They also learned that serious disturbances, famines, and insurrections were ravaging the countryside. Not long thereafter, local Japanese urged the *Morrison* to depart immediately, and their warning was quickly followed by artillery fire from shore. Only after eighteen hours of fright and peril did they manage to escape out to sea, shaken but unharmed. The Japanese seamen recommended that the mission be abandoned and declared that they would under no circumstances allow themselves to be put ashore, so the *Morrison* turned back toward China, arriving at Macao at the end of August 1837.[69]

67. Martin, *China*, 1:329.

68. King, *Claims of Japan and Malaysia*, 1:116-19. The statement about transgressing Japan's laws refers to the Jesuit missionaries of the sixteenth century.

69. "Journal of Mr. Parker on a Voyage to Japan," *Missionary Herald* 24 (June 1838): 203-7; S. W. Williams, "Narrative of a Voyage on the Ship *Morrison*," *CRep* 6.5 (November 1837): 209-29; *CRep* 8 (December 1837): 353-80.

King concluded his report on the mission with an impassioned plea for action by the American government to open Japan now that the private effort had failed. "[T]hat the only flag fired on in the harbors of Japan should be that of the only nation which maintains no church establishment, forms no offensive leagues, holds no foreign colonies, grasps at no Asiatic territory; and whose citizens present themselves at the capital unarmed and with every pledge of peaceful, humane, and generous intentions, that the American flag should be so dealt with . . . calls for acknowledgment. . . . As a friend of freedom and amelioration in this part of the world, I hope the time is near when my own country will be prepared to cast the first stone at Japan, unless she will sin no more against the dearest human interests." If the American government will not act, "then friends of civil and religious liberty must prepare the Bible and lessons of universal instruction for distribution in the Japanese language."[70]

The mission, though a failure, did feed already existing appetites for the opening of Japan to foreign intercourse and Christian evangelism. It also stimulated two young Tokyo students of "Western learning" to issue a pamphlet criticizing the Japanese government's exclusion policy, for which audacity they were imprisoned.[71] For the guidance of future vessels, Ingersoll made detailed nautical observations of the Ryukyu Islands as well as the bays of Tokyo and Kagoshima.

Two of the Japanese sailors continued to teach Williams and Gützlaff Japanese and aided them in preliminary translations of Genesis, Matthew, and the Epistles of John into katayama characters. When the U.S. president decided to send Commodore Matthew C. Perry in 1853 to demand the right to diplomatic relations, Williams was official interpreter and one of the Japanese sailors was his assistant. The next year, one of the shipwrecked sailors was employed on the British expedition under Admiral Sir James Stirling to negotiate a treaty with Japan. Two of the Japanese continued to work in Gützlaff's office. At least one accompanied Gützlaff north during the Opium War of 1840-42, and he would subsequently gain a responsible position under Gützlaff in the Hong Kong government. Five of the seven accepted Christian-

70. King, *Claims of Japan and Malaysia*, 1:168-94.

71. Reinhard Zöllner, "Gützlaffs Japanreise 1837 und das *Bojutse yume monogatai*: Zur japanischen Fremdenpolitik am Vorabend der 'Öffnung,'" in *Karl F. A. Gützlaff*, ed. Thoralf Klein and Reinhard Zöllner (Nettetal: Steyler Verlag, 2005), pp. 21-40; George B. Sansom, *The Western World and Japan* (1949; New York: Vintage Books, 1973), pp. 261-63. The Dutch alone were permitted to trade at Nagasaki Bay under strict conditions, and their factory was the principal source of "Western Learning." For further detail on the *Morrison* Expedition, see Jessie G. Lutz, "Japanese Castaways, China Missionaries, and Renga Kusha in the Opening of Japan" (forthcoming).

ity, and one or more assisted Gützlaff in evangelizing tours. In America, interest in the possibility of evangelism in Japan was aroused, and women's mission circles adopted Japan as the object of prayer.[72]

Western Perceptions of the Opium War, 1840-1842

In September 1840 Elijah Bridgman lamented over the conflict between China and Great Britain: "No war in modern times, or perhaps in any age since the world began, has involved the weal or woe of so many human beings, as are now likely to be affected for good or for evil by the present struggle; yet never was there a war undertaken, about which there was so much ignorance as to its causes, its objects, the manner of its being conducted, etc. as there now is with regard to this war."[73] Despite the exaggerated drama of the statement, it was undoubtedly true that diverse groups held variant views of both the sources and the goals of the conflict. The differing Chinese and English interpretations are familiar: opium versus conditions of trade and intercourse, the label "Opium War" versus "Anglo-Chinese War." Such national disparity was not, however, the object of Bridgman's concern, for he offered selections from British parliamentary debates of April 1840 as proof of the ignorance. Bridgman had in mind only the Western contingent.

During parliamentary debate a member of the opposition had presented a motion censuring the British cabinet for having blundered into conflict; he accused the administration of a lack of foresight regarding the opium trade and of failure to provide the superintendent at Canton with adequate powers and instructions. Not included was any condemnation of the war itself. In fact, one critic stated: "he could not conscientiously say that some further continuation of hostilities, however culpably they were originated, might not . . . be now unhappily necessary."[74] He asked only that the war be pursued without revengefulness or undue feelings of hostility toward the Chinese people.

Not even the opponents of Her Majesty's government questioned whether or not England's national honor should be upheld. In an era when a voyage for communication with China averaged six months or more round-trip, guidelines from London were often quite general, and diplomats had to be allowed considerable leeway. Upon events overtaking instructions, officers in

---

72. Edward Gulick, *Peter Parker and the Opening of China* (Cambridge, MA: Harvard University Press, 1973), pp. 62-70; "American Tract Society," *New York Observer* 15 (13 May 1837): 74.

73. Elijah Bridgman, "War with China," *CRep* 9.5 (1840): 241.

74. Bridgman, "War with China," p. 249.

the field took the initiative, and London was left with the choice of repudiating or backing its representative abroad. Such was the case with the opening of the Opium War, as Foreign Secretary Lord Palmerston opted for dispatching a fleet to China and mobilizing troops in India to support the actions of Superintendent Charles Elliot in Canton. That Commissioner Lin Zexu had insulted an emissary of the British government and had infringed on the inalienable rights of British citizens by holding them hostage at Canton was common parlance. The conflict, even if unpremeditated and regrettable, had to be carried forward to an honorable settlement. National dignity and international reputation required it.

Generally accepted also was the thesis that expansion of trade with China was both possible and desirable. Textile manufacturers needed new outlets as Europe and the United States industrialized. In their opinion, huge markets awaited fabricators of cotton textiles and yarns if Chinese restrictions on trade could be eliminated. The inherent right to free trade was very much a part of the expansionism given expression in British nationalism, imperialism, and evangelism. Upon learning of the conflict, English traders and chambers of commerce of the manufacturing cities launched a major lobbying campaign. William Jardine even made a trip to London to have his say.

Lord Henry Palmerston might have decided to provide Elliot with military force no matter what the common wisdom regarding the China market, the opium trade, or Chinese military strength. Nevertheless, the arguments he employed in replying to the motion of censure paralleled many of those expounded by Gützlaff, Lindsay, and others in the field. In treating the censure motion as an attempt to bring down the cabinet rather than as opposition to the conflict itself, Palmerston was hardly forthright in his reply; indeed, he came close to flippancy.[75] To those worried about the economic consequences of trade stoppage, he insisted, "Up to the latest period at which we had received any advises, there had been no permanent interruption of our commercial relations, and that the truth was, that those relations in the year that had passed had been more prosperous, more profitable, and more successful than in any former year."

With regard to the opium trade, Palmerston pronounced, "The Chinese were not in earnest in the wish to prohibit opium. Why had they not put down the cultivation of the poppy in China? (Hear, hear) No, it was with them a bullion question and there was perhaps a [Chinese] poppy agricultural interest concerned in excluding the foreign opium. (Cheers)." The Chinese government, not the British, had the obligation to end smuggling.

75. Bridgman, "War with China," pp. 249-51.

Lord Palmerston justified the resort to force on a number of counts: to prevent British citizens from starving as a consequence of the withdrawal of all Chinese servants and suppliers, to retaliate for the alleged poisoning of drinking water, and to protect Elliot's ship from threatened attack. In summary, he quoted from a public statement by British merchants in which they contended that trade with China could no longer be conducted with security to life and property or with credit and advantage to the British nation unless the government responded to the Chinese outrages with firmness and energy. With soothing reassurances, Palmerston opined that "the object of this expedition would probably be accomplished without resorting to warlike operations" and that "these disputes might yet be brought to an amicable and happy termination." Even so, the censure motion lost by only nine votes. The close vote was indicative of the confusion and dissatisfaction surrounding the issues. Matters of Britain's honor and profits saved Palmerston's cabinet from defeat.

Once the conflict was joined, the consensus was that while the Chinese only respected force, they were so divided and so weak militarily that a minimal demonstration of firepower would be sufficient. Warships were slow in arriving and, initially, were few in number.[76] The loss of a bargaining position by Elliot after evacuating troops from Zhoushan in 1841 was interpreted as further confirmation of the supposition that force was the one effective instrument in dealing with the Chinese and that any sign of weakness revived Chinese arrogance and obstinacy.

When Sir Henry Pottinger replaced Elliot as new chief superintendent and plenipotentiary in mid-1841, the local Britishers, along with Gützlaff and Bridgman, were heartened by the perception that they now had a leader who would at last make war. Sir Pottinger, according to reports, "is up to all the tricks and chicanery of the native courts, and rely on it will not allow himself to be humbugged."[77] He was under instructions to launch a naval expedition north to retake Zhoushan. He should carry forward operations so that he could negotiate from a position of strength, and he should parley only with Chinese officials holding plenipotentiary powers. Pottinger would, the following year, demand the opening of China at least to the extent of free trade

76. The slowness of response and the initial minimal military commitment were partly due to communication and transportation problems. An additional factor was the channeling of responsibility through the Indian command at a time when the latter was involved in the Afghan conflict.

77. Fay, *The Opium War*, p. 312. For Gützlaff's criticisms of Elliot, see his *Chinesesiche Berichte von der Mitte des Jahres 1841 bis zum Schluss des Jahres 1846* (Cassel: Vorstand der Chinesischen Stiftung, 1850) (published under the name Gaihan), letter of 17 October 1842, pp. 21-23.

with private merchants at five ports. In addition, the ceding of a secure harbor was considered essential as security against future interruption of trade.

Gützlaff and the Prosecution of the Opium War

British ships fired their first shots of the war on 5 September 1839, with Gützlaff acting as interpreter and intermediary for Superintendent Elliot.[78] Lin Zexu, having helped persuade the emperor that suppression of opium traffic and consumption rather than legalization was the proper course of action, had been sent to Canton in March 1839 to carry out the mandate. Lin worked first with Chinese officials, gentry, and merchants, ferreting out names of major opium dealers, arresting over one thousand Chinese, and confiscating large quantities of opium and opium pipes. Next, he turned to the Westerners, demanding that they turn over all opium chests in port and pledge that they would cease trading in opium. Suspension of trade and blockade of the factories persuaded Elliot to direct that the opium be handed over for destruction, but some merchants refused to cease trading in opium. Further complicating relations was an affray between sailors and Kowloon residents in which one Chinese was killed. When Elliot refused to turn over a culprit, all Britishers were ordered off Macao, and several thousand Britishers found themselves crowded on ships with limited provisions.[79] Lin Zexu had, furthermore, forbidden Chinese to sell goods to or perform services for the English, and signs had been posted over coastal wells warning that they had been poisoned. After protests and petitions, Elliot, Gützlaff, and Captain Henry Smith sailed toward the Kowloon battery with a cutter and an armed opium brigantine. Three armed junks met them. Five to six hours of negotiation ensued as Gützlaff made impassioned pleas to three different Chinese naval officers, but all his bombast, threats, and calls for humanity toward fellow starving humans availed nothing. After Gützlaff warned Commissioner Lin's deputy that the Chinese would bear responsibility for any "mischief" arising from their refusal to permit provisioning, Elliot sent a boat to a village some distance up the bay. Though the local inhabitants were willing to sell supplies, Chinese police runners quickly moved in and halted the exchange. Elliot, by his own admission, then lost his temper and ordered his men to open fire on the Chinese warships.

---

78. For Gützlaff's and Elliot's reports on the event, see "Review of Public Occurrences during the Last Ten Years from 1832 to 1841," *CRep* 11.5 (1842): 466-69.

79. Gützlaff was so closely identified with the English that he had to evacuate along with British citizens.

Despite the fact that the British guns were the more effective, Elliot seemed abashed at this opening of hostilities on his initiative. He deterred Captain Smith from returning in force to complete the destruction of the junks and to blow up the battery, while he dispatched an apologetic note to Lord Palmerston explaining his action. Both Lin and Elliot subsequently adopted a more conciliatory stance, so that negotiations were resumed. Not only were supplies for the British forthcoming, but their troops and officers were shortly able to return to Macao.

Each side put its own interpretation on the contest, neither of which was conducive to peaceful resolution of the ongoing dispute. Lin sent to the emperor the Chinese naval commander's report that numerous barbarians had been killed and a two-masted vessel sunk, a signal victory for the Cantonese. Captain Smith, Gützlaff, H. H. Lindsay, and many British merchants expressed dismay that Elliot had not followed through with his advantage. In their view, England's credibility and security were at stake. Lindsay concluded that the appearance of provisions four days later "was a practical confirmation of the received opinion among foreigners that much more could be gained from the Chinese by 'bearding' them . . . than could possibly be expected from the most humble entreaties." Gützlaff, as a missionary, expressed sorrow over the bloodshed, but he did not alter his view that the British should be adamant in insisting on their right to trade and to evangelize. Elliot's dilatoriness and readiness to compromise would only prolong the warfare, in Gützlaff's opinion. Perhaps overestimating Gützlaff's influence on British policy, Commissioner Lin was said to have been determined to have Gützlaff's head.[80]

Not, however, until the next military encounter on 2 November 1839 did it become clear that England and China would go to war. This time Captain Smith succeeded in gaining Elliot's permission to fire the big guns of his frigate *Volage* and the corvette *Hyacinth* on a massed group of sixteen war junks and a dozen fireboats. Despite Elliot's qualms of conscience regarding the military encounters, he was not repudiated by the home government. By mid-June 1840, almost a year and a half after Lin's appointment as commissioner to suppress opium, a British war fleet had assembled near Macao ready for a military expedition north.

Since almost none of the commanders or soldiers knew Chinese, interpreters would be called upon for a multitude of duties: parleying with Chinese officials and commanders, securing provisions for the troops from the

---

80. S. Fay, "The Protestant Mission and the Opium War," *Pacific Historical Review* 40 (May 1971): 153. Lin had been governor of Jiangsu when Gützlaff made one of his exploratory journeys up the Yangxi River.

local populace, gathering intelligence and navigational information, administering captured cities, collecting monies to help pay for the expedition, superintending the Chinese laborers who served the British military, and more. John R. Morrison, the chief interpreter, devoted most of his time to the translation of official dispatches; he was also the interpreter of choice in formal negotiations with high-level officials. Much of the day-to-day work was the responsibility of the co-secretaries Robert Thom, a Jardine-Matheson clerk, and Gützlaff. Further assistance came from a Chinese Catholic named Rodriges and from Bu Dingbang, a comprador who employed pidgin and some English. Thom was useful primarily in matters requiring a knowledge of Cantonese, while Gützlaff's proficiency in dialects meant that he was needed in relations with Chinese outside the Canton region. Gützlaff, for example, was given responsibility for collecting the ransom levied on the businessmen of Ningbo and other cities. He also interpreted in negotiations with lower-level officials and military commanders. Interpreters were overworked and were permitted considerable latitude in defining and executing their responsibilities — they were, in other words, much more than interpreters.

The extent to which the lack of linguistic expertise influenced the British campaign and contributed to the hardships inflicted on the Chinese people would be difficult to specify. An English officer, suddenly coming upon a body of Chinese, was reported to have exclaimed à la Shakespeare: "An interpreter! An interpreter! My regiment for an interpreter!"[81] Other sources expressed regret over the numerous misunderstandings between the troops and the populace derived from their inability to communicate. An anonymous correspondent mentioned temporarily aiding Gützlaff in his work as civil magistrate after the capture of Zhoushan, a thankless task that the writer gladly abandoned. "[I]f a man could speak good mandarin, I would listen to his complaint; but if he could only speak the patois of the place — which none of us can understand well — I was obliged to dismiss him with his grievance unredressed."[82] He then gave several instances in which the innocent suffered while thieves profited because of the inadequate knowledge and understanding by those in authority. During much of the British occupation of Ningbo, Gützlaff was the only resident Westerner with a knowledge of Chinese, and a naval commander who kept a journal of the second northern expedition noted regretfully the kidnapping of those in the employ of the British and the widespread robbery and looting in the suburbs of Ningbo, especially by Chinese. "How is it possible to do much with one interpreter?

81. "A Chinese Chrestomathy in the Canton Dialect," *CRep* 11.3 (1842): 158.
82. "Hostilities with China," *CRep* 9.4 (1840): 231.

All that one man can do, more than any other, perhaps, could do, Gützlaff does; but he is not an Irish bird, and cannot be in even two places at once, far less in four or five as is desirable."[83]

As aide to one of the British senior commanders, Gützlaff participated in both the first northern expedition of June 1840 and the second of August 1841. He, along with pilots and captains from opium runners, provided navigational information for the fleet. He put his previous experience in the coastal waters and port towns to use as he joined scouting forays to collect information regarding troop deployment, military fortifications, and the topography of proposed attack sites. He delivered ultimatums and bargained with Chinese officers to surrender in order to avoid bombardment. He accompanied initial landing forces, bringing with him posters designed to reassure the Chinese inhabitants, to invite merchants to trade, and to justify the British cause.[84] As the British second northern expedition approached Shanghai during the summer of 1842, Gützlaff heard about panic in the city and the flight of the wealthy. Taking advantage of the chaos, British ships reconnoitered the route from Wusong to Shanghai and came upon numerous merchant vessels, many of them loaded with fish packed with ice. Gützlaff, on board the *Nemesis,* assured the merchants that they would not be harmed, but that they would have to give up their cargo. The merchants, according to a naval official, were so relieved over not being blown to bits that "they refused all kind of payment." The British, for their part, were delighted to obtain fresh provisions.[85]

At Zhapu, Zhejiang, and Zhenhai, the British discovered that Manchu commanders frequently put up stiff resistance, for they were defending both China and their dynasty. Han Chinese commanders, many of whom were less than enthusiastic about Manchu rule, were more apt to retreat upon discovering that they had little chance in the face of British arms. When Zhapu and Zhenhai fell despite a bloody defense by the Manchus, most of the commanders committed suicide and encouraged their wives to do the same. Gützlaff, in the advance force, personally entered Manchu dwellings in generally unsuccessful attempts to persuade Manchu women not to destroy themselves and their children after the retreat of imperial troops.[86] Some Chinese officers did, of course, resist even

83. Granville G. Loch, *The Closing Events of the Campaign in China: The Operations in the Yang-Tze-kiang and Treaty of Nanking* (London: J. Murray, 1843), p. 43.

84. Williams, *The Middle Kingdom,* 2:536.

85. William Bernard, *The Nemesis in China, comprising the history of the late war in that country; with an account of the colony of Hong-Kong,* 3rd ed. (1846; New York: Praeger Publishers, 1969), p. 322.

86. John Francis Davis, *China, during the War and since the Peace,* 2 vols. (London: Longman, Brown, Green, & Longmans, 1852), 1:248-49.

unto death. In July 1840, for example, the Chinese leader in charge of the Dinghai, Zhoushan, garrison was invited on board the *Wellesley* by Sir George Bremer. He was shown the ship's guns and, according to Gützlaff, remarked, "It is very true that you are strong and I am weak. Still, I must fight."[87]

Between military campaigns, Gützlaff acted as civil magistrate in several occupied cities: Dinghai from July 1840 until evacuation in February 1841, Ningbo from October 1841 to May 1842, and Zhenjiang near Nanjing for a brief period in 1842. He participated in numerous negotiating sessions, including those terminating with the Treaty of Nanjing. On occasion, when the Chinese tried to employ individuals without full plenipotentiary powers, Gützlaff or Thom took over as negotiators rather than interpreters, for Pottinger refused to meet with those lacking equal authority. In June 1842, for example, the Manchu mediator Yi Li Bu sent a subordinate to parley; the latter was assigned to Gützlaff, who lacked the power to negotiate peace terms but who did make arrangements for mutual exchange of prisoners.[88] At the signing of the Treaty of Nanjing on 29 August 1842, Gützlaff continued his dual role, handing out copies of the New Testament to each of the Chinese negotiators. Of interest is the fact that it was Gützlaff, rather than Morrison, who interpreted Pottinger's post-signing declamation that the responsibility for suppressing opium rested with the Chinese, not the British. Gützlaff was civil magistrate of Dinghai, Zhoushan, a second time from September 1842 until the death of John Morrison in August 1843; he was then called to succeed Morrison as Chinese secretary to Her Majesty's government in Hong Kong.

Throughout all of these developments, Gützlaff was advertising his evangelistic activities and the opening of China in reports to mission societies and magazines. Though his mission correspondence conveys a distorted impression, he did devote much of his spare time to preaching visits to Chinese homes, chapel services, and distribution of tracts and Bibles. He even managed to publish several Chinese-language pamphlets on both secular and religious topics.[89] During Gützlaff's second tour of duty at Dinghai, Zhoushan experienced a devastating drought, and the inhabitants appealed to Gützlaff

87. "Hostilities with China," *CRep* 4 (1840): 231; S. Fay, *The Opium War*, p. 222.

88. Gützlaff [Gaihan], *Chinesesiche Berichte*, 23 June 1842, pp. 9-10; John K. Fairbank, "Chinese Diplomacy and the Treaty of Nanking, 1842," *Journal of Modern History* 12.1 (1940): 12-13. There seems to be some confusion about the emissary. Gützlaff says that Yi Li Bu himself came, but without plenipotentiary powers. Yi Li Bu reported to the emperor that he sent an emissary "well acquainted with the barbarian nature."

89. Lockhart to London Missionary Society (hereafter LMS), Tinghai, 26 October–11 November 1840, CWM, LMS, S. China, Incoming, 1840-1847, Box 4; Lockhart to Directors of LMS, Macao, 22 March 1841, CWM, LMS, S. China, Incoming, 1840-1847, Box 4.

for help. He reported that he held a public prayer session and offered numerous private prayers and was gratified when the Savior performed a miracle and sent a deluge. Unfortunately, he remarked, the people held a procession for their idols, and these, rather than the true God, received the credit.[90]

The British occupation also opened up the possibility of evangelism by other resident Westerners. Missionaries, both Roman Catholic and Protestant, quickly arrived on the scene. One evangelist noted that some Chinese took them for government emissaries. Mary Gützlaff came to Dinghai and was soon gathering Chinese children in order to start a school. Dr. William Lockhart, first British medical missionary to China, was met by Gützlaff, who, though seriously ill, immediately took him on preaching tours. According to a report by the American Tract Society, some ten thousand volumes were sent to Zhoushan during 1840-1841 for distribution by Gützlaff and Lockhart on daily tours.[91] Dr. Lockhart also opened a medical clinic, which helped to create a more favorable attitude toward the occupying foreigners. The clinic was short-lived, however, since Lockhart left Zhoushan when the British evacuated in February 1841.

The Significance of Gützlaff's Role

In warfare, adversity for the defeated is the general rule, of course, and it is rare that excesses are not committed. The extent of wanton violence during the Opium War and the responsibility for excesses are not easy to determine. To assess Gützlaff's role is doubly difficult. Conflicting reports abound, and Gützlaff's own writings are full of contradictions. In reporting on the occupation of Dinghai in 1843, for example, Gützlaff stated that he left in place a governing council of responsible citizens, something of a little republic; other records described those who assumed control as the scum of the land who preyed on their fellow villagers.[92]

90. Gützlaff [Gaihan], *Chinesesiche Berichte*, 10 July 1843, pp. 37-40.

91. American Tract Society, *Sixteenth Annual Report*, 1841, p. 104; Suzanne Hoe, *The Private Life of Old Hong Kong: Western Women in the British Colony, 1841-1941* (Hong Kong: Oxford University Press, 1991), pp. 27-28; "Dr. Lockhart Writes from Chusan, Nov 5, 1840," *Missionary Register* October 1841, p. 465. Lockhart married Mary Gützlaff's relative, Catherine Parkes, in 1841 and soon transferred to Shanghai, where he spent most of his career.

92. Gützlaff [Gaihan], *Chinesesiche Berichte*, 12 June 1843, pp. 32-33; "Reminiscences of Chusan," *CRep* 10.9 (1841): 498; Loch, *Closing Events*, pp. 34-35; Carl T. Smith, *Chinese Christians, Élites, Middlemen, and the Church in Hong Kong* (Hong Kong: Oxford University Press, 1985), p. 241.

Chinese officials and gentry lost more than their authority and social status during the British occupations; because many fled precipitately, leaving home and goods unprotected, their property was subjected to looting by both Chinese and foreigners.[93] When winter came, many buildings became a resource for firewood. British troops had to be provisioned off the land, at least partially. Though some farmers and middlemen might profit from the higher prices charged the "foreign barbarians," many suffered. A villager reluctant to sell his draft ox or breeding sow was given no choice; resistance could result in seizure without payment or even violence. At Dinghai, farmers presented Gützlaff with a petition asking that soldiers be ordered to stop seizing bullocks necessary for plowing the fields and that documents of protection be posted. Since most merchants had shuttered their shops and the British army was desperate for fresh food supplies, remedial action was beset with difficulties. To make matters worse for the peasants, the provincial governor issued a proclamation threatening any Chinese who sold oxen to the British with dire punishment.[94] Villagers might be required to furnish labor service, while fishermen might be drafted for navigational duty. The limited ability of the occupying forces to maintain order and security brought misfortune to large segments of the population. Marginal elements, the poverty-stricken, and camp followers took advantage of the administrative vacuum to rob and plunder.

At Dinghai, the first occupation of 5 January 1840 to 23 February 1841 got off to an unfortunate start.[95] After landing, British troops bivouacked for the night in a suburb that happened to be a center for the manufacture and storage of a strong Chinese liquor. Even though British officers had so many jars broken that the liquor flowed through the streets, many soldiers became intoxicated. In the early morning, a fire broke out and destroyed much of the suburb; plunderers and pillagers from both sides completed the destruction. When the British entered Dinghai the next day, it was a mute city, with shops shuttered and houses abandoned. Gützlaff and other British officials strug-

93. Loch, *Closing Events*, pp. 32-33; R. Jocelyn, *Six Months with the Chinese Expedition, or Leaves from a Soldier's Notebook* (London: John Murray, 1841), pp. 59-60, 74; Henry Charles Sirr, *China and the Chinese, Their Religion, Character, Customs, Manufactures: The Evils arising from the Opium Trade*, 2 vols. (London: William S. Orr & Co., 1849), 1:134-35, 231-35.

94. "Petition from Chusan Peasants, 24 October 1840," Gough Papers, #8303-105-697, National Army Museum, Dept. of Records; Gützlaff translation for Caine, 15 November 1840, #8303-105-739, National Army Museum, Dept. of Records.

95. Jocelyn, *Six Months with the Chinese Expedition*, pp. 58-59; John Ouchterlony, *The Chinese War: An Account of All the Operations of the British Forces from the Commencement to the Treaty of Nanking*, 2nd ed. (London: Saunders and Otley, 1844), pp. 47-49; Sirr, *China and the Chinese*, 1:231.

gled to restore order and confidence. A comprador who had accompanied the expedition north, Bu Dingbang, helped in persuading villagers to bring goods to market and merchants to reopen stores. Gützlaff recruited local Chinese to guard against thieves and looters, while he himself functioned as magistrate, dispensing a ready justice. A popular and somewhat malicious poem depicted "Daddy Kuo" on his dais:

> Up to his high dais
> Daddy Kuo comes.
> If you are in trouble
> He'll get things straight,
> If you have been wronged
> He'll come to the rescue,
> If you have got into difficulties
> He'll arrange things for you.
> He's a master at speaking the Chinese language,
> There is not an ideogram he cannot read.
> Daddy Kuo is nothing short of a genius!
>
> Big trouble about a bull,
> Small trouble about a chicken —
> He'll settle the case with a pen
> that seems to have wings!
> And sooner will the Southern Hills move
> than this decision be altered. . . .[96]

About the time that there seemed hope of achieving a degree of stability, Chinese officials offered large sums for captured foreigners and sent undercover agents to report on Chinese cooperating with the occupation. Shops closed down again and supplies disappeared from the market. Frequent kidnappings occurred. Bu Dingbang was one of those abducted and, after being employed in questioning captured Westerners, he was decapitated and his entire family suffered punishment. After the capture of Bu, recruitment became more difficult, so that the British had to pay handsomely, at least by Chinese standards. One eyewitness, who sympathetically credited Gützlaff with doing the best he could under near impossible circumstances, called Gützlaff's informants and police "a sad set of rogues" and related one instance in which some of Gützlaff's police joined in the plunder.[97]

96. Translated in Waley, *The Opium War through Chinese Eyes*, pp. 230-31.
97. Loch, *Closing Events*, pp. 32-35.

The British initially had relatively little difficulty hiring needy Chinese for manual work such as transporting supplies and providing services.[98] Where there was hesitancy, it was more apt to derive from fear of "foreign devils" than from nationalistic opposition to the foe (except perhaps in Canton). But the British needed intelligence as well, along with procurators and policemen. Gützlaff in particular recruited spies, constables, and other aides. Eventually he was employing some forty Chinese and receiving daily reports on Chinese troop activity and morale, imperial proclamations, and communications sent by provincial officials and commanders. All of these he duly translated and transmitted to the office of the army commander, Sir Hugh Gough.[99]

After Captain Anstruther, Mrs. Noble, and other Britishers were captured and imprisoned in Ningbo, Gützlaff established contact with Anstruther via a spy and learned that the captain and Mrs. Noble were being decently treated. Soon, however, came word that the provincial lieutenant governor had received permission to execute the captives. Elaborate plans for the scout to bribe the prison guards and arrange the escape of the captives were drawn up. Fortunately they did not have to implement the risky abduction, because the 1841 truce secured the return of the prisoners.[100] Mary Gützlaff took the pregnant Mrs. Noble under her care and offered passage on the ship taking the Gützlaffs back to Macao.

In several instances, Chinese collaborators furnished valuable information. Chen Bingzhun helped guide British warships into Dinghai harbor. Another reported that the Chinese were busily fortifying Ningbo and recommended that if the British intended to take the city, they should do so as quickly as possible.[101] After the capture of Wusong, collaborators revealed that many of Shanghai's leading citizens had decamped, such that Shanghai could probably be taken without bombardment and with minimal force. The spies also intercepted correspondence between the emperor and his local officials and commanders that allowed the British to gain some insight into the inability of the Chinese to pursue a consistent strategy. With spies in the commanding general's headquarters, British officers claimed that sometimes they knew as much about Chinese battle plans, military emplacements, and troop strength as the Chinese commanders themselves.

Gützlaff may have influenced British strategy in an even more significant

98. Letter of Rev. W. M. Lowrie, 11 June 1842, *Foreign Missionary Chronicle* 11 (1843): 43; Martin, *China*, 2:380-81.

99. See the Gough Papers, 1840-1842, at National Army Museum.

100. Gützlaff to Gough, 28 December 1840, #8303-105-747; 4 January 1841, #753; 16 January 1841, #756; 4 February 1841, #773, 775; 5 February 1841, #777, National Army Museum.

101. Gützlaff to Gough, 5 February 1841, #777.

way. Among the Gough correspondence is a position paper by Gützlaff submitted to headquarters in 1842. Gützlaff recommended that the British bypass Hangzhou and other cities to move directly up the Yangtze and take Nanjing.[102] Such a strategy would cut China in half, block shipping on China's greatest waterway, and bring transport of rice and salt to the capital on the Grand Canal to a standstill. The emperor would be forced to sue for peace. How much the essay influenced General Gough and Sir Henry Pottinger in their battle plans is impossible to determine, but Gough did read the paper and comment favorably on it. The strategy they followed coincided closely with that recommended by Gützlaff.

One of the more dramatic events of the war was the Chinese surprise attack on Ningbo in March 1842.[103] Scouts had repeatedly brought Gützlaff word of massing Chinese troops in the environs, and British search and destroy missions had been dispatched, only to have the Chinese soldiers fade away. By March 8 Gützlaff had received further indications of a possible night attack on Ningbo and reported the same to the military commander. Whether Gützlaff had cried wolf too often to be taken seriously or Gützlaff was too tentative in his report is not clear, but only minimal extra precautions were taken. By the time the British headquarters became aware of the attack, hundreds of Chinese soldiers had already breached the south city gate and others threatened the west gate. Fearful carnage, with hand-to-hand combat, occurred; Chinese soldiers, their retreat cut off, fought desperately and received no quarter. Pillage and arson only made the disaster worse. Whereas the early occupation of Ningbo had been relatively orderly under Gützlaff, hostility and suspicion now reigned on both sides. Enlisted British soldiers, when not in the presence of officers, took revenge on innocent victims. Chinese reprisals took the form of renewed kidnapping and murder of isolated soldiers and camp followers. At one point there was even an attempt on the life of Gützlaff himself.

After the assault, Gützlaff and the military commander had difficulty restoring credibility. According to one witness, when it became known that the British planned to evacuate Ningbo and would no longer be able to protect collaborators, the British ceased to have a friend in the city.[104] On the other

---

102. Gützlaff, "Remarks upon the Occupation of Nanking," #8303-105-856, National Army Museum. See also John Nicolson, "The Reverend Charles Gützlaff, the Opium War and General Gough," *Missiology* 13.3 (1985): 353-61.

103. J. Ouchterlony, *The Chinese War*, pp. 228-34; Bernard, *The Nemesis in China*, pp. 288-89; Davis, *China, during the War*, 1:226-33; Gützlaff to Gough, n.d., #8303-105-790; 1 February 1842, #803; 11 March 1842, #850, National Army Museum.

104. Loch, *Closing Events*, pp. 45-46.

hand, W. A. P. Martin, who worked in Ningbo from 1850 to 1860, reported, "The people of Ningpo were well disposed toward us, because, as they said, they had 'experienced kind treatment at the hands of the British during the war'. . . . They were never tired of telling how Dr. Gutzlaff . . . had been installed in the yamen of the prefect, and how careful he was to see justice done, so that if a soldier bagged a fowl it had to be brought back and paid for. Not only did this state of feeling make it safe and pleasant for us to promenade the streets — it opened to us the doors of many families."[105]

Among the masses outside Canton, cooperation with the British seems initially to have carried few overtones of treason to the state. But the combination of hardships and humiliations suffered during the occupation and the venality of spies and police in British employ activated popular hostility toward the "barbarians." As Frederic Wakeman has noted, strangers had been at the gate of Canton for a long time, so the Cantonese were ahead of the populace elsewhere in developing an identity vis à vis the outsider.[106] The experiences of the war accelerated the evolution of conscious Chinese exclusivism beyond Canton and helps to explain the great reluctance of Chinese to allow Western settlement within the gates of the new treaty ports after 1842. Like the skirmish between Canton braves and British troops in May 1841, the Ningbo surprise attack entered the mythology of Chinese patriotism. At Ningbo the Chinese had come perilously close to destroying the occupying troops. In the case of Sanyuanli the Cantonese were convinced that victory would have been theirs without the negotiated truce.

John Fairbank has argued, furthermore, that the number of lowly Chinese who acted as spies for the British tarnished any official having intercourse with the victors.[107] Peace negotiations and subsequent implementation of the Nanjing treaty were thereby made more difficult. Caught between hostility toward the British and the weakness of the Chinese position, the Chinese plenipotentiary Qiying could be forthright with neither his emperor nor his British counterpart. Officials rose and fell according to Beijing's perception of the strength and determination of the British, the influence of conservative factions at court, the threat of domestic rebellion, and a multitude of other pressures. Despite the Opium War, relations with Western barbarians continued to have low priority except during emergencies. Not only did "foreign

---

105. W. A. P. Martin, *A Cycle of Cathay,* 2nd ed. (New York: Fleming H. Revell, 1897), pp. 66-67.

106. The phrase comes from Frederic Wakeman, *Strangers at the Gate: Social Disorder in South China, 1839-1861* (Berkeley: University of California Press, 1966).

107. Fairbank, "Chinese Diplomacy," p. 8. There were, of course, many additional reasons why Chinese "foreign experts" were vulnerable.

specialists" command little prestige, but Chinese officials assigned to such work endangered their careers. They lacked the institutional structure of a foreign office from which they might build a support group. The consequences were a lack of continuity in responsible and experienced foreign officers at the helm and a lack of consistency in Chinese policy toward the West. Qiying, under arrest, was ordered to commit suicide in 1858. At a much lower level than Qiying was a medical practitioner visited by a missionary in Zhoushan several years after the Treaty of Nanjing. One of Gützlaff's former spies, he had conveyed information from Ningbo to the British at Dinghai. He was now isolated, resented by the British because of continuing importunities and shunned by Chinese suspicious of his "patriotism."[108] His fate was more typical than unique.

Chinese Secretary in Hong Kong

Before the transfer of the British administration from Macao to Hong Kong in 1842, the latter's population stood at about eight thousand Chinese inhabitants, two thousand of them boat people and the remainder laborers, small farmers, tradesmen, pirates, and brigands. As plenipotentiary and first governor of Hong Kong, Sir Pottinger faced enormous problems. He needed to place Sino-British relations on a new footing.

On Hong Kong, no government institutions and few legal guidelines were in place; tax resources were minimal; roads and substantial buildings were lacking; and the population was overwhelmingly male, most of them concerned with their own economic betterment rather than the public welfare. About the only assets seemed to be an excellent harbor and lovely scenery. Many British merchants and officials, like Gützlaff, were unhappy that Pottinger had opted for Hong Kong rather than Zhoushan as a permanent base.[109] They contended that Zhoushan had a better location because it was closer to the potential market of central China and to the source of tea, China's main export to Britain. It was thought to have a healthier climate than Hong Kong, and it was removed from Canton, with the latter's legacy of antiforeignism and trade restrictions.

By 1845 Hong Kong's population had tripled, but its reputation had not

108. Smith, *Chinese Christians,* pp. 185-86. For Qiying, see Fang Chao-ying, "Ch'i-ying," in *Eminent Chinese of the Ch'ing Dynasty,* 2 vols., ed. Arthur Hummel (Washington: U.S. Government Printing Office, 1943-1944), 1:130-34.

109. See the extended discussion on the advantages of Zhoushan over Hong Kong in Martin, *China,* 2:330-92.

improved. Illness and death decimated the British troops during the summers. As an open port where opium had been legalized as a tax source, Hong Kong had become a principal entreport for transshipment of opium and illegal salt and also a haven for pirates and secret societies. Neither European nor Chinese commerce had grown significantly. Marginal men, many hoping to make a fortune before returning home, accounted for most of the increase in population. Western sailors who disembarked after months at sea did little to contribute to civil order or the moral climate. Prostitution, gambling, and alcohol ruled the night; piracy, brigandage, and highway robbery were rampant. Westerners slept with a revolver at their bedside and dared not venture out unarmed in the evening; private watchmen guarded their residences and business establishments. Representatives of the leading British firms protested to the governor in 1845 that "Hongkong has no trade at all and is the mere place of residence of Government and its officers with a few British merchants and a very scanty and poor population."[110] Only when Triad uprisings in Guangdong and the Taiping rebellion made life and property on the mainland insecure did Hong Kong's fortunes improve significantly.[111] Substantial Chinese merchants, not just petty tradesmen, then began to invest in business in Hong Kong and even transfer their families there. Tens of thousands of refugees and emigrants took passage in Hong Kong for California, Southeast Asia, and the West Indies, and Hong Kong became the center of trade catering to their needs.

As Chinese secretary in Hong Kong, Gützlaff, along with Robert Thom and other Western interpreters, maintained a considerable staff of Chinese clerks. Among those assisting Gützlaff were Zheng Chiyao, secretary of the Chinese Union, and one of his loyal Japanese sailors. They were responsible for making English translations of edicts and other communications by the emperor and local officials and of responses by British officials. These covered a wide range of issues: correspondence about the frequent instances of violence between Chinese and Westerners, inquiries as to whether the emperor's 1844 edict of toleration for the Tianzhu religion (Roman Catholicism) extended to Protestants, matters of trade and currency, attempts to extend the territory of the Western factories in Canton, and so forth. The Chinese secretary's office also made regular translations of the *Jing bao (Peking Gazette)* and local Chinese publications. Gützlaff compiled an annual record of Hong Kong shipping. These detailed lists of vessels docking at Hong Kong, their or-

110. Quoted in E. J. Eitel, *Europe in China: The History of Hongkong from the Beginning to the Year 1882* (1895; Taipei: Ch'eng-wen Publishing Co., 1968), p. 241.
111. Eitel, *Europe in China*, pp. 239-59; Smith, *Chinese Christians*, pp. 103, 113-14.

igin and destination, cargo and tonnage, became part of the governor's yearly report to London and provide an overall view of the nature of Britain's commerce with south China. In this connection, Gützlaff also wrote for the governor specialized reports on salt smuggling, piracy, and the Chinese junk trade, including the transport of "coolies" to Southeast Asia and the West Indies.

A Danish visitor, Steen Anderson Billie, described Gützlaff at work:

> Among my few acquaintances in Victoria on the island of Hongkong was my friend, the learned missionary Gützlaff. . . . He was constantly active. One could enter his bungalow in the heat of the day and always find him busily engaged. A dozen Chinese sat and wrote in the office. Letters were received and letters were sent out, and everything that was sent out was a product of Gützlaff's mind. He seldom erred in his choice among the fifty thousand [Chinese] characters. In order to avoid misunderstanding or lack of clarity, he had taken a very fastidious Chinese into his service. The latter was obliged to read through each of his drafts before it was sent to the copier. None of this activity hindered him from receiving visitors. He engaged in the most lively conversation with his guests, all the while writing ceaselessly and issuing orders and instructions right and left. Conversations would include his work as secretary, in which he took special pleasure, events of interest in China, and inquiries regarding developments in Europe, of which he was abysmally ignorant.[112]

Gützlaff participated in the lengthy and ultimately unsuccessful negotiations with Qiying and Xu Guangjin to secure foreign residence within the walls of Canton. One revelation was the continued operation of Gützlaff's spy network; Chinese subclerks smuggled copies of memorials and decrees out of yamens and passed them to the Chinese secretary's office.[113] In March 1849 Gützlaff obtained a copy of an imperial rescript permitting the foreigners to enter the city temporarily. Xu, however, under intense pressure from the Cantonese and the local militia, substituted a forged imperial rescript stating "The Central Empire cannot oppose the People in order to yield to the men from a distance."[114] Uncertain about the authenticity of the smuggled document, the plenipotentiary Sir George Bonham protested, but backed down rather than initiate military action. Antiforeignism and local officials sup-

---

112. Anonymous author quoting Billie, a Danish admiral, in "Die Insel Hongkong," *Quartal-Berichte der Chinesischen Stiftung* 3.1 (March 1853): 25-26.

113. Wakeman, *Strangers at the Gate*, pp. 93-105.

114. Quoted in Wakeman, *Strangers at the Gate*, p. 103; the emperor rescinded the permission in an order of 14 April 1849.

ported by gentry militia had won a battle, but at the expense of imperial power and festering British resentment.

Gützlaff also took part in Britain's abortive attempt to thwart France's monopolistic influence in Vietnam. Though the probe was rebuffed, the knowledge of the Annamese rulers about international affairs and empire-building by Britain and France in China and India was impressive. It was in March 1847 that Gützlaff accompanied Governor Sir John F. Davis on a trip to Vietnam (Annam) to gain information about French activities in the region and attempt to open relations. Gützlaff practiced his usual bluffing tactics in the face of obstruction. "Mr. Gutzlaff went twice on shore for the purpose of delivering the Plenipotentiary's letter, but no one would receive it, being in terror of the consequences; and it was only by an ingenious device of the Chinese Secretary that it was at length left upon the person of a petty mandarin. . . ."[115] The party was then permitted to confer with the provincial treasurer and to make several short sightseeing excursions. They were royally dined, but not allowed to proceed to the capital to present their request for intercourse. The Annam official denied any possibility of opening diplomatic or commercial relations, citing as reasons the recent interventions by French naval commanders on behalf of Christians and the fate of India and China following the opening of trade.

Gützlaff's ambitions, interests, and thirst for knowledge about China seem unlimited. He translated dynastic histories and other imperial compilations and composed a biography of the Daoguang emperor, details from which continue to be cited upon occasion.[116] Upon hearing in 1842 that the Yellow River had overflowed with great loss of life, Gützlaff requested the Dutch to send him books on hydraulic engineering so that he could offer his services to the Chinese government. Though it is most unlikely that the Chinese were interested in hiring Gützlaff as an adviser on water control, he did send the Dutch materials with his comments to the Chinese.[117] In August 1848 Gützlaff presented a paper to the Hong Kong branch of the Royal Asiatic Society recommending the establishment of a botanical garden in Hong Kong to collect specimens of native plants. The suggestion was warmly applauded, and the RAS appointed a committee to inquire regarding site and cost. Despite delays because of financial stringency, the Zoological and Bo-

---

115. "Journal of Occurrences," *CRep* 16 (December 1847): 614-15; Davis, *China, during the War*, 2:303-18.

116. Fairbank, "Chinese Diplomacy," p. 13, n. 37.

117. Gützlaff to NZG, Hong Kong, 28 September 1845, NZG Archives, Kast. 19, No. 1, Doss. G.

tanical Garden was founded under Governor Sir John Bowring and still remains a green oasis in Hong Kong.[118]

As in so many aspects of Gützlaff's life, his relations with his Western co-workers and superiors abounded with contradictions. The British administrators depended on him for a great variety of information as well as for interpreting and translating, and they apparently accepted his data as reliable. They might caution against his optimistic interpretations, but they passed his reports along to the Foreign Office and Parliament. As already noted, Chinese statistical data included in *China Opened* (1838) was deposited with the British Foreign Office and later incorporated in the Blue Book on events leading to the Opium War. In 1846 G. T. Staunton, a participant in the 1792 Maccartney embassy, co-founder of the Royal Asiatic Society, and member of Parliament sent Gützlaff thirty-three questions about Hong Kong, Zhoushan, and China in general. Later published in the *Journal of the RAS*, Gützlaff's responses covered a wide spectrum: the potential market for British goods, the prevalence of crime, piracy, and infanticide, the consumption of opium, the operation of Chinese law courts, the nature of Chinese charity facilities, the educational level of Chinese, religious and recreational activities, and the attitude of the populace toward their Manchu rulers.[119] Members of the British government obviously felt the need for basic factual data about China and considered Gützlaff an informed source. Gützlaff's replies are notable in that he often distinguished among the conditions and practices of various Chinese regions rather than offering broad generalizations, and he differentiated between the literati, who frequently were antagonistic toward the Manchu rulers, and the populace, who were primarily concerned with local governance.

Gützlaff was awarded letters of commendation by the Hong Kong governor for his work with the Chinese. Gützlaff, in turn, identified with the English nation. He admired Great Britain as a leader of progressive, prosperous, and expanding Western Christendom. He Anglicized his name to Charles Gutzlaff and composed many of his works in English; he married three English women. But Gützlaff was always an outsider, never a part of Hong Kong colonial society. Partly, this was because he was German. Among the Hong Kong social elite, he was considered an uncouth German, coming from the lower classes and lacking the social graces. Though Sir Pottinger considered

118. Eitel, *Europe in China*, p. 284; foreword by James Hayes in Smith, *Chinese Christians*, p. viii.

119. Gützlaff, "Replies to Queries in Relation to China, Proposed by Sir G. T. Staunton," *Journal of the RAS* 12 (1852): 386-400.

appointing Gützlaff as British consul at Fuzhou, he decided that it would be inappropriate, since Gützlaff was not a British citizen. When Gützlaff proposed to revise Robert Morrison's translation of the Bible, LMS officials expressed indignation that this German activist would presume to improve upon the work of Morrison and thereby discredit him. In addition, Gützlaff had little time to participate in Hong Kong's social life, because he spent every waking hour outside his office in evangelistic work.

Gützlaff's alienation, however, was also a function of his character and personality. Despite his seeming assurance and omniscience, he was simultaneously an insecure loner, sensitive and quick to perceive offense in relations with equals or those in authority. His exaggerated form of expression, whether demeaning his accomplishments or claiming great success in conversions, whether presenting the possibilities for trade and evangelism or relating his harrowing experiences in which he was saved by God's intervention, struck many as insincere. He seemed unable to steer a middle course between servility and arrogance.

In correspondence with William Jardine, whom he considered his patron, he was deferential. "With many excuses for giving the king of merchants so much trouble," concluded one letter in which Gützlaff had requested Jardine to take care of certain financial transactions.[120] He thanked Jardine for a contribution to a hospital fund: "Whatever is in my power (and this is very little), I will seek every opportunity to cooperate for the extension of our trade. I hope you will give me an opportunity to show that I am not ungrateful for your repeated kindness."[121] Any indication that Jardine was displeased elicited profuse apologies and an expression of hope for Jardine's continued esteem.[122]

In contrast, Gützlaff engaged in a very public quarrel with James Legge of the LMS in 1848. The specific occasion was disagreement over translation of a Chinese phrase in a government proclamation to Chinese seamen visiting Hong Kong harbor, but relations between the two had already become so embittered over differences related to mission methodology and publicity that both reacted immoderately.[123] Legge wrote a highly critical letter to the *China Mail* accusing Gützlaff of mistranslation.[124] Gützlaff then called in two missionaries as witnesses to his declaration that he bore no malice to-

120. Unplaced, 572, #719, 19 May 184[?], J-M Archive.
121. Pvt. Macao, #98, 1 November 1835, J-M Archive.
122. Pvt. Macao #96, 19 December 1834; Hwuylau, 495, P18, 19 September, 1834, J-M Archive.
123. See chapter 8 on the Chinese Union.
124. Legge to Arthur Tidman, Hong Kong, 29 November 1848, CWM, LMS, South China Incoming, Box 5, Folder 1a.

ward Legge and could not be held responsible if parliamentary inquiry led to accusations against Legge. Rumors that Legge had transposed certain Chinese characters began to circulate, and Legge naturally attributed these to Gützlaff. The matter was brought up at the governor's office, where Legge's conduct came in for criticism, but the issue died down after Legge wrote the governor and was assured of his confidence in Legge. On another occasion, in 1850, Gützlaff engaged in an extended dispute with the Hong Kong auditor-general over the amount of income tax he owed, and he again resorted to accusatory language.[125]

Gützlaff, nevertheless, held the office of Chinese secretary until his death in August 1851. Leading government officials and Hong Kong merchants as well as Chinese and Japanese attended his funeral, where he was praised as zealous in prayer, tireless in work, and great in generosity. A choir of Chinese converts concluded the service with a funeral hymn.[126]

Gützlaff's Relations with the Chinese

Gützlaff's relations with the Chinese often appear inconsistent and have been given varying interpretations. Some of the contradictions were of his own making while others derived from his civil office and evangelical goals. Gützlaff perceived himself as a sympathetic advocate of the Chinese, and indeed Chinese plaintiffs in Dinghai, Ningbo, and Shanghai turned to Gützlaff for redress of their grievances. Partly they did so because he was the only available administrator who spoke the language, but Chinese also turned to Gützlaff because he acquired a reputation as a friend of the Chinese. Westerners depicted Chinese as flocking around Gützlaff with petitions, in the belief that he would protect them against the "barbarians."[127] An official Chinese captured document was said to have mentioned Gützlaff's kindness toward Chinese prisoners.[128] Though Gützlaff was criticized for his summary justice, Chinese defendants may have found that it compared favorably

125. Original Correspondence, CO 129/33-35, Colonial Office, Public Records, Hong Kong.

126. "Rede des Englischen Caplans Dr. Moncrieff," *Neueste Nachrichten aus China* 1 (1 November 1851): 113-17; Schlyter, *Karl Gützlaff als Missionar in China* (Lund: C. W. K. Gleerup, 1946), p. 277.

127. Stanley Lane-Poole, *The Life of Sir Harry Parkes*, 2 vols. (London: Macmillan Co., 1894), 1:25, 55-56; Charles Toogood Downing, *The Stranger in China; or the Fan Qui's Visit to the Celestial Empire in 1836-1837*, 2 vols. (Philadelphia: Lea & Blanchard, 1838), 2:9.

128. Loch, *Closing Events*, p. 39.

with the treatment they would have been accorded in a magistrate's court. Dr. William Parker of the CES reported that Ningbo Chinese were "agreeable and friendly to foreigners" partly as a consequence of Gützlaff's brisk and impartial justice.[129] Even the fact that Gützlaff was more successful than most in recruiting Chinese spies and police was indicative of his ability to communicate with Chinese and attract them to his entourage. In the Nanjing settlement, Gützlaff insisted that amnesty be guaranteed those who had worked in his employ. Whether accurate or not, Gützlaff boasted that the inhabitants of Zhoushan had petitioned to have him remain as magistrate and regretted his departure for Hong Kong in the summer of 1843.[130] Indeed, Gützlaff tended to be naive and overly trusting of those Chinese who offered their services for evangelistic or political purposes. In his recruitment of police, aides, and evangelists, Gützlaff was frequently taken advantage of by the unscrupulous.[131]

Gützlaff, on the other hand, adopted an authoritarian stance toward most Chinese. He was, in his mind, the teacher of truth to misguided pupils, and he acted on the assumption that Chinese respected authority and hierarchy. One military officer remarked that Gützlaff was very precise about the exact rank of Chinese sent to negotiate with the British and on one occasion insisted that an individual was only the equivalent of a corporal despite the latter's assumption of the title of captain. When Gützlaff helped secure a tutor for a British naval officer, Gützlaff warned the Englishman against letting the tutor become too familiar. On Gützlaff's advice, therefore, the British officer would not let the tutor walk abreast of him but insisted that he follow several steps behind.[132]

Perhaps coincidentally, but perhaps not, those British officials Gützlaff tutored in Chinese and socialized to the Chinese scene were among the most knowledgeable, most skilled linguistically, and most self-assured of England's representatives in China during the second half of the nineteenth century. They include Sir Harry Parkes, Shanghai consul and British minister to China; Thomas F. Wade, British ambassador to China and professor of Chinese, Cambridge University; and Horatio N. Lay, first inspector general of Chinese Imperial Customs. All three lived for a time in Gützlaff's home and received regular instruction from him. Parkes, a cousin of Mary Gützlaff,

---

129. Quoted in Broomhall, *Hudson Taylor and China's Open Century,* 2:349.

130. Gützlaff [Gaihan], *Chinesesiche Berichte,* 30 November 1843, pp. 45-46.

131. "Hongkong, Letter of Mr. Johnson," 5 May 1851, *Baptist Missionary Magazine* 31 (1851): 381; American Baptist Missionary Union, "Thirty-eighth Annual Report: Hongkong," May 1852, p. 75; Loch, *Closing Events,* pp. 32-35.

132. Loch, *Closing Events,* pp. 34, 38.

acted as clerk to Gützlaff during the second occupation of Zhoushan, and he noted in his diary and in letters to his sisters that Gützlaff was strict about his Chinese lessons, expecting him to apply himself daily to Chinese study and to make steady progress. In addition, Gützlaff insisted that Parkes learn several dialects along with Mandarin and that he mingle regularly with the Chinese populace to converse with them and become acquainted with their customs.[133] Likewise, several of the more aggressive, bold, and innovative missionaries were either instructed by Gützlaff or inspired by his example; they include Issachar Roberts of Taiping fame, the individualistic Scotch Presbyterian William Burns, and J. Hudson Taylor of the China Inland Mission.

During Gützlaff's tenure as Chinese secretary in Hong Kong, he often assumed the role of intermediary in relations with the growing Chinese community. He even began to be identified as spokesman for Chinese interests and views despite the fact that many of his responsibilities involved regulating the Chinese inhabitants and seamen. One of the early tasks assigned to Gützlaff and Chief Magistrate W. Caine was to investigate claims by local fishermen in the frequent feuds over fishing rights and to bring some order to the coastal waters. Out of this came a proposal by Gützlaff for a Chinese Department of Marine and Harbour Regulations.[134] As organized, the separate division under the Chinese secretary had its own budget, with its own Chinese clerks, messengers, patrol boats, and police, who had the right of boarding all junks coming into harbor. The assignment of numbers to all boats and installation of buoys helped to regulate movement, while all new statutes for shipping and fishing were to be translated into Chinese by Gützlaff and posted.[135] Though the Hong Kong government claimed control over all island residents and the application of British law and justice to all, the administration, in actuality, encouraged the Chinese community to police itself. By setting up separate departments for regulating the Chinese, the government hoped to limit expenses, overcome some of the problems of ruling people from a different culture, and reduce Chinese antagonism. The Chinese Department of Marine and Harbour Regulations was one of the first examples of this policy. Along the same lines was the establishment of a division of the Municipal Police with Chinese constables and sub-constables "mutually bound for themselves and the people under their supervision."[136] Subject to government approval, Chinese were permitted to select their own constables,

133. Lane-Poole, *Life of Sir Harry Parkes,* pp. 27, 54, 57.

134. Woosnam to Gützlaff, 25 March 1844, CO129/10E, #121, Hong Kong, Colonial Outward Correspondence, Public Record Office.

135. CO129/10, 21 January 1844, 25 March 1844, CO, Public Records, Hong Kong.

136. "Government Notification," *Hong Kong Register* 17 (23 April 1844): 63.

and in many ways, they functioned like headmen in the old *bao chia* system. Certain customary Chinese punishments such as flogging were permitted.[137]

Gützlaff's acquaintance with the local Chinese and his forceful personality frequently served him well in mediating disputes. In April 1844, for example, a riot almost erupted as a consequence of a Westerner hiring outside carpenters, probably non-Hakka, to work on his house. The local artisans resented the outsiders and stole property. When police came to search their sheds they resisted, and the sheds were set on fire. Caine and Gützlaff arrived with six European policemen the next morning to find shops shuttered and four to five hundred Hakka stonecutters gathered to support the local workers. Caine and Gützlaff arrested seven ringleaders and ordered the rest of the imported supporters home, conspicuously accompanying them for two miles on their way.[138]

Despite temporary improvement, piracy, robbery, and blackmail by Triad chiefs remained intractable problems. Pirate fleets numbering up to 150 fighting ships preyed along shipping lanes. Hong Kong-registered vessels dared not make the short run to Canton unless armed, and Chinese traders resorted to hiring armed foreign ships as convoys or else sailing under the British flag, both practices subject to serious abuse.[139] In 1856 an incident involving a Chinese vessel under British flag provided the excuse for the opening of the Arrow War. Chinese shippers, merchants, and tradesmen generally deemed it prudent to pay the protection money demanded by Triad leaders. Gützlaff might be able to provide general information about secret societies and pirate fleets, and he often became involved in cases where individuals had been apprehended, but suppression was another matter. Attempts to rid Hong Kong waters of brigands often drove them out to sea or up rivers on the mainland where they undermined the authority of local Chinese officials and terrorized the countryside.

Two challenging assignments were determining the compensation of rice growers whose fields were to be drained and the removal of vagrants and undesirables from the central market. Following registration of the Chinese population, a drive was launched to clean up the bazaar, where brothels and gaming houses outnumbered all other establishments. Even shopkeepers engaged in legitimate businesses but lacking residence certificates were to be moved, though they were to be compensated. Caine and Gützlaff were given the task of deciding which individuals would be expelled from the bazaar and

---

137. Ordinance #10, 1844, CO129/5; Davis to Stanley, 1 June 1844, Public Record Office.
138. *Hong Kong Register,* Supplement, 7 May 1844.
139. Grace Fox, *British Admirals and Chinese Pirates* (London: Kegan Paul & Co., 1940).

which allowed to remain, the rate of reimbursement, and the locale of the new Chinese settlement. Great dissatisfaction arose, so that Gützlaff was assigned to meet with the inhabitants and explain the reasons for the government action, but the issue dragged on. Eventually the governor ruled that the two magistrates had already allowed sufficient time for the people to move and action was imperative. He did agree that those resettled would be exempt from rent on their new holdings for four years.[140]

Because of the prevalence of malaria and other illnesses among British troops, the Hong Kong administration decided to drain rice fields near the barracks; also, the construction of roads and bridges often necessitated filling ditches and elimination of paddy fields. Caine, Gützlaff, and W. J. Gordon, land and road inspector, were assigned to recommend a sale price per mow and the annual value of the rice harvest according to paddy quality. Based on Gützlaff's consultation with the farmers, the three recommended a price that the Hong Kong government found excessive, and so lengthy negotiations with the Chinese ensued. The farmers were eventually compensated at a rate somewhere between Gützlaff and Caine's estimate and that advocated by the government.[141] More healthful conditions did prevail, but, unfortunately, many of the Chinese were said to have dissipated their remittance rather than investing it.

In December 1845 Gützlaff proposed that the Hong Kong government provide small subsidies to Chinese schools. Only in the late nineteenth century did the English government assume responsibility for a state-supported national educational system. Before that, most elementary education was provided by religious and charitable organizations or was left to private initiative, though the government did grant aid to certain institutions for school buildings. Gützlaff reported in his request that of the local Chinese schools he had visited, most were held in miserable hovels and enrolled only a few forlorn pupils, but they had intelligent teachers. If the government would provide small sums to a few well-conducted schools with enrollments of at least fifteen, the expense would be minimal and it would "do great good for the children and make a favorable impression on the parents."[142] Gover-

140. CO129/10, 17 April 1844, CO, Public Record; Woosnam to Davis, 2 April 1844, CO129/6; Woosnam to Caine, Gützlaff, and Gordon, 17 April 1844, CO129/10; Answer to Proposals of Committee of Caine, 22 July 1844, CO129/6; Davis to Stanley, 29 October 1844, CO129/6.

141. Woosnam to Caine, 9 February 1844; 17 March 1844, CO129/10E, CO, Public Record; 14 May 1844, CO129/10, Public Record.

142. Gützlaff to Davis, 13 December 1845, CO129/6; Davis to Gladstone, 22 June 1846, CO129/6, CO, Public Record; CO129/16, 20 January 1846, CO, Public Record. Legge had

nor Davis endorsed the proposal and sent it to the Colonial Office with the recommendation that a very limited contribution be made. A lengthy correspondence ensued, with queries about curriculum, teachers, and the amount to be contributed by the pupils. Finally in July 1847 came London's authorization to spend up to one hundred pounds a year in subsidies to three Chinese schools. Gradually the number of subsidized schools increased, while many of the traditional Chinese teachers were replaced by Christian converts; by 1869 a school for girls had been founded in Victoria.[143] Hong Kong's complex school system was slowly being pieced together: a Chinese stream and a Western stream, government schools, grant schools generally of missionary origin and eventually largely funded by the government but administered by religious organizations, subsidized schools receiving a lower level of aid, and private schools, mostly Chinese.[144] This diversified system would last until the People's Republic took control of Hong Kong in the late twentieth century.

Gützlaff's relations with Chinese appear to have been more amicable than those of many Western missionaries, merchants, or government officials. He was fascinated by all things Chinese and delighted in learning all he could about Chinese history, culture, and customs, whether through the written word or direct experience. He visited Chinese temples and homes; he observed and wrote about Chinese festivals such as New Year's or a village's celebration of the birthday of their local deity; he described funerals, theatrical performances, fishing techniques, government organization, treatment of women, salt works, medical practices, and a host of other facets of Chinese society. He adopted Gaihan (Ai Han zhe), "lover of the Chinese," as his pen name, and he insisted that he had been adopted into a Chinese lineage and made a naturalized citizen of Fujian province. In his visits to the province, he consistently identified himself with his "fellow Fujian citizens," and on his first coastal journey he wore local Fujian dress, including even the turban. He delighted in those occasions when he was mistaken for being Chinese, and he bragged about being received as an old friend at Xiamen and other ports he

---

earlier in 1845 proposed that the Hong Kong government found a free school for Chinese, but the government had rejected the proposal as too costly. Legge went home on sick leave in 1846, so it was Gützlaff who followed through on the grant-in-aid program. Wong Man Kong, *James Legge: A Pioneer at Crossroads of East and West* (Hong Kong: Hong Kong Educational Publishing Co., 1996), pp. 67-68.

143. George B. Endacott, *A History of Hong Kong* (Hong Kong: Oxford University Press, 1973), pp. 135-43.

144. Anthony Sweeting, *A Phoenix Transformed: The Reconstruction of Education in Post-War Hong Kong* (Hong Kong: Oxford University Press, 1993), pp. 6-8.

revisited on his numerous voyages.[145] After the death of his second wife in 1849, he called China his "bride" and asserted that he had no other wish than to live out his life in service to China.[146]

As a Protestant evangelist, on the other hand, he was committed to the thesis that the Chinese were depraved heathens. Without the civilizing agency of Christianity, Chinese were backward, cruel, and dishonest. The "debased idolatry" of the Chinese he illustrated with descriptions of Chinese temples and monasteries and accounts of the "superstitious" rituals performed there. As a father figure to the Chinese, however, Gützlaff could be forgiving of Chinese errors. In his paternalism, he expected less of his Chinese assistants than of Westerners. His relations with Chinese were not as between equals; both sides operated according to hierarchical precepts. Gützlaff's workers were loyal to him and he, in turn, supported and protected them. In a sense a relationship based on such an assumption was the ultimate insult, but Chinese understood and accepted inequality between those with authority and wealth and those who were poor and dependent. Gützlaff's encounters with Chinese literati might be abrasive, but he was a friend and patron of his Chinese assistants and catechists, and he felt no threat from most Chinese. When he left Hong Kong in September 1849 for his first home visit after twenty-three years in East Asia, he was presented with a testimonial that read: "His official character has been as spotless as water; and not a single cash has he received as a bribe."[147]

145. Gützlaff [Gaihan], *Chinesesiche Berichte*, 23 June 1842, pp. 7-9; Gützlaff, *Journal of the Three Voyages*, p. 415; Gützlaff quoted in "China and India beyond the Ganges," *Missionary Register*, January 1833, p. 39.

146. John Kesson, *The Cross and the Dragon, or the Fortunes of Christianity in China* (London: Smith, Elder & Co., 1854), p. 231.

147. Kesson, *The Cross and the Dragon*, p. 231.

CHAPTER 5

The West Learns about China:
Karl Gützlaff's Western-Language Writings

Missionaries as Purveyors of Information about China to the West:
Images and Orientalism

For three centuries after the arrival of the Roman Catholic missionary Matteo Ricci in China in 1583, missionaries were the primary purveyors of information about China to the West. Likewise, they served as a major conduit for the flow of Western learning to China. As John Fairbank noted in 1968, the only Westerners in daily contact with individual Chinese were the missionaries; they sent regular reports to their home boards, and frequently they maintained a voluminous correspondence with family, home congregations, and supporters.[1]

The missionaries, of course, had their own agenda. They were in China to convert "heathens" to Christianity, and they had no doubt about the ultimate truth of Christianity as the universal religion. Desperate for coworkers in their task of converting 350 million Chinese, the Protestant missionaries of the nineteenth century tailored their writings to stimulate support at home. They could best justify their work, their sacrifices, and the Chinese need for Christianity by painting a bleak picture of heathen society. Even if many missionaries residing in China and studying the Chinese heritage learned to appreciate Chinese achievements in art, literature, and philosophy, they could

---

1. John K. Fairbank, "The Many Faces of Protestant Missions," in *The Missionary Enterprise in China and America,* ed. John K. Fairbank (Cambridge, MA: Harvard University Press, 1974), p. 6; "Assignment for the '70s," *American Historical Review* 74.3 (December 1969): 480-511.

not abandon their faith in the uniqueness and superiority of Christianity so long as they remained evangelists.

Chinese who incorporated materials from missionary works into their world geographies and treatises on maritime countries beyond China also had an agenda; they hoped the information would be useful in strengthening China against the incursion of the Western "barbarians."[2] They had no doubt about the superiority of the Confucian way and no thought of altering the fundamentals of their great heritage. Both were selective in their writings.

Cultural and historical traditions provided the context for the perceptions and interpretations of each party to the informational exchange. The Chinese literatus who was willing to abandon the Middle Kingdom perception of foreign relations or the centrality of Chinese tradition was rare indeed until the twentieth century. Chinese culture equated to civilization. Perhaps the mid-nineteenth century Protestant missionaries came closer to purveying Orientalism as defined by Edward Said than any other propagandists of China to the West.[3] China was heathen and therefore, other; as heathen, it was inferior to the Christian West. The West was the baseline against which Chinese civilization was to be judged, and political events and economic practices were important insofar as they affected Christian missions and free intercourse with China. Praise for selected aspects of Chinese culture could not alter their conviction that the future belong to Western technology, institutions, and Christianity. Despite the accumulation of data, therefore, images of China in the West and images of the West among the Chinese were amalgams of myths, preconceptions, prejudices, and factual information.

Images did, nevertheless, change during the three-hundred year period, more so in the Western picture of China than the reverse. Harold Isaacs, in his classic study, *Images of Asia,* called the era from 1840 to 1904 the "Age of Contempt," whereas he labeled the earlier period the "Age of Respect." As late as the 1820s and 1830s, China was for many Westerners a faraway land conjuring up a generalized picture of exotica: silks, teas, porcelains, and masses of black-

2. Suzanne W. Barnett, "Practical Evangelism: Protestant Missions and the Introduction of Western Civilization to China, 1820-1850" (Ph.D. diss., Harvard University, 1973); Jane K. Leonard, *Wei Yüan and China's Rediscovery of the Maritime World* (Cambridge, MA: Harvard University Press, 1984); Fred W. Drake, *China Charts the World: Hsü Chu-yü and His Geography of 1848* (Cambridge, MA: Harvard University Press, 1975); Wang Jiajian, *Wei Yüan dui Xi-fang di renshi ji chi haifang suxiang* [Wei Yüan's understanding of the West and his ideas of coastal defense] (Taipei: Taiwan University, 1964).

3. For the concept of Orientalism, see Edward W. Said, *Orientalism* (New York: Vintage Books, 1979). Said deals primarily with the West's perceptions of the Middle East, but the concept has also been applied to Western images of East Asia.

haired people. Among the well-educated, the romanticized vision of China fashioned during the Enlightenment was still pervasive. Roman Catholic missionaries of the sixteenth and seventeenth centuries, concentrating on work among the educated elite, had found much to admire in Confucian ethics and Chinese political doctrines. As scholars with a mastery of classical Chinese, the Jesuits searched for and found concordances between Confucian and Christian teachings. Associating initially with Chinese literati at the capital, they were impressed by the seeming lack of "superstitious" beliefs among the scholars.

The reports of these early missionaries to Europe had not been uncritical, however, for they had been frustrated in their evangelistic efforts by the stubbornness of Chinese tradition, the opposition to heterodoxy, and the gap between theory and actuality among both officials and civilians. It was rather eighteenth-century philosophers such as Voltaire, Leibniz, and Quesnay who had drawn from the Catholic writings an idealized picture of China. In contrast to European religious warfare, they had found China to be home of a great civilization that practiced religious tolerance. As a critique of European despotism, they had portrayed a China that was ruled by philosopher-kings and a meritocracy selected by civil-service examinations.[4]

By the 1850s the popular image of China was that of a corrupt and tradition-bound oligarchy sustained by oppressed, impoverished peasants. China was considered weak, not only militarily but also politically. Available were detailed, if prejudicial, descriptions of Chinese religious beliefs and practices, magistrates and courts of punishment, the position of women, and the lives and attitudes of merchants and villagers. Popular works on China's geography, history, literature, and languages had appeared. The generally negative view derived in part from changes in the relative power and wealth at the disposal of China and of the Western states. China had by the nineteenth century entered upon a period of dynastic decline, whereas the Western states, especially Great Britain, had at their disposal greater political power, technological expertise, and economic wealth; accompanying these were increased self-confidence and expansiveness. Evangelical Protestants, furthermore, had brought to China their own rather puritanical and millenialist interpretation of Christianity, which ran counter to the this worldliness of many Chinese. Contributing to the change as well was the fact that Christian missionaries during the nineteenth century were working among the middle and lower classes, not the educated elite. They were largely confined to south-

---

4. Zhu Weizheng, *Coming Out of the Middle Ages: Comparative Reflections on China and the West,* trans. Ruth Hayhoe (Armonk, NY: M. E. Sharpe, 1990), pp. 14-15.

east China, where Confucian tradition was less deeply embedded and mercantile interests were strong. Many, including Gützlaff, were critical of views based primarily on Chinese written sources and considered as unwarranted "that obsolete admiration which was once so fashionable." Gützlaff frequently contrasted his experiences with venal officials and impoverished villagers with the idealized picture of earlier writers like Jean-Baptiste Du Halde.[5]

Karl Gützlaff, with his flair for publicity, contributed to the transformation of the West's image of China and to attempts to alter Chinese perceptions of the West. He spared no effort to make China known in the West and to bring both Christianity and Western secular learning to the Chinese. And remaining true to form, he maintained an output that was prodigious. The most nearly complete bibliography of Gützlaff's publications, compiled by Hartmut Walravens, lists 188 items.[6] In the Chinese language there are over sixty religious tracts plus translations of the Bible, and secular works that included a world history, a universal geography, a history of England, a booklet on commerce, a tract advocating reciprocal trade between China and foreign countries, *Shifei lüe* (A general discussion of right and wrong), and the editorship of a magazine, *Dong-Xiyang kao meiyue tongjizhuan* (*The East-West Monthly Magazine*). In Dutch, English, German, and other European languages there were his histories of China, biographies of Chinese emperors, journals of Gützlaff's residence in Southeast Asia and his voyages along the China coast, official reports as a British civil servant, essays on the Chinese language and grammar, reviews of Chinese classics and literary works, and commentaries on Chinese religious practices. In addition, Gützlaff translated the Gospel of St. John and the Epistles of John into Japanese and the Gospels of St. Luke and St. John into Thai. As an aid in learning Korean, he edited a comparative vocabulary of Chinese, Korean, and Japanese languages, adding the English meaning, the sound in Korean, and indices.[7] He published innumerable appeals on behalf of Christian missions in European and American magazines, many of which are not even listed in Walravens's bibliography.

5. Gützlaff, *Journal of Three Voyages* (1834; Taipei: Ch'eng-wen Publishing Co., 1968), pp. 13-15.

6. Hartmut Walravens, *Karl Friedrich Neuman (1793-1870) und Karl Friedrich August Gützlaff (1803-1851): Zwei deutsche Chinakundige im 19. Jahrhundert* (Wiesbaden: Harrassowitz Verlag, 2001).

7. "Review," *Chinese Repository* (hereafter *CRep*) 4 (1835): 195-96.

Popularizer of China Missions and Image-Maker

Among Gützlaff's earliest and most popular publications were the journals of his three-year residence in Thailand (1828-1831) and his first three trips along the China coast. The journal of Gützlaff's Thailand residence and of his first trip was originally serialized in the *Chinese Repository*,[8] a magazine that published information on Christian missions and Chinese civilization and politics for merchants and missionaries in Canton and Southeast Asia as well as supporters in the West. According to founder and editor Elijah Bridgman, the founding of such a magazine had been under consideration for some time, and Gützlaff's offer of his manuscript provided the necessary impetus to undertake the project. Journals of the subsequent voyages on the East India Company vessel *Lord Amherst* and the opium trader *Sylph* also furnished copy for later volumes of the *Repository*.[9] Numerous editions of the journals came out in England and the United States, and translations in Dutch, German, and Norwegian soon appeared; there was even a juvenile edition in German. Dozens of church magazines of various denominations in England, Europe, and the United States reprinted extensive excerpts; secular periodicals such as *The Literary Gazette, Journal of the Royal Geographical Society,* and *Das Ausland* considered the reports of such general interest that they quoted at length from them.[10]

8. Charles Gutzlaff, "Journal of a Residence in Siam, and of a Voyage along the Coast of China to Mantchou Tartary," *CRep* 1 (1832-33): 16-25, 45-64, 81-99, 122-40, 180-96.

9. "Journal of a Voyage along the Coast of China from the Province of Canton to Leaoutung in Mantchou Tartary," *CRep* 2 (1833-34): 20-32.

10. "Report of Proceedings on a Voyage to the Northern Ports of China, in the Ship, *Lord Amherst,*" *The Literary Gazette*, 24 August 1833, pp. 530-32, and 31 August 1833, pp. 551-52; "Review of New Books," *The Literary Gazette*, 3 May 1834, pp. 305-6; "Reisen eines deutschen missionärs an der Küste von China," *Das Ausland*, 1834, pp. 1043-44, 1047-48; "Extract from the Journal of a Residence in Siam and Voyage along the Coast of China," *Journal of the Royal Geographical Society* 3 (1834): 291-310. The list of religious periodical printing excerpts is so long that only a sample can be given: *New York Observer* 10.48 (1 December 1832): 189-90; 11.6 (9 February 1833): 21-22; 11.7 (16 February 1833): 28; 11.13 (30 March 1833): 50-54; "Review," *Baptist Missionary Magazine* 15 (1835): 62-79; "Voyage of Rev. Charles Gutzlaff along the Coast of China," *Missionary Herald* 29 (1832): 140-46, 174-78, 213-17, 249-52, 277-82; "Netherlands Missionary Society," *Missionary Record* 1 (1833): 109-11, 125-27, 138-40, 155-58; "Experimental Voyage to the Northeast Coast of China," *Asiatic Journal and Monthly Register* (hereafter *AJMR*) 12 (1833): 94-107, 157-73; "Missionar Gützlaff's dreijähriger Aufenhalt in Siam und seine erste Reise nach China," *Magazin für die neuste Geschichte der evangelischen Missions- und Bibelgesellschaften*, 1835, pp. 3-176; "Missionar Gützlaff's zweite und dritte Reise nach China," *Magazin für die neuste Geschichte der evangelischen Missions- und Bibelgesellschaften*, 1835, pp. 179-336.

The immense popularity of the journals stimulated interest in China and became an inspiration to mission and Bible societies. Among the pious, they expanded horizons and created high hopes for evangelism in China. The American Board of Commissioners for Foreign Missions (ABCFM) reported that "The late voyages of Mr. Gutzlaff . . . will probably constitute an era in the commercial and religious history of [China]; their effect was almost like the discovery of a new coast of some fertile and prosperous continent for the mercantile and religious community."[11] A father named his son for Gützlaff, and upon the death of little Charles Gützlaff Hildrent at the age of three the father sent the five-dollar savings account set up for the son to the American Tract Society for Gützlaff's distribution of religious tracts in China. Gützlaff replied with a small Chinese tract based on the quotation, "Come unto me all ye who are heavily laden and I will give you rest," expressing the hope that the death of the child would contribute to life eternal for millions.[12] A review of the third edition of the journals in the *Evangelical Magazine and Missionary Chronicle (EMMC)* stated that "More of the real character of the Chinese may be learned from the pages of Mr. Gutzlaff than from all the accounts of all the embassies which have been sent by the various nations to that country. He came into contact with the China-man, and not with the mere governmental automaton."[13]

In 1832 the American Bible Society (ABS) voted to extend their efforts overseas and in 1835 the American Tract Society (ATS) authorized funds for the development of movable metallic Chinese type in order to facilitate and expedite the production of tracts — more specifically so that Gützlaff might have tens of thousands to distribute.[14] The Church Missionary Society (CMS) took under consideration a proposal to establish a China mission and consulted Gützlaff, who of course assured them of its feasibility and desirability.[15] Gützlaff followed up the enthusiasm by correspondence with dozens of potential donors ranging from King Frederick William III of Prussia to secretaries of Bible, tract, and mission societies, to contributors of only a few dollars. Letters and articles went out to mission magazines, local and Western

11. American Board of Commissioners for Foreign Missions (hereafter ABCFM), *Annual Report*, 1833, p. 2.

12. "Receipts," *American Tract Magazine* (hereafter *ATM*), 15 (April 1840): 46; "Cheering Anonymous Letter," *ATM* 12 (March 1837): 49; American Tract Society (hereafter ATS), *Annual Report*, 1841.

13. "Review of Religious Publications," *Evangelisches Missions-Magazin* 17 (1839): 179.

14. Henry O. Dwight, *The Centennial History of the American Bible Society* (New York: Macmillan Co., 1916), pp. 112-18; ATS, *Tenth Annual Report*, 1835, pp. 87-95.

15. Gützlaff to CMS Committee of Correspondence, Macao, 13 October 1835, Church World Mission Society, CH, Ch/047.

newspapers, and secular periodicals such as the journals of the Royal Asiatic and geographical societies, and *Das Ausland.*

How does one explain the popular acclaim? Earlier Protestant missionaries to China such as Robert Morrison, William Milne, and Walter Medhurst had all reported extensively on their work among the Chinese in Southeast Asia and the Macao-Canton complex, while David Abeel and Elijah Bridgman soon joined the effort to arouse interest in China and China missions. Even though they had been effective propagandists, none of their works offered the excitement and appeal of Gützlaff's journals. Gützlaff was a master at popularizing missions, albeit at times a somewhat unscrupulous one. An advertisement for the first New York edition of two voyages predicted that the work would be read with "a thrilling interest in the author's personal adventures and an earnest desire for the success of his truly apostolic efforts."[16]

The prediction proved accurate. Gützlaff presented a personal narrative of hazardous exploits undertaken in the cause of Christ. Westerners, especially Americans, could identify with his enterprising spirit. He not only articulated the populist, pioneering ideal; he lived the life of an adventurer, deliberately courting danger, enduring hardships, and reveling in the challenges. Gützlaff, for example, described an episode in which the *Sylph* ran aground in the Gulf of Liaodong. Before long a fierce cold wind had disabled the Indian sailors and iced the ship. Since they were unable to right the vessel, Gützlaff typically gathered a group of volunteers to seek help. Land was twenty-five miles distant, and by the time their rowboat had reached shore the crew and the boat were entirely encased in ice. One Indian froze to death even though Gützlaff gave him his own wraps; the others, in the words of Gützlaff, "were on the verge of eternity." Though they obtained no aid from the mandarins, "the ship got off by the interposition of God, who had ordered the south wind to blow. . . . His name be praised to all eternity."[17] On a trip to interior Fujian, Gützlaff and a Chinese guide led the way as the group traipsed up hilly footpaths until their feet were so swollen that they could no longer walk. They hired chair carriers, and Gützlaff felt such compassion for them that he treated them to pork and as much rice as they could eat. Once, the party had to negotiate the narrow footpaths by moonlight before they finally reached a village; here, Gützlaff managed to find lodging with a friendly peasant, though they had to share the quarters with the farmer's pigs.[18]

16. *Journal of Two Voyages along the Coast of China in 1831 and 1832* (New York: J. P. Haven, 1833), p. iii.

17. *Journal of Three Voyages*, pp. 421-33.

18. G. J. Gordon, "Visit to the Ankoy Tea District," *AJMR* 16 (1835): 281-89.

Gützlaff's unbounded optimism and his assurances of the superiority of Western civilization to that of China spoke to the expansive, self-assertive, and self-confident mood of Great Britain and America. In calls for volunteers, Gützlaff's glowing accounts of the great opportunities in China were more impelling than Bridgman's frequent laments about the difficulties of the task.[19] Readers were more apt to admire than censure Gützlaff for boldly bearding mandarins. They may even have shared Gützlaff's pleasure in matching wits with two military officials who received H. H. Lindsay and Gützlaff at Xiamen.

> The tung-ping . . . manifested the most decided spirit of hostility towards us. A conversation ensued between himself and Mr. Gutzlaff in the Fokien dialect, in which he roundly declared that our plea of wanting provisions was merely a pretence to veil some sinister purposes; but Mr. Gutzlaff was not the person to be brow-beaten by angry words; and he replied to his accusations with so much tact and spirit, that we had the satisfaction to see his opponent completely foiled in his arguments. On this the tung-ping [was unable to] moderate his anger, which appeared to be greatly increased by seeing that the bystanders evidently enjoyed his discomfiture, and were much amused by some of the apt remarks made by Mr. Gutzlaff.[20]

Western merchants, missionaries, and officials applauded Lindsay and Gützlaff's insistence on their right to be seated in the presence of seated Chinese officials. That the Westerners won the contest was a source of satisfaction; more important, it provided a precedent for future audiences with Chinese.[21]

Gützlaff, almost invariably critical of the mandarins, expressed sympathy for the masses even as he described their lack of cleanliness or candidness. A constant theme of his journals was the basic goodwill of the general populace; they welcomed him with his medicines and tracts, some even accepting him

---

19. According to Michael D. Lazich, *E. C. Bridgman (1801-1861), America's First Missionary to China* (Lewiston: The Edwin Mellen Press, 2000), Bridgman suffered from bouts of depression, and this is confirmed by reading his correspondence with the ABCFM. On the other hand, Bridgman rarely allowed his depression to interfere with his demanding work schedule. Under his editorship, *The Chinese Repository* became an important source of information on China missions and Chinese civilization for a diverse audience.

20. Lindsay and Gutzlaff, *Report of Proceedings on a Voyage to the Northern Ports of China in the Ship Lord Amherst* (London: B. Fellowes, 1833), pp. 124-25, 185-86.

21. Lindsay and Gutzlaff, *Report of Proceedings,* pp. 122-23, 255.

as an adopted citizen of Fujian. Villagers offered him tea and shelter, once warning him that chair carriers were plotting to take advantage of him. He contrasted the eagerness of the masses for both trade and tracts with the hostility and opposition of the "despotic" emperor and high officials. Oppressed by the magistrates, villagers revealed little sense of loyalty to the government; the affairs of the Beijing rulers elicited only minimal interest among them. Gützlaff speculated, in true democratic fashion, that the central government could not enforce prohibitions against foreign contacts in the face of popular will.

Through on-site descriptions of farmers' efforts to wrest a living from sandy, infertile soil, of the sailors' harsh existence, of emigrants in Southeast Asia who skimped on food in order to save enough to send a dollar or two home, Gützlaff humanized the Chinese.[22] His portrayal might convey a mixed image with many shadows, but for his readers, Chinese became more than exotic, inscrutable stereotypes. They were individual human beings deserving of attention and a chance to hear the promise of salvation. Gützlaff, for example, vividly described seamen indulging in alcohol, gambling, and debauchery, but he also depicted individual sailors who were repentant and willingly risked their lives on seagoing junks in order to bring home a bag of rice to their family. He was touched by their gratitude to him for ministering to their eye and skin diseases. He marveled at the small patches of land that were cultivated with great care by the Hakka of Haifeng, Guangdong, and he admired the farmers for being cheerful and communicative even though "clad in rags, and scarcely provided with the necessities of life."[23] In Shandong he reported that he was invited to dinner and treated with much kindness by individuals who lived in tiny houses with minimal furniture and subsisted on a diet of ground millet.[24] In Korea he described the heated brick kangs or beds on which families spent much of winter, barely surviving on stored grain until spring. Their skin was encrusted with dirt and many were covered with vermin. He concluded, "Would their present state have been what it is, had they been allowed intercourse with foreigners? 'Exclusion' may have kept them from the adoption of foreign customs, but had not meliorated their condition."[25] Reiterated throughout the journals was the theme that all of his sacrifices were in the noble cause of making the gospel of salvation known and of fostering free intercourse, which would benefit all humanity,

---

22. *Journal of Three Voyages,* pp. 61, 85-88, 166-67.
23. *Journal of Three Voyages,* pp. 156-57.
24. *Journal of Three Voyages,* pp. 102-3.
25. *Journal of Three Voyages,* pp. 345-46.

East as well as West. While he believed that the task of the missionary was to evangelize, not reform, he took for granted that conversion to Christianity and knowledge of Western civilization would inevitably lead China toward a society resembling that of the West.

Gützlaff often tailored his correspondence to his specific audience. In writing to officials of American religious societies and to American journals, Gützlaff deliberately cultivated the notion that God had a special mission for Americans. On America, God had abundantly poured out His divine spirit. To America, God had granted religious liberty. A letter to the American Bible Society secretary described Americans as a "great and free people eminently blessed by the Lord on high." [26] Gützlaff's obvious conclusion was that such a favored people incurred a unique obligation to extend the blessings of God to all the peoples of the world. America, of all nations, was destined to engage in the noble endeavor to communicate knowledge of the truth to those in darkness. Consciously or instinctively, he appreciated the sense of superiority that accompanies charity, and he fed a growing sense of a distinctive American identity. Gützlaff, a German, articulated a developing American national pride that was intertwined with a sense of mission.

For English readers he pointed out that Great Britain was the political and economic leader among the Western powers in Asia. As an industrializing nation, she was growing in wealth and advancing in technology. When she demanded the right of free intercourse among all nations, according to Gützlaff, she was not merely seeking material benefits for herself; she was exercising an inherent human right which was necessary to progress. She upheld the Protestant religion, the only true Christianity. She was the most civilized of all peoples, and as such she should take the initiative in bringing the benefits of Western civilization, including Christianity, to China.[27] Gützlaff challenged the Germans by pointing out that England and America were about to send several missionaries to China. Would not his own country accept its moral obligation?

26. Gützlaff to Secretary of the American Bible Society, Macao, 5 March 1836, ABS Archives; "Evangelization of China: Letter from Rev. Mr. Gützlaff," *Foreign Missionary Chronicle* 5 (October 1837): 147; "China and Its Vicinity: An Appeal from Charles Gützlaff," *Evangelisches Missions-Magazin* 15 (October 1837): 137-40.

27. This was a frequent theme in both Gützlaff's Chinese- and English-language writings. See "Mouyu" (Trade), *Dong-Xiyang kao meiyue tong ji zhuan* [The East-West monthly magazine] (1838); *Da Yingguo tongji* [Short account of England] (Malacca: LMS, 1834), 5:22; *Sketch of Chinese History, Ancient and Modern: Comprising a Retrospect of the Foreign Intercourse and Trade with China*, 2 vols. (London: Smith, Elder, & Co., 1834), 2:291; *Journal of Three Voyages*, pp. 261, 269.

During the early 1830s Gützlaff also composed a two-volume history of China, which appeared in both English and American editions and later in German translation. The full title of the work is indicative of its intent and content: *A Sketch of Chinese History, Ancient and Modern, Comprising a Retrospect of the Foreign Intercourse and Trade with China*. He dedicated the book to the president of the East India Company Board of Control, Charles Grant: "As you have, moreover, always taken a deep interest in the important trade with China (the success of which it is the aim of my humble labours to promote), I know of no public man to whom these volumes can be more appropriately dedicated." Over three-fourths of the second volume is devoted to two topics: the propagation of Christianity in China and the foreign intercourse of China, with particular attention to Anglo-Chinese relations.[28] Gützlaff's goal was to present a popular history in order to stimulate interest in China. He would extend the vista of Western Christians who had only recently accepted responsibility for foreign missions. Since the Western public knew so little about China, basic factual data had to be included, filtered of course through the eyes of a Western missionary. In both his history and his journals, he continued to juggle his dual roles of evangelist and employee of British merchants. He wished to correct the idealized image of China by the seventeenth-century Jesuits, who relied on Chinese theory and philosophy rather than practice. He would, he stated, demonstrate the fallacy of two widespread misconceptions: (1) that the Chinese are a peaceable people whose history has been torn by fewer wars and revolutions than in the West, and (2) that Chinese military power is a colossus that no European power can overcome.

Another theme, frequently repeated here and elsewhere, is the degradation of women in Chinese society. Foot binding, concubinage, and slave girls were some of the practices deplored by Gützlaff; infanticide, he insisted, was widespread, especially in south China. Citing Confucian teachings as sanctioning both the denial of education to women and the subordination of women successively to father, husband, and son led Gützlaff into his argument that Christianity was essential to raising the status of Chinese women. Just as Christian women were crucial to the founding of Christian families, so educated wives and mothers were necessary to creating a civilized society. The education and conversion of women should have high priority. China needed devout women from the West to come to China to help raise up their heathen sisters; an opportunity for great good work awaited them.[29]

28. See chapter 4 on Gützlaff's civil career for an analysis of this section. Gützlaff was in the employ of Jardine, Matheson & Co. during the composition of this work.

29. Gützlaff, *Sketch of Chinese History,* 1:55-56, 197; *Journal of Three Voyages,* pp. 384-85;

Unlike Gützlaff's journals, which are based on his personal experience, his *Sketch of Chinese History* makes use of both Chinese and Western historical works. At the end of most chapters, he lists his sources, though he does not provide footnotes, a common format at the time. Gützlaff never lost his craving for knowledge nor his desire for recognition as a scholar as well as an evangelist. Despite his criticism of the Jesuits, he praised them for their mastery of the Chinese language, and he relied on their writings. The book's map, for example, is one drawn by the Jesuits, but corrected on the basis of Gützlaff's coastal journeys. Other items he mentioned are the writings of French geographers and historians: Jean Baptiste B. d'Anville (1697-1782), Antoine Gaubil, S.J. (1689-1759), Jean Pierre Abel Remusat (1788-1832), Barthetemy de Herbelot (1625-1695), and Jean Baptiste Du Halde, as well as Marco Polo's *Travels*. For the dynastic history sections, Gützlaff also referred to Suma Qien, *Shi Zhi* (Historical memoirs), and specific Chinese dynastic histories. Gützlaff's own journals provide copy for some of the general introductory material, though only the *Chinese Repository* is mentioned, not the author.

The first volume of the history begins with chapters on Chinese geography, government and laws, language, learning, and religion. For Western readers just becoming cognizant of China, these were doubtless among the most interesting and informative sections. The Orientalism pervading the descriptions probably enhanced the work for Western audiences rather than offended them. The geographical features of each province are followed by brief characterizations of its inhabitants and major products, all presented in a simple, readable style. For example, the Fujianese are a commercial, enterprising people, many of them emigrating to Southeast Asia; they are friendly toward foreigners; Fujian is a major source of the black teas. Zhejiang has good harbors and is the locale of China's finest cities; it exports green teas and silk. In accepting the Chinese government's population estimate of 367 millions, questioned by many Westerners at that time, Gützlaff stated that he had checked Chinese census figures for several small districts and found them accurate. In his publicity, he would cite over and over again the 350 million Chinese awaiting the gospel of salvation.

His summary description of Chinese government structure, with emperor, boards, censors, Hanlin Academy, civil and military ranks, is accurate

---

"Das weibliche Geschlect in China," *Evangelischer Reichsbote* (hereafter *ER*) 2.2 (February 1852): 3-7; *China Opened, or, a Display of the Topography, History, Customs, Manners, Arts, Manufactures, Commerce, Literature, Religion, Jurisprudence, etc. of the Chinese Empire*, 2 vols., revised by Andrew Reed (London: Smith, Elder & Co., 1838), 1:490-508.

and would be useful for a beginning student of China, though Gützlaff was not hesitant about offering his personal assessment. "One remark, in regard to all Chinese institutions, which applies also to the emperor, may here be made: the theory is, in many instances, very excellent, but the practice is generally exceedingly defective. A crafty, lying, base spirit pervades the court and all the officers of the government."[30]

In the section on Chinese character and learning, he again offered a picture full of contradictions. He commended the emphasis given to filial piety, which is the foundation of both the polity and society and which also fosters the Chinese fondness for their children and respect for the aged. But he also stressed the indifference to suffering by non-kin, the "mental lethargy" of the Chinese, and the political tyranny of officials despite a cloak of paternalism. Perhaps because his contacts had been primarily with southerners, particularly the Cantonese and the Fujianese, he argued that a mercantile spirit pervaded all; the Confucian theory that merchants ranked at the bottom of society had no basis in reality. Neither here nor elsewhere is the interplay between doctrine and actuality examined. As for learning, he contended that however rich China was in literature, she was defective in science.

As might be expected, Gützlaff's depiction of Chinese religion was censorious, and his attitude altered little during his quarter-century of residence in East Asia. Even though he became somewhat more understanding of the trials faced by Christian converts and of their failings, he did not and could not change his overall assessment of the Chinese religious beliefs and practices. Like most of the Protestant pioneers, he adopted a confrontational approach toward Chinese religions; they were Christianity's competitors. Negative adjectives abounded in his writings on Chinese Buddhism, Daoism, religious festivals, and ancestor worship: idolatrous, sensual, superstitious, full of absurdities, gross. Only when discussing the teachings of Confucius did Gützlaff moderate his language. Confucius, he wrote, was practical and advocated a morality conducive to order and social happiness; his theory of good government had much to recommend it. Even so, Gützlaff concluded, the classics reveal the vanity of relying on human doctrine without the aid of divine revelation. "Though the notion of a Supreme Being glimmers faintly through the doctrines of the ancient sages," Confucius kept a studied silence on the existence of God and the immortality of the soul.[31] Such a this-worldly

---

30. *Sketch of Chinese History*, 1:38.

31. *Journal of Three Voyages*, pp. 373-79; 386-87; "Remarks on the Religion of the Chinese," *CRep* 4 (1835): 272; *Sketch of Chinese History*, 1:68; "Protestantische Missionen in China," *Evangelisches Missions-Magazin* 1 (1840): 35-37.

philosophy could never satisfy the populace and, furthermore, it bore heavy responsibility for the great discrepancies between theory and actuality in Chinese society.

The masses, and even the supposedly agnostic literati, demonstrated their true religious attitudes in folk festivals, Buddhist funeral ceremonies, ancestor worship, and geomancy. Though indifferent toward the Divine and disdainful toward priests, the populace delighted in religious celebrations because they meant days of pleasure: gambling, smoking, feasting, theatricals, pageantry, and noise. Coming out of a conservative Protestant background, Gützlaff found such festivities repellant. Their rituals and prayers, he reported, were mechanical; appeals to deities were entirely in terms of earthly concerns; worship and offerings were on a quid pro quo basis. Yet, Gützlaff's descriptions of the propitiation of Ma Zu by sailors, of funerals, of commemoration of New Year's, and of the Buddhist center at Putuo are vivid and informative. He even admired the magnificent setting and architecture of Putuo, and he managed to conclude his description of sailors' offerings to Ma Zu with an admonition to Christians: "Christians are the servants of the living God, who had created the heavens and earth; at whose command the winds and the waves rise or are still . . . how much more, then, should they endeavour to conciliate the favour of the Almighty! . . . If idolaters feel dependent on superior beings; if they look up to them for protection and success; if they are punctual in paying their vows; what should be the conduct of nations who acknowledge Christ to be their Saviour?"[32] Pervading all was the assumption that Christianity was the one true religion and the Christian God the one true God. Appealing to Ma Zu for protection on the seas was idolatrous superstition; appealing to the Christian God for protection simply acknowledged the power of God over all creation.[33]

Gützlaff employed a Western context for his narrative of Chinese history, and the historical section of *Sketch* begins with an attempt to use Western periodization. He divided China's history into mythological, ancient (2207 B.C.–A.D. 263), middle (264-1367), and modern ages (1368-present). Having done this, he added, "But that their empire existed before the flood, and even before the era which we assign for the creation of the world, is as extravagant and unfounded as the mythical stories of the Hindoos and the Greeks."[34] The truth of biblical history he could not question.

32. *Journal of Three Voyages*, p. 60.

33. Gützlaff, *Sketch of Chinese History*, 1:197; "Remarks on the Religion of the Chinese," pp. 271-76; "Protestantische Missionen in China," pp. 35-36; "Das Chinesische Neu-Jahr," *ER* 1.10 (October 1851): 5-7; "Die Feste der Chinesen," *ER* 1.3 (March 1852): 1-4.

34. *Sketch of Chinese History*, 1:71.

Gützlaff then resorted to the compartmentalizing that characterizes many of his actions and his writings. Within the Western framework, he employed Chinese dynastic dating and methodology — in order to avoid confusion, he wrote. The story is told dynasty by dynasty, and within each dynasty, emperor by emperor, the Chinese characters and transliteration given for reign names. The more important emperors are briefly portrayed; a few anecdotes or episodes from the emperor's life are related. Internal warfare, campaigns to expand the Middle Kingdom, and conflicts with the peoples of the Inner Asian Frontiers, along with political intrigues and power struggles with eunuchs and pretenders to the throne, all receive attention. The two monarchs to whom he assigned the greatest merit are Kubilai Khan of the Yuan dynasty and the Kangxi emperor of the Qing. Both were talented and brave warriors who became effective and just rulers once they had attained the throne. More important to Gützlaff, however, was the fact that both were receptive to foreign learning and practiced religious tolerance, at least initially.

Gützlaff insisted that once the imperial system had been established, Chinese civilization stagnated. In contrast to the variety and multitude of competing states in West Europe and North Africa, Gützlaff found only monotony, an undifferentiated civilized mass in East Asia. By the Ming period, Gützlaff maintained, the hand of tradition had become so heavy that no new ideas or inventions were possible and closure impeded enlightenment from outside. By mid-Qing, population growth, corruption, and general dynastic decline had made a shambles of China's political and military system.[35]

As a skilled publicist and fundraiser, Gützlaff played a few notes that he repeated over and over in his journals, his *Sketch of Chinese History,* and other popular writings. China, he insisted, was not shut. God has opened China's doors to the courageous and faithful. Only the emperor and his officials were hostile toward foreigners, trying to keep them with their message of salvation out of China. The millions of ordinary Chinese citizens were friendly. A minister of God, furthermore, was subject to a higher authority than that of a despotic emperor who did not abide by Christian and Confucian teachings on the brotherhood of all mankind. If a Westerner avoided the cities where mandarins resided, he could live in interior China and spread the gospel, and in any case, the Protestants should be able to equal the Roman Catholics by enlisting recruits willing to sacrifice all in the great cause. Not only were the Chinese a reading people, but one written language served all China. Translations of the Scriptures and religious tracts, therefore, could carry the Word of God to the far reaches of the nation, where the works were welcomed by villagers.

35. *Journal of Two Voyages,* p. iii.

Never for a moment does Gützlaff seem to have doubted the linkage of Christianity, science and technology, political stability and power. Since Christianity was the ultimate source of the West's power and progress, material rewards would naturally accompany spiritual blessings. China as well as the West had much to gain from free intercourse between the two. As a matter of fact, stagnant China required the influence of external forces — Christianity and Western knowledge — for its rejuvenation. Who would support the greatest of all mission challenges? Who would join the crusade to redeem the most numerous and most advanced peoples of Asia? These themes Gützlaff returned to again and again. By the time of Gützlaff's death in 1851, fifteen Protestant mission societies were supporting some seventy missionaries in China.[36] Many China missionaries had contributed to the growth of interest in China among Western Protestants. Gützlaff was certainly not the least of the publicists.

China Missionaries Learn about China

Despite the limitations imposed by the Christian viewpoint and mission, it would be inaccurate to give the impression that Gützlaff and his colleagues remained unchanged by their China experiences. During the early nineteenth century most Western evangelists sailed for China with little or no knowledge of Chinese language and culture. They might have read the reports of their predecessors; a few, like Robert Morrison, had begun to learn Chinese, but their studies in seminary had provided no special training for a specific field. Frequent misunderstandings and misinterpretations were the consequence. Abandoning the assumption that Western civilization was the norm was difficult. Residence in China and daily interaction with Chinese, nevertheless, led many to the realization that China was home to a great civilization; they even learned to appreciate Chinese literature, ethical teachings, administrative structure, and more. During the 1830s, for example, Gützlaff began a reading program that embraced the Chinese classics, novels, histories, poetic works, historical biographies, collections of legends, and accounts of gods. On the basis of his perusal of these works, many of them multi-volumed, he published a dozen and a half reviews in the *Chinese Re-*

---

36. In addition, there were forty missionary wives plus several printers and physicians who were not officially listed as missionaries. See "China," in *A Cyclopedia of Missions*, ed. Harvey Newcomb, rev. ed. (New York: Charles Scribner, 1856), p. 294. Except for the high attrition rate due to death, retirement for health reasons, and other losses, the total figure would have been considerably higher.

pository, thereby drawing attention to a literary corpus largely unknown to most *Repository* readers.[37]

His reviews summarize the contents of the works, but provide relatively little interpretation or analysis. Commentaries consist, in many instances, of criticism from a European Christian point of view, and it is clear that Gützlaff sometimes only skimmed the volumes. Such must have been the case with *Honglou meng* ("Dream of the Red Chamber"), where he mistakes the main character for a female.[38] Despite being offended by what he considers the coarse sexuality of the novel, Gützlaff does acknowledge that one can learn about female society of the higher classes and also gain a fairly accurate picture of Chinese judicial proceedings from the manslaughter trial it describes.

Though Gützlaff read the works of Su Shi (Su Dongbo) and other poets, he had difficulty initially in acquiring an appreciation of Chinese poetry, with its concise style and use of allusion and alliteration. *Sanguo shi tongsu yanai* ("Romance of the three kingdoms") rated high praise by Gützlaff. Not only did he recommend it as providing a faithful picture of the tumultuous political scene of third-century China, but he also endorsed it as an example of good literary style that was accessible to the general reading public. A beginning language student, he said, would profit more from reading the Three Kingdoms and the *Da Ming Zhengde Huang you Jiangnan zhuan* (later translated by He Jinshan and James Legge as "The Rambles of the Emperor Ching Tih in Keäng Nan") than from starting with the classics, an observation that still has considerable merit.[39] Gützlaff also applauded *Nan Song zhizhuan* (History of the southern Song dynasty), which was not only interesting but also a model of lucid writing. "The book is well suited for beginners, and the best sinologue may learn from it the secret of writing a flowing style and using elegant expression without pedantry."[40]

Predictably, Gützlaff's review of *Shi Xian tong Jian* (A general account of the gods and the genii) was laden with sarcasm: "And now we are at once introduced to the genii, who inhabit hills and valleys, and most materially influence human affairs. Let it be remembered that they are immortal, and more-

---

37. See *CRep* 3.3 (1834)–12.2 (1843); also, Patrick Hanan, "The Missionary Novels of Nineteenth-Century China," *Harvard Journal of Asiatic Studies* 60.2 (December 2000): 426.

38. "Hung Lau Mung, or Dreams in the Red Chamber," *CRep* 11.5 (1842): 266-73; Hanan, "The Missionary Novels," pp. 425-26.

39. "Notice of the San kwo che or History of the Three Kingdoms," *CRep* 7 (November 1838): 233-49; "Chingtih hwang yew Kuangnan: The Rambles of the Emperor Ching-tih in Keangnan," *CRep* 9 (1840): 57-63.

40. "Nan Sung Ch-chuen or History of the Southern Sung Dynasty," *CRep* 11.10 (1842): 540; Hanan, "The Missionary Novels," p. 426.

over very talkative, of which our author has availed himself to fill many a volume. The only question arising is, whether they kept a recorder, who was always at hand to write down their dialogues, and as soon as he heard of the intention of our compiler forwarded to him the voluminous manuscript."[41] Yet Gützlaff noted the importance of becoming acquainted with the work in order to understand Chinese religious beliefs, and he expressed the view that the traditional division of Chinese religions into Confucianism, Buddhism, and Daoism had little reality, particularly among the masses. Their religion consisted of an amalgam and was more concerned with ritual than ethics.

Gützlaff undoubtedly enhanced his mastery of the Chinese language through his reading program, and the fact that his disparaging comments became less frequent as he proceeded may indicate a growing appreciation and understanding. At any rate, he had no doubt about the importance of the works to the comprehension of Chinese culture and history, and he hoped that his reviews would motivate *Chinese Repository* readers to study them. "We cannot sympathize with this almost innumerable people," he wrote, ". . . unless we view them in their true character and condition." Even "their government, as bad as it is, had stood the test of ages and deserves the attention of every thinking man."[42] He recommended also that Westerners visit the famous Buddhist temples and monasteries for the unequaled beauty of their sites and the harmony of their layout as well as for an understanding of the popular appeal of Buddhism.

Most controversial of Gützlaff's publications was *China Opened*, printed in 1838. The British journal *The Athenæum*, which had praised Gützlaff's *Sketch of Chinese History* as the "most clear and intelligible account of Chinese civilization that has yet appeared in any European language," characterized *China Opened* as a mere compilation, exhibiting "very little skill, no powers of condensation."[43] It is true that the title *China Opened* appeared to fly in the face of reality, since Gützlaff had previously raised high expectations about the possibilities of evangelizing within China only to have the hopes dashed by imperial edicts and local opposition. The work, furthermore, gave greater evidence of haste and impatience than any of Gützlaff's previous publications. Even though the structure was new, segments were patched in from his earlier writings; material was occasionally repeated, and the whole lacked

41. "Review of the Shin Seen Tung Keen: A General Account of the Gods and Genii," *CRep* 7 (1838): 508-9.

42. "Character of Chinese Historical Works: Inducements to Study Them," *CRep* 3 (1834): 54.

43. "Reviews," *The Athenæum* 363 (10 October 1834): 744; and 569 (22 September 1838): 695-96.

integration. At the same time, the title was meant to carry a second meaning, that of opening China to Western understanding. The subtitle and organization of the work make the double entendre clear: *A Display of the Topography, History, Customs, Manners, Arts, Manufactures, Commerce, Literature, Religion, Jurisprudence, etc. of the Chinese Empire.* In contrast to the *Sketch of Chinese History,* only one chapter was devoted to dynastic history; instead, successive chapters discuss the items listed in the subtitle. Throughout the work Gützlaff expressed the hope that increasing Western understanding of China would inspire the home churches to support new volunteers to bring the gospel of salvation to China.

Gützlaff had continued to read about China and to gain understanding; the number of sources referred to, both Chinese and Western, is impressive. New information had been added and interpretations had been refined. Gützlaff no longer contended that the imperial government as devised in the Qin-Han era remained static. Changes during the eighth century, he wrote, had brought consolidation of the emperor's power at the expense of feudal overlords. Imperial appointment had displaced heredity in determining office, and the result was a more stable imperial system. Material on the role and power of clans, even at the expense of formal government, indicates Gützlaff's greater understanding of Chinese society in southeast China. In the chapter on religion, Gützlaff expanded material previously presented on Chinese religious sects and on Chinese Catholic communities and evangelists during the previous hundred years; both were unexplored subjects until the twentieth century. Using a biblical text, he demonstrated various styles of Chinese calligraphy in the section on Chinese language and literature. He had even gained an appreciation of Chinese poetry, which is "interwoven with so many strange and original metaphors and figures of speech, and contains such various allusions to history and deified heroes, that at first sight it appears mere jargon. But when a sufficient acquaintance with these peculiarities has enabled the reader to penetrate into the spirit, a splendid vista opens, and the most sublime images present themselves."[44]

Gützlaff provided a detailed and useful description of the operation of Sino-Western trade during the 1830s: the role of the hong merchants licensed to trade with Westerners, and their difficult position because of government requisitions and the fact that they were held responsible for anything relating to the Western traders. The function of pilots, compradors, and revenue

---

44. Quoted in Henrietta Shuck, *Scenes in China: or Sketches of the Country, Religion, and Customs of the Chinese* (Philadelphia: American Baptist Publication Society, 1852), pp. 220-21.

agents; articles of export and import, the quantity of each item, and the customs levied on each, plus the customary irregular charges, are all spelled out. He notes that contraband trade along China's coast probably exceeded the legitimate trade through Canton, a fact not always recognized. He also contended that continued growth in opium smuggling and the abolition of the East India Company monopoly in favor of individual merchants would lead to direct confrontation unless changes were negotiated. And he believed that Sino-Western trade had to be placed on a new footing.

For Gützlaff, there was no question that opium was an addictive, death-dealing drug, and he expressed the wish that the British would cease to sponsor its production in India, but he was fully aware that this was a pious hope. In an attempt at an impartial account of current Sino-British relations, including the opium issue, and various proposals for change, he related the British resident merchants' grievances and their justification of aggressive action. Then he presented rebuttals by members of the British foreign office, opium opponents, and merchants fearing interruption of trade. It is an interesting summary of contemporary opinion, though Gützlaff's biases are evident. He identified completely with the British and their demand for free trade, even using such pronouns as "our" and "we" when referring to the nation. He contended that merchants on the scene understood the situation better than the home office. He repeated old themes: most Chinese actually desire to expand trade; Chinese respect firmness, not compromise. The Chinese military is so weak that the mere threat of force will lead to negotiation and change; bloodshed will not actually be required. And, most important of all, opening China to free intercourse, including Christianity, will serve the Chinese well.

Why, one may ask, did Gützlaff issue such a work, one that incorporated previously published materials, that needed reworking, and that by its very title would elicit criticism? Gützlaff, as even his critics noted, was capable of much better; few Westerners could equal Gützlaff in knowledge of Chinese and Western sources, in mastery of the oral language, and in direct contact with Chinese individuals. The origins of the work lay with Sir G. H. Robinson who, upon being appointed superintendent of trade in 1835 and knowing little about China, requested Gützlaff to furnish him with any information that might be useful. Gützlaff's reports to Robinson were relayed to the British foreign office and became the basis for *China Opened*.[45] Even so, one can only speculate as to why Gützlaff would publish such an unfinished manuscript.

45. Letter of Robinson quoted in *The Friend of China and Hong Kong Gazette*, 2 November 1850, p. 350; also Chang Hsin-pao, *Commissioner Lin and the Opium War* (Cambridge, MA: Harvard University Press, 1964), p. 66.

Perhaps he needed to demonstrate his continued commitment to the cause of China missions despite being a full-time civil servant. Perhaps it was simply his zeal and sense of urgency that drove him to try to impress the West with the promise of China's millions. New missionary recruits supported by congregations awakened to Christ's commission could carry the message of salvation to interior China even if his own range of activity was restricted. Another publication on China would maintain Western interest in China and stimulate a greater sense of responsibility to bring Christian civilization to the "benighted heathen." He assumed that the stimulus for change in China must come from outside; caught in a pre-modern mode, China lacked the internal resources to arouse herself. Whatever the merits or demerits of the book, the data and the themes were available to members of the British Parliament and foreign office. They became part of the background to the Opium War of 1840-1842.

Scholarly and Semi-scholarly Works

Among Gützlaff's scholarly works is *Geschichte des chineseschen Reiches von den ältesten Zeiten bis auf den Frieden von Nanking (History of the Chinese Empire from Ancient Times to the Treaty of Nanjing, 1847).*[46] Even though Gützlaff stated that his goal was a popular history that would arouse interest in China in his Fatherland, he introduced his history with an annotated bibliography of his Chinese sources. The list is long and runs the gamut from *Chun qiu* (Spring and Autumn Annals) and *Zuo zhuan* (Narratives of Zuo) to the writings of Suma Qian and Ban Gu, the official dynastic histories, and numerous historical novels. His commentary on Chinese histories is better informed and less prejudicial than in his earlier *Sketch of Chinese History* or his reviews for the *Chinese Repository*. Gützlaff then plunged directly into China's past, instead of beginning with broad generalizations about China's geography, government, and society. He apparently anticipated a more knowledgeable audience than for his previous history in English. *Geschichte* is, like most histories of the nineteenth century, imperial history, not social history, and so Gützlaff proceeds dynasty by dynasty. In contrast to *Sketch of Chinese History,* material on the earlier period is shortened while that on the Song, Ming, and Qing dynasties is greatly expanded. The work concludes with a long chapter on the Opium War.

Gützlaff contended that for decades the Daoguang emperor did not en-

46. There was also a Dutch translation of the work.

force the prohibition on Christianity and its propagation so that, contrary to the current opinion, small Roman Catholic communities and even isolated families survived in China, sometimes with only a lay leader and sometimes with priests visiting them only rarely to perform baptisms and hold mass. He describes the flow of European priests into interior China and the surreptitious journeys of Chinese candidates to seminaries in Macao, India, and Europe. The instances of persecution are seen as exceptions, often launched by local mandarins. Such a view of continuing Chinese Catholicism during the period of prohibition has found confirmation in recent scholarship.[47]

Based on personal experience, Gützlaff remarked on the expansion of the opium trade, the course of the war of 1840-1842, and the personalities of some of the leading players. His account is lively and at times touched with humor, but it never mentions his own role in the opium trade or war. Though Gützlaff acknowledged that conflict became inevitable once Westerners began to convey the opium ashore in their own armed boats and that China's loss of bullion had become serious, he joined many Europeans of the time in blaming the growth of the imports on the Chinese appetite for the drug and on corruption by participating officials. Commissioner Lin Zexu is characterized as a brave and honorable mandarin who was, unfortunately, ill informed about Westerners, to whom he tried to apply traditional Chinese techniques of threats and punishment. Captain Charles Elliot, though well intentioned, increased the likelihood of conflict by his vacillation. Sharing the opinion of many Europeans that China only responded to force, Gützlaff censured Elliot's agreement to withdraw British troops from Canton upon payment of $6 million and also Elliot's willingness in 1840-1841 to retire from Ningbo and Zhoushan and to transfer negotiations to Canton. The Cantonese interpreted the British withdrawal as a victory, while both the Chinese emperor and the British prime minister repudiated the terms of the Elliot-Qishan agreement. The result was that Elliot was dismissed; aggressive warfare was renewed under the command of Sir Henry Pottinger, and the terms of the 1842 Treaty of Nanjing were even harsher than those previously negotiated. Gützlaff perceived both Qishan and Qiying as tragic figures, caught between the conser-

47. See, for example, Robert E. Entenmann, "Catholics and Society in Eighteenth-Century Sichuan," in *Christianity in China, from the Eighteenth Century to the Present,* ed. Daniel Bays (Stanford: Stanford University Press, 1996), pp. 8-23; "Christian Virgins in Eighteenth-Century Sichuan," in Bays, ed., *Christianity in China,* pp. 180-93; David E. Mungello, *The Forgotten Christians of Hangzhou* (Honolulu: University of Hawaii Press, 1994); John Witek, "Creating an Image of Nineteenth-Century China from Catholic Missionary Publications" (paper presented at Neuvième Colloque International de Sinologie de Chantilly, 7-9 September 1998).

vatism and hypocrisy of the imperial court and the power and expectations of the British.

Gützlaff concluded that the Chinese were an extraordinary people with a great civilization and great potential, but the West remained for him the standard against which China was viewed. He reiterated his belief that China would move forward only when open to the stimulus of Christianity and free intercourse. Even so, special pleading in the cause of free trade and missions is minimal in this work. As a summary of contemporary Western views on the opium trade and the Opium War, the *Geschichte* is a useful primary source.

A number of Gützlaff's essays were published in the *Journal of the Royal Asiatic Society (JRAS)* and the *Journal of the Royal Geographical Society*. Significant was Gützlaff's article on the powerful and expanding secret society popularly known as the Triads.[48] Gützlaff noted that the Triads thus far had rarely engaged in political action despite their commitment to political reform. He concluded, nevertheless, "Their power . . . is now on the increase, and it is by no means improbable that they will one day or other fraternize with some of the patriotic societies, which are now forming in every part of China. . . . [I]t would not be at all extraordinary, if these ambitious incendiaries should use the Triad Society as an instrument for carrying their designs into execution."[49] In the light of subsequent attempts at Taiping-Triad cooperation for purposes of overthrowing the Qing dynasty, Gützlaff's understanding of certain aspects of the current Chinese scene is impressive.

The Triad essay consists of a translation of Triad papers found in Hong Kong, plus commentary by Gützlaff. Included are an account of the origins of the society; rituals, verses, and oaths used in the induction of new members; songs to accompany various ceremonies; rules governing membership; and the religious principles of the society. Though William Milne had written a brief sketch on the nature and goals of the Triads and Robert Morrison had translated a forty-character manifesto found in Macao in 1828, Gützlaff provided the first English translation of a Triad manuscript from China itself. Gützlaff also added the first English-language descriptions of Triad meetings, their secret identification signs, their organization into lodges, and their financial support drawn from both member contributions and robberies labeled patriotic levies. The manuscript related the traditional story of the founding of the Triads by a young Ming descendent and five Buddhist monks wrong-

---

48. Gützlaff, "On the Secret Triad Society of China," *Journal of the Royal Asiatic Society* (hereafter *Journal of the RAS*) 8 (1846): 361-67. The paper was read before the Hong Kong branch of the Royal Asiatic Society on 15 February 1845 and published in the *Journal of the RAS* the following year.

49. Gützlaff, "On the Secret Triad Society of China," p. 367.

fully accused of rebellion. This version, previously accepted in both Chinese and Western scholarship, has recently been challenged by Dian H. Murray and Qin Baoqi in *The Origins of the Tiandihui*.[50] Their monograph, on the other hand, confirms Gützlaff's observations concerning the makeup and appeal of the society: "All classes are permitted to join; and amongst the Triad Society, there are at present mandarins of low degree, police runners, soldiers, merchants, brothel-keepers, gamblers, and needy characters of every description; for the association promises mutual support in every emergency."[51]

Useful but more ephemeral were articles in the *JRAS* and the *Journal of the Royal Geographical Society* on Chinese medicine, Buddhist writings, the present status of Buddhism in China, Chinese mines, Tibet, Laos, the language and geography of Thailand, Chinese language and grammar, the languages of Japan and Korea, and more. One indication of the need for basic information about China was a series of thirty-three questions sent to Gützlaff in 1846 by Sir George T. Staunton, member of Parliament. Many of the queries were elementary: What are the geographical and geological features of your district? What are its chief productions and manufactures? Are any of them likely to suit the British market? Are the natives, generally speaking, obedient to the government, or are insurrections frequent? How are cases handled in Chinese courts? Is mendicancy very prevalent? What is the condition of the people as to education? Gützlaff's replies were generally factual and judicious, and they were considered informative enough to be printed in the *JRAS*.[52] Gützlaff also compiled a large manuscript for an English-Chinese dictionary that was never completed or published. These writings, despite Gützlaff's evangelistic agenda, served as introductions to China for missionaries, diplomats, and other residents in China. The works also laid the groundwork for subsequent generations of China scholars.

A study of enduring value, published posthumously, was Gützlaff's *The Life of Taou-Kwang, Late Emperor of China: Memoirs of the Court of Peking* (1852). Gützlaff's introduction offers a perceptive commentary on the position of the Chinese emperor, who was all-powerful in theory and both political and ceremonial leader of China, but whose actual power and initiative were severely restricted by custom, ritual, and astrology. Ensconced in the Imperial City or traveling only with a large entourage along a prescribed route, the emperor was dependent on information conveyed to him by individuals

50. See the comments of Dian Murray on the contributions of Gützlaff's paper in Dian H. Murray and Qin Baoqi, *The Origins of the Tiandihui: The Chinese Triads in Legend and History* (Stanford: Stanford University Press, 1994), pp. 94-95.

51. Gützlaff, "On the Secret Triad Society," p. 364.

52. "Replies to Queries in Relation to China," *Journal of the RAS* 12 (1852): 386-400.

over whom he had the power of life and death. Another paradox that Gützlaff noted was the fact that a high official or eunuch, despite the vast wealth and influence he might amass, remained totally dependent on the emperor's favor. Leaders holding positions of great responsibility could be reduced overnight to imprisonment or exile, their property confiscated, and their families in danger of their lives. Yet, the possibility of rehabilitation within a few months existed. Such, Gützlaff points out, was the fate of Commissioner Lin Zexu and special negotiator Qiying, both of Opium War fame.

The Daoguang emperor (1821-1850), as Gützlaff depicted him, was attentive to his administrative responsibilities and quite parsimonious in his personal life, but he inherited a kingdom with such intractable political and economic problems as to thwart resolution: a far-flung empire with restive minorities and frontier peoples, a heavy population burden, an unfavorable trade balance with the West attributable largely to opium imports, and pressures from a maritime power that he ill understood. Daoguang's attempts to raise revenue through special levies and sale of ranks and offices only increased political tension and undermined the integrity of officials. The emperor's ability to obtain accurate information about conditions in the countryside or military expeditions rapidly declined. Themes such as these, though refined and amplified by later historians, have stood the test of time.

Despite being critical of Daoguang's reliance on astrology and geomancy, Gützlaff offered a sympathetic and, on the whole, balanced evaluation of the emperor. Pious hopes for the Christianization of China are not overly obtrusive and are frequently tacked on at the conclusion of a chapter or section. Unlike many of Gützlaff's publications, the biography is not primarily a propaganda vehicle. Daoguang is presented as a Manchu with a classical education, but also with the requisite military skills. An honest individual who remained loyal to his friends, he did not relish devious political intrigues. He was more conscientious than brilliant. Scattered throughout the history are extensive translations of imperial edicts and memorials to the emperor. For nineteenth-century readers, they provided valuable insights into the worldview of the Chinese emperor and his officials.

Gützlaff did exaggerate the impact of the Opium War on China, especially interior China. Expressing views typical of Westerners on the fringes of China, he found the Treaty of Nanjing a watershed and the Daoguang era "the most important period of Chinese history" because China ceased to be isolated. Relations between China and the West would henceforth be on an entirely different footing. He censured Cantonese opposition to foreigners residing in Canton and the antiforeign attacks instigated by mandarins, but he did not blame Daogaung, who, he explained, was unable to obtain the true facts. In the long run, Gützlaff concluded, steam navigation and the expansion of the British, Russian, and Chinese empires had brought their peoples into such close proximity that the exchange of information and goods would inevitably set China on the path of progress.

To ascertain the number of readers of Gützlaff's study of the Daoguang emperor is, unfortunately, impossible. Perhaps it is some indication of the German assessment that an eminent professor at the University of Munich translated and edited the history, and it was published in Tübingen by the prominent house of J. G. Cotta. A Lutheran minister at The Hague translated it into Dutch, and a professor of theology, H. C. Millies, wrote the introduction to the Dutch edition (1852), praising it as an important contribution to the cause of China missions. John Fairbank called Gützlaff a well-informed contemporary of the statesman Qiying and cited Gützlaff's *Life of Daoguang* as a source in discussing Qiying's background.[53] Fang Chao-ying also lists the *Life of Daoguang* as a source in his biography of the emperor in *Eminent Chinese*.[54]

Both the merits and the flaws of Gützlaff's writings were, in many ways, a function of his personality and his work habits. He read voraciously and he enjoyed accumulating information; he was interested in all aspects of Chinese life and culture. His journals, therefore, are more than a diary of his daily activities; data based on Chinese histories and previous reports as well as his personal observations and experiences are incorporated. On the other hand, he did not distinguish among his sources; he worked with great speed, rarely revising and often relying on his memory rather than rechecking his sources. The published journals of his first trips apparently were based on notes taken during the treks, but were composed after their completion. He frequently recycled material from his previous publications. Elijah Bridgman complained that the manuscripts submitted by Gützlaff to the *Chinese Repository* resembled drafts and that as editor he sometimes felt that he spent as much time as Gützlaff in readying them for publication.[55]

The journals and the histories do provide valuable and specific information, particularly about Chinese conditions during the 1830s, an era when sources were limited and basic information was not readily available. Elizabeth L. Malcolm in her essay "The *Chinese Repository* and Western Literature on China, 1800-1850," for example, points out that *The Classified Index to the*

53. Fairbank, "Chinese Diplomacy and the Treaty of Nanking," *Journal of Modern History* 12 (March 1940): 13.

54. Fang, "Min-ning," in *Eminent Chinese of the Ch'ing Dynasty*, 2 vols., ed. Arthur W. Hummel (Washington: U.S. Government Printing Office, 1943-1944), 1:576.

55. Barnett, "Practical Evangelism," p. 100.

London Catalogue of Books Published in Great Britain, 1816 to 1851, listed only thirty-six works published on China during the thirty-five-year period; she concludes that by 1850 the British public had ready access to about forty books on China.[56] As indicated in chapter 6, more accurate navigational information about harbors, shoals, passageways, and so forth proved of value to subsequent merchants and British naval expeditions. The discerning reader could even distinguish regional differences in climate and typography, agricultural crops and manufacturing specialties, architecture, and social organization, so that China was not simply an amorphous mass.

Even today it would be hard to find a better description of the tragic consequences of lineage feuding in south China and government reprisal than that offered by Gützlaff:

As we advanced, the appearance of the country grew worse, and we observed, to our great astonishment, whole patches uncultivated. . . . We moreover espied several hamlets in ruins, whilst the inhabitants passed us in gloomy silence: a rare thing with a Chinaman, who has generally a smile in store. . . . We finally came to a hamlet which was nearly deserted, and inhabited only by old women and children. . . . [W]e made inquiries of a gentleman, whom curiosity had brought into our company. . . . "These evils," he said, "have been occasioned by war. Two rival clans, Wang and Jin, have risen in open hostilities against each other. Behold," he continued, pointing to an extensive encampment, surrounded by some entrenchments, "their fortifications; and the field of battle upon which they fought only a short time ago. It is on this account that the region around has been laid waste, and that many inhabitants have fled, or are roving about as desperadoes! The government, during the heat of the contest referred to, did not dare to interfere; but since the fury has abated, the chief magistrate . . . has just made his appearance, to extort fines and apprehend some of the guilty. For this unseasonable officiousness, several of his mymidons have been killed, and things are again ripe for revolt. The whole populace, in the meanwhile, are ready to rise in arms, and most of the peasantry have provided themselves with matchlocks and swords."[57]

56. Elizabeth L. Malcolm, "The *Chinese Repository* and Western Literature on China, 1800-1850," *Modern Asian Studies* 7.2 (1973): 177.

57. "Gützlaff in Interior of China," *New York Observer* 14.2 (13 January 1838): 5. Also quoted in Walter H. Medhurst, *China: Its State and Prospects, with especial reference to the spread of the Gospel* (Boston: Crocker & Brewster, 1838), pp. 416-17.

Useful information about Chinese junk trade with Southeast Asia during the 1830s, the products of exchange, navigational techniques, the life of sailors, their relationship with the ship's captain, and their devotion to Ma Zu, the protector of seamen, is all available in Gützlaff's first journal. Chinese emigration to Southeast Asia, the life of the overseas Chinese, and the importance of their remittances to the families at home are also described.

Gützlaff was prone to exaggeration and, as an astute publicist, he recognized that dramatizing an encounter kindled interest. He painted in broad strokes and he played to his audience and their biases. The seriousness of the sailors' plot to kill Gützlaff during his first journey and of his ability to out-bluff the seamen may be questioned, for instance. On the other hand, it is unlikely that Gützlaff simply invented incidents, dangers, and confrontations. Too many of these tales were corroborated by the reports of such companions as H. H. Lindsay, G. T. Gordon, Charles W. King, and Edwin Stevens.[58] Contributing to the sense of veracity are occasional candid comments in which Gützlaff acknowledged that curiosity and a desire to obtain free books motivated the crowds who gathered around him or he admitted that many merchants who expressed a willingness to trade were primarily interested in opium.

As Gützlaff acquired familiarity with the Chinese literary and historical heritage and also as a consequence of years of interaction with individual Chinese, his image of China became less dark. He employed a more nuanced canvas, and in his histories, his proselytizing became less blatant. Reviewers and scholars often recommended Gützlaff's publications while advising that his specific data should be checked for accuracy against other sources. Hosea Morse wrote that Gützlaff's works were full of valuable information, but required some checking on point of accuracy; Earl Pritchard concurred and added that personal observations were often blended with documentary evidence.[59] S. Wells Williams, author of *The Middle Kingdom,* sharply criticized Gützlaff's haste and carelessness in publishing, but both Williams and W. A. P. Martin in *A Cycle of Cathay* cited Gützlaff as an authority for information on frequent occasions. Sir John Francis Davis in *The Chinese: A General Descrip-*

58. See Lindsay and Gützlaff, *Report of Proceedings;* Gordon, "Visit to the Ankoy Tea District," pp. 281-89; Edwin Stevens, "Expedition to the Bohea (Wooe) Hills," *CRep* 4 (1835): 82-96; Charles W. King, *The Claims of Japan and Malaysia upon Christendom exhibited in notes of voyages made in 1837 from Canton in the ship* Morrison *and Brig.* Himmaleh, 2 vols. (New York: E. French, 1839).

59. Morse, *The International Relations of the Chinese Empire,* vol. 1, *The Period of Conflict, 1834-1860* (London: Longmans Green, 1910), p. 604; Earl H. Pritchard, *Anglo-Chinese Relations during the Seventeenth and Eighteenth Centuries* (Urbana: University of Illinois, 1930), p. 231.

tion of China and Its Inhabitants, along with many other reporters on nineteenth-century China, relied heavily on Gützlaff's writings for data.

Circulation figures for most of Gützlaff's writing are unfortunately lacking. The *Chinese Repository,* in which many of Gützlaff's essays first appeared, printed only about eight hundred copies per issue. The magazine was, nevertheless, widely read by members of the Canton-Macao community, including merchants and government officials as well as missionaries. It also gained a small but influential audience in the West; the *North American Revue, Edinburgh Quarterly,* and *Blackwood's Magazine* all indicated that they received copies of the periodical. The several editions and translations of Gützlaff's journals must have run into the thousands, not counting the dozens of excerpts in mission periodicals. For some lower middle-class families a religious magazine was the only subscription of the household, and Gützlaff's descriptions of his adventures undoubtedly extended horizons as they entertained and created images of heathen lands.[60] It can be assumed that Gützlaff's histories reached a more limited audience, but the fact that his study of the Daoguang emperor and other writings were translated into German and Dutch would indicate that Gützlaff's name commanded an audience. According to Walravens, it was the interest in China missions aroused by Gützlaff's *Geschiche des Chineseschen Reiches* that prompted the establishment of the Cassel foundation for the evangelization of China.[61] *Das Ausland* reprinted several of Gützlaff's more substantive compositions: the section on Chinese administration in *China Opened,* Gützlaff's essays on Tibet and on the geography of Cochin China from the *Journal of the Royal Geographical Society,* and Gützlaff's paper on Chinese medicine from the *JRAS.* Gützlaff's works would quickly be superseded, but during the second half of the nineteenth century, Gützlaff's perceptions and data, whatever their accuracy, exercised considerable influence.

Gützlaff was, of course, a product of his times, even if sometimes in magnified form. The fact that he, like other missionaries, applied European culture and values as the norm may be cause for criticism today, but in Gützlaff's era, they enhanced the popularity of the journals and histories. His writings may still be read with profit because they illustrate so well the mindset of Westerners regarding China during the "Era of Contempt."

60. Though we do not have figures for the circulation of most mission and church magazines, it is indicative of their popularity that in 1824 the Religious Tract Society of London published 40,000 copies of its journal per month, and the American Tract magazine had to print second editions of the first numbers issued; see *ATM* 1.8 (August 1825): 24.

61. Walravens, *Neumann and Gützlaff,* p. 115. Walravens also says that the book sold well, but provides no documentation for the statement.

CHAPTER 6

Translating Christianity for China

The Centrality of the Bible in Protestantism

For pietist missionaries of the nineteenth century, Christianity was a universal doctrine, the Lutheran Bible was the ultimate source of truth, and European Protestantism was its orthodox interpretation. Despite their claim of returning to the basic teachings of Christ, their definition of Christianity actually included multiple heritages: the monotheism of Judaism, the savior doctrine of the New Testament, the concept of orthodoxy from the classical era, the emphasis on community from the Germanic tribes, the idea of the individual and its religious corollary of a personal relation with God from the Renaissance and Reformation, and Puritanism and the work ethic of Calvinism.[1] Even though nineteenth-century Protestantism had evolved out of a very different cultural context than that of China, Western missionaries found it difficult to agree on the translation process that had to occur in China. As had been true of Roman Catholic missions during the seventeenth century, controversies arose over how far they should go in accommodating Christianity to Chinese religious teachings and practices. What was the essence of Christianity? How much leeway should Chinese evangelists and converts be permitted in interpreting Christianity to make it meaningful and understandable to Chinese?

During the nineteenth century these questions came to the fore over the translation of the Bible. Despite the fact that many missionaries became less rigid after residing in China, differences survived. Karl Gützlaff was among those finding a minimalist Christianity acceptable. In the final analysis, of

---

1. Andrew Walls, *The Missionary Movement in Christian History: Studies in the Transmission of Faith* (Maryknoll, NY: Orbis Books, 1996), pp. 16-23.

course, Chinese Christians themselves would translate Christianity according to their needs.

Today the Bible remains at the core of Chinese as well as Western Protestantism. Chinese Protestants remain "people of the Book," and the Bible is central in their Christian literature. At a recent exhibition in Hong Kong on the history of the translation, printing, and distribution of the Bible in China, Rev. Cao Shengjie, president of the China Christian Council, stated that the Bible is "the essential spiritual food for Christians in China."[2] Since biblical revelation is considered the primary basis of religious truth and knowledge, church sermons ordinarily consist of explicating scripture verses. The Amity Foundation and other Christian organizations have expended large sums in printing and distributing copies of the Bible, so that now a significant proportion of Christian families possess their own prized copy of the scriptures.[3] For many church members and leaders of "house churches," the Bible is the only Christian work available to them. Recognizing the importance of the Bible in the history of Western civilization, the Institute for the Study of Christian Culture of the People's University in Beijing announced in December 2001 that it was planning a translation of the Bible into modern Chinese, to be sold for the first time in the free market. The demand for Christian literature is so great that even commercial presses are finding it profitable to sell Christian works.[4]

There are numerous possible explanations for the centrality of the Bible to Chinese Protestantism. In neither Confucianism nor Chinese folk religion is theology emphasized; ethics and ritual, rather than theories concerning the nature of the divine, the origin of the earth, or the afterlife, are the focus of attention. In 2001 over 80 percent of China's Christians lived in rural areas.[5] Impoverished, isolated, and poorly educated, many Christians in the interior are deeply conservative. Not only are they uninterested in doctrinal theology, but they often lack the educational background to appreciate its intricacies.

---

2. "Bible Exhibition Draws Hong Kong Crowds" and "Bible Stories: Reactions to 'A Lamp to My Feet. A Light to My Path,'" *Amity News Service* 13 (9 October 2004): 2-5.

3. "No Ordinary Day," *Amity News Service* 8.3/4 (1999): 1-3, reports on a meeting held in celebration of the printing of the twenty millionth copy of the Bible in China. Of the organizations sending Bibles to China, many were overseas groups.

4. "Bibelübersetzung für den freien Buchmarkt geplannt," *Actuelle China-Nachrichten* 53 (14 January 2002): 1; Wing N. Ping, "Christian Publications in China," *International Bulletin of Missionary Research* 28.1 (January 2004): 36-37.

5. Gao Shiming, "Christemtum und modernes China," trans. Monika Gänssbauer, *Actuelle China-Nachrichten* 51 (17 September 2001): 1. This figure is changing as urbanization continues.

For them, the Bible provides instant access to truth and offers guidance in making decisions. Decades of repression and persecution of Christians after 1949 have created a severe shortage of trained Christian ministers, so that many of the house church leaders are lay members or pastors with minimal knowledge of Christian theology and literature.

Pioneer Protestant missionaries of the nineteenth century shared with present-day Chinese Protestants their emphasis on the Bible. For most Protestant evangelists of that era, the Bible was the divine word of God — or as the American Bible Society (ABS) described it, "a Book transmitted from Heaven."[6] Since the Bible was thought to be the revealed Word of God, both its history and its teachings were to be accepted literally on faith. When Gützlaff sought to explain Bible stories, such as the descent of all humankind, including the Chinese, from Abraham, he resorted to a leap of faith, stating that all things are possible with God. Pietists, furthermore, believed that the Word of God had great power; those who read and understood the gospel could not but be impelled to accept its truth. But the Bible was considered more than the *means* of awakening Chinese; it was also the *teacher*. Not the priest, as in Roman Catholicism, but the Sacred Book was the primary source of Christian teachings for believers. Ever since Luther, therefore, the translation of the Bible into the vernacular has held priority. Every inquirer and convert should have direct access to the scriptures, and if possible, should be provided with the means to literacy.

Translating the Bible

With such a frame of reference, early Protestant missionaries devoted great effort to composing Chinese religious tracts and even to trying their hand at translating the Bible. Writing tracts amounted to a form of language study for a newly arrived missionary in that it helped with expanding Chinese vocabulary and learning Chinese syntax. During the year or more that it took to acquire the facility in oral Chinese essential for public preaching, a missionary could, with the aid of Chinese assistants, write simple Chinese pamphlets. Producing a Chinese publication became for new arrivals almost a badge of initiation, as John Fairbank noted years ago.[7] Gützlaff collaborated with Wal-

6. American Bible Society (hereafter ABS), *Twentieth Annual Report*, 1836, p. 24.
7. Fairbank, "Introduction: The Place of Protestant Writings in China's Cultural History," in *Christianity in China: Early Protestant Missionary Writings*, ed. Suzanne W. Barnett and John K. Fairbank (Cambridge, MA: Harvard University Press, 1985), p. 13.

ter Medhurst in translating the Bible and then produced almost a dozen revisions of the translation.

The first Protestant missionaries had additional reasons for concentrating so heavily on translating, publishing, and distributing Christian works. Not only were the evangelists forced to operate on the fringes of China, but public preaching was restricted even in their "harborside ghetto" in Canton. Among the Protestants, only a few intrepid propagandists like Gützlaff ventured illegally into coastal villages to hand out scriptures and tracts. Despite the multiplicity of spoken dialects, the written language was the same throughout China, so that a translation of the scriptures could bring the glad news to the far reaches of the "vast empire." Chinese colporteurs could carry Christian works into the interior even if the Westerners couldn't. The press would be "the great engine with which to batter the walls of separation, superstition, and idolatry."[8] Finally, the conviction that Buddhism had gained acceptance in China primarily through the written word became a part of mission wisdom during the 1830s, the implication being that Christianity could do the same. Despite the paucity of converts and the restrictions on their activities, missionaries fed their hopes and spirits by producing Chinese Christian literature; they believed they were thereby laying the foundation for the conversion of China. In actuality, the dispersion of hundreds of thousands of religious tracts and Chinese Bibles without follow-up instruction appears to have yielded few converts, but the production of religious tracts and translations of the Bible did contribute to the development of a Christian vocabulary, a process that the Jesuits had begun centuries earlier.

The London Missionary Society's commission to Robert Morrison as he sailed for China in 1807 was to learn Chinese and to translate the Bible into Chinese. Once in China, he set about these tasks promptly and conscientiously, pursuing them steadily until his death in 1834. The first two translations of the Protestant Bible into Chinese were completed almost simultaneously, one by Robert Morrison in Canton and another by Joshua Marshman in Serampore, India. Marshman published the last volume of his five-volume edition in 1822, while Morrison's translation in twenty-one volumes was published in 1823 in Malacca.[9] It was, however, to be the Morrison version rather than the Marshman version that would become the baseline

8. Philosinesis [Gützlaff], "Christian Missions in China: Remarks on the Means and Measures for Extending and Establishing Christianity," *Chinese Repository* (hereafter *CRep*) 3.12 (April 1835): 566.

9. A. J. Garnier, *Chinese Versions of the Bible* (Shanghai: Christian Literature Society, 1934), pp. 14-22; Eric M. North, ed., *The Book of a Thousand Tongues* (New York: Harper & Bros., 1938), p. 84.

for most subsequent revisions.[10] Even before completion of the translations, the British and Foreign Bible Society had been founded to finance the translation, printing, and distribution of the Bible in Chinese. The East India Company would also contribute funds.

Though Morrison and Marshman are listed as authors of the two translations, both Westerners were heavily dependent on their Chinese-speaking assistants, as few missionaries acquired the ability to compose in acceptable Chinese style. The translations might be more accurately described as collaborative works, but unfortunately, the identity of most Chinese associates is not easily discovered. Marshman was assisted by Johannes Lasser, a Macao-born Armenian Christian who had moved to Calcutta to become professor of Chinese at the College of Fort William; also of aid were a Roman Catholic missionary from Beijing and a Chinese dictionary. Morrison benefited from what is known as the British Museum manuscript, a translation by a Roman Catholic priest of the Harmony of the Gospels, the Acts of the Apostles, Paul's Epistles, and the first chapter of the Epistle to the Hebrews. The author of the British Museum manuscript was Jean Basset, who had been born in Lyon around 1662 and had served in China as missionary of the Société des Missions Étrangères de Paris. Basset had drawn much of his religious terminology from Buddhism, and Morrison, in turn, would adopt many of Basset's religious terms for his own translation.[11] Before departing for China, Morrison had been assisted by a Chinese in transcribing the Basset manuscript as well as much of a Latin-Christian manuscript dictionary; once in China, Morrison hired several Chinese to tutor him in the language and help with his translation. In 1816 another Catholic priest supplied Morrison with a manuscript version of the Gospels made by a Catholic missionary then living in Beijing. For a brief period, China's second Protestant missionary, William Milne, also worked with him on the project.

The pattern ordinarily followed by a missionary was to read verses aloud in English or, if possible, in oral Chinese, as the Chinese scholar transcribed them in classical Chinese. The classical version was then read by both Westerner and Chinese, and its meaning checked by the missionary against the original Hebrew or Greek. Then, the Chinese assistant might be asked to explicate questionable phrases or words to see if they conveyed the meaning intended. Finally, a Chinese would go through the manuscript to eliminate or alter foreignisms

10. Perhaps Morrison's version benefited from the fact that Morrison was actually in China rather in India; also, he had the powerful backing of the London Missionary Society (LMS). In addition, Morrison produced a Chinese dictionary and a grammar, which were used by missionaries as they developed their language skills.

11. Thor Strandenaes, *Principles of Bible Translation* (Stockholm: Almqvist and Wikell, International, 1987), pp. 22-23, 43-45.

and infelicitous expressions insofar as the missionary deemed it consistent with the original.[12] The missionary, in the final analysis, controlled the outcome, for few trusted a Chinese, even a convert, to understand fully the meaning of Christian terms and concepts. According to Morrison, "A less pure and idiomatic translation, made by a Christian missionary of sound judgment and moderate acquirements, is likely to convey the sense of divine revelation better than a translation made by the most accomplished pagan scholar, who has not studied the sacred writings," and who rarely comprehends "clearly the sacred text."[13]

Despite Morrison's painstaking efforts, it soon became evident that his version required revision. His Chinese vocabulary was still limited, and his syntax was often more Western than Chinese. He had frequently opted for literalism, for he had a deep "sense of the awesome responsibility" of translating the sacred text.[14] Biblical imagery derived from a herding, dry grain, and vineyard culture conveyed little to Chinese, whose economy was based on stable, intensive agriculture. Liang Fa, as devoted as he was to Morrison, wrote, "The style . . . is far from being idiomatic, the translators having sometimes used too many characters, and employed inverted and unusual phrases, by which the sense is obscured. The doctrines of scripture are in themselves deep and mysterious; and if in addition to this, the style be difficult, men will be less likely to understand the book."[15] A Chinese transcriber wrote, "Having perused the present translation of the scriptures into Chinese, I find it exceedingly verbose, containing much foreign phraseology, so contrary to the usual style of our books, that the Chinese cannot thoroughly understand the meaning and frequently refuse to look into it."[16] Robert Morrison readily acknowledged that his was a pioneering work, but he was not given the time to undertake the revision himself.

Gützlaff and Biblical Translation

Gützlaff, having worked on a translation of the New Testament into Thai with the cooperation of Jacob Tomlin, began a translation of the New Testament into Chinese in collaboration with Walter Medhurst. The production of revised versions, unfortunately, became enmeshed in national rivalries, per-

---

12. E. C. Bridgman, "The Chinese Version of the Bible," *CRep* 4 (October 1835): 249-61.

13. "Book Review and Tribute, *Memoirs of the Life and Labors of Robert Morrison, compiled by his widow*," *CRep* 10.1 (January 1841): 30.

14. "Book Review and Tribute, *Memoirs*," p. 30.

15. Quoted in W. Medhurst, *China: Its State and Prospects, with especial reference to the spread of the Gospel* (Boston: Crocker & Brewster, 1838), pp. 442-43.

16. Medhurst, *China*, p. 443.

sonal antagonisms, and disagreements over the translation of such key terms as God, Holy Ghost, the soul, and baptism.[17] Should priority be accorded to fidelity to the Bible or to idiomatic Chinese? Should the translator strive for formal correspondence with the original or functional equivalence, that is, express the sense of the text in idiomatic Chinese? Should the translation be directed toward an educated audience, who would respect only the classical style, or toward the general public, who would find a style closer to oral Chinese more comprehensible? The story is not a happy one — not even a very Christian one, it is tempting to say. On issues of faith and truth, commitment could be deep and uncompromising. On the assumption that the Bible was the direct word of God, some missionaries considered it sacrilegious to tamper with imagery, phraseology, or syntax.

Not long after Robert Morrison's death in 1834, his son J. R. Morrison, Elijah Bridgman, William Medhurst, and Gützlaff began a joint effort at revision. The secretary of the LMS immediately sent out alarm signals. He wrote to J. R. Morrison: "London Missionary Society does not recognize Gützlaff as its agent . . . nor has it any connection with American missionaries who appear to be sanctioning Gützlaff's impositions and delusions and pursuing a course which is calculated to discredit all that your father did, as if nothing had been done, and to transfer to America the credit and control. . . . We recommend you therefore to consider the revision of your father's work as your own higher office, and not to be confided to others. . . . In the interim keep your father's revision with care and do not let Gützlaff or anyone else forestall you by obtaining access to them."[18] J. R. Morrison's reply was moderate and conciliatory. To recognize the need for revision of his father's translation was not to deny its great contribution. As to Gützlaff's ability and knowledge in Chinese, he was qualified to undertake revision, even if he was well known for his imprudence and impatience. The LMS could rest assured that Medhurst and Morrison were deeply involved in the project, and that Bridgman gave as much assistance as his other commitments would allow.[19] The ecumenism

17. Irene Eber, "The Interminable Term Question," in *Bible in Modern China: The Literary and Intellectual Impact,* ed. Irene Eber et al. (Sankt Augustin: Institut Monumenta Sinica, 1999), pp. 135-61 and Jessie G. Lutz, "Western Nationalism, Chinese Assistants, and Translations of the Chinese Bible." Paper delivered at conference on "A Bridge between Cultures: Commemorating the 200th Anniversary of Robert Morrison's Arrival in China," University of Maryland, March 15-16, 2007.

18. Thomas Fisher to John R. Morrison, London, 30 July 1835, Church World Mission Society (hereafter CWM), LMS, China Personal, Box 2, R. Morrison, Letters.

19. Morrison to Fisher, Macao, 2 December 1835, CWM, LMS, China Personal, Box 2, R. Morrison, Letters.

that had developed among the small community of Western missionaries in Canton-Macao, sometimes labeled "Zion's Corner," did not characterize denominational mission societies in the West.[20]

The carefully worded joint letter of Medhurst, Bridgman, Gützlaff, and J. R. Morrison to the British and Foreign Bible Society requesting support for the revised translation of the New Testament underlined the delicacy of their task. They accorded credit to Robert Morrison and acknowledged their debt to him: "To the excellent and venerated father of the Protestant mission to China, we are indebted for having more than twenty years ago produced a version of the New Testament in Chinese. . . . These first attempts [by Morrison and Marshman] have met with their due acknowledgment, and remain standing memorials of the zeal and fidelity of their authors. It has, however, never fallen to the lot of man, to bring work to perfection, without repeated efforts." They then reiterated the reasons for a less literal translation that would be more acceptable to the Chinese. They assured the Bible society that the "greatest harmony has prevailed among us" as they tried to steer a middle course between fidelity and comprehensibility.[21]

In the quartet's new translation, the basic and final revisions of the New Testament were primarily by Medhurst, while the committee of four collaborated on the Old Testament up through Joshua. Gützlaff completed the remainder of the Old Testament when the other three could no longer give the project their attention. Their revised New Testament (*Jiu shizhu yesu xin yizhaoshu*), published in 1837, and the Old Testament (*Jiu yizhao yizhaoshu*), published a couple of years later, became the principal translation in use among Chinese Protestant churches during the next decade.

Gützlaff continued to revise the translation in an effort to make it more idiomatic and understandable. His goal for the New Testament, he said, was to make as literal a translation of the Greek as the genius of the Chinese language would permit. Despite his protestations that the Word of God was perfect and needed no embellishment, he was willing to go further than many translators in sinifying the style.[22] Nothing was to be gained by producing a translation that was unacceptable and unintelligible to the Chinese, and he cautioned

20. The phrase "Zion's Corner" comes from Murray Rubinstein, *The Origins of the Anglo-American Missionary Enterprise in China, 1807-1840* (Lanham, MD: Scarecrow Press, 1996).

21. Medhurst, Gützlaff, J. R. Morrison, and E. Bridmann to A. Bandram, Canton, 21 December 1835, copy of letter to British and Foreign Bible Society (hereafter BFBS) in ABS Archives.

22. Philosinensis [Gützlaff], "Christian Missions in China: Remarks on the Means and Measures for Extending and Establishing Christianity," *CRep* 3.12 (April 1835).

against considering the Word of God so sacred that one must translate it literally, word for word.[23] Chinese word order, which differed from the Hebrew, Greek, and English, should be adopted, for it often served as a substitute for Western grammatical distinctions. Reduplication, antithesis, and climax might seem mere affectation to foreigners, but to Chinese, "all writing which is destitute of them seems loose and spiritless."[24] His pietist emphasis on a minimalist theology helped in the justification of such a position.

Throughout the 1840s Gützlaff continued to revise and publish translations of the New Testament in his effort to provide the Chinese with an accessible text free of "foreignisms." In all, he produced ten or more editions of the New Testament, while also bringing the cost of the New Testament down to nine cents by using wood blocks and yellow paper. He had, he said, tried out his revision on Chinese scholars, on workers, and even on children to determine if they were comprehensible, and by 1850 he could write that he believed he had achieved a "faithful verbal translation."[25]

During the course of his revisions, Gützlaff made repeated pleas to the BFBS for aid toward the publication and distribution of his translation, even providing testimonials as to its merits. The Bible Society, however, preferred to await the production of a union revision (later known as the Delegates' Bible) and declined support.[26] Despite the fact that Gützlaff was no longer formally associated with the Dutch Missionary Society, he secured significant sums from the NZG and the Dutch Bible and tract societies during the 1840s.[27] In view of the long delay in completion of the Delegates' Bible, occasioned by the "interminable term question," the BFBS finally relented in 1848 and sent a grant of £100 to Gützlaff for printing his New Testament, Psalms, and certain books from the Old Testament. While acknowledging that it was undesirable to have two or more versions of the Bible circulating in a country,

23. Gützlaff, "Remarks on the Chinese Language," *China Mission Advocate* 1.8 (August 1839): 225-27.

24. Gützlaff, "Revision of the Chinese Version of the Bible," *CRep* 4.9 (January 1836): 393-98.

25. Gützlaff to A. Brandram, BFBS, Islington, England, 21 January 1850, BFBS Archive, Cambridge University, Foreign Correspondence, Inwards, 1850, #98.

26. Gützlaff to A. Brandram, BFBS, Hong Kong, 19 July 1848. The correspondence concerning support for Gützlaff's translations lasted from 25 January 1844 to 21 January 1850 and may be consulted at the BFBS Archive.

27. Gützlaff to Mackay, 1 March 1840, *Extract-Akten*, p. 76, Gützlaff to Mr. Vorstman, Macao, 1 March 1840; Gützlaff to Ledeboer, 12 March 1840; Ledeboer to Gützlaff, Rotterdam, 17 November 1840; Gützlaff to Ledeboer, Hong Kong, 24 May 1845; 29 December 1845; 26 February 1846; 20 May 1846; 27 October 1846; Gützlaff to NZG, Victoria, 23 December 1846, HKI, NZG.

the society justified several subsequent contributions to the Chinese Union by citing the size of the country and population; "no opportunity should be foregone."[28] During the late 1840s, therefore, the Chinese Union distributed tens of thousands, perhaps hundreds of thousands, of Gützlaff's scriptures and religious tracts in interior China.

A Western student without knowledge of Hebrew and Greek and lacking mastery of classical Chinese is hardly in a position to assess the merits of the Gützlaff Bible. His 1847 revision of the New Testament was the one adopted by the Taiping revolutionaries, though this could have been as much a consequence of its accessibility to Chinese leaders as of its comprehensibility. In 1847 Hong Xiuquan, the Taiping founder, had studied with the Baptist missionary Issachar Roberts, who used the Gützlaff version and undoubtedly provided Hong Xiuquan with a copy. The Taipings would subsequently print thousands of copies of Gützlaff's New Testament along with books from the Old Testament.

Praise for the version did come from both Chinese and Westerners. In November 1847, Theodor Hamberg of the Basel Society reported that Gützlaff's translation was generally regarded as the best available and was generally used by most missionaries.[29] In 1848 Presbyterian missionaries at Ningbo published Gützlaff's New Testament on movable type.

Two assessments from the 1850s indicate both the assets and the deficiencies of the Gützlaff version. George Smith, bishop of Victoria, urged W. Lobschied to reprint Gützlaff's Old Testament, stating, "The LMS [Delegates'] version might be for the more educated scholars, Dr. Gützlaff's for the more plain and less educated reader." Charles Taylor of the Methodist Episcopal Church, South, reported, "I put the book [Gützlaff version] into the hands of my Chinese teacher, whose opinion of it is that it is both the very best version, and the very worst. It conveys the very idea of the original, but it is not a classical version; it is the most faithful one; but in adhering to fidelity it departed from style. I think I would put Dr. Gutzlaff's version into the hand of an educated Chinaman, in order to give him *the clearest view of the original scriptures*."[30] Other Westerners maintained that Gützlaff departed far from the revealed scripture in an effort to make it understandable to the Chinese. Medhurst reported in 1849 that Gützlaff's revision of the Old Testament had eliminated some of the defects of

28. BFBS, *Forty-fourth Annual Report,* 1848, p. ci; *Forty-fifth Annual Report,* 1849, p. cxxxii; *Forty-sixth Annual Report,* 1850, pp. cvii-cix.

29. Hamberg to Barth, Hong Kong, 28 November 1847, Hamberg correspondence, Archives of Basel Missions Gesellschaft (hereafter BMG).

30. Charles Taylor, "The Bible in China," *China Missionary Gleaner* 1.16 (September 1854): 124-45.

earlier texts but still contained many impurities and inelegancies; learned scholars objected that many phrases and expressions did not employ correct, classical style.[31] The search for a middle ground continued.

The Delegates' Bible and the Term Question

By 1843 China missionaries had generally agreed that yet another revision of the Chinese Bible was necessary. The opening of five treaty ports in the Treaty of Nanjing with widening opportunities for evangelism enhanced the sense of urgency. A group of leading missionaries in August 1843 laid down guidelines for the production of a new translation. In a spirit of optimism, they called on every missionary who could to contribute, and they divided up the translation of the books of the Bible among the various mission stations. Once a mission station had completed its work, the revised section would be circulated to the other stations for comment. Finally, a committee of delegates from various denominations and mission societies would meet to coordinate the submissions and draw up the final version.

The delegates, with their Chinese language assistants, convened at Shanghai in June 1844. Despite discussions extending over several days, they found themselves unable to reach a consensus on appropriate Chinese terms for *God, Holy Ghost,* and *baptism.* They therefore recommended a formal investigation of the issues with the arguments presented in writing. The debate in the form of essays in the *Chinese Repository,* position papers, pamphlets, and even whole books by Medhurst and Legge, extended over several years and produced much heat and antagonism but no agreement. The ramifications of the voluminous literature are beyond the scope of this monograph; only a greatly simplified summary is possible here.[32] The two principal contenders for God were

31. Medhurst to Tidman, Shanghai, 30 June 1849, CWM, LMS, Central China, Incoming; Extract of letter from Rev. Dr. Medhurst, 8 October 1848, CWM, LMS, Central China, Incoming.

32. For excellent discussions, see Eber, "The Interminable Term Question," in *Bible in Modern China: The Literary and Intellectual Impact,* ed. Irene Eber et al. (Sankt Augustin: Institute Monumenta Sinica, 1999), pp. 135-61, and Douglas G. Spelman, *Papers on China* (Harvard University Center for East Asian Studies) 22A (1969): 25-52. For samples of contemporary literature, see "Remarks on Shangti and Shin" (Comments and letters by Medhurst and Gützlaff), *CRep* 16 (January 1847): 36-39; W. J. Boone, "Essay on the Proper Rendering of the Words Elohin and Deos into the Chinese Language," *CRep* 17 (February 1848): 61-70; Medhurst, "Reply to Dr. Boone's essay," *CRep* 17 (November 1848): 569-74; Medhurst, *A Dissertation on the Theology of the Chinese, with a view to the elucidation of the most appropriate term for expressing the Deity in the Chinese language* (Shanghai: Mission

Shen (spirit) and *Shangdi* (supreme ruler). The Roman Catholic term, *Tian Chu* (Lord of Heaven), came under brief consideration, but was rejected — primarily, it seems, because it was too closely associated with Catholicism. For the Holy Ghost, there were *ling* (guide, lead) and *feng* (wind), while the question concerning baptism was whether the Chinese word should convey the idea of total immersion or simply of washing clean. A whole host of issues arose. A Chinese repertoire of religious and ethical vocabulary already existed in Buddhist, Daoist, and Confucian literature. How much of it should be adopted? Did the Chinese have such concepts as a creator God, a being self-existent in eternity, or even monotheism? What did the term *Shangdi* mean when employed in the early Chinese classics? What do the terms *Shangdi* and *Shen* convey to contemporary Chinese? The Protestants, as Arthur Wright noted, were wrestling with dilemmas that had been faced centuries ago by translators of Buddhist texts into Chinese and by the Catholic missionaries of the seventeenth century.[33]

In choosing Chinese terms, translators had at least four options. (1) They could select an existing Chinese term that seemed to have an equivalent meaning. The concept might appear less foreign, but there was the risk that the accumulated Chinese meanings would obscure the uniqueness of the Christian concept. (2) They could adopt a Chinese word but employ it in a specific technical sense different from Chinese usage. (3) They could create a new combination of characters, as the Roman Catholics had done with *Tian Chu*. (4) Or they could resort to transliteration of the sound. For the names of the prophets and apostles, transliteration was ordinarily the option without causing controversy, though initially different characters might be chosen. Members of the delegates' committee were also at odds over whether they should lean toward free translation for the sake of comprehension and literary respectability or give priority to a faithful rendering of the wording of the original Hebrew and Greek.

Division tended to coincide with national origin. The Americans E. Bridgman, William J. Boone, and M. S. Culbertson preferred *Shen* and a more literal version, and they received support for their position from the American Bible Society. The English, William Medhurst, W. C. Milne, and John Stronach, with the backing of the LMS and the BFBS, favored *Shangdi* and a freer translation.

Press, 1847); James Legge, *The Notions of the Chinese concerning God and Spirits, with an examination of the defense of an essay, on the proper rendering of the words Elohim and Theos, into the Chinese language by William J. Boone* (Hong Kong: Hong Kong Register, 1852), esp. pp. 159-66.

33. Wright, "The Chinese Language and Foreign Ideas," in *Studies in Chinese Thought*, ed. Arthur Wright (Chicago: University of Chicago Press, 1953), pp. 288-93.

The delegates' committee split, with the LMS missionaries and the Americans working separately.[34] The Baptists went their own way because of their practice of total immersion and requested that Rev. J. Goddard undertake a revision of the Marshman-Lasser translation. Despite the disagreements, work continued, but the unhappy outcome was the publication of variant versions of the Bible, in which *baptism* was translated by two different characters and *God* was rendered in two different terms by the Protestants and by yet another term by the Roman Catholics.[35] The Delegates' Bible, nevertheless, gradually displaced other translations and would remain the most widely used text until it too was displaced by the Union Mandarin version published in 1919.[36]

Though Gützlaff was not a member of the delegates' committee and did not participate directly in the revision, he did enter the debate over terminology. He was in essential agreement with Medhurst and his colleagues in preferring *Shangdi* and in arguing against *Shen*. Both he and Medhurst had originally used *Shen*, but as they had acquired greater knowledge of Chinese religion and the Chinese classics, they had come to prefer *Shangdi*. "These two, being the best and most experienced Chinese scholars, had of course great weight," wrote W. M. Lowrie of the delegates' committee.[37] *Shen*, Gützlaff wrote, was a generic term for spirit and therefore seemed at first suitable for the variety of terms referring to God in the Old Testament. Among Chinese, however, it was used for all manner of false deities, glorified heroes, special trees or places, and even for spirits. It carried such a broad range of meanings that it would only mislead Chinese concerning the nature of the transcendent, omnipotent God. *Shangdi*, on the other hand, referred to the Supreme Being in early Chinese writings. Even if it might not completely convey the spiritual nature of God, a being self-sufficient in all eternity, and despite the fact that it had largely fallen into disuse, it was an authentic Chinese term and the one

34. Since the home societies provided the support for both the missionaries and their publications, the views of the societies, conveyed in frequent letters of instruction, carried considerable weight. This may have contributed to the split along national lines.

35. The Delegates' version of the New Testament was published in 1852 and of the Old Testament in 1858. Bridgman and Culbertson's version came out in 1863, and the Baptists' version of the New Testament was published in 1853. See Garnier, *Chinese Versions of the Bible*, pp. 73-77.

36. For an excellent discussion of the process of translating the Delegates' Bible, see Jost Zetzsch, *The Bible in China: History of the Union Version; or: The Culmination of Protestant Missionary Bible Translation in China*, Monumenta Serica Monograph Series 45 (Nettal: Monumenta Serica, 1999).

37. Walter M. Lowrie, "Letter of 23 July 1847 to John C. Lowrie," in *Memoirs of the Rev. Walter M. Lowrie, Missionary to China*, ed. by his father (New York: R. Carter & Brothers, 1850), p. 441.

closest to the Christian perception.[38] Such a bare summary does justice neither to the defenders of *Shen* nor to the complexities of the discussion, but *Shangdi* did gradually gain acceptance as the Protestant term for God.[39] Several of the participants in the debate, in examining the Chinese classics for references to the supreme deity, gained greater understanding of early Chinese philosophical writings and a new appreciation of Chinese ethical ideals.

Evangelism via Chinese Tracts; Christianity as Presented in Gützlaff's Tracts

Despite the seeming preoccupation with producing a satisfactory Chinese Bible, missionaries also devoted vast amounts of time and energy to composing Christian pamphlets and books. The number and volume of tracts produced by the small number of Protestant missionaries in China during the 1830s and 1840s is astonishing.[40] Medhurst estimated in 1837-1838 that 2,000 complete Bibles, 10,000 New Testaments, 30,000 separate books of the Bible and scriptures, and 500,000 copies of tracts had been printed, amounting to 20,000,000 pages.[41] According to an ABS report for 1840, the ABCFM Press in Singapore had issued eighty-two titles, which broke down into 295,000 copies or 12,775,000 pages. About half of the tracts were by Gützlaff.[42] These statistics do not include the works published by the LMS Press in Malacca nor those printed in China. Such productivity attests to the deep commitment of the missionaries to their cause and also to the strength of their work ethic. It also indicates a desire for a sense of accomplishment amidst frustrations over the indifference or hostility of the Chinese to Christianity.

The missionaries concentrated on the production of religious tracts for many of the same reasons already mentioned for translating the Bible: restrictions on their activities, faith in the persuasiveness and power of the written word, and a desire to make the gospel message known as rapidly and ex-

---

38. "Remarks on Shangti and Shin," *CRep* 16 (January 1847): 36-39; An Impartial Reader [Gützlaff], "Chinese Terms to Denote the Deity," *CRep* 16 (March 1847): 121-22.

39. Recently, Roman Catholics and Protestants in China have held conversations in the hope of reaching agreement on a single Chinese term for God.

40. The *Records of the General Conference of Protestant Missionaries of China, 1877,* reported that a total of 1,036 separate Christian works in Chinese had appeared between 1810 and 1875; of these, only 126 were Bibles or portions of the Bible. Cited by Daniel H. Bays, "Christian Tracts: The Two Friends," in *Christianity in China, from the Eighteenth Century to the Present,* ed. Daniel H. Bays (Stanford: Stanford University Press, 1996), p. 20.

41. Medhurst, *China,* Appendix II, List of Books, pp. 586-92.

42. "Mission to Singapore," *ABS Report,* 1840, pp. 139-41.

tensively as possible. Tracts supplemented and to some extent substituted for the Bible, whose bulk in Chinese made it unwieldy. The New Testament alone ran to more than 300 leaves. Tracts were less expensive to print and more portable; a colporteur could transport thousands of short pamphlets, but only a few sets of the Bible or New Testament.

While the evangelists acknowledged the Bible as the sole source of Christian truth, they recognized that certain doctrines required explication for individuals reared in a non-Christian culture. The Bible is a protean work, written and compiled over hundreds of years, an expression of changing religious beliefs meeting the needs of diverse cultures. Its teachings were subject to varying interpretations, as the numerous heresies of early Christianity indicate. Believing in the universality of their Christianity, many pioneer missionaries showed little tolerance of Chinese converts who evolved their own interpretation, especially if it meant accommodation with Confucianism. One function of the tracts was to guard against heresy, as defined by the Westerners, and to present their version of Christianity to the Chinese. A content analysis of the tracts, therefore, shows the particular interpretation of Christianity that the Protestant missionaries expounded to the Chinese, not how the message was understood by the receptors.

During the early 1830s, tract production and distribution aroused increasing enthusiasm and gained significant financial support. The Dutch tract society, the American and British tract societies, and the denominational mission associations raised their budgets for the "silent messengers" almost every year, while the British and Foreign Bible Society and American Bible Society steadily increased their contributions for the printing and circulation of the scriptures. Gützlaff assiduously cultivated all of these organizations, dashing off letters of publicity and appeal almost every evening; a packet of his letters went out with almost each Western ship. It was partly his demand for ever-increasing numbers of publications to distribute on his coastal journeys plus his assurances that the Chinese gladly welcomed the publications that encouraged the home societies to make available growing sums. He succeeded in securing funds for printing and disbursing tens of thousands of brochures from various Western agencies and societies.

Gützlaff wrote or translated dozens of religious works in Chinese.[43] Dur-

---

43. For a list of Gützlaff's Chinese-language publications as well as his works in European languages, see Alexander Wylie, *Memorials of Protestant Missionaries to the Chinese: Giving a List of Their Publications, and Obituary Notices of the Deceased, with Copious Indexes* (1867; Taipei: Ch'eng-wen Publishing Co., 1967), pp. 56-66. Hartmut Walravens provides an updated list of Gützlaff's writings and also secondary works on Gützlaff, in *Karl Friedrich Neumann (1793-1870) und Karl Friedrich August Gützlaff (1803-1851): Zwei*

ing his most prolific period, 1834-38, he composed original works focusing on basic Christian teachings and practices, and on the blessings they promised. Between 1836 and 1843 he published booklets on the life of Jesus, along with *Youtaiguo shi* (A history of Judea) and a half-dozen narratives of the lives of the prophets and apostles.[44] In a five-volume work on the biblical patriarchs, *Shengshu liezhu quanzhuan,* Gützlaff recounted the history of the eminent ancestors of the Jewish people from Abraham through Jacob. He also issued short pamphlets entitled *Yesu sheji zhi zhuan* (Miracles of Jesus) and Yesu zhi baoxun (Precious teachings of Jesus), the latter a translation of the discourses of Jesus and some of his apostles. These were essentially compilations from the scriptures with brief commentaries or amplifications of biblical texts; some were recycled materials from earlier publications. *Shengshu hezhu quanzhuan,* for example, was largely drawn from articles in his magazine *Dong-Xi.* The declining proportion of original texts may have been a consequence of his increasing administrative responsibilities associated with the Opium War and his preoccupation with revision of his Bible translation. Also, he was studying the Japanese language in the hope of translating the Bible into Japanese.

From 1843 until 1849 Gützlaff concentrated on works that would aid in formation of congregations and would guide their worship services. Among these were translations of two brief catechisms, *Jin yao wanda* (Catechism of essentials) and *Tianjiao getiao wanda jieming* (Luther's small catechism), along with the Sermon on the Mount with commentary *(Shanshang xuan dao),* the Augsburg Confession of Faith *(Huangcheng xinshi),* and selections from the Church of England liturgy *(Shenghui daozhi).* In addition, he trans-

---

deutsche Chinakundige im 19. Jahrhundert (Wiesbaden: Harrassowitz Verlag, 2001). For the analysis that follows, I have read some but far from all of the more than fifty religious tracts by Gützlaff. For others I have relied on the brief descriptions by Wylie and Walravens. Also, I have drawn from the excellent discussions of Patrick Hanan, "The Missionary Novels of Nineteenth-Century China," *Harvard Journal of Asiatic Studies* 60.2 (December 2000): 413-43, and of Suzanne W. Barnett, "Practical Evangelism: Protestant Missions and the Introduction of Western Civilization to China, 1820-1850" (Ph.D. diss., Harvard University, 1973).

44. *Yesu jiangshu zhi zhuan* [Birth of Jesus] (Singapore: ABCFM, 1836); *Yesu shenji zhi zhuan* [Miracles of Jesus] (Singapore: ABCFM, 1836); *Yesu zhi baoxun* [Precious teachings of Jesus] (Singapore: ABCFM, 1836); *Yesu fusheng* [Resurrection of Jesus] (n.d.); *Yesu shousi* [Death of Jesus] (n.d.); *Yesu shui ye?* [Who is Jesus?] (n.d.); *Yohan yanxing lu* [Life of John] (Singapore: ABCFM, 1837); *Yosifuyan yanxing lu* [Life of Joseph] (Singapore: ABCFM, 1838); *Danyeli yanxing quanzhuan* [History of Daniel] (Singapore: ABCFM, 1837); *Bidelo yanxing quanzhuan* [Complete account of the life of Peter] (Singapore: ABCFM, 1838).

lated from German a theological work on nineteen basic Christian teachings (*Jiantao*) and composed a history of the church, *Shenghui zhi shi*. He used the four-character format in his translation of Christian Barth's history of the scriptures, *Shengjing zhi shi*, in order to make it easier to memorize, and he used tetrametric verse for a brief outline of Christian doctrine. The latter, quoting Genesis, opened with the words *Shangdi chuangtao* (God created); though it is undated and untitled, it may well be from the 1840s.

By this time Gützlaff had turned to Chinese converts as the primary instruments of evangelism, and he wanted manuals to guide the Chinese workers and their Western supervisors in establishing Christian communities. Some of the works were also used as texts in mission schools and seminaries. The Rhenish missionaries, for example, included Barth's history of the scriptures in their curriculum, as did the Berlin missionary August Hanspach in the schools he sponsored.[45] The difference between the writing before 1837 and those that followed seemed to be signaled by his change of pen name from *Aihan che* (Lover of the Chinese) to *Shande* (Admirer of virtue) for most of his later Chinese writings.

Many of the most interesting and creative publications were written during the first period. Gützlaff asked his new converts to accept only a few basic doctrines at first: recognition of one's sin, the assurance of salvation through Christ's sacrifice, repentance, rebirth through the Holy Spirit, and a determination to lead a new life. Gützlaff offered a Christocentric Christianity. Unlike the Christocentric Christianity of liberals during the 1920s, however, Gützlaff's major theme was individual salvation through Christ, not national salvation; Jesus as a social reformer was an important but not central doctrine. More of Gützlaff's tracts dealt with Christ, his life, his teachings, and above all his redemption of humankind through his death on the cross, than with any other topic. Perhaps Gützlaff best expressed his viewpoint when appealing to the American Tract Society for support in printing his Japanese booklet "Life of the Savior": "I thought it best to begin with the adorable Savior, knowing that in Him alone is our strength, and salvation through His name is also promised to this remote people. . . . The chapter upon the sufferings of the Savior is longer than any other, for the heart must be moved by contemplating His dying love."[46]

A number of Gützlaff's pamphlets narrate stories of individuals who are greedy and arrogant, given to sexual license and gambling. Those who refuse

45. Julius Richter, *Geschichte der Berliner Missionsgesellschaft, 1824-1924* (Berlin: Verlag der Buchhandlung der ev. Missionsgesellschaft, 1924), p. 512.

46. ATS, *Twelfth Annual Report, 1837*, pp. 116-17.

to repent and reform, as well as those who seek solace from their guilt in Buddhism or opium, are fated to remain unhappy and die without hope. For those who acknowledge their sins and mend their ways, there is Jesus, who looks down in mercy. If they turn to him in faith, he will forgive them and reward them with a blessed life in heaven. Jesus, in some senses, resembles a new and accessible Guan Yin, the goddess of mercy, at least in the minds of many Chinese. Gützlaff must have accepted the doctrine that original sin is the root of all evil, but he did not emphasize it, and Chinese may well have viewed the avariciousness and dissipation depicted by Gützlaff as social crimes, cause for shame and a sense of guilt. In *Huimo xindao* (Persuasion and instruction), for example, Gützlaff tells the story of a selfish and rapacious merchant in Shanghai.[47] Despite the remonstrances of Christian friends, he does not reform, and when he dies, his sons quickly begin to dissipate his fortune. A Christian is able to persuade the eldest son to give up his evil ways, and he dies with the hope of eternal life in heaven; the youngest son also repents and converts to Christianity. The middle son, who ignores the admonitions of the Christian, dies of syphilis.

Changhuo zhi dao zhuan (The doctrine of eternal life) depicts a high official named Li Rui, who despite his indulgent life, is unhappy and guilt-ridden. He attempts to reform, but also seeks relief in opium. Accused of a crime by his fellow officials, he is sent into exile. When he is mistreated there, he is befriended by a Christian doctor, who converts him before his death. His son visits his father's grave and he too is converted and eventually goes to heaven.

Another of Gützlaff's tracts on redemption is entitled *Zhuanhuo wei fu zhi fa* (The way from misery to happiness). It is presented as a dialogue between two Chinese, one a Christian and one a non-believer. After discussions in which the Christian presents the need to believe, repent, and reform if one hopes for reward in heaven, the booklet concludes with a pointed admonition to the reader: "Pay attention to the teachings of Jesus if you desire to avoid misery and enter into happiness. Do your best to be faithful unto death and valiantly witness to your faith. Then, misery will become happiness."[48] Gützlaff's message is clear: the faithful, though they may suffer, are rewarded in heaven; evildoers are punished and die condemned.

Jesus, as the perfect man, was also the source of moral instruction. In *Fuyin zhi jingui* (Gospel precepts), Gützlaff collated Christ's teachings on so-

---

47. For further detail, see Hanan, "The Missionary Novels," pp. 427-30.
48. See *Zhuanhuo wei fu zhi fa* [The way from misery to happiness] (Singapore: ABCFM, 1838), p. 5b.

cial relations. Sections on proper conduct are presented within the categories of the Confucian bonds, that is, prince-subject, father-son, husband-wife, elder brother-younger brother, and friend-friend. Noting Jesus' admonition to love thy neighbor as thyself, Gützlaff asserts that the concept of universal brotherhood was expounded by both Jesus and Confucius, an argument he employed in several works. Kindness and universal love are also highlighted in an address ostensibly delivered in a Fujian village.[49] In *Yesu biyu zhushuo* (Parables of Jesus) and *Shanshang xuandao* (Sermon on the mount), Gützlaff quotes verses from the Gospels, adding his own explanations and exhortations. Such virtues as charity, peaceableness, forgiveness, humility, truthfulness, and filial piety comprise Christian morality as set forth by Jesus. Also, Gützlaff wrote *Gaixie guiyi zhi wen* (Abandoning depravity and turning to righteousness), a booklet of eleven pages illustrating the evils of opium smoking and assuring the reader that Jesus would assist him in giving up this vice.

God the Father is the subject of several tracts. In these, God is presented as creator of the universe, the almighty maker of heaven and earth and all therein. One should, therefore, look to God with praise and thanksgiving. Worshipping God will be rewarded.[50] One's fate lies in God's hands, and if one has faith in God, all things are possible. Though Jehovah is the God of justice, he is also the God of mercy, and he has sent the Holy Spirit to operate on this earth as guide and protector.[51] For many Chinese, God must have seemed less approachable than Jesus; yet many converts found the story of creation fascinating, especially the creation of Eve out of the rib of Adam. It was frequently the subject of sermons by Chinese evangelists.[52] They also emphasized that God the omnipotent was more powerful than any of the Chinese deities. The Christian God, not the Chinese deities, could promise them protection and reward.

Gützlaff was uninterested in either complex theology or denominationalism. His goal was to spread the glad tidings far and wide. The basic message was for him a glorious one full of hope for all. He did not dwell on hell and the suffering of the damned, even though he accepted the teaching that heathens stood condemned. Once an individual had been awakened and determined to lead a new life, he should be baptized and welcomed into the Christian community. The time for instruction in doctrine and church formation

49. *Zihui boai* [Kindness and universal love] (Singapore: ABCFM, 1839).

50. See *Songyan zanyu* [Eulogy and praise] (Singapore: ABCFM, 1838).

51. See *Shangdi wanwu zhi dazhu* [God, the great Lord of all creation] (Singapore: ABCFM, 1838[?]), and *Shangdi zhenjiao zhuan* [Theology] (1834).

52. Philipp Winnes to Inspector, Pukak, 2 February 1855, BMG, A-1.3, no. 33.

would follow after baptism. Such an approach was derived from his Herrnhutter training and his own personal experience. The Jänicke school he attended offered no erudite or modernist theology, and in fact Gützlaff had been criticized for his interest in learning while there; he had found acceptance in the community only after a conversionary experience and rebirth in Christ. In China he came into conflict with his fellow workers in part because of his rejection of denominationalism and his simplified definition of Christianity. As for his scholarly interests, he found outlets elsewhere, specifically in secular writings about and for the Chinese.

Most of Gützlaff's tracts are in the modified literary style generally called easy *wenli*. He used relatively few technical theological terms, but instead offers simplified narrative. A writer of tracts, according to Gützlaff, was not formed in the study; rather, the writer learned from the mouths of the Chinese, discovered their prejudices, witnessed their vices, and listened to their defenses in order to meet their arguments more effectively. "To clothe our ideas in genuine Chinese is the study of a lifetime, and despite zeal to expunge foreignisms, they cleave to us. I would like to leave the work to instructed natives, but their thoughts are confined, their minds a stranger to logic, and their expressions often savor too much of paganism; they do not comprehend the *whole* Gospel."[53] For the present he would continue to compose Christian works in Chinese with the aid of educated Chinese, while hoping that Chinese could take over the task in the future. Gützlaff worked with great speed. Except for the Bible, he spent relatively little time checking sources and revising; erroneous characters occur here and there in the Chinese texts. Even so, according to one Chinese scholar experienced in translating Christian literature, "Most readers could understand all of the treatises with little or no difficulty, if they are literate at all."[54]

As indicated in the above analysis, Gützlaff employed a variety of formats for his religious writings: biographies of biblical figures, sermons or discourses, histories, and collations of scriptural passages concerning the same doctrine, with or without commentary. Sometimes he invented a central character, who goes abroad and so is able to correct the mistaken notions of his home folk about Western customs, institutions, and beliefs. *Cheng chong bai lei han* (Faithful letters) is one such work. The eldest son of a Fuzhou family is writing to family from England. He discusses the basic Christian doctrines and contrasts them with heathen beliefs; he also describes his life

---

53. "Mr. Gutzlaff's Letter," Macao, 26 March 1837, *New York Observer* 15 (9 September 1837): 144.

54. Personal communication, Samuel Chao, 3 January 1999.

abroad and moralizes about the differences between Chinese and Western societies. Two difficult styles that foreigners rarely mastered, according to Gützlaff, were verse and the classical sententious style employing aphorisms, rhythms, and references to the Confucian classics. Since such literature was highly esteemed by Chinese scholars, Gützlaff recommended that Western writers strive to acquire the ability to use them.[55] He himself composed one work in each style: *Shangdi chuangzao* in verse and *Shangdi Zhengjiao zhuan* in the ornate classical style.

Of the original tracts composed by Gützlaff as distinct from translations or collations, the dialogue was his favorite form. It was a convenient mode, he explained, for countering the arguments of Confucian scholars and convincing the reader of the superior truth of Christianity. Often, one conversationalist is a convert who engages in discussions with critics or skeptics. Doubtless, Gützlaff was also influenced by the popularity of William Milne's *Zhang Yuan liang you xiang lun,* copies of which he had distributed on his coastal voyages.[56] Gützlaff was influenced, furthermore, by the popularity of Chinese historical novels, many of which he reviewed in the *Chinese Repository* during 1838-1839; these works, he stated, were the ones most widely read by Chinese. Typical of this genre are *Zhendao zizheng* (Proofs of truth) and *Zhengxie bijiao* (Orthodoxy and heterodoxy compared).

Zhendao zizheng opens with the son of a Mr. Zhuang meeting Mr. He, a Christian, and lamenting that he is most unhappy because he is confused about the nature of heaven; he is not truly virtuous; he does not understand the way *(Dao)* and he is incapable of following it. Mr. He assures him that the way of heaven is the way of man, but that it is much more. Heaven finds expression everywhere; it cannot be understood solely from books. Then Mr. He explains the nature of Shangdi as the creator of the universe, the nature of man, his sinfulness, and the need for redemption. He offers comfort to Mr. Zhuang by telling the story of Jesus, the great redeemer who is the means to salvation. In *Zhengxie bijiao,* Gützlaff sets the scene in Suzhou. Three educated gentlemen who have discovered truth, He Zhanneng, Ma Fuling, and Chen Chengdo, meet daily with people who come to ask questions. During the discussions that ensue, a wide range of Chinese religious doctrines and practices are brought forward, and the enlightened gentlemen are able to demonstrate their errors and contrast them with the true teachings of Chris-

55. "Mr. Gutzlaff's Letter," p. 144.
56. *Zhang Yuan liang you xianglun* [Conversations between two friends, Zhang and Yang] (Singapore: ABCFM, 1836) went through at least seventeen editions and was still being used in the twentieth century; a minimum of several hundred thousand copies were put into circulation, according to Bays, "Christian Tracts: The Two Friends," pp. 22-24.

tianity. The impotence of false deities is juxtaposed against the omnipotence of God. As for the ethical teachings of the Chinese sages such as Mencius, they are incomplete without divine revelation. Worthy as the writings of the classical philosophers are, their rational this-worldliness can never lead to ultimate truth and eternal life.

The narrative and dialogue formats were designed to present the Christian message within a Chinese context insofar as possible. Traditional Chinese dating was adopted, and often the events were situated in a specific locale in China. The speakers were individualized by name and background, with each addressing the other by the deferential terms appropriate to status. Sometimes the participants followed the Chinese custom of exchanging pleasantries and drinking tea before taking up the subject of concern. Chinese aphorisms and quotations from Chinese literature adorned their conversations. Gützlaff's style, in fact, has been criticized for awkward overuse of traditional narrative devices.[57] His goal was to diminish the foreignness of Christianity by treating it as a world religion, superior to Confucian teachings but sharing many of its moral values. Simultaneously, Christian teachings could be presented in a less confrontational manner as Chinese speakers themselves replied to queries and criticisms by fellow countrymen.

How successful was this approach? There is little way of knowing, but it is true that tracts employing the dialogue approach, especially Milne's "Two Friends," enjoyed greater popularity than most Christian works in Chinese. The use of dialogue or narrative is one more indication that the China mission was a two-way process. The outlook of many missionaries was altered by residency in China and daily contact with Chinese. Though the Westerners might staunchly hold to their Christian theology, the Chinese were no longer completely "other," no longer the heathen masses living in darkness. They were living individuals with whom one interacted on a daily basis. They were, Bridgman wrote home, "human beings, not celestial or infernal."[58] As John Fairbank once wrote, a Western Christian in the non-Christian society of China was not the same as a Western believer in the Christian culture of nineteenth-century Europe and America.[59]

A byproduct of the missionary emphasis on production of tracts was the development of movable lead type for the Chinese language. Wood block printing, though inexpensive and attractive to the Chinese, was slow, and

57. Hanan, "The Missionary Novels," p. 427.
58. Quoted in Fred W. Drake, *China Charts the World: Hsü Chi-yu and His Geography of 1848* (Cambridge, MA: Harvard University Press, 1975), p. 92.
59. Fairbank, "Introduction," in *Christianity in China*, p. 4.

An illustration of woodblock printing, 1890s

only a limited number of impressions could be made before new blocks had to be cut. For the printing of tens of thousands of copies of a tract or New Testament, missionaries endeavored for decades to produce cheap movable type. Gützlaff even sent a set of characters to Germany to have individual metal characters cast, but the work of the German craftsmen was so inaccurate and ragged that the font was not usable. It was Samuel Dyer of the LMS who, with the aid of skilled Chinese artisans in Singapore, created the first practicable metal font at mid-century. Intrinsic to this was the design of a standard modern Chinese font based on the 214 radicals of the Kangxi dictionary. Chinese printing houses quickly adopted the new methods, though mission presses remained among the most active printing establishments throughout the nineteenth and early twentieth centuries.[60] The simplified Chinese style that was developed in translating the Bible became one of the models used by advocates of *baihua* in the second decade of the twentieth century. It was during the New Culture Movement that the Bible first enjoyed a degree of popularity outside the Christian community.[61]

For Chinese readers, tracts such as *Cheng chong bai lei han* and *Youtaiguo shi* presented lands beyond China, civilizations whose beliefs and values, social mores, and governments differed from those of the Middle Kingdom. The English people were prosperous and orderly despite their ignorance of Confucius. Judea produced great men like Moses, who set forth a high standard of morality comparable to that of Confucius.

The number of Chinese readers of Christian literature during the nineteenth century is unknown. Missionaries occasionally were gratified when an individual who had read a scriptural translation or a tract sought them out for further information, but this did not happen very often.[62] Hong Xiuquan is, of course, the most famous example of an individual attracted to Christianity as a consequence of reading a Christian tract, in this case *Chuanshi liangyan* (Good words to admonish an age) by Liang Fa. One missionary reported having seen Christian pamphlets in the library of an educated Chinese, while another noted several on the bookshelves of a Chinese bookseller.[63] These instances seem to have been the exception rather than the rule.

Limiting the appeal of Christianity and the Christian tracts was the primacy given to individual faith and morality as the means to individual salvation and eternal life. In the Confucian canon the individual was enmeshed in society, so that individual morality was essential to social order, but individual ethics was not separable from social ethics. For Chinese, *luan* (disorder, confusion) was fearful indeed, and individualism in the Western sense was often equated with selfishness. Any decision regarding loyalty or belief in a par-

60. Barnett, "Practical Evangelism," p. 84; Roswell S. Britton, *The Chinese Periodical Press, 1800-1912* (Shanghai: Kelly & Walsh, 1933), pp. 83-84; Ho Herbert Hoi-Iap, *Protestant Missionary Publications in Modern China, 1912-1949: A Study of Their Programs, Operation, and Trends* (Hong Kong: Chinese Church Research Centre, 1988).

61. Other works, especially Chinese popular novels, also served as models.

62. George Smith, *A Narrative of an Exploratory Visit to Each of the Consular Cities of China and to the Islands of Hong Kong and Chusan in Behalf of the Church Missionary Society in the Years, 1844, 1845, 1846* (New York: Harper & Bros., 1847), p. 138; "China-Letter of Dr. Macgowan," *Baptist Missionary Magazine* 30 (October 1850): 315.

63. Medhurst, *China*, pp. 334-35; "Survey of Missionary Stations, Religious Tract Society," *Missionary Herald*, March 1844, p. 128.

ticular ideology was a family matter as well as an individual concern. Veneration of the ancestors, forbidden by the missionaries, was a family
responsibility considered essential to the well-being and identity of the
group. Those Chinese who were disoriented as a result of personal tragedies
or psychological trauma might find the Christian message attractive, and
other converts hoped that Christianity would be a means to renew Chinese
society. Always there was an additional obstacle: the contrast between Christianity as portrayed by the missionaries and the behavior of Western merchants and sailors coming from a supposedly Christian civilization to China.
The burden of the opium trade and Western expansionism was heavy. For
many Chinese, the latter represented the West more accurately than the
Christian tracts.

The era of such heavy reliance on tracts as a primary instrument of evangelism was relatively brief. Despite the fact that Christians continued to produce Christian literature for instructional purposes, missionaries had begun
to realize the limitations of tracts by the late 1830s. Serious doubts about the
effectiveness of tract distribution unaccompanied by personal evangelism began to arise; it became increasingly clear that foreign doctrines without supplementary explanations were incomprehensible to most Chinese.[64] The
Christian concepts were apt to be misunderstood and distorted, especially
since most Chinese lumped them into the same category as the heterodox
writings of Chinese religious sects. Without further instruction, few Chinese
readers could understand the Christian import of such concepts as redemption, the Trinity, or the dual nature of Jesus. The Taiping leader Hong
Xiuquan, along with many other Chinese inquirers, assumed that if God had
a son, He must have had a wife and perhaps other children as well. Though
stories of virgin birth could be found in Chinese Buddhism, educated Chinese had difficulty accepting the virgin birth of Jesus, who was both human
and divine.

The imperfections of the tracts and their lack of literary elegance offended
many Chinese, and even those who had clamored for the booklets quickly
discarded them or used them for waste paper. In an ironic twist, money for
opium was sometimes wrapped in tract sheets preparatory to transfer. Some
concluded that the missionaries had been misled regarding the high rate of
literacy among Chinese males, for many who claimed literacy only remembered a few hundred characters, hardly enough to read either Chinese or

64. S. Wells Williams, "An Account of China: Macao and Its Population," *Missionary
Herald* 25 (February 1839): 54-55; "Journal of the Rev. R. W. Orr," *Foreign Missionary
Chronicle* 7 (April 1839): 121-22.

Christian literature. It was true that an occasional inquirer sought out a missionary or Chinese convert, but conversion and rebirth required follow-up instruction and guidance. It was also true that the tracts aggravated the hostility of the imperial court and of the Chinese literati to Christianity. Missionaries increasingly turned to supplementary means of evangelism, especially after the cession of Hong Kong and the opening of the five treaty ports for residency and evangelism.

CHAPTER 7

New Horizons

Neither Chinese literati nor Western missionaries were ready for cultural exchange during the first half of the nineteenth century. Despite challenges from abroad as well as at home, the Middle Kingdom and the Confucian way seemed intact. Even defeat in the Opium War of 1839-1842 was incorporated into theories about taming barbarians. As had been the practice in relations with the peoples of Inner Asia, the Chinese would buy off the foreign warriors with trade privileges and friendship. Protestant missionaries, for their part, came to China to teach, not to learn; their commission was to preach the true and unique gospel, the source of Western greatness. Yet interchange between East and West occurred. Not only did Western supporters of Christian missions learn about China, but small numbers of Chinese on the coast learned about Western geography, history, and culture.

Various explanations have been offered for Beijing's minimal response to defeat in the Opium War. The failure to perceive the necessity for basic change was rooted in the Middle Kingdom perception of a world of inferior cultures, with the major threats coming from the inner Asian frontiers, according to John K. Fairbank. Non-Chinese who came from overseas and knocked at China's door on the southeast coast were not perceived as belonging to the same category as the non-Han peoples from the steppes of Asia. Joseph Levenson stressed the incompatibility of Confucian political and cultural ideals and the statist orientation of the Western powers. Frederic Wakeman Jr. pointed to the domestic distraction of the Taiping rebellion and the rise of regional centers of power. James M. Polachek emphasized the factionalism at court and political inertia fed by a growing uneasiness among Manchus about their ability to retain the loyalty of Han officials as the source of Beijing's failure to follow a consistent policy of self-strengthening and reform.[1]

1. John K. Fairbank, *The United States and China,* 4th ed. (Cambridge, MA: Harvard

It can be argued, nevertheless, that the Opium War marked a turning point in China's relations with the West, whether Beijing recognized it or not. China would face an increasingly aggressive West, not only in terms of opening China to Western goods, but also in the form of growing numbers of missionaries and merchants residing on the mainland. Though there were only a couple of dozen Roman Catholic priests and forty Protestant missionaries in China in 1845, the numbers grew during the 1850s. In 1860 there were about 190 Protestant missionaries, and by 1866-1867, 42 European priests. The evangelists, furthermore, could no longer be confined to Canton or even the treaty ports. They were carrying their subversive message and lifestyle into interior China. Translations of Western works became more readily available. Western states demanded treatment as equals, while they would soon be treating China as less than equal in international relations. Domestic pressures for change in the form of rebellion, piracy, secret societies, administrative corruption, and unfavorable ratios of arable land to population were mounting. Alternate strains of Confucianism were gaining followers.

In the 1860s the tears in the Chinese fabric were small, more apparent in the south than elsewhere. As devastating as the Taiping Rebellion was, the Taipings were finally defeated, and the Tongzhi Restoration of the 1860s seemed to promise reform and self-strengthening. The fissures, however, would grow larger and more numerous as the century progressed. Not by coincidence did southeast China become the initiator of change during the nineteenth and twentieth centuries. The peoples of this sector of China had never been as fully incorporated into the Confucian mainstream as those of the Yellow and Yangzi river valleys. Various minority and ethnic groups lived in uneasy relationship with the dominant Han Chinese. In addition, the southeast coastal cities had long conducted a brisk trade with Southeast Asia, so that they faced seaward rather than landward toward the interior. Western contacts had further contributed to the commercialization of the economy, and the inhabitants had seen firsthand the economic strength and military power of Great Britain. Missionary writings offered alternate views and values; their secular works presented new horizons.

For Gützlaff and other Protestant pioneers, Western Christendom was

---

University Press, 1983), chs. 6 and 7; Frederic Wakeman, *Strangers at the Gate: Social Disorder in South China, 1839-1861* (Berkeley: University of California Press, 1966); Joseph R. Levenson, *Confucian China and Its Modern Fate,* 3 vols. (Berkeley: University of California Press, 1964), vols. 1 and 2; James M. Polachek, *The Inner Opium War* (Cambridge, MA: Council on East Asian Studies, Harvard University Press, 1992), pp. 4-10. For a revised view by Fairbank, see *The Great Chinese Revolution, 1800-1985* (New York: Harper & Row, 1986), pp. 4-9, 84-121.

both a repository of religious truth and a source of useful knowledge. They, like most Protestant missionaries during the first half of the nineteenth century, had been sent out with little or no specialized instruction concerning the specific civilization where they were to work. Whether they were assigned to China, with its complex culture and historical mindedness, or to Africa, where oral history and tribal organization were more typical, or to the Americas, with their varied native nations and cultures, their training was essentially biblical and theological. Evangelistic methodology merited little attention, and specific methodology tailored to particular regions was practically non-existent. Though a missionary might volunteer for a certain country, the mission boards frequently appointed a missionary to a field shortly before departure, and the destination depended on the board's estimate of need at that time. Gützlaff, for instance, briefly considered the Middle East and even began learning Turkish, but the Dutch Missionary Society sent him to the Dutch possessions in Southeast Asia, an assignment which he soon rejected in favor of becoming an independent missionary to the Chinese. Inspired by Gützlaff, the pioneer Protestant missionary to Japan Guido Verbeck volunteered for China, but instead he was assigned to Japan, where he had an influential career as educator of samurai sons and adviser to government officials.

In contrast to the Jesuit missionaries of the seventeenth century, most early Protestant missionaries came to China with little knowledge of the Chinese language, and certainly they had not received advanced instruction in mathematics and science in order to appeal to Chinese scholars.[2] Once a volunteer knew that he would be working in China, he might read one or more relevant mission works — Gützlaff's journals of his voyages or Medhurst's *China, Its State and Prospects,* for example. These furnished some useful factual information. Often the new missionary began study of the Chinese language only during the long sea journey to East Asia. For the pioneer Protestant missionaries, expounding the Good News of salvation and converting lost souls was the all-encompassing goal.

Expanding Perceptions of Mission Methodology

More than one Protestant evangelist began expanding his perception of his mission soon after arrival in East Asia. The publication of secular works in Chinese by Morrison, Milne, Medhurst, Bridgman, and Gützlaff was one in-

2. Robert Morrison, to some extent, was an exception in that he used the British Museum manuscript to begin his study of Chinese in London.

dication of broadening goals. Even though such activity was far from the activist reformism of the Social Gospel mission at the turn of the century, the writers did envision an "enlightened" China transformed by Christianity and by the arts and sciences of the West. They had come to appreciate the fact that the Chinese, though heathen, were members of a sophisticated civilization. They soon learned that most Chinese were unimpressed by the message of outsiders who claimed to preach a superior religion and morality. Certain missionaries had also become convinced that the Chinese view of the Westerners as barbarians was a deterrent to Chinese acceptance of Christianity. The Chinese worldview, with the Middle Kingdom as the locus of civilization, had to be altered; they needed to be compelled to recognize that other civilizations existed and were viable alternatives to Chinese culture. Respect for the West, they concluded, could be engendered by making the Chinese aware of European achievements in science, technology, and the arts. Demonstration of the validity of the Western experience would thereby pave the way for Christianity. As Chinese learned of the potential benefits of free exchange of knowledge and material goods, they would adopt a more open commercial and foreign policy. They would awaken and follow the West down the road of progress. *Awaken, enlighten,* and *civilize* were key words in justifying to the home boards their devotion of time to composing secular educational works.

In actuality, the line between secular and religious was not sharply defined in the minds of mid-nineteenth-century Protestant missionaries. Christianity may not always be obtrusive in their essays on geography, history, or government, but it is rarely absent. Labeling their writings as secular is, to some extent, misleading. For many Westerners during the first half of the nineteenth century, the equating of progress, Westernization, and Christianization appeared valid. Products of a middle-class and evangelical Protestant background, they accepted Western civilization as a meaningful and coherent entity. Within this holistic view, history was the working out of God's will and a means of moral instruction. All within the universe was God's creation, and the phrases "natural law" and "God's design of nature" were interchangeable. Ethics and politics were intertwined, so that rulers who followed the path of truth became instruments of progress while depraved and heretical leaders contributed to their nation's decline.[3] Knowledge and science, wrote Gützlaff, were the handmaidens of true religion. They fulfilled God's plan for the progress of mankind and so could become a means to convincing Chinese of the omniscience and benevolence of Jehovah.

---

3. Philosinensis [Gützlaff], "The Diffusion of Knowledge in China," *Chinese Repository* (hereafter *CRep*) 2.11 (March 1834): 508-9.

Gützlaff's *Dong-Xi* and Potrayal
of the West for the Chinese

On 1 August 1833 Gützlaff published the first issue of his magazine, *Dong-Xi yang kao meiyue tongjizhuan* (The East-West examiner and monthly magazine). According to Suzanne Barnett, the title was based on a seventeenth-century Chinese geographical work, *Dong-Xi yang kao* (A study of eastern and western oceans) by Zhang Xie; Gützlaff probably hoped thereby to give legitimacy to his magazine and to distinguish it from earlier geographical writings by the Jesuits.[4] In November 1833 a group of missionaries met to discuss the formation of a Society for the Diffusion of Useful Knowledge (SDUK), and in March 1834 the *Chinese Repository* printed Gützlaff's rationale for the establishment of such a society.[5] The purposes of the magazine and the society, as enunciated by Gützlaff, were the same. The SDUK held its first meeting on 19 October 1835, Gützlaff writing both the preamble and the statement of goals to be adopted.[6] The SDUK would sponsor the production of Chinese-language materials, with priority given to a universal history, a world geography with atlas, and the development of a uniform nomenclature based on the Beijing dialect. *Dong-Xi* was soon thereafter placed under the auspices of the SDUK, though Gützlaff remained the principal source of copy for the magazine. From mid-1833 through 1835 *Dong-Xi* was edited by Gützlaff and published in Canton, but no issues came out in 1836, possibly because of imperial edicts leading to the arrest of wood block cutters and printers of mission works in Canton. The magazine resumed in 1837, but henceforth it was printed at Singapore. All of the writings were published anonymously, and Gützlaff was no longer listed as editor on the title page, but he continued to provide many of the articles through the final issue of 13 February 1839. Bridgman, J. R. Morrison, and Medhurst were also important contributors. Between 1839 and 1842 Gützlaff was preoccupied with his responsibilities as interpreter and adviser to British commanders during the Opium War, so *Dong-Xi* ceased publication.

In the belief that the war had stimulated a desire among Chinese officials to learn more about the Western nations, Gützlaff attempted in 1842 to revive

4. Suzanne W. Barnett, "Practical Evangelism: Protestant Missions and the Introduction of Western Civilization to China, 1820-1850" (Ph.D. diss., Harvard University, 1973), p. 177.

5. Philosinensis [Gützlaff], "The Diffusion of Knowledge," pp. 508-9; "Periodical Magazines," *CRep* 2.4 (August 1833): 186-87.

6. "Proceedings Relative to the Formation of a Society for the Diffusion of Useful Knowledge in China," *CRep* 3.8 (December 1834): 378-84.

Dong-Xi under the title *Qianlijing* (Telescope or, literally, "thousand li glass").[7] The preface to the first issue noted the desirability and advantage of Chinese acquiring more accurate knowledge of foreign countries; it also explained that the title of the publication indicated its purpose, namely, to provide a close-up view of regions beyond China. Included in the introduction was a description of a telescope and its design. A comparative Chinese-English almanac, an article on the geography of Asia, and a few news items made up the contents. Though officials in Nanjing and Ningbo were reported to have welcomed the magazine, Gützlaff abandoned the venture after only one or two issues. Upon J. R. Morrison's death in 1843, Gützlaff acquired new responsibilities as Chinese secretary to the Hong Kong government. Furthermore, a decline in both financial and literary contributions led to the demise of the SDUK in the early 1840s. During its existence the SDUK sponsored the publication of nine titles plus *Dong-Xi.*

The contrast between the goals of *Dong-Xi* presented to Chinese readers and the goals *Dong-Xi* and the SDUK outlined for Western readers of the *Chinese Repository* reveals a certain dualism.[8] For the Chinese audience Gützlaff stressed the brotherhood and friendship of all peoples, the need for Chinese and foreigners to regard each other as members of one family, and the hope that knowledge of the various nations would contribute to peace under heaven. This statement of goals deliberately paraphrased Confucius. The first issue of *Dong-Xi* after it resumed publication in 1837 also assured Chinese readers that the peoples of Europe were constantly developing new technology, which they would gladly share to the benefit of all.[9] Western readers of the *Chinese Repository,* on the other hand, were reminded of their blessings as members of a progressive Christian civilization; they were under obligation to share their knowledge with those sunk in ignorance and to bring truth to

---

7. I have not seen an issue of *Qianlijing,* though Wu Yixiong of Zhongshan University in Kuangzhou reported having located a copy: "Xinjiao chuanjiaoshi yu yapin zhanshi quan hou di xixue shuru" [Protestant missionaries and the importation of Western learning before and after the Opium War], paper presented at the Conference on Modern Science and Technology and Sino-Western Cultural Communication, Wuhan, 15-20 August 1999. E. C. Bridgman also reported having received a copy of *Qianlijin* in 1843, "Journal of Occurrences," *CRep* 12.2 (February 1843): 111.

8. "Proceedings Relative to the Formation of a Society," pp. 378-84; "Periodical Magazines," pp. 186-87; *Dong-Xi yangkao meiyue tongji zhuan* (East-West monthly magazine, hereafter *Dong-Xi*) 1833.6:2b-3.

9. *Dong-Xi* 1837.1. From the Chinese style of the introduction to the 1837 issue, Lazich concludes that it was written by Bridgman. See Michael Lazich, *E. C. Bridgman (1806-1861), America's First Missionary to China* (Lewiston: The Edwin Mellen Press, 2000), pp. 135-36.

those unaware of their wretchedness. The arts and sciences would overcome the empty conceit of the Chinese and perhaps even prove to the Chinese that foreigners were not their enemies but their friends and beneficiaries. Only Western knowledge could end China's stagnation so that it could take its rightful place among the great civilizations of the world. Special emphasis should be placed on the usefulness of the information to Chinese leaders.

The membership of the SDUK and the financial support for both the SDUK and *Dong-Xi* illustrate the symbiotic relationship of the missionary and merchant communities of Canton. The leading British merchant of Canton, William Jardine, was initially the main supporter of *Dong-Xi;* as a matter of fact, Jardine had promised aid to *Dong-Xi* when requesting Gützlaff to serve as interpreter on his opium clippers. British merchants also provided the primary backing for the publications of the SDUK, while James Matheson, Jardine, and John Green were successive presidents of the society. Canton merchants actually composed the majority of the SDUK's executive board, and the British superintendent of trade was also an honorary member; Gützlaff and Bridgman were Chinese secretaries and J. R. Morrison was English secretary.

The SDUK publications should be aimed at China's reading public, not scholars, wrote Gützlaff; they should, therefore, be written in a plain readable style, and they should be printed as cheaply as possible. Every effort should be made to circulate the works throughout China. Until Christian schools could furnish Chinese writers acquainted with the Western and Christian heritage as well as their own, Westerners would have to be the authors even though they would inevitably employ foreign modes of thought and expression. Insofar as they were capable, however, the writers should take Chinese works as their models and conform to "their dress."[10] Yet, for masters of classical Chinese, the Protestant writings seemed vulgar and inelegant, as Xu Jiyu, author of *Yinghuan zhilüe* (Survey of the maritime circuit), remarked.[11]

Precedents for Chinese secular publications by missionaries existed. Nineteenth-century Protestant missionaries were well aware both of the works on astronomy, mathematics, and gunnery by sixteenth- and seventeenth-century Jesuit missionaries and of their success in gaining a hearing at the highest administrative levels. Gützlaff cited the example of the Jesuits in justifying composition of secular works by Protestant missionaries.

10. "Proceedings Relative to the Formation of a Society," pp. 378-84; Philosinensis [Gützlaff], "Christian Missions in China," *CRep* 3 (1834): 566-68.

11. Quoted in Fred Drake, *China Charts the World: Hsu Chi-yü and His Geography of 1848* (Cambridge, MA: Harvard University Press, 1975), p. 54. Obviously, there is some ambiguity as to the audience since Gützlaff hoped to influence Chinese leaders and yet insisted on using a popular style.

At one point, he even suggested that Protestant mission societies follow the Jesuit example by stationing a missionary-mathematician in Beijing. Gützlaff's praise of the Jesuits was always tempered with criticism, however. It was unfortunate, he wrote, that such courageous, dedicated, and intelligent evangelists as Matteo Ricci (1552-1610), Ferdinand Verbiest (1623-1688), and J. Adam von Schall (1591-1666) worked in the cause of popery. They refused to give the gospel to the masses; they were only concerned with the elite. The science they brought was so enmeshed in Romanism that both Western secular knowledge and true Christianity acquired an unfortunate reputation in China.[12] Protestant missionaries, he hoped, will "show that the spread of divine truth opens the door for every useful art and science; that unshackled commercial relations will be of mutual benefit; and that foreigners and Chinese, as inhabitants of the same globe, and children of the same Creator, have an equal claim to an amicable intercourse, and a free reciprocal communication."[13] Gützlaff was expansive in his ambitions and also in his definition of Western Christendom.

From 1815 to 1822 William Milne had published *Chashisu meiyue tongjizhuan* (World examiner and monthly record), and Medhurst had continued the periodical under a new name for a brief period after Milne's death. Stationed in Malacca, Milne had circulated the periodical via missionary friends, travelers, and Chinese trading vessels operating within Southeast Asia and between Southeast Asia and China. The LMS missionaries, answerable to their home board, apparently did not feel as free as the independent missionary to limit the religious content. *Chashisu* included occasional historical extracts, notices of current affairs, and geographical and astronomical data; for example, there were articles on European principles of astronomy and on goods produced by England. Most of the essays, however, were "of a religious and moral kind."[14] According to Milne, the promotion of Christianity and morality was the primary purpose of the magazine; other things of general knowledge were to be treated as subordinate, but not overlooked.[15]

On the *Lord Amherst* voyage of 1832, Gützlaff had distributed old copies of *Chashisu*, along with another "secular" work, *Da Yingjili liguo renpin guoshi lüeshuo* (A brief account of the people and affairs of the great English nation), written by Charles Marjoribanks of the East India Company and translated by

12. Gützlaff, "Remarks on the History and Chronology of China," *CRep* 2.3 (July 1833): 123; Gützlaff, *Journal of Three Voyages along the Coast of China in 1831, 1832, and 1833* (1834; Taipei: Ch'eng-wen Publishing Co., 1968), pp. 16-17, 393-98.

13. Gützlaff, *Journal of Three Voyages*, p. 64.

14. "The Chinese Magazine," *CRep* 2.5 (September 1833): 234-36.

15. "The Chinese Magazine," p. 235.

Robert Morrison. The central thesis of the pamphlet, as indicated earlier, was that both the Chinese and the English people are refined, civilized, prosperous, and highly capable. The English are especially skilled in maritime affairs, and they desire trade and diplomatic relations as between equals, but they have no territorial designs on China. If China and England established friendly relations and mutually respected each other, both countries would prosper. Gützlaff had been impressed by the ready reception of both Milne's magazine and the Marjoribanks pamphlet. The Chinese, he concluded, were gaining a new worldview and were learning to respect foreigners. Such secular works could be a new way to approach the Chinese, to interest them in the Western heritage, and to persuade them of the advantages of free intercourse.[16]

Listed on the title page of each issue of *Dong-Xi* is a table of contents, doubtless in the hope of enticing readers to peruse some of the articles. As further encouragement, Gützlaff adorned the title page with quotations from the Chinese classics, for instance, from the *Analects* of Confucius: "[W]hen I walk along with two others, they may serve me as my teachers; I will select their good qualities and follow them, their bad qualities and avoid them." Most of the numbers contain one or more historical essays, an article on the geography and culture of a country or region, brief news items, and a record of current commodity prices for goods traded in Canton.[17] The April 1834 issue, for example, gives a factual if sympathetic account of the arrival of the first British superintendent of trade, Lord Napier, of the mission's failure, and

---

16. Barnett, "Practical Evangelism," pp. 89-93.

17. Though I have examined many of the issues of *Dong-Xi* and have translations of many of the articles, I have not read the entire run. The following analysis benefits from the following works: Fred Drake, "Protestant Geography in China: E. C. Bridgman's Portrayal of the West," in *Christianity in China: Early Protestant Missionary Writings,* ed. Suzanne W. Barnett and John K. Fairbank (Cambridge, MA: Harvard University Press, 1985), pp. 89-106; Suzanne W. Barnett, "Wei Yuan and Westerners: Notes on the Sources of the *Hai-kuo T'u-chih*," *Ch'ing-shih wen-tí* 2.4 (November 1970): 1-20; Barnett, "Practical Evangelism"; and Lazich, *E. C. Bridgman,* pp. 111-64, 182-88. See also Jessie G. Lutz, "Karl Gützlaff: Missionary Entrepreneur," in Barnett and Fairbank, eds., *Christianity in China,* pp. 61-87; Lutz, "Karl Gützlaff and Changing Chinese Perceptions of the World during the 1840s," in *Jidujiao yu Zhongguo wenhua congkan* [Christianity and cultural communication], ed. Ma Min (Hubei: Hubei Jiaoyu chubanshe, 2003), pp. 354-92; and Cai Wo, "Tantan 'Dong-Xi yang kaomeiyue tongjizhuan': Zhongguo jingnian diyizhong xiandai Zhongwen qikan" [Comments on the "East-West Monthly Magazine," the first modern Chinese periodical published in China], *Guoli zhongyang tushuguan quankan* [National Central Library Bulletin], new series, 2.4 (April 1969): 23-46; Ch'en Kuan-sheng (Kenneth Ch'en), "The Growth of Geographical Knowledge concerning the West in China during the Ch'ing Dynasty" (M.A. thesis, Yenching University, 1934); Tsien Tsuen-hsuin, "Western Impact on China through Translation," *Far Eastern Quarterly* 13.3 (May 1954): 305-27.

the death of "the brave man [who] did not attain what he sought."[18] Other is-sues reprint Qing edicts and memorials on opium importation as well as items on public events in Europe.[19] Most of the world regions or nations are described in either historical or geographical essays. An issue of 1834 prints the letter of a fictional Chinese traveling in South America to his father in China; the writer comments on the mines of Chile and the city of Lima as well as his ship and the weathering of a storm. The following year, a series of essays on India began, covering its peoples, languages, classes, and religious practices, the major administrative and pilgrimage centers, and a short his-tory with special attention to the Mughal empire and the founding of the British empire.[20]

Beginning in 1837, a column entitled *Shichi* (Historical records) presented historical materials and information on recent events in the world beyond China. The cultural/geographical essays turned increasingly to the West. Arti-cles on Spain, Portugal, France, Holland, Germany, Greece, Italy, Russia, Swe-den, and Ireland briefly summarize the history of each, list their capitals and major products, and comment on their national politics and position in the international community. A letter from a hypothetical Chinese scholar travel-ing in Europe discusses education and scholarly work in Germany. There, the study of religion is a scholarly discipline conducted by highly trained teachers with a knowledge of several languages and able to interpret the meaning of the Bible and of Christ's life.[21]

Appearing also in 1837 are three essays on the United States, introduced by Gützlaff, but actually written by E. J. Bridgman, who was then composing *Meilige heshengguo zhilüe* (A short account of the united provinces of Amer-ica).[22] Typically, Gützlaff's introduction has a Chinese scholar inquire of a friend about the "flowery flag" (*huaqi* — the stars and stripes) he sees flying in Canton and the country it represents. The friend, a Mr. Wu, then summa-rizes the geography of the United States, as well as the Spanish explorations leading to the discovery of the American continent and the circumnavigation of the globe. The colonization of the east coast began with English settlers seeking the right to worship as they pleased, but peoples from Holland, Swe-den, and France soon came to establish their own settlements. In discussing the American revolution, Bridgman emphasized the unfair taxes imposed by

18. "Xinwen," *Dong-Xi*, 1834.4:52.

19. For the opium edicts, see "Yan duce" [Registration of opium], *Dong-Xi*, 1835.5:12-13; "Feng wei yapian" [Edict regarding opium], *Dong-Xi*, 1837.4:14-15; 5:12-13; 6:14-15.

20. "Tianzhu huo wuduguo zonglun" [General account of India], *Dong-Xi*, 1835.5.

21. "Shu" [Correspondence], *Dong-Xi*, 1837.4:1-2b.

22. See numbers 5, 6, and 7 of *Dong-Xi*.

the British monarch, particularly the tax on Chinese tea. He then described the creation and the structure of America's democratic government. Like Gützlaff in his history of England, he paid special attention to the system of justice, the limitations on the executive, and America's conduct of foreign relations and its commercial exchange with all nations. Obviously, Bridgman cherished the hope that these would serve as models for China. As free, enterprising adherents of orthodox Protestant Christianity, Americans had prospered and expanded. China too could come out of its deep sleep.

Coverage of the Middle East was primarily via biblical history: the history of the early descendants of Noah and Abraham, of Judea and the descent into Canaan.[23] Here was proof that the West had an ancient history, one even predating that of China. Articles entitled "Hongshui zhi hou" (After the flood), "Hongshui zhi xianji" (First records of the flood), and "Solomen wang ji" (Records of King Solomon) note that both the Bible and early Chinese works record a great flood.[24] Before the building of the tower of Babel, all peoples spoke the same language, but because they offended God, the various races were scattered, with some of Abraham's descendants becoming the inhabitants of East Asia. Sharing origins from Abraham, the Han Chinese and all the peoples of the world are therefore related. "The races of men are, like the four limbs of the body, of the same trunk, all interconnected." A second theme is that God is active in history, as indicated in both His protection and His punishment of the Jews.

Early issues of *Dong-Xi* reprinted sections of Medhurst's comparative chronology of the origins of Chinese civilization from Pan Gu to the Song dynasty and of Western civilization from Adam to the first English kings. Medhurst's intent also was to illustrate that the West as well as the Middle Kingdom had an ancient history. "I have been led," he explained, "to draw up this work from . . . the practice of the Chinese boasting of their high antiquity, looking with contempt on the comparatively modern dates of Europeans. I have, therefore, endeavored, by a regular exhibition of dates . . . and incidents, to show them that we have a system of chronology that can be depended on, more authentic and ancient than their own . . ."[25]

23. "Hongshui zhi xian" [Before the flood], *Dong-Xi*, 1833.7:4-7; "Yuesheya jiang Jiananguo" [Joshua sent down to Canaan], *Dong-Xi*, 1837.9:117.

24. See "Hongshui zhi hou" [After the flood], *Dong-Xi*, 1833.8:16-19; "Hongshui zhi xianji" [First records of the flood], *Dong-Xi*, 1835.5:4; "Solomen wang ji" [Record of King Solomon], *Dong-Xi*, 1838.5:83. "Hongshui zhi hou" was reprinted in the first issue of 1837. See also Lazich, *E. C. Bridgman*, p. 137.

25. Letter of Medhurst, July 1828, *Missionary Herald* 24.1 (January 1829): 193. Quoted in Lazich, *E. C. Bridgman*, pp. 117-18.

As the most progressive and powerful nation of the West, England was accorded the greatest coverage. There were not only compositions on the geography and history of Great Britain, but three installments on the British Parliament, and special essays on London, the English halls for the worship of Shangdi, English female society, and education.[26] In several essays on commerce, England was the primary illustration of the benefits of free trade and international relations.[27] Some of this material was later included in a separate pamphlet, *Mouyi tongshi* (Treatise on commerce), that also abstracted the principles of John R. MacCulloch's commercial dictionary of 1832.

The editors stated that they also hoped to bring to people's attention the sages and worthies of all countries. Accordingly, one number in 1837 includes an essay on the book of Zhuangzi in which Zhuangzi is commended for appreciating the importance of enriching the country and pacifying the people.[28] Mencius is also presented favorably, partly because quotations from his sayings could be interpreted to suit Gütlaff's purposes. Magazine issues occasionally contained biographical sketches of Western heroes, most notably Napoleon and George Washington. Washington's leadership in America's fight for liberty against great odds and his refusal to accept a position as permanent emperor merited high praise. Institutions such as Western newspapers, the postal service, and the judicial system warranted attention. Not to neglect moral issues in the emphasis on things of this world, Gützlaff included essays illustrating Western philanthropy and bravery — for example, the recovery of the drowning victims instead of ignoring them for fear of accepting responsibility and becoming involved, the building of hospitals, and provision of education for the poor. The essay on bravery allowed Gützlaff an opportunity to illustrate once again God's protection of followers of orthodox Christianity, that is, Protestantism. It relates the history of the Dutch Protestants in their struggle for independence from the oppressive rule of the Spanish and Spain's imposition of Roman Catholicism, that is, *yiduan* (heterodoxy).[29] Avarice, autocratic rule, torture of criminals, and idolatry were condemned. Also printed were miscellaneous articles that appear designed to titillate the interest of readers, though some were listed under the category of natural history.

26. "Da Ying bai Shangdi zhi tang" [English halls for worship of Shangdi], *Dong-Xi*, 1837.9: 124-25b; "Landun jingdou" [London, the capital], *Dong-Xi*, 1838.4:69-71; "Yingjili zheng gonghui" [The English parliament], *Dong-Xi*, 1838.4:64b-65a; 5:81-83.

27. "Tongshang" [Commerce], *Dong-Xi*, 1837.12:160-62; "Mouyi" [Trade], *Dong-Xi*, 1838.1:8-11.

28. "Lun Zhuangzi zhi shu" [Discussion of the book of Zhuangzi], *Dong-Xi*, 1837.9:116-17.

29. "Xiadan" [Bravery], *Dong-Xi*, 1835.6:8b-9b.

Among these were short essays on polar bears, fleas, ostriches, the birds of the Philippines, the hippopotamus, and the lion, king of beasts but the object of cruel sport in Rome.[30] For Chinese interested in virility, there was the report of a 105-year-old Polish man who fathered a child by his fourth wife, a woman of twenty-two.

Perhaps least successful were essays comparing Chinese and Western literature.[31] Asserting that all peoples need to feed the spirit as well as the body, the authors assured readers that the West had a rich literary tradition, embracing many different forms of literature. Unfortunately, until now the Chinese have not been interested and have not translated the great Western classics. Despite such prompting, it is unlikely that many Chinese literati were attracted to comparisons of the Four Books and Five Classics with the writings of Greek and Roman authors such as Herodotus, Plato and Aristotle, Virgil, and Tacitus. Contrasting the goals and methods of the poet Li Bo and Homer may well have been lost effort.

In accord with the stated goals of *Dong-Xi* and the SDUK, the scientific and technological achievements of the West were not neglected, though Gützlaff was capable of presenting only elementary information. Explanations of solar and lunar eclipses and the changing phases of the moon were given — even an essay on the physical geography of the moon. Other pieces offered explanations of human anatomy, icebergs, earthquakes, volcanoes, and the variations in the length of day and night.[32] There were descriptions, sometimes with illustrations, of the steam engine, railway, underwater diving equipment, or a passenger balloon. For any Chinese desiring information on the principles and manufacture of Western steamships and weaponry, the *Dong-Xi* offered an introduction, but only limited specific detail.

Gützlaff made an effort to provide a Chinese context for most of the articles. The title page and many of the historical articles employed Chinese dynastic dating rather than the Christian calendar. Jesus was born in the first year of the reign of the Han emperor Ping, for example. Countries and cities were located with reference to China or other identifiable places. The 1835 essay "Lun Ouluobu shiqing" (Discussion of European affairs) identified Europe with Da Xiyang guo (Great western ocean countries), a Chinese term for the north Atlantic region, and located it beyond the western province of Xinjiang, but different from Nanyang (Southern ocean or region). The author

30. See, for example, "Lüsong niaodeng zonglun" [General account of the birds of Luzon], *Dong-Xi*, 1833.8:21; "Tiaofeng lun" [Discussion of fleas], *Dong-Xi*, 1835.5:13.

31. "Lun shi" [Discussion of poetry], *Dong-Xi*, 1838.8:1-2.

32. "Dizhen" [Earthquakes], *Dong-Xi*, 1838.3; "Huoshan" [Volcanoes], *Dong-Xi*, 1837.6; and "Yue mian" [Surface of the moon], *Dong-Xi*, 1837.4 are typical.

then discusses Europe's expansion to many parts of the world. The Europeans are constantly searching for new places to trade and are eager to bring *Yesu zhenjiao* (The true religion of Jesus) — that is, Protestant Christianity — to all peoples. They therefore inform themselves about the world beyond Europe and its inhabitants. The implication, of course, is that China would be wise to do the same.[33] Even though the magazine's cover page ordinarily included a quotation from the Chinese classics and many of the articles began with a quotation from China's sages, Gützlaff tailored the comparative approach and interpreted the quotation to substantiate his major themes. Most quotations were appeals for change or improvement; Gützlaff even incorporated an evolutionary and progressive outlook. Protestant Christianity was always essential to the wealth and greatness of Western civilization.

The essay on London, the capital, compared London with Beijing and Tokyo; it was founded during the reign of the Ming De emperor of the Eastern Han. A quotation from Mencius to the effect that emperors should exhibit humanity and concern for the people's welfare introduced the discussion, as Mencius becomes an advocate of a form of paternalistic populism. A benevolent emperor attracts people of culture and talent to its borders so that the capital prospers. The populace will be industrious; education will flourish, and the capital will serve as a model, an influence for good throughout the land. Corrupt officials and residents, on the other hand, bring calamity, as was the case three times when God sent the plague to punish the English people, who had forsaken righteousness. Only when they returned to charity, morality, and the teachings of Jesus did they enjoy peace and prosperity.[34]

In Gützlaff's essay illustrating the benefits of trade for both the government and its citizens, he contrasts the prosperity and progressiveness of the coastal Fujianese, who dominate trade between China and Southeast Asia, with the poverty and backwardness of the inhabitants of Guizhou and Guangsi, who concentrate solely on agriculture.[35] Trade, for Gützlaff, is evidence of civilization, for savages live off the land and do not need to exchange goods. Quoting from Mencius on the efficiency of division of labor, he contends that trade develops naturally as civilization develops. The more trade, the greater the prosperity. China has long engaged in commercial exchange with Southeast Asia and her border countries. Now, with modern trains and steamships making transportation fast and cheap, trade between China and Great Britain will become as easy as trade between China and her neighbors.

33. "Lun Ouluobu" [Discussion of European affairs], *Dong-Xi*, 1835.5:1-4.
34. "Landun jingdou" [London, the capital], pp. 69-71.
35. "Mouyi" [Trade], 1838.1:8-11.

The result will be that people will learn from one another; knowledge will be broadened, and intellectual activities quickened.

The essay on commerce opens with a quotation from the *Shujing* (Classic of documents or book of history) encouraging the transportation and exchange of goods; Gützlaff then reiterates his theme that the benevolent ruler is one who fosters trade because it brings stability and order and it benefits both the upper and lower classes. Forbidding trade would be like trying to "catch the moon at the bottom of the water."[36] Gützlaff contrasts the value of China's annual foreign trade, which he estimates at $30 million in 1837, with that of Great Britain, estimated at $187 million imports and $255 million exports. Fast ships, made possible by modern technology, a liberal trade policy, and the king's patronage explain the rapid expansion of British commerce.

Shifei lüelun (Correction of erroneous impressions) is also a plea for reciprocal trade relations between China and foreign countries, particularly Great Britain.[37] Here too historical and geographical material is conveyed through a dialogue between two fictional Chinese conversationalists. A Mr. Chen Zeshan, who had been a merchant in London for twenty-five years, has returned to his Guangzhou home. On the basis of his experiences abroad, he counters the xenophobic prejudices of his friend Mr. Li. Chen insists that the British are not barbarians, but are citizens of a prosperous and powerful country with a stable government. It is wrong to treat Great Britain as a tributary state, to restrict Westerners to the port of Guangzhou, to suspect foreigners of spying on China. Chen's theme is "Within the four seas, all men are brothers," a Confucian saying that Gützlaff employed on numerous occasions. The final chapter on British education, language, marriage customs, and women apparently recapitulated materials that had been published earlier in *Dong-Xi* and *Da Yingguo tongzhi* (Short account of England).

As was true in some of Gützlaff's religious tracts, the Chinese speakers observe the courtesies of Chinese social relations. Before broaching the object of their meeting, they inquire about each other's health, comment on the weather, have a cup of tea, or stroll in the host's garden. The younger conversant, even if he is the primary source of information, addresses his elder with deference and proclaims his desire to learn from his senior. Both, of course, sprinkle their conversation with familiar Chinese maxims and quotations from the Chinese classics. They exhibit the Chinese love of numerical clusters

36. "Tongshang" [Commerce], 1837, 12:160-162.

37. I have not seen a copy of this pamphlet of thirty-eight leaves, and I depend here on P. Hanan's description of its contents; see "The Missionary Novels," pp. 428-29. According to Hanan, a copy is located in the library of the American Philosophical Society.

as in their references to the five bonds, the five constants (humanity, righteousness, propriety, knowledge, sincerity), and the six virtues (harmony, wisdom, humanity, sincerity, moderation, righteousness).

In *Da-Yingguo tongzhi* (A short account of England), a certain Ye Duhua has returned to Guangdong after more than twenty years' residence in England, and he shares his observations about this alternative culture with fellow villagers. A series of articles on British parliamentary government in *Dong-Xi* depict Su Faling, the teacher, discoursing with Zhang Xiande, his pupil, on the British legal system and political institutions. Ye Yunzheng, who spent eight years abroad, explains individual rights in England.[38] Gützlaff was obviously trying to establish a bond with his Chinese readers and to lend credence to the accounts by employing a Chinese mouthpiece. Since the hypothetical speakers were in most instances respected scholars able to quote the great poets and essayists, their favorable comments about the West should be doubly impressive.

Such a tactic required sophistication and tolerance on Gützlaff's part; the approach was possible only for a missionary who had acquired a dual vision as a consequence of residence in China. Certainly Gützlaff's Chinese speakers seemed to be remarkably open-minded upon encountering the exotic ways and customs of England. As Chinese scholars, on the other hand, they were cognizant of the merits of their own heritage. Even Mr. Ye, who expressed the hope that all peoples would eventually follow the way of Shangdi, praised Confucius and quoted Mencius with approval.[39] Christianity and Confucianism are not opposites even if Christianity is the universal and true teaching. Gützlaff admittedly retained his Protestant commitment, which limited his ability to use the comparative approach without bias, but he realized that a wholesale condemnation of pagan China, its beliefs and customs, by a Chinese scholar would ring false.

The comparative technique may have served Gützlaff better than he realized, for it required him to view English history and institutions from within the Chinese context. A traditional narrative of kings and wars would hardly explain the strengths and virtues of Western civilization. A more analytical and broadly descriptive discussion that included economics, religion, social customs, and government was necessary. History could not be equated with either Western or Chinese history, but would have to encompass both. Morality and culture were not synonymous with Western Christendom, even if the Chinese speaker went so far as to acknowledge Western superiority in certain

38. *Da Yingguo* [Short account of England] (Malacca: LMS, 1834), 1:1-4a; "Yingjiliguo zenggonghui" [English Parliament], *Dong-Xi,* 1838.4:42-44; 5:63-65, 81-83.
39. *Da Yingguo,* 1:4a; 3:7-8b.

realms. The differences between Gützlaff's writings on England, where the dialogue form is used, and his world history, *Gujin wanguo gangjian*, where there is no intermediary, illustrate the significance of the device.

For Gützlaff, Old Testament history is universal history, so that without a Chinese narrator, *Gujin wanguo* opens with the story of creation 5,840 years ago.[40] Approximately one-third of the work is devoted to the period of the Old and New Testaments, one-third to the era from the Roman Empire through the voyages of discovery, and one-third to Western national history during the modern age. Though such small states as Switzerland, Sweden, and Denmark rate separate treatment, there are no chapters on China, Japan, or India; they enter the narrative primarily as they are subsumed under Western events. In discussing the migration of the Huns, for example, Gützlaff speculates about their origins in East Asia, but it is European expansion that brings Asia to the forefront. The bulk of the work is organized along political lines, that is, empires and peoples during the pre-modern period and nation-states during recent times. As was true of much Western history of the mid-nineteenth century, monarchs, wars, and religious conflicts dominate the story.

Not only is the proselytizing obtrusive during the discussion of the biblical epoch, but it continues to intrude frequently throughout *Gujin wanguo*. The chapter on England, for instance, begins with Henry VII ascending the throne; after a brief characterization of the king and his political opposition, there is a flashback to John Wycliffe.[41] Gützlaff, by making Wycliffe's teachings almost identical with those of Martin Luther, launches into an exposition of the essential doctrines of the Protestant Reformation. Men, he cautions, should not harden their hearts against the truth, as the Romanist priests did, but should surrender themselves to God. Such a statement was, of course, intended as an admonition to the Chinese.[42] The history of the English Reformation and subsequent conflicts centers around the succession of rulers, with those following orthodoxy — Protestantism — generally bringing prosperity and greatness to the English people and those rulers favoring heterodoxy — Roman Catholicism — causing troubles.[43] Mary Tudor's persecution of Protestants provides an opportunity for a disquisition on the rewards of martyrs, and Gützlaff offers an extended description of the blessed

40. The first chapter is simply entitled "Old Testament."

41. *Gujin wanguo* [Ancient and modern history of the world] (Singapore: ABCFM, 1838), pp. 52b-53b. Wycliffe is not mentioned by name, but the reference is clear.

42. In reports to home boards, missionaries frequently explained the paucity of converts by stressing the hardness of hearts of the Chinese.

43. *Gujin wanguo*, pp. 55-56b, 59-60b.

in heaven washed clean by the Blood of the Lamb, dressed in white robes, and singing praises before the throne of God. Mention of England's expansion in India under George III allows Gützlaff to inject a paragraph on the ascension of Christ and his commission to preach the gospel to all mankind.[44] The doctrine of atonement, with Jesus as the only gate to heaven, is repeated once again.

It is instructive to contrast this ethnocentric and Christocentric approach of *Gujin wanguo* with Gützlaff's treatment of England in other works. When Ye is spokesman in *Da Yingguo*, the evangelizing persists but is more subtle. Lengthy expositions of Protestant doctrines are infrequent, and biblical quotations are rare. Despite a dangerous storm on his trip from England back to China, Ye states that he was not frightened because he entrusted himself to God who rules all the earth.[45] He also volunteers that Britain has rejected Buddhism and regards the worship of idols as heresy. Buddhism and Daoism are condemned as fallacious during his discussion of English religion, but Confucius, Mencius, and the classical authors are quoted favorably; their sayings sanction English practices.[46] In response to a question on the influence of the priesthood, Ye briefly summarizes Christian teachings, and the work concludes with an assurance of the brotherhood of all peoples under the Heavenly Father, who created heaven, earth, and all creatures. When all races follow His rule, the world will enjoy peace.[47]

In *Da Yingguo* as well as the chapters on England in *Dong-Xi*, Gützlaff reveals that religion plays a significant role in the lives of the English.[48] Bride and groom take vows of marriage before a priest and promise to follow God's commandments; some ten days after the birth of a baby, the infant is baptized in the Christian ritual of rebirth instituted by Jesus. The faithful have built many churches where they gather to hear the scriptures and to sing praise to God. Despite repeated destruction by fire and invasion, the English people reconstructed St. Paul's Cathedral, each time grander than the last. Gützlaff hoped that Chinese readers would conclude that Protestant Christianity is good and true, but his discussion is even-handed and friendly rather than pervaded by the battle metaphors of his *Gujin wanguo* and of some of his English-language works.

When Gützlaff employs the Chinese narrator, China becomes the base-

---

44. *Gujin wanguo,* pp. 64-65b.
45. *Da Yingguo,* 1:4a-b.
46. *Da Yingguo,* 2:1b-4a.
47. *Da Yingguo,* 5:45-46.
48. *Da Yingguo,* 1:5a; 3:2-3a; 4:14b-15a; "Da Ying bai Shangdi zhi hui" [English halls for the worship of God], *Dong-Xi,* 1837.9:124-25b.

line. Explanations of the English fiscal and tax structure are in terms of similarities or differences with the Chinese.[49] The English, like the Chinese, for example, pay heavy taxes, but the British government's income is derived primarily from commercial tariffs rather than charges on salt and grain. In the discussion of foreign affairs, the English are contrasted with the primitive peoples with whom China has traditionally conducted foreign relations. Great Britain is put on a par with the Qing empire; both have numerous tributary states, the major distinction being that China's colonies are contiguous whereas England's colonies are scattered and diverse.[50]

A second Chinese in the audience sometimes enters the conversation and expresses typical Chinese reservations. Gützlaff uses this technique to try to offset prejudices and alter stereotypes. The viewpoint remains that of a Chinese looking outward, however, and comparison is still utilized to make the information understandable. For example, Ye states that the English, like the Chinese during the Song period, use paper money. When a Mr. Zhen interrupts to predict that the money will become worthless just as the Song certificates had, Ye assures him that the British government backs up the paper money and the people can always cash it in.[51] To a query as to whether there could really be another civilized country like "ours" with laws and officials, Ye answers in the affirmative. He offers proof that the English are an orderly people by listing the ranks of the nobility and the titles and offices of the government administrators; one can see the similarity with China, says Ye. When the narrator discusses the evolution of Parliament and popular sovereignty, a Chinese pupil inquires why this does not lead to confusion; the doubter is reassured that the king is head of Parliament, and the people delegate authority to scholar officials who maintain order.[52]

Though comparisons often lead to explanations of differences between English and Chinese customs, common features are also noted in order to attest to the legitimacy of English ways. The degree of similarity that Gützlaff finds is greater than one might expect and reminds us that his vision of nineteenth-century Europe and China is not necessarily identical with that of a scholar of over a century and a half later. The intermeshing of political and social structure, government and ethics, so often considered characteristic of Chinese culturalism, is for Gützlaff also true of Europe. He believes in the organic unity of Western civilization, even if he is, in actuality, selective; for in-

49. *Da Yingguo*, 2:6a-b.

50. *Da Yingguo*, 4:14a; 5:18b-21b.

51. *Da Yingguo*, 2:6a-7a.

52. *Da Yingguo*, 1:6a-7a; "Yingjiliguo zenggonghui" [English Parliament], *Dong-Xi*, 1838.4:64b.

stance, he makes England the exemplar of the West. He also favors those Chinese classics that he finds congenial. The *Book of History, Mencius,* and *Zhuangzi* are frequently cited to sanction Western values and practices and to explain the glories of England.

Both China and England are said to have kings who receive their mandate from heaven and who acknowledge the obligation to rule for the benefit of the people. A class society with administration in the hands of the educated and virtuous and with the masses trusting in the paternalism of their betters is the norm. Ethics and politics become linked as true leaders foster orthodoxy and guide their people through their example. Gützlaff's description of British government presents the king as the keystone and opens with a quotation from the "Great Declaration" of the Zhou ruler in the *Book of History:* "Heaven, for the help of the inferior people, made for them rulers and made for them instructors that they might be able to aid God and secure the tranquility of the four quarters of the Kingdom."[53]

The English monarch, according to Gützlaff, is both symbolic and functional head of the realm, assuming overall control and responsibility for government operation.[54] As in Chinese dynastic histories, the effectiveness and popularity of the government are directly related to the moral character of the king. In the section on England in *Gujin wanguo,* comments by Gützlaff on the monarch's personal qualities set the stage for a favorable or unfavorable evaluation of each reign.[55] Parliament, when summoned by the king, can discuss and examine the affairs of the country; it must authorize taxes, but it is dependent upon the king's leadership. Though Parliament contributes stability to the system in that the people feel that they have a channel of communication, the House of Lords and the House of Commons are clearly the province of the leadership class. When Gützlaff discusses the political role of the average citizen, he concentrates on the obligation to pay taxes and serve in the military.[56] As in Chinese politics, Gützlaff's view is ordinarily from the top down. Leaders who demonstrate concern for the people's welfare can expect to have a free hand.

Respect for scholars, commitment to education, and filial piety also exemplify common values. English parents, like the Chinese, will sacrifice much in order to provide their children with an education, though attaining literacy is easier in English than in Chinese, for English has, according to Gützlaff, only

---

53. *Da Yingguo,* 1:4b. Gützlaff does not actually identify the source of the quotation.

54. *Da Yingguo,* 1:4b-5, 7a; "Yingjiliguo zenggonghui," *Dong-Xi,* 1838.4:64b-65a; 5:81-83.

55. In Gützlaff's histories of China for the Western public, he also emphasizes the morality of Chinese emperors when evaluating them as rulers.

56. *Da Yingguo,* 1:4b-5a; "Yingjiliguo zenggonghui," *Dong-Xi,* 1838.4:64b-65a; 5:81-83.

twenty-four letters.[57] In both societies, education includes instruction in the rules of correct behavior, along with the teaching of reading and writing; study of sacred literature and history trains people to seek righteousness and harmony among the classes. Not objectivity but inculcation of the accepted morality should be the goal of instructors.[58] Cognizant of the esteem accorded literati, the Chinese narrator likens English clergymen and physicians to scholars rather than to their occupational counterparts. Protestant ministers are comparable to Chinese scholar-officials in that they study, take examinations, and have the duty of leading the people in the way of *ren* (humanity) and *de* (virtue). A bit of didactic evangelism enters: just as England, which nourishes scholars, has accepted the truth, so any society which cultivates learning — for example, China — has already prepared the way for the gospel. When scholars uphold correct doctrine, the masses will follow their example. A people who revere filial piety could find no greater model than Jesus, who accepted his Father's will even unto death.

Despite the use of China as a baseline and the attention to shared values, Western Christendom emerges as a distinctly different society from that of China. It is also a superior society, according to Gützlaff, and has much to teach stagnant China. True liberty is the soul and source of every improvement, and included in true liberty is religious freedom, with the leaders allowing individuals to worship according to their conscience. Gützlaff was undoubtedly trying to encourage China's administrators to permit Christian evangelism. On the other hand, he accepted the right of the government to favor orthodoxy so long as it allowed all doctrines a hearing.

English law and justice are examined in several items: Gützlaff's essay on "Individual Rights," a significant portion of the second chapter of *Da-Yingguo*, and sections of *Dong-Xi* articles on Parliament.[59] Gützlaff's two major points are the supremacy of law and the impartiality of justice in England. In Britain, judges are well paid so that they are not subject to bribes, and they must ensure that an impartial investigation is conducted and proof of guilt is furnished. Punishment may vary according to circumstances and intent, but not according to status. Even the ruler is subject to law. In unfavorable contrast, China has a government based on persons rather than law, and the law is designed to repress and control the people. The accused, says Gützlaff, has little or no legal protection; he is subject to physical punishment to obtain

---

57. *Da Yingguo*, 3:26.

58. *Da Yingguo*, 2:1b-2a, 4a; "Yingjili gonghui," *Dong-Xi*, 1837.11:157-58.

59. *Dong-Xi*, 1838.4:64b-65a; 5:81-83; "Zizhu zhili" [Individual rights], *Dong-Xi*, 3:42-44b; *Da Yingguo*, 2:5a-b.

confession; bribes to ensure a favorable verdict often consume his wealth. Gützlaff concludes this idealized description of British law and justice with the comment that culture flourishes and the economy prospers only under such a system.

The nation-state, according to Gützlaff, is a sovereign entity, and the king follows the directives of no foreign country.[60] As a native of Germany, which was still struggling toward nationhood, Gützlaff admired Britain's political system and could appreciate the relationship between her nation-state structure and her political and economic strength. For him, the sovereign nation-state was the norm, with England representing the most advanced model. The power and prosperity of Great Britain rest on the triple foundations of orthodox Christianity, sound political institutions, and an expanding commercial economy.

In the idealized pictures of the West drawn by Gützlaff, Bridgman, and others, revolutionary upheavals, warfare, slavery, and similar dark aspects of Western civilization were minimized. Their criticisms were largely limited to aspects that directly affected the Chinese: the behavior of sailors newly arrived on Chinese shores or the failure of English and American merchants to observe the Sabbath. Such an emphasis derived in part from the missionaries' attempt to offset the negative image of the West held by Chinese and to inspire respect for Western civilization. But there was also a natural tendency to ignore current problems which lacked immediacy for the missionaries, stationed as they were thousands of miles from home. In reaction to the hardships of living in a different culture and a difficult climate, they viewed their native land through rose-tinted glasses.

For Gützlaff, Western Christendom was both the home of universal Christianity and a repository of useful knowledge. By offering the Chinese the latter, he hoped to persuade them to accept the former, to acknowledge a new basis for authority in understanding nature, man, and society. The religious and the secular complemented one another, and England was the prototype expressing the harmony of the whole. China, of course, never accepted the whole. A few Chinese scholar-officials during the 1840s did select for incorporation in their writings certain information deemed useful in strengthening China. The translations themselves tell us much about the intent of the authors, but nothing about the perceptions of the readers. It is by examining the materials excerpted for inclusion in Chinese geographies that we learn what meaning the missionaries' secular writings held for Chinese scholars.

60. *Da Yingguo,* 1:4b.

The Chinese Audience

The Chinese audience for the early Protestant secular writings was much smaller than the missionaries had hoped. How widely the works circulated is impossible even to estimate, but editions were generally small: 300 copies of Gützlaff's *Gujin wanguo* and 600 copies of the first issue of *Dong-Xi*, for example. There were, however, reprints. Because the first volume of *Dong-Xi* was disposed of so quickly, a second edition of 300 was reprinted, and subsequently the number of copies per issue was raised to 1,000; also, the SDUK voted in 1837 to finance a 1,000-copy reprint of the first volumes of *Dong-Xi*.[61] A new edition of Gützlaff's *Gujin wanguo* came out in Ningbo in 1850. Bridgman's *Meilige heshengguo zhilue* (A short account of the united provinces of America) went through four editions between 1838 and 1862 and was also translated into Japanese. For the first generation of Chinese and Japanese scholars seeking information about America, it became a basic source.[62] Some of the works were sent to Nanjing and Beijing, and Gützlaff distributed copies to the signers of the Treaty of Nanjing. He also dispersed volumes during his brief forays into coastal towns. Other evangelists and Chinese colporteurs carried a few of the secular works with them and reported that Chinese were much more interested in these than in the religious tracts. It seems unlikely, nevertheless, that many works penetrated far into interior China. Literate Chinese interested in Western culture and civilization were few, and even those who might be curious about such exotica found the awkward style of the writings and their Christian orientation unattractive.

Some specific motivation was required if an educated Chinese were to seek out and peruse the missionaries' publications. The Opium War served as that stimulus. Certain Chinese officials, mainly those stationed in southeast China, entered of necessity into communication with the foreigners. Observing the Westerners' firepower, they came to appreciate the importance of learning about the enemy in order to strengthen and protect China. Impressed with how much Westerners seemed to know about China, they sought to make available to their compatriots data on the world beyond China.

Among the best known of those who solicited information about the West was Commissioner Lin Zexu (1785-1850) of Opium War fame; he compiled a digest of translations from the foreign press on Chinese affairs which circulated among local officials.[63] Among the most influential mid-nineteenth-

---

61. "Periodical Magazines," *CRep* 2.4 (August 1833): 186-87; "First Report of the SDUK," *CRep* 4.8 (December 1835): 356.

62. Lazich, *E. C. Bridgman*, pp. 154-55.

63. Tsien, "Western Impact on China through Translation."

century Chinese works were *Haiguo tuzhi* (Illustrated treatise on the maritime kingdoms) by Wei Yuan (1794-1856) and *Yinghuan zhilüe* (A brief survey of the maritime circuits) by Xu Jiyu (1795-1873).[64] But there are evidences of others who had become curious about the West. A non-commissioned officer garrisoned in Kowloon intercepted Gützlaff on one of his itinerations to remind him of the promise of a geography.[65] A Ningbo official in 1843 requested William Milne to insert Chinese characters in a Western map of China, and several other members of the literati queried Milne about England and Europe; one had already obtained accounts of travelers abroad and desired confirmation of the information therein.[66] Zhen Keyao, secretary of the Chinese Union, reported that in April 1851 a Chinese Union member had given a copy of Gützlaff's *Wanguo shizhuan* (Universal history) to the magistrate at Jiangmen, Guangdong, a port where Chinese junks assembled for their journey to Southeast Asia.[67] In 1854, Dr. Benjamin Hobson reported giving out tracts to his patients. Though they accepted the religious tracts with little enthusiasm, they frequently requested works on geography, natural history, the calendar, and medicine, and so he distributed them along with the scriptures and religious tracts.[68] Wilhelm Lobschied wrote that he had given the New Testament, *Wanguo shizhuan,* and a geography to the secretaries of the Fukong magistrate when they visited.[69] Finally, Robert Neumann of the Berlin mission stated that

64. Drake, *China Charts the World;* Drake, "A Nineteenth-Century View of the United States of America from Hsü Chi-yü's *Ying-huan chih-lüeh*," *Papers on China* (Harvard East Asian Research Center) 19 (1965): 30-54; Jane Leonard, *Wei Yuan and China's Rediscovery of the Maritime World* (Cambridge, MA: Harvard University Press, 1984); Suzanne W. Barnett, "From Route Books to International Order: The Early Protestant Missionary Press and Chinese Geographical Writings," History of Christianity in China Project, 1990; Barnett, "American Missionaries and Chinese Officials in the Context of the Opium War" (paper delivered at the Conference on the Impact of American Missionaries on U.S. Attitudes and Policies toward China, San Diego, October 1987); Zhang Mingjiu, "*Yinghuan zhilüe* yu *Haiguo tuzhi* bijiao yanjiu" [A comparative analysis of *Yinghuan zhilüe* and *Haiguo tuzhi*], *Jindaishi yanjiu* 67 (January 1992): 68-81; Ch'en, "The Growth of Geographical Knowledge"; Tsien, "Western Impact on China through Translation."

65. Ferdinand Genähr, "Tagebuch," No. 5, Hong Kong, 28 May 1847–19 June 1847, Vereinte Evanglische Mission, Archives of Rheinische Missionsgesellschaft (hereafter VEM), Genähr Korrespondenz und Tagebucher.

66. W. C. Milne, "Notes of a Seven Months' Residence in the City of Ningpo, from December 7th, 1842 to July 7th, 1843," *CRep* 13.1 (January 1844): 14-18; 3 (March 1844): 127.

67. "Tagebuch des Chinesichen Verein," *Neuste Nachrichten aus China* 1.4 (July 1851): 50.

68. Hobson to Tidman, Canton, 20 January 1854, Church World Mission Society (hereafter CWM), London Missionary Society (hereafter LMS), Box 3D, #5, South China, Incoming.

69. "Journal of Missionary Labour in China," *The Gleaner* 2.3 (August 1852): 19.

800 copies of Gützlaff's geography had been printed and were being distributed along with thousands of religious works; also, two cases of books and pamphlets had been packed for transport to San Francisco.[70]

The Geographies of Lin Zexu, Wei Yuan, and Xu Jiyu

Almost immediately after arriving in Canton in March 1839, Lin Zexu had recruited four Chinese with missionary training to aid him in obtaining and translating writings about the West. An elderly man known as Aman had attended mission schools and worked with Dr. Marshman in Serampore; Yuan Dehui (Shaou Tih) had studied at a Roman Catholic school in Penang and the Anglo-Chinese College in Malacca; and another translator, Alum, apparently had been enrolled at a church school in Cornwall, Connecticut, during the 1820s. The fourth translator was Liang Jinde, son of evangelist Liang Fa and also a student and literary assistant of Elijah Bridgman. He was particularly helpful, for he was able to provide Lin with copies of *Dong-Xi*, the *Chinese Repository*, and other mission publications. He had worked with Bridgman in writing the *Meilige heshengguo* and undoubtedly made this history of the United States available to Lin.[71] These four transmitted and provided Chinese summaries from commercial newspapers, books published in London and the United States, and items from the missionary press. Lin also requested regular translations from the newspapers of Macao, Canton, Singapore, and India. On the basis of these materials, Lin circulated among local officials a digest of translations from the foreign press on Chinese affairs.[72] Lin himself also took the initiative in requesting foreign books from Bridgman and in purchasing from the ABCFM a copy of Hugh Murray, *An Encyclopedia of Geography* (London, 1834), which he had Liang Jinde translate. On the basis of the latter, he drafted *Sizhou zhi* (Geography of four continents).[73]

70. "Ein allgemeine Bericht des Missionars Neumanns," *Evangelischer Reishsbote* 3.10 (October 1853): 6; 4.9 (September 1854): 70.

71. Carl Smith, *Chinese Christians: Élites, Middlemen, and the Church in Hong Kong* (Hong Kong: Oxford University Press, 1985), pp. 52-62; "Journal of Occurrences," *CRep* 17.6 (1848): 318; Lazich, *E. C. Bridgman*, pp. 185-88.

72. Tsien, "Western Impact on China through Translation," p. 315.

73. At a meeting with Bridgman in connection with the destruction of confiscated opium, Lin acknowledged having received foreign books from Bridgman. Most of Lin's writings were published by his family only after his death. Du Lianzhe, "Lin Tse-hsü," in *Eminent Chinese of the Ch'ing Dynasty*, 2 vols., ed. Arthur Hummel (Washington: U.S. Government Printing Office, 1943-1944), 1:512-14. Only a brief extract from Lin's *Sizhou zhi*

He applied to Dr. Peter Parker (1804-1888) for a translation of paragraphs in Emeric de Vattel's *Law of Nations* dealing with war, blockades, and the right to interdict trade and confiscate smuggled materials. Parker also offered to send Lin a world atlas, a geography, and a globe; later, Lin asked Parker to make an English translation of his famous letter to Queen Victoria protesting British transport of opium to China.[74]

By September 1840, when Lin was dismissed from office for the disasters of the Opium War, he had amassed an unprecedented collection of materials on the West. These he turned over to a fellow official and admirer, Wei Yuan, whom he met on his way to exile in June 1841, and they formed the basis for Wei Yuan's *Haiguo tuzhi*. In fact, so important were Lin's contributions that Gützlaff in his review of Wei's work for the *Chinese Repository* mistakenly attributed it to Lin.[75] Materials from Lin and Wei Yuan were, in turn, included in Xu Jiyu's geographical treatise printed four years later. Lin's collection apparently was never published, but the works of Wei and Xu would be expanded and reprinted several times.

All three were civil officials who spent part of their careers in east China. Here they had become deeply disturbed by China's internal weakness and by the simultaneous threats of the opium trade and Western expansionism. Unique circumstances called for learning factual data about the world beyond China and even for new directions in policy. They had to understand the enemy; they needed to discover the sources of the West's strength. Nurtured on Confucian texts, they continued to accept the superiority of the Confucian moral way and to believe that guidance could still be found in the classics. Wei and Xu, however, belonged to the "Modern Text" school, with its emphasis on critical scholarship, and all three were members of the "statecraft" *(jingshi)* circle, which advocated "learning of practical use to society"

discussing Russia and its expansion under Peter the Great appears to survive as a separate publication today.

74. Edward V. Gulick, *Peter Parker and the Opening of China* (Cambridge, MA: Harvard University Press, 1973), pp. 88-91, 232 n. 22. This was one of two translations, for Lin also requested one of his aides to make another translation of his letter to Queen Victoria. One reason for Parker's access to Lin was that Parker had treated Lin, by proxy, for hernia and had provided information about opium addiction and its cure. Bridgman published an English translation of Lin's letter in *CRep*, but the British foreign office apparently never delivered it to the Queen.

75. "Hai kwoh Tu chi, Statistical notices of the ocean kingdom with maps," *CRep* 16.9 (September 1847): 417-24. A few sections of the compilation were indeed credited to Lin by Wei Yuan. According to Bridgman's introduction to Gützlaff's review, the only copy yet seen by the missionaries was one sent to Gützlaff from Shanghai. Gützlaff and a few friends had an opportunity to peruse it briefly before it was taken to Europe by a Frenchman.

(*jingshi zhi yong*). Metaphysical speculation and textual criticism should give way to administrative reform, social participation, and this-worldly activism. The goal of all three was to make China wealthy and strong again in order to protect its heritage against Western incursions. The perception as to what was required to defend the Middle Way, however, broadened as one moved from traditional Chinese geographies to the works of Lin and then to Wei and to Xu. As Suzanne Barnett has pointed out, guidebooks for dealing with foreigners and collections of data on the physical and cultural geography of non-Chinese countries gave way to "treatises intended to inform political debate and policy making."[76]

Simultaneously, the interpretive input of the authors increased. Lin's work was a compendium with little organization or commentary. Wei selected his materials and grouped them according to the traditional Chinese division into maritime kingdoms; while he added his own notes and commentary, he did not alter the quoted texts. Xu attempted to evaluate his sources, incorporating what seemed creditable and omitting the marvelous. He sometimes edited out of missionary writings the disquisitions on Christianity, though he did use biblical stories and emphasize Jewish history in the geographical sections on the Middle East. In explaining his methodology, Xu wrote that the Jesuits were well versed in the language so that their style was clear and agreeable, but their presentations were not always forthright. The Protestant writings were mostly vulgar and inelegant, but he concluded that their facts regarding the rise and fall of states were reliable. The elegance of the former could not replace the candor of the latter.[77] Both Wei and Xu did, however, rely on Jesuit works for selections on mathematics and some of their maps and materials on physical geography, including Ricci's Sinocentric map of the world. Despite Ricci's placement of China at the center of the universe, he had introduced latitude and longitude line in his maps.[78] Other Jesuit sources employed were Giulio Aleni's 1623 *Zhifang waiji* (Further notes on foreign geography) and Ferdinand Verbiest's 1624 *Kunyu quantu* (Illustrated map of the world).[79]

All three authors made use of a variety of sources, both Chinese and West-

76. Barnett, "From Route Books," p. 37.

77. Xu, in the journal *Yinghuan zhilüe*, 1: 2b, quoted in Drake, *China Charts the World*, p. 54.

78. Ch'en Kuan-sheng, "Matteo Ricci's Contribution to, and Iinfluence on, Geographical Knowledge in China," *Journal of the American Oriental Society* 59.3 (September 1939): 325-59.

79. It is possible that the Chinese authors had access to the revision of Verbiest's map by Michel Benoist, 1760, which rearranged the hemispheres in the European way.

ern. Lin relied heavily on gazetteer records on trade and maritime defense compiled in the 1830s by Liang Tingnan, a member of the statecraft circle and a close friend of Lin. Xu turned to *Tianxia junguo libing shu* by New Text author Gu Yanwu (1613-1682) for much of his material on Japan and Southeast Asia, though he supplemented it with information from Gützlaff. Both Xu and Gützlaff noted that the Fujianese in Nanyang were mostly traders, the Cantonese were artisans and laborers, and those from Chaozhou, Guangdong, were farmers. All three included selections from Gützlaff's essays on political economy, though it is not always clear whether they came from *Dong-Xi* or from *Mouyi*, the booklet largely composed of reprints of *Dong-Xi* articles. All three included lengthy quotations or paraphrases from Elijah Bridgman's *Meilige heshengguo zilue* for their history and geography of the United States; the result is a laudatory picture of a peaceable kingdom and a courageous, self-sacrificing George Washington. Other Western sources were Divie B. Bethune, *Pingan tongshu* (Peace almanac), 1850-1853; Richard Q. Way, *Diqiu tushuo* (Illustrated discussion of the world), 1848; and Majishi (Marques), *Waiguo dili beikao* (A study of foreign geography), 1847.[80] In the sections on Europe and the Middle East, Lin, Wei, and Xu were heavily dependent on writings by Westerners even if they incorporated them into their own conceptual framework.

Determining the exact locale of their data is not easy, for they might give the title, sometimes abbreviated, of the work used, but they rarely cited the author or specific pages. They freely reproduced excerpts used by previous authors, and they often tailored passages, sometimes to eliminate Christian proselytism and sometimes to condense a section. Both Wei and Xu also obtained information directly from foreigners. Wei, for example, requested permission to question the British captain Peter Armstruther, who was captured and imprisoned in Ningbo during the Opium War and Armstruther provided Wei with information on English history, geography, and customs. England, Wei concluded, "produced powerful ships and enterprising merchants."[81]

One of the few Westerners whose assistance Xu acknowledged was the Reformed Church missionary David Abeel (d. 1846). During 1844 Xu met with Abeel and William J. Boone in Xiamen (Amoy) on several occasions. Abeel described Wei as "the most inquisitive Chinese of high rank I have yet met"

80. Suzanne W. Barnett lists thirteen Western sources used by Wei Yuan; "Wei Yuan and Westerners: Notes on the Sources of the *Hai-kuo T'u-chih*," *Ch'ing-shih wen-tí* 2.4 (November 1970): 1-20. Little is known about Majishi since the author's English name is not given; internal evidence would indicate that he was a Westerner and a Roman Catholic.

81. Leonard, *Wei Yuan*, p. 88.

and gladly answered Xu's questions regarding foreign countries. Abeel also leafed through a Western atlas with Xu, pointing out the position and territorial boundaries of various states, and he provided Xu with maps on which he had written place names in Chinese.[82] In accord with his own agenda, Abeel presented Xu with copies of the New Testament and several religious tracts, along with copies of *Dong-Xi*, but he regretfully concluded that Xu was more intent on learning about the kingdoms of this world than about the way to the Kingdom of Heaven.

Xu wrote, "I sought all kinds of writings on [world geography], and . . . I made extracts from all of them upon slips of paper of what was worthy of being retained; and whenever I saw men from the West, I improved the opportunity to ask them concerning the accuracy of my notes."[83] Xu talked with the independent missionary, Dr. William Cummings, who lauded the beauties of the Swiss landscape and the peaceful character of the inhabitants. From a sub-prefect, Xu obtained two large Western maps and several books written by Westerners in Chinese. He established a brief but friendly relationship with British Consul G. Tradescant Lay, whose spoken Chinese was quite good.[84] From Lay and his successor Rutherford Alcock, Xu garnered additional data about the history and geography of Europe and the Middle East as well as about the empires of Britain, France, and Russia. Mrs. Alcock drew for him a map indicating the areas controlled by each of the three imperial powers. The fact that these Western gentlemen, though lacking knowledge of the Confucian classics and reared outside the Middle Kingdom, seemed well informed, courteous, and acquainted with the Chinese language, impressed and pleased Xu. He was inclined to trust their data even if it conflicted with information from Chinese authors; for instance, he accepted the existence of Antarctica even though he found no record of it in Chinese works.

As for Karl Gützlaff, there is no record of his having personal contact with any of the three, despite the fact that he was Chinese secretary with the British administration and often acted as interpreter in negotiations with Chinese officials. As noted above, however, Lin's "Western experts" made available to him *Dong-Xi* and probably Gützlaff's publications on world geography and history, the history of England, and economics. Abeel, Lay, and Alcock may

82. "Extracts from the Journal of the Rev. D. Abeel at Amoy," *CRep* 13.5 (May 1844): 234-37.

83. Quoted in S. Wells Williams, "The Ying Hwan Chi-lioh, or General Survey of the Maritime Circuit, a Universal Geography by His Excellency Sü Ki-yü," *CRep* 20.4 (April 1851): 171.

84. Lay had studied Chinese under Gützlaff and had remarked on how demanding he was as a teacher.

well have included some of these works among the items they supplied to Xu. Xu cited *Wanguo dili* at least twice. In an era when there was no uniformity in Chinese names for Western states, the Chinese characters that Xu and Gützlaff used to designate the European countries were identical in most cases. Internal evidence also indicates reliance on Gützlaff's writings. Xu, for example, presented quite a favorable description of Gützlaff's homeland, Prussia, calling it an illustrious Western state. The Prussian ruler "encouraged the farmers and artisans, established centers of learning, and gave aid to traveling merchants. The common people, therefore, felt close to him."[85] This connection between prosperity and a good governor who fostered agriculture and commerce was a theme that ran through many of Gützlaff's essays.

Xu also contrasted Protestant north Germany with Roman Catholic south Germany and Austria. "Those who live in the North are all strong and healthy; they are pure and good by nature. and they love to study the arts. The Southerners' habits are wasteful; their day is spent in drunkenness and over-eating, and they have no plans for the future."[86] Such bias had pervaded Gützlaff's views of continental Europe as well as his comparisons of England and Ireland. Throughout the sections on the West, Xu exhibited a more positive attitude toward Protestantism than Catholicism. Like Gützlaff, he associated Protestantism with an industrious, frugal, and ingenuous people. Under Protestant rulers like Queen Elizabeth, England was prosperous and powerful, while rule by Catholic kings often meant difficult times: conflict between the papacy and state rulers, religious wars, and plagues. Similar correlations had been detailed in Gützlaff's *Da Yingguo, Dong-Xi,* and *Gujin wanguo.* Xu's more lenient view of Protestantism was also based on the fact that the bulk of his contemporary Western contacts were Protestants such as Abeel, Lay, Boone, and Cummings.

Xu's section on the Middle East is similar to that of Gützlaff in *Gujin wanguo* and *Wanguo diliguanji* (Universal geography) in that the Old Testament is the basis for the early history of the region. Xu relates the life of Abraham and his descendants, including the story of Daniel's interpretation of the strange dream of the king of Babylon. Xu was skeptical, however, of the claim that Moses received the stone tablets engraved with the Ten Commandments directly from God. His geography of Greece and Italy also begins with the ancient period. The section on contemporary Turkey, however, emphasized the current imperialistic designs of England, France, and Russia on the country.

Like Gützlaff, Wei and Xu accorded England greater attention than any

85. Quoted in Drake, *China Charts the World,* p. 145.
86. Drake, *China Charts the World,* p. 146.

other Western state. The Chinese writers had a specific purpose for emphasizing England. A major theme of Wei's *Haiguo tuzhi* was that Western expansionism via the sea posed a grave threat to China. Western advances in communication and transportation had lessened the distance between China and Europe, and Chinese rulers needed to take cognizance of the fact. Though Wei employed the traditional Chinese framework of dividing the world beyond China into maritime kingdoms, one of his valuable contributions was his thesis that China must cease to concentrate so exclusively on the inner Asian frontiers and acknowledge the importance of the maritime kingdoms to China's security and prosperity.[87] China must build up her maritime power, using Western weapons and ships as necessary, and she should "use barbarians to control barbarians" — that is, induce Western powers to checkmate each other. Before China could devise effective policies to thwart the Western menace, however, she must correct and update her information on the sea regions. Wei directed attention to Nanyang and India, whose history and cultural geography receive detailed treatment. The six sections on India, while containing data on China's earlier relations with India and information on the opium poppy, were primarily designed to illustrate the methods by which Great Britain had recently expanded its control in the region: trade, missions, and armed force were all a part of Great Britain's arsenal. Since Chinese information on the Indian subcontinent was sparse and outdated, Wei had to rely heavily on writings by Westerners. Particularly useful was the series of essays on India in *Dong-Xi*, later revised and included in Gützlaff's *Gujin wanguo*; in addition, the last chapter of *Da Yingguo* discussed the "tributary countries" of Great Britain, comparing them with China's tributary states.

According to Wei, the fate of India should be a warning to China, for Western tentacles had already reached into Southeast Asia. China had neglected for too long its strategic and commercial advantages in Nanyang. Since China had a heritage of tributary and trade relations with peninsular Southeast Asia, Wei and Xu turned to Chinese works for its history and geography. They had, however, to depend on other sources for information on the islands of the Pacific as well as for recent events in Nanyang. Wei, apparently, did interview several Fujian merchants who traded regularly with Nanyang, but Gützlaff's writings furnished material on the current activities of Chinese

---

87. Two earlier works by Wei Yuan were more traditional in that they advocated defense of the homeland via a war of attrition, the enemy exhausting and overextending himself in the vastness of China. Paramilitary troops such as the heroes of 1841 at San yuan li, Guangdong, would further harass the enemy forces. See Polachek, *The Inner Opium War*, pp. 194-200.

in Southeast Asia and on the islands of Borneo, Java, the Philippines, and Singapore. *Mouyi* and the record of commodity prices of goods traded in Canton, a regular feature of *Dong-Xi,* proved valuable for trade statistics, including the relative importance of each country, articles of export and import, and sea routes.

A second theme running through both Wei's and Xu's works was, in fact, the importance of trade and commerce to China. As Gützlaff had often reiterated, the gross national income of China was not dependent solely upon agriculture, as Confucian theory would seem to indicate. Rather, commerce provided a livelihood for many Chinese, especially those of southeast China. Again, there was the example of England.[88] England, despite having limited arable land, had built a great empire relying heavily on commerce and shipping. The British government, instead of viewing merchants as objects for extracting funds, aided them by creating a favorable environment for trade, protecting its overseas merchants, and adopting a laissez-faire policy of free trade. The Chinese government, according to Wei and Xu, needed to adopt policies beneficial to the commercial sector of the economy. Instead of ignoring the Fujian sailors who traded with Nanyang and treating overseas Chinese as disloyal, China should regard them as important actors in maintaining its presence in Nanyang and countering Western penetration. Wei, furthermore, recommended that the government establish a translation institute and build a shipyard and arsenal at Canton; French and American engineers should be hired to guide construction and teach navigation.[89]

By expanding the realm of competition beyond commerce, Xu went a step further than Wei. Whatever the opinion of most Chinese, Xu acknowledged that centers of culture and civilization existed outside China. They might not be the equal of the Chinese, but it behooved Chinese to learn about them, to study their sources of strength in order to checkmate them. Xu had moved to a global perspective. He had not gone so far as to depict a world of equal, sovereign nation-states, but he did recognize Abeel, Lay, and others as products of societies with their own literature, technology, government, and mores. He wanted to know why their governments could exercise such power; in particular, how had Great Britain managed to become the leading nation of Europe and the greatest threat to China? Like Gützlaff, he found the explanation only

88. "Lun Ouluoba shiqing," *Dong-Xi,* 1835.5:1-4; "Tongshang" [Commerce], *Dong-Xi,* 1837.12:160-62; "Mouyi" [Trade], *Dong-Xi,* 1838.1:8-11.

89. Wei did not recommend the use of British advisers since he viewed the policy as one of using barbarians to control barbarians *(yi yi zhi yi).* Both of Wei's recommendations would be implemented by the government at a later date, though not necessarily as a consequence of Wei's advocacy.

partially in economics and technology. There was also the people's sense of identity with their government. Xu's description of rule by the British king and Parliament closely paralleled the accounts of Gützlaff in *Da Yingguo* and *Dong-Xi*. Rule lay in the hands of an educated elite, whose policies were designed to bring security, prosperity, and justice to the populace. The masses were recipients rather than active participants in the governing process. Even the sections on the United States, based on Bridgman's *Meilige heshengguo*, featured a noble, courageous, and unselfish George Washington aided by a leadership group representing the people. As in the case of Gützlaff, Xu probably conveyed to his Chinese readers an image of modified gentry rule rather than a democratic government.

Though the works of Wei and Xu are generally called geographical works, they actually include a wide range of topics in addition to physical geography: history and government, religion and language, natural resources, industry, finance, and commerce, size and composition of the military, and foreign relations, especially those with China. Many sections, especially those on the status of women, education, social courtesies, and marriage customs, relate details identical with those in *Dong-Xi* and *Da Yingguo*. However, despite Gützlaff's essays in *Dong-Xi* comparing Chinese and Western literature, Wei and Xu believed that the West had nothing to offer China in the realms of art and literature and included little on these aspects of Western civilization. Neither Wei nor Xu was concerned with the specifics of latitude and longitude in their maps; their purpose was not so much to make a contribution to scientific knowledge as to serve the political needs of China. They did, consequently, incorporate materials on steamships, railways, and weaponry. Xu noted that knowledge of cannon and gunpowder had originated with China, but Westerners, with their ingenuity, had transformed them into effective modern arms. Xu provided extensive information on British warships, describing the number of cannon, the heights of the masts, and the draughts of the various battleships. He even included data about their keels, the sails, the wood used, and the metal sheathing of recent vessels; he expressed awe over the ability of the steamships to travel over 1,000 li in 24 hours.[90] The essays might make Chinese readers aware of the importance of such vessels to China's defenses, but the sketchy diagrams without detailed explanation or accurate pictures of the engines and their operation could convey only a hazy understanding of their mechanics.[91]

90. Drake, *China Charts the World*, pp. 113, 141.

91. The translations of Li Shanlan (1810-1882), Joseph Edkins (1823-1905), and Alexander Wylie (1815-1887) on mathematics and mechanics during the 1850s and those of Hua

The Significance of the New Geographies

As one would expect, all these works were China-centered. China was the measure, so that the importance and the amount of text accorded states and regions were a function of their significance for China. Dynastic dating was routine; states were located in terms of their distance from some point in China; comparisons with Chinese customs and institutions were employed in attempts to make Western society and mores understandable. But then, Gützlaff had used the same techniques in hopes of Sinifying his writings and attracting an audience. Even Xu knew no Western language and was in no position to invent new character combinations for foreign concepts; instead, he relied on Chinese terms that inevitably carried Chinese connotations. Democracy, nationalism, Asia as operative categories of analysis — none of these ideas find clear expression in Xu.[92] Xu did call attention to the confusing diversity of names for Western countries, attempting to correlate synonyms, and S. W. Williams in his review of *Yinghuan* expressed the hope that Westerners would adopt Xu's terminology so that "we can adhere to one name for a country."[93] Nothing suggests that either Xu or Wei was personally attracted to Christianity or that they thought the Christian religion had anything to offer China. Neither Lin nor Wei nor Xu saw any need to alter the fundamentals of Confucian society and government.

What these works could do was broaden horizons. Sinocentric maps could be compared with Western maps depicting the size of China in relation to that of Russia, Europe, America, and the rest of the world. Xu's *Yinghuan zhilüe* included forty-four maps, many of them using the Western style. More accurate information about the world beyond China and even about the Chinese coastline was rapidly being made available. Comparative chronologies as well as the sections on the Middle East, Greece, and Italy revealed that the West had a long history. To a great extent, the ancient civilizations of China and the West that were the foundation for current institutions and cultures had developed independently; thus, they were qualitatively different. By 1861 twenty-two works on world geography and some

---

Hengfang (1833-1902), Xu Shou (1818-1884), Xu Jianyin (1845-1901), John Fryer (1839-1928), and Young J. Allen (1836-1907) for the Jiangnan Arsenal during the 1870s would be more useful to individuals seeking to upgrade China's military capabilities. Several of these were appended to the 1895 edition of Xu's work.

92. Drake, *China Charts the World*, pp. 57-59, 194; Rebecca E. Karl, "Creating Asia: China in the World at the Beginning of the Twentieth Century," *American Historical Review*, October 1998, pp. 1096-1118.

93. See Williams, "The Ying Hwan Chi-lioh," p. 171.

two dozen publications on Western military technology and artillery tactics had appeared.[94]

For a book to be influential, however, a receptive environment is required. Such did not exist in China during the 1840s. Lin, Wei, and Xu were not alone in their curiosity about the West, but they belonged to a tiny minority of China's elite. During the 1840s and 1850s distribution of the works depended on personal contacts among scholars. One Meixian prefect was reported to have read Lin's or Wei's geography and to have issued a proclamation refuting in detail the author's depiction of Christianity.[95] S. W. Williams stated in his review of Xu's geography that several Cantonese had expressed surprise at statements it contained and inquired whether they could really be true.[96] Wei's *Haiguo tuzhi* was reprinted in expanded editions in 1847 and 1852, but it became popular in Japan long before it was finally republished in China in 1895. Both an abridged edition and a full translation of *Haiguo tuzhi* and a reprint of *Yinghuan zhilüe* came out in Japan during the 1850s.

Limiting the influence of these geographies were factionalism among officials and difficulty in gaining access to the throne. Too often, the emperor was told what officials thought he wanted to hear. Xu, who had rashly acknowledged that an alternative if less worthy civilization existed outside China, aroused the enmity of conservative Chinese officials and was cashiered. Xu would hold several relatively minor posts during the 1850s, but he was not fully rehabilitated until the Tongzhi reform movement of the 1860s. In 1865 Xu was recalled from retirement to membership in the Zongli Yamen, established to supervise relations between China and foreign states. Although he was seventy years old and largely a figurehead, his reinstatement signaled recognition of the importance of learning about the West. He was, furthermore, in communication with leaders of the Self-Strengthening Movement and constantly urged a foreign policy based on a realistic assessment of factual data instead of grand theory. A reprint of *Yinghuan zhilüe* in 1866 included a complimentary preface by the reformer Dong Xun (1807-1892) and became a text at the Tongwen guan, the school founded to train "Western experts." Both the great statesman Zeng Guofan (1811-1872) and Guo Songdao (1818-1891), the first Chinese ambassador to Great Britain, consulted Xu's work for information about the outside world. Finally, Kang Youwei (1858-1927) and Liang Qichao (1873-1929), leaders of the 1898 Hundred Days of Reform, read

94. Yen-p'ing Hao and Erh-min Wang, "Changing Chinese Views of Western Relations, 1840-95," in *The Cambridge History of China*, ed. J. K. Fairbank and Kwang-ching Liu (Cambridge: Cambridge University Press, 1980), 11.2:147-49.

95. "Proclamation by the Prefect of Meihsien," *Hong Kong Register*, 29 October 1850.

96. Williams, "The Ying Hwan Chi-lioh," pp. 169-94.

the book and found its information about the strength of the West and the weakness of China alarming. Change, including institutional change, was necessary.[97]

Lin Xezu had collected information about the West with specific and limited goals in mind; he wanted to learn enough about Westerners' values and social customs to be effective in negotiating with them. What kinds of appeals and threats would they respond to? How could he convince them of the necessity of ceasing the opium traffic? Once warfare began, he recognized the need to learn more about the West's cannon, warships, and other weaponry. This viewpoint, arising out of military conflict, contributed to the persistent Chinese image of Westerners as ingenious in technology and enamored of trade and profit.

Wei Yuan likewise acquired a respect for Western ships and weaponry, but he also acknowledged the importance of commerce in the West, and he came to appreciate its contribution to the West's wealth and strength. Wei went further; he urged Chinese to reconsider the role of commerce in China's economy and its potential contribution to China's influence overseas — in other words, to alter traditional agrarian economic theory. As Jane Leonard noted, the *Haiguo tuzhi* was one of the earliest Chinese works "to make a realistic geopolitical assessment of the worldwide dimensions of Western expansion and of its implications for Asian trade and politics."[98]

Xu Jiyu recognized the existence of alternative centers of civilization, as the Protestant missionaries had desired. To Wei Yuan's emphasis on trade and technology as a basis for the West's prosperity and potency, Xu added the sense of identity between the people and their government. None of the three, however, found much to admire in Christianity, at least as far as China was concerned. Xu might depict Protestantism as preferable to Roman Catholicism for the Germans and the British, but neither teaching was considered to have anything to offer China, with its superior Confucian ethic. The hopes of Gützlaff, Bridgman, and Abeel that secular writings would pave the way for acceptance of Christianity went unfulfilled. Nor did the three Chinese writers advocate free trade or the Western form of international relations. Already, as Abeel had sensed, Chinese were demonstrating selectivity in what they chose to adapt.

The influence of Lin's, Wei's, and Xu's changing perspectives of the West in China was limited during the 1840s and 1850s. The weight of tradition was heavy, and the inertia of the bureaucracy was great. Not only did Lin's collec-

97. Drake, *China Charts the World*, pp. 186-88, 195-97.
98. Leonard, *Wei Yuan*, p. 4.

tion remain unpublished, but Wei's and Xu's works attracted relatively few readers at mid-century, and those readers interpreted the data from within a Chinese context. Only as a propitious intellectual environment evolved would the writings truly acquire significance.

Chinese were interested in those fields that could be used as tools of statecraft. In the case of the Jesuits of the seventeenth century, Western mathematics and astronomy became absorbed in the Chinese corpus of knowledge without altering the basic Confucian cosmology. In the case of the Protestant writings, the new political geography acknowledging Western civilizations and new economic theories had greater corrosive potential.[99] They met initially with resistance, indifference, or rejection by the majority of scholars and bureaucrats. Even when Tongzhi leaders tried to implement certain policy changes arising from the new knowledge, Beijing was unwilling or unable to pursue a consistent reform program. Vast changes had occurred in the West between the 1600s and the 1800s, however. A gap in the wealth and power at the disposal of Chinese and Western governments had opened up during the two centuries. New developments in the technology of communications and transportation negated attempts at isolation. Just as the new electronics of today are undercutting China's control of the media, so the growing numbers of Western missionaries and traders in China brought new challenges as the century wore on. Cultural interaction between China and the West was embryonic during the mid-nineteenth century, but momentum was building. Missionaries, particularly Karl Gützlaff and Elijah Bridgman, helped fuel the momentum.

99. Copernican theory certainly had corrosive potentialities, but in the seventeenth century it had not yet completely displaced Ptolemaic theory and was not pushed by the Jesuits. See Nicole Halsberghe and Keizô Hashimoto, "Astronomy," in *Handbook of Christianity in China*, ed. Nicolas Standert (Leiden: Brill, 2001), vol. 1, pp. 715-17.

CHAPTER 8

Karl Gützlaff and the Chinese Union

The Nature of Conversion

In recent years, scholars have reexamined both the definition of the term *conversion* and the actual process of conversion. Works on conversion from Buddhism to Christianity or Christianity to Buddhism, from an animistic religion to Islam or Christianity, or from "mainline" Christianity to a "faith" sect, all have contributed to a better understanding of conversion.[1] Indigenization, enculturation, and adaptation of Christianity in a non-Christian culture have also been the subjects of numerous works.[2] To the surprise of many scholars, there has been a resurgence of interest in religion, especially in conservative interpretations of Judaism, Islam, and Christianity.

These recent developments shed new light on Karl Gützlaff's Chinese Union, an attempt to convert all China to evangelistic Christianity by means of Chinese proselytizers. Generally judged a scandalous failure, the Chinese Union included some forty preachers who were trustworthy, many of these becoming valued workers with other mission societies after the demise of the Chinese Union. Chinese evangelists, especially members of the Chinese

---

1. Lewis R. Rambo, *Understanding Religious Conversion* (New Haven: Yale University Press, 1993); Robert W. Hefner, ed., *Conversion to Christianity: Historical and Anthropological Perspectives on a Great Transformation* (Berkeley: University of California Press, 1993); Christopher Lamb and M. Darrol Bryant, eds., *Religious Conversion: Contemporary Practices and Controversies* (London: Cassell, 1999).

2. See, for example, Daniel H. Bays, ed., *Christianity in China* (Stanford: Stanford University Press, 1996); Lin Zhiping, ed., *Jidujiao yu Zhongguo bense hua* [Christianity and Chinese indigenization] (Taipei: Yuchouguang, 1990); Ku Wei-ying and Koen De Ridder, eds., *Authentic Chinese Christianity: Preludes to Its Development* (Leuven: Leuven University Press, 2001).

Union during the 1840s and 1850s, exercised greater responsibility than would be accorded to Chinese assistants in later decades of the nineteenth century, by which time the missionary community had increased and Westerners were permitted to reside in the interior so that they could maintain closer supervision.[3] As the Chinese Union workers of the 1840s had itinerated through China, interpreting Christianity according to their own understanding and employing their own metaphors and vocabulary, they were already adapting Christianity to Chinese mores and environment. Instead of formal preaching, they often employed a one-to-one conversational approach; rather than doctrinal instruction, they emphasized narrative and ritual, so characteristic of traditional Chinese religions. Repetition of the Lord's Prayer, the Apostles' Creed, and the Ten Commandments, and the telling of biblical stories with a moral admonition at the conclusion were favored. They emphasized the efficacy of Christianity in addressing practical concerns. Though the Westerners' goal was to transmit a holistic, universal Christianity, Chinese inevitably were selective. New information and concepts were understood within an existing mindset. One baptismal candidate, in assessing Christianity, remarked that Christianity was useful insofar as it instilled morality and offered the protection of a powerful God. Rudolf Lechler reported with some dismay that when he asked a recently baptized scholar about his beliefs, the convert replied that as compared with actual Chinese mores and practices, Christianity was superior, but as compared with the teachings of Confucius and Mencius, it was superfluous.[4]

Several Chinese Union preachers who later became outstanding Chinese assistants had originally sought baptism and union membership for personal economic reasons. They internalized their Christianity only as they assumed the role and responsibilities of an evangelist. How then does one define a Christian? When could one say that the conversion of these "rice Christians" occurred? Or is such a question inappropriate?

Pure transmission of a religion is, of course, impossible, because communication inevitably happens in context and through persons.[5] The personali-

3. This was true of both the Chinese Union members and some Chinese assistants associated with other mission societies in the mid-nineteenth century. See Jean-Paul Wiest, "Was God Partial to the Hakka People?" pp. 87-106, and Jessie G. Lutz, "A Profile of Chinese Protestant Evangelists in the Mid-Nineteenth Century," pp. 67-86, both in Ku and De Ridder, eds., *Authentic Chinese Christianity*.

4. Lechler, "Dritter Quartalbericht," Hong Kong, 1866, Basler Missionsgesellschaft Archives, China (BMG), A-1.5, no. 21; Eppler, *Geschichte der Basler Mission, 1815-1899* (Basel: Verlag der Missionsbuchhandlung, 1900), p. 227.

5. Andrew F. Walls, *The Missionary Movement in Christian History: Studies in the Trans-*

ties and cultures of the evangelist and the inquirer enter into the conversion process. This was especially true during the initial stages of the Protestant mission in China, for many of the pioneer generation of Protestant missionaries were strong, high-achieving individuals.[6] Among these, Karl Gützlaff was doubtless the prime example. This advance guard might not have been highly educated or have attended elite colleges, but quite a few were ambitious, interested students who continued their self-education. Products of the revivalist traditions, they came out of evangelical backgrounds and shared a common cultural framework that equated Western civilization with Christendom. The first English missionaries to China, for example, all belonged to dissenting churches rather than the established Church of England. Yet there was room for differences in methodology and interpretation. Few precedents guided their work, since they considered Roman Catholicism to be heresy. Their inclination was either to ignore previous Catholic missions or to treat them as negative examples. The China field, furthermore, was so replete with unknowns that the sending societies could offer only minimal guidelines. During the 1840s an exchange of letters between China missionary and home society could take up to six months. Slow communications meant that the first Protestant missionaries had considerable freedom to adjust praxis to context.

In such an environment, numerous questions inevitably arose. Which should receive priority, spreading the Good News to as many Chinese as quickly as possible, replicating Western denominational churches, or founding Christian communities? For those who believed that all heathens stood on the brink of damnation, choosing between extensive and intensive evangelizing could be stressful. What was necessary to merit baptism? Who had the authority to baptize — only institutionally ordained ministers, or could designated Chinese assistants baptize as well? What was acceptable proof of conversion? What degree of adaptation was permissible? Should one build on Chinese teachings or was a confrontational, displacement approach required?

Mid-nineteenth-century Protestant missionaries customarily hoped for a conviction of sin, a personal spiritual awakening, acceptance of Christ as the means to salvation, and a determination henceforth to lead a moral life. For

---

mission of Faith (Maryknoll, NY: Orbis Books, 1996), pp. xvii, 51; Nicolas Standaert, "Christianity in Late Ming and Early Qing China as a Case of Cultural Transmission," in *China and Christianity: Burdened Past, Hopeful Future,* ed. Stephen Uhalley Jr. and Xiaoxin Wu (Armonk, NY: M. E. Sharpe, 2001), pp. 81-116.

6. Daniel Bays, "Missions and Christians in Modern China, 1850-1950" (paper delivered at the Symposium on American Missionaries and Social Change in China, Linfield College, OR, 14-17 July 1994).

Protestants, this emotional experience constituted conversion; it could be dated from a moment in time. Conversion as viewed by many scholars today, however, is more commonly considered a process involving several stages, often beginning with a quest for meaning in life and an encounter with a religious teacher. These experiences could occur in either order, and sometimes they were preceded by a personal crisis. Interaction ensued as the inquirer learned of new doctrines, participated in rituals, and formed new relationships. Commitment might follow, with rituals of incorporation such as baptism, but even this was sometimes only the first step toward a personal transformation. Rejection or temporary reversion was possible during any stage.[7]

In a non-Christian society, the conversionary process, rather than the conversionary event, was typical. For the first Chinese converts, socialization into Christianity was not a possibility, and there was no nominal Christianity to act as a reference group. Converts were often subjected to ostracism or persecution by kinfolk, so that it behooved a Chinese evangelist to concentrate first on converting his own family. Only later in the century do we find instances of socialization into Christianity within Chinese Christian families, and even today Christianity is a minority religion in China. Chinese society in the nineteenth century, as today, lacked support mechanisms for members of non-orthodox groups. Whether a Confucian society as in the nineteenth century or a communist society today, aid has to be provided by the religious community itself, with the result that Christian communities, like Chinese sect groups, assumed a variety of functions beyond religious worship and instruction.

China missionaries constantly complained that the Chinese lacked a sense of sin. Largely absent from Chinese thought was the dualism so pervasive in the West: good versus evil, God versus Satan, absolute truth versus absolute falsity. More typical was the principle of complementarity, as in the concepts of yin-yang and the five elements. Theodor Hamberg reported his conversation with a baptized assistant:

> "Zhen! Are you a sinner?" At this question he looked astonished and answered in the negative. "Have you no sin?" "No, none." "And have you never sinned earlier?" "No, Never." I now went through the Ten Commandments with him and attempted to make it clear to him that he was a sinner. All this was in vain. He stuck to his position that from his youth on he had worshiped the one true God and adhered to His commandments.

7. Lewis Rambo and Charles E. Farhadian, "Converting: Stages of Religious Change," in Lamb and Bryant, eds., *Religious Conversion*, pp. 23-34.

"In that case, can you say that you need no Savior?" "It is good to pray to Him; He wants us to believe in him as a Savior in tribute to His holiness." All this disappointed me very much, but I, nevertheless, still love him and I am convinced that he is more righteous than many of the others. May the Lord bring him to the realization that he is a sinner.[8]

Not only was Zhen unable to understand the Western concept of original sin, but he retained the Chinese perception that deities needed the attention of human disciples.

Such experiences presented Protestant missionaries with a dilemma as to when they should administer baptism, signifying acceptance as a converted Christian and granting church membership. Despite their claim to the right of definition, they could reach no consensus on the criteria and timing of baptism. What was the proper response when faced with an apparently sincere profession of faith lacking a conviction of sin and an expression of repentance? One American missionary acknowledged, "I have come to the conclusion that deep and pungent convictions are not to be looked for in the heathen when they first become converts to Christianity. . . . It has not had time to work down into the heart."[9] In the baptism of Zhen, who admitted no sin, the pietist definition of conversion had obviously been compromised. Other missionaries delayed baptism until the inquirer had undergone extensive instruction in Christian doctrine.

Western missionaries who accepted Chinese as converts and baptized them often did so with strong misgivings. The converts did not correspond to the European idea of a Christian convert, but they were as close as the European missionary could expect within the context of the Chinese environment. Does this mean that the Western missionaries accepted Chinese Christianity as fully authentic? The answer is no. For all of them, a conviction of personal sinfulness was a major prerequisite of conversion. The whole Protestant process of conversion hinged on this. Without a sense of personal and original sin, one could not seek repentance and salvation. Consequently, to baptize someone who had not gone through the stages of guilt, repentance, and acceptance of divine forgiveness was a violation of Christian standards. Yet the missionaries did baptize Chinese who did not meet this standard, and these missionaries had strong guilt feelings over their administration of bap-

8. Hamberg and Lechler to Inspector, Hong Kong, 21 September 1847, BMG, A-1.1 (1B), no. 14. Hamberg is the author, though there are interjections by Lechler. Also quoted in translation in Jessie G. Lutz and R. R. Lutz, *Hakka Chinese Confront Protestant Christianity, 1850-1900* (Armonk, NY: M. E. Sharpe, 1998), p. 241.

9. Quoted in Walls, *The Missionary Movement*, p. 85.

tism to such Chinese. Rudolf Lechler remarked that he could not rely on Gützlaff's Chinese Union members in his work in northeast Guangdung because these Chinese Union members were not full fledged Christian. [10] In fact, however, Lechler did rely on such members to teach school, to gain entré to villages and initiate contacts, and to assist him in numerous ways.

These may have been Chinese Christians, but they weren't Christians in the Western sense. Their understanding of Christianity did not conform to the Western idea of Christianity. Later, when the Western missionaries stood in judgment on the Chinese Union members during Gützlaff's absence from China, they did not accept the outlook and knowledge of the Chinese Union members as authentically Christian. Yet these Union members knew the familiar stories of the Bible, especially the story of Jesus' life; they knew the Ten Commandments and they knew the Creed. For the Western evangelicals, however, the memorization of biblical stories, the Ten Commandments, and the Creed did not equate to Christianity. Even if the knowledge of these things went beyond memorization, knowledge and faith were two entirely different matters. Most nineteenth-century Protestant missionaries adhered to this point of view even when they permitted conversion to take place. As a result, the missionaries of the mid-nineteenth century were not especially impressed by the fact that Gützlaff's former converts were willing to help them and to shield them from possible detection.

The Founding of the Chinese Union

Like the majority of early Protestant evangelists, Gützlaff initially assumed that the conversion of China to Christianity would be achieved by Western missionaries. His 1835 essay in the *Chinese Repository* discussing the means of extending and establishing Christianity was entirely devoted to the recruitment of qualified missionaries and the nature of their work in China.[11] Crucial for effective China missionaries were both a facility for languages and a willingness to reside in the interior, even at the risk of losing one's life. Though Gützlaff condemned the "heretical doctrines" of the seventeenth-century Jesuit missionaries, he admired their dedication, zeal, and courage.

10. See Lechler's comments in Lechler to Inspector, Yamtsau, 30 October 1852, and his comments during the joint meeting with Hamberg and Winnes, 17-18 December 1852, in Hong Kong, BMG A1.2, nos. 12 and 17.

11. Philosinensis [Gützlaff], "Christian Missions in China: Remarks on the Means and Measures for Extending and Establishing Christianity," *Chinese Repository* (hereafter *CRep*) 3 (1834): 559-68.

Surely Protestants could recruit their equals in love of the Savior and readiness to give all to China. He was critical of missionaries who lived in the "English style" and of those scholarly types who concentrated their energies on mastering written Chinese. The Chinese language was difficult, and to be effective, a missionary must master spoken mandarin and also a Chinese dialect; the latter was something that few of the current missionaries had achieved. Those without linguistic skills should be sent to other fields. In recommending educational work, Gützlaff was interested only in the training of Chinese assistants; he did not accept education as a means of conversion. Secondary, not primary schools, should be fostered by missionaries, for Chinese workers ought first to gain competency in classical Chinese, best mastered in traditional schools. Gützlaff did make an exception for women's education; he was an early advocate of schools for women. The conversion of China required that "the female sex obtains its proper rank in society," he wrote.[12]

Gützlaff stated that a convert should be judged by his deeds, not by his knowledge of Christian doctrine: "Who shall be considered converts, and what rites they shall relinquish, and what retain, can be determined only by the rules of the Gospel. If none but those who are under the influence of the divine Spirit are to be admitted as candidates for baptism, and these tried by our Savior's test, 'ye shall know them by their works,' a distinct line will be drawn between the pagan and the Christian."[13] Despite the fact that Gützlaff believed in the pietist definition of conversion, with its stress on repentance and a conviction of sin, his optimistic temperament encouraged him to emphasize the positive aspects of Christian teachings. His list of fundamental Christian doctrines included redemption through the Savior, grace, sanctification, an all-powerful God, and human obligation to Him.

Gützlaff had been training Chinese to assist him in spreading the gospel ever since the beginning of his mission in Asia. When Gützlaff departed Southeast Asia in 1831, he left behind a Chinese convert whom he had dispatched to Annam to carry the message of salvation. Preaching assistants accompanied Gützlaff on his visits to villages in the Macao-Canton region, and he often provided newly arrived missionaries with assistants as well as language teachers. In 1838 Gützlaff sent two of his assistants to the border of Jiangxi and Guangdong to proselytize, and when they returned with glowing reports of converting relatives, they received funds to repeat the journey. The outbreak of the Opium War in 1839, however, interrupted his experiment with Chinese evangelists working on their own in the interior. Placing his as-

---

12. Philosinensis, "Christian Missions in China," p. 564.
13. Philosinensis, "Christian Missions in China," p. 560.

sistants under the care of the Baptist missionary Issachar Roberts, Gützlaff accompanied the British north to the Yangtze and acted as civil magistrate at occupied Zhoushan and Ningbo. He returned to Macao in 1841 to find his little band largely dispersed, though a few of his converts welcomed him. Once again, he gathered Chinese believers for early morning and evening instruction leading toward baptism, and he had some of his converts accompany him on local weekend itinerations preparatory to independent work as colporteurs and preachers. In 1844 Gützlaff gave his corps of assistants the title Chinese Association for Propagating the Gospel, later changed to Chinese Union or *Han hui*. The union motto, provided in both English and Chinese, came from Isaiah:

> Behold these shall come from far; and lo, these from the north and from the west; and these from the land of Sinim. Sing O Heavens; and be joyful, O earth; and break forth into singing, O mountains; for the LORD has comforted his people and will have mercy upon his afflicted. (Isaiah 49:12-13)

In the union's first year, members reported a total of 262 baptisms, mostly in Hong Kong and its environs; a significant proportion came from the Hakka ethnic minority.[14]

For many reasons Gützlaff had become convinced that Chinese, not foreigners, must effect the conversion of China. By the 1840s he was isolated from the missionary community in Hong Kong and Canton and rarely joined in its activities. Yet, despite holding a full-time civil job, he was driven by a sense of urgency to bring salvation to the heathen. The Chinese masses must be rescued from damnation and be morally reformed by Christianity. But foreigners were permitted to reside only in the five treaty ports, while his own civil service position restricted the radius of his mission work to the Hong Kong–Canton nexus. He, along with all other Protestant missionaries in China, had converted only a handful of Chinese. The minimal fruits of three decades of missionary efforts, furthermore, had been immensely costly; after years of language study to ready themselves, missionaries all too often had their careers terminated by illness, death, or resignation. Gützlaff craved success after years of frustration and disappointment. "The evange-

14. Gützlaff, *Chinesesiche Berichte von der Mitte des Jahres 1841 bis zum Schluss des Jahres 1846* (Cassel: Vorstand der Chinesischen Stiftung, 1850), pp. 1-2, 50-53, 68; Schlyter, *Karl Gützlaff als Missionar in China* (Lund: C. W. K. Gleerup, 1946), p. 98; A. H. Broomhall, *Hudson Taylor and China's Open Century*, vols. 1-3 (London: Hodder and Stoughton, 1981-1982), 1:311-17.

lization of the world in this generation" would become a popular slogan during the late nineteenth century. "Evangelization of China in my lifetime" had been Gützlaff's driving ambition ever since he first arrived in East Asia in 1827.

Gützlaff's plan was to recruit missionaries to instruct, supervise, and sustain a corps of national preachers who would do the actual evangelizing. He believed that the cultural gap between Westerner and Chinese and the difficulties of attaining true language facility were so great that few missionaries could ever communicate effectively with the masses. A Chinese Christian could always interact with the populace more effectively than a foreign missionary. As evidence, he could point to the fact that the majority of Christian converts thus far had actually been made by Chinese workers rather than by missionaries. Chinese, moreover, were free to travel throughout China, and they could often make contacts through kinship ties. The gospel must be presented as God's gift of grace, not as the gift of foreigners or as a teaching of the foreign world, a translation process more easily achieved by Chinese than Westerners. Missionaries, however, could mitigate their foreignness by going Chinese: wearing Chinese-style dress, including the queue, adopting Chinese cuisine, and living among the Chinese, preferably in the interior.[15]

Theologically, Gützlaff advocated extensive, as opposed to intensive, evangelization. Jesus had commanded his followers to carry the gospel to all peoples. Establishing denominational churches was not his goal. Converting Chinese through primary schools was too slow. Christian communities would come into existence and continuing instruction would occur after baptism, but a Christian as defined by Gützlaff was one who had seen the light and accepted Jesus' offer of grace. Gützlaff did not require competence in the theology of Western Christianity before acceptance as a Christian, nor was he interested in the teachings and rituals specific to denominations. He believed that the greater the simplicity and earnestness with which the doctrines of a crucified Christ were taught, the more effective would be the message. With his conviction that the Holy Spirit was the ultimate source of all conversion and could accomplish all things came an unbounded faith in the power of the Word. The work of the Chinese preachers, therefore, could be supplemented by Chinese colporteurs to distribute thousands of Bibles, New Testaments, and religious tracts. Each of these stimuli to the founding of the Chinese Union — personal, methodological, and theological — left ample room for controversy. At the same time, such a minimalist theology enabled Chinese evangelists to adapt teachings and rituals to their clientele.

15. Gützlaff, *Chinesesiche Berichte*, p. 256.

Chinese evangelists with the Basel Mission Society   (Source: Basel Mission Archive)

In the beginning Gützlaff gave careful attention to the selection and training of Chinese Union workers. They should, he wrote, be deeply imbued with Christian grace and able to communicate religious truth.[16] If they were to attract listeners, they should be educated, for the Chinese disdained the illiterate. They were to go through a three-stage trial period, from probationer to candidate to preacher; an examination, which consisted of discoursing on an assigned subject, was required to attain preacher status and a salary.[17] In several instances, Gützlaff refused baptism until the probationers had received further instruction. During their training they attended regular prayer ses-

16. "Requisites for the foreign preachers of the Gospel who wish to combine their efforts with the Associations now forming for the conversion of Eastern Asia," Archive of the Missions Library of Selly Oak College, photocopy of Gützlaff materials from Overseas Missionary Fellowship Archives (hereafter Selly Oak, OMFA), manuscript, n.d.

17. Genähr, "Tagebuch," 26 May 1847, Vereinte Evangelishe Mission, Archives of Rheinische Missionsgesellschaft (hereafter VEM), Genähr Korrespondenz and Tagebucher. Genähr remarked, however: "To my way of thinking, this examination bears no resemblance to a German examination."

sions and instruction classes held by Gützlaff, while in the early evening and on Sundays they accompanied him on preaching tours. Often they visited Hakka laborers, who seemed more receptive to the gospel than most Chinese. Once a Chinese preacher began to journey into the interior on his own, he was accompanied by a partner, so that each could check on the other, and he was obliged to keep a daily journal to be presented to Gützlaff on return. Compensation was to be sufficient to cover travel expenses only, for a larger salary might attract unworthy candidates. If God brought the Chinese preacher success in attaining converts, and if he was willing to suffer for the cross, he might be looked upon as having been called to the work, according to Gützlaff.[18]

Detailed records in English and Chinese conveyed the impression of authenticity. The name of each evangelist, the date of his departure, his destination, and the estimated length of his assignment were registered. Another list gave, province by province, the identity of each station, its latitude and longitude, the workers there, and a brief comment on accomplishments. Every reported baptism, with name and location in Chinese, was enumerated.[19]

Expansion

Gützlaff, meanwhile, cultivated support in Great Britain and Europe. He regularly spent his evenings writing to every missionary society and friend of missions he knew. The imperial edicts of 1844 and 1846 had granted tolerance to Catholics, and soon thereafter this was interpreted to include Protestants as well. Buoyed by assurances of legality, Gützlaff waxed eloquent about the possibilities of penetrating all of China's provinces, and even Tibet, Korea, and Japan. Evangelists had only to follow the example of the apostles, and China's millions would receive the glad news of salvation. A conscious effort was made to present the Chinese Union as a Chinese enterprise, in both leadership and membership. Reporting under Gützlaff's Chinese name Gaihan (*aihan*, lover of the Chinese), he repeated claims of Chinese converts forsaking their idols and the rise of numerous Chinese Christian communities.[20]

18. "Requisites for the foreign preachers," Selly Oak, OMFA.

19. Chinese Union Members, Selly Oak, OMFA. These records are one of the few places where one can find the full Chinese names, with Chinese characters, for Chinese Christians. Many mission reports either do not provide the names of Chinese assistants and converts or provide the transliteration for only part of the name, sometimes the surname and sometimes the given name.

20. Gützlaff, *Chinesesiche Berichte*, pp. 124, 186, 191, 203-4, 291. These reports were pub-

He sent translations of letters attributed to Chinese Union members in which they expressed joy upon receiving promise of redemption and ventured to hope that all Chinese might be so privileged.[21] Records of the evangelists sent out, payments to Chinese, and lists of converts were signed by Zhang Qiyao, secretary of the union, or by the Chinese auditor rather than Gützlaff.[22] Funds to support hundreds of Chinese evangelists and tens of Western mentors ready to sacrifice all in a heroic crusade were required.

Gützlaff's astute and ever-sanguine publicity fell on fertile ground. The Second Great Awakening had generated a new awareness of the Christian obligation to missions. Moreover, churches had discovered that sponsoring overseas missions often vitalized home congregations. Appealing to a rising German nationalism, Gützlaff noted that Germans were far behind Americans and British in recognizing their moral duty to the heathen. Why not take advantage of the opportunity to rectify their neglect by supporting the Chinese Union? The Opium War had further aroused interest in China, as it had raised hopes of an open door for Bibles and missionaries along with British cottons and other trade items.

One of Gützlaff's most enthusiastic supporters and publicists was Christian G. Barth, author of a popular compilation of biblical stories, a history of the church, and editor of *Calwer Missionsblatt*. The lead article of the 1 November 1844 issue of the magazine carried the title "Morgenroth in China's Nacht" (Dawn in China's night).[23] It commended to its readers the needs of China and called attention to Gützlaff's project. Letters and reports by Gützlaff and Chinese Union members became regular features of the *Calwer Missionsblatt*. Barth urged the Basel and Rhenish mission societies to answer Gützlaff's call for Western evangelists to work with Gützlaff and the Chinese Union. Other magazines opened their pages to Gützlaff's exhortations, and

lished by Christian G. Barth in *Calwer Missionsblatt* before being issued as a separate volume in 1850. See also the frequent quotations from Gützlaff's letters in *Jahresbericht des evangelischen Missions-Verein in Kurhessen*, 1846, 1847.

21. Journals and letters of Chinese Union members, Selly Oak, OMFA. There are both Chinese and English versions in many cases. Some of the letters and journals were published in Gützlaff, *Chinesesiche Berichte;* see, for example, pp. 149-50, 156-57, 163-79.

22. Sometimes the reports were transcribed by one of the rescued Japanese sailors. The Chinese Union's secretary and auditor and the converted sailor were all employees in Gützlaff's secretarial office.

23. Barth had known Gützlaff personally before Gützlaff left for China, and he had earlier publicized many of Gützlaff's writings, including Gützlaff's journals of his trips along the China coast. Gützlaff translated Barth's history of the church from German into Chinese, under the title *Shenghui zhishi,* and distributed it widely.

numerous church congregations expressed interest and support. The king of Prussia donated 400 dollars to the great cause.

Reward came with the departure in November 1846 of four missionaries consigned to Gützlaff and the Chinese Union: Theodor Hamberg and Rudolf Lechler of the Basel Missionary Society and Ferdinand Genähr and Heinrich Köster of the Rhenish (Barmen) Missionary Society. In March 1847 Gützlaff welcomed them to Hong Kong and almost immediately sent them to Chinese quarters with their language teachers and assistants.[24] Each was allocated Chinese Union helpers, with whom he was to go on a preaching tour the following Sunday — the assistants and not the Westerner, obviously, doing the evangelizing. Gützlaff assigned them to begin reading his Chinese translation of the Gospel of John, write 300 characters a day, study his Chinese grammar, and practice the spoken dialect. Each was to learn a different dialect of southeast China. In the evenings they were to go out among the populace with Chinese Union members from the preparatory class. Total immersion indeed!

The Chinese Union expanded rapidly. Gützlaff had suffered several bouts of illness during his years in China, and now both he and his wife were in declining health. He was in a hurry and threw caution to the winds. Baptisms came quickly as workers were appointed after a few weeks of instruction. Evangelists were dispatched deep into China despite the impossibility of supervising them. They allegedly distributed tens of thousands of Bibles and tracts on stopovers and at examination sites. Gützlaff began to envision his dream becoming a reality, his twenty years of labor for the Chinese justified. As Genähr wrote, "China's conversion and the conversion of the Chinese, that is the refrain of his pronouncements, deeds, and prayers. It goes to bed with him and rises with him, and he finds rest only when something is accomplished to bring his goal closer."[25] Though the figures are incomplete and differ according to source, the table on page 228 approximates the claims. Generally, about 40 percent of the evangelists, stations, and baptisms were credited to Guangdong, but Guangxi, Fujian, and Jiangxi were well represented. By 1849 Gützlaff reported one or more representatives in twelve provinces, with some as far afield as Sizhuan, Yunnan, Gansu, Hainan, and Liaoning.

The Chinese Union also published its own literature for distribution and, according to Gützlaff, several stations arranged for local printers in the interior to issue cheap woodblock editions. Funds came from the British and For-

---

24. Lechler to Inspector, Victoria, 22 March 1847, BMG, A-1.1, 1846-1847, no. 4; Hamberg to Inspector, Hong Kong, 27 March 1847, BMG, A-1.1, 1846-1847, no. 6; Genähr to Deputation, Hong Kong, March 1847, Vereinte Evanglische Mission, Archives of Rheinische Missionsgesellschaft (hereafter VEM), Genähr Korrespondenz.

25. Genähr to Inspector, Hong Kong, 23 April 1847, VEM, Genähr Korrespondenz.

Chinese Union Membership and Converts[26]

	Members	Preachers	Converts	Stations
1844	20	—	262	—
1845	80	—	88	—
1846	179	36	601	—
1847	366	50	655	31
1848	1,000	100	487	—
Jan.-Sept. 1849		130	695	113

eign Bible Society and the American Bible Society, which were eager to have the Bible circulated throughout China. Most of the works were Gützlaff's translations: the Old and New Testaments, the History of the Bible (Shengshu zhi shi) and History of the Church (Shenghui zhi shi), the Augsburg Confession (Huangheng xinshi), selections from the Anglican prayer book (Shenghui daozhi), and religious tracts such as "Lord Jesus, Savior of the World" (Jiu shi zhu Yehsu), "God, the Creator" (Shangdi chuangdao), and "God, the Great Lord of All Things" (Shangdi wanwu zhi dazhu). In addition, several of Gützlaff's secular works were printed and distributed: "Universal Geography" (Wanguo dili quantuji), "A Comprehensive Account of England" (Da Yingguo tongzhi), and "History of the World" (Gujin wanguo gangjian).[27]

Expenses were running into thousands of dollars. Yet Gützlaff had lost the personal funds that he had invested in Australia for support of the Chinese Union. Repeated inquiries to his Australian agent brought only reports of the bursting of the real estate bubble and widespread bank failures.[28] Driven by his vision of a Christian China, he would go to Europe to found support societies for thousands of Chinese evangelists and he would recruit dozens of men and women to instruct the national preachers. Lonely after the death of his wife in April, he would visit family, friends, and patrons for the first time in twenty years.

26. Sources: Selly Oak, Papers Relating to Gützlaff; Jahresbericht des evangelischen Missions-Verein Kurhessen, 1846, p. 54; A. J. Broomhall, 1: 317; Schlyter, Karl Gützlaff, p. 297; Genähr, Tagebuch, 2 April 1847, VEM.

27. "Books and Tracts published by the Chinese Union," Selly Oak, OMFA. Gützlaff reported in 1849 that the Chinese Union had published more than fifty tracts.

28. Jardine Matheson Archives (hereafter, J-M Archives), S 1, 462, 3 March 1846; 10 June 1849. The microfilm is almost illegible, so it is not possible to provide full documentation.

The European Tour

Gützlaff's tour of England and Europe opened on a triumphal note.[29] Preceded by an aura of romance and fame, Gützlaff was equal to expectations. He had a genius for inspiring confidence and enthusiasm upon initial contact, and he made the most of it. Often he wore Chinese garb; he identified himself as a Chinese citizen and spoke of "our Emperor," "our country," and "our people." He was, according to one writer, like electricity.[30] Setting himself a brutal schedule which required travel by night after twelve-hour days of lectures, meetings with executive committees of mission societies, sermons, and more, he conducted a whirlwind tour of Europe.

The tour was remarkably comprehensive. In the British Isles it included England, Ireland, and Scotland. On the continent it included Holland, Belgium, Paris, France, Switzerland, many of the German principalities, parts of Bohemia, Moravia, Austria, Hungary, and parts of the Russian Empire, including Poland, Lithuania, Finland, and the Russian capital, St. Petersburg. He also visited Sweden, Denmark, Italy, a Greek island, and the coastal strip of Greece's Peloponnesian Peninsula. The only major European countries Gützlaff omitted were Norway, Spain, Portugal, and European Turkey. This extensive tour he completed in less than a year's time.

Gützlaff began his mission tour of Europe in London, where he arrived in January 1850. The first mission supporter to greet him was Charles Young, who in turn put Gützlaff in contact with Richard Ball, leader of a group of Chinese Union supporters located primarily in southwest England. Ball arranged to have Gützlaff attend a meeting of China mission supporters at the home of the Howard family in the London suburb of Tottenham. Under Gützlaff's influence, the Howards founded the second major support organization for the Chinese Union (the first was the *Chinesische Stiftung,* founded some years earlier in Cassel, capital of Electoral Hesse). The new organization adopted the name "Association for Furthering the Promulgation of the Gospel in China and the Adjacent Countries by Means of Native Evangelists." Later the name was changed to "Chinese Evangelization Society." Two Howards, Eliot and Luke, were present, and the Howard home in Tottenham served for a time as the major center of the organization. Richard Ball and

---

29. Detailed coverage of Gützlaff's European tour is provided in H. Schlyter, *Der China-Missionar Karl Gützlaff und seine Heimatbasis: Studien über das Interesse des Abendlands an der Mission des China* (Lund: C. W. K. Gleerup, 1976).

30. A. Tidman to J. Legge, London, 24 January 1850, Church World Mission Society (hereafter CWM), London Missionary Society (hereafter LMS), East China, Outgoing Correspondence, Box 4.

George Pearse were elected to the shared position of secretary, with Ball playing the leading role as spokesman and fundraiser for the organization. The founding group was made up, for the most part, of lawyers, stockbrokers, businessmen, and Protestant ministers. Among its members was the Rev. Dr. C. F. A. Steinkopff, cofounder and member of the British and Foreign Bible Society.[31] Though Gützlaff's first direct encounter with Steinkopff occurred during his trip to Europe, the two had often corresponded with one another regarding the publication and distribution of Bibles. Richard Ball served during Gützlaff's Europe tour as a sort of clearinghouse for correspondence aimed at the missionary and for published articles that referred to Gützlaff's activities or publications. Gützlaff frequently wrote him and asked him to supply printed materials to newly founded support societies.[32]

One important aspect of the Chinese Evangelization Society is deserving of special attention. Gützlaff was a pietist, and as such was uninterested in denominational theology. The major support organizations he founded, especially the ones that survived, attracted dissenters in Great Britain. In Germany, most were affiliated with the Evangelical Alliance, a loose European association of interdenominational evangelical Protestants. This orientation was reflected in the British society's founding document, co-written by Richard Ball and George Pearse, the two secretaries:

> The promoters of it [the Association] have no desire to interfere with any existing Societies, or trench upon their means. They [the promoters] earnestly desire the cooperation of all who love the Savior and who can cordially combine, *on purely unsectarian grounds,* for the spread of the knowledge of the divine Savior. The Association will in no way be responsible for, or interfere with, the internal organization or arrangements which are or may be adopted by those on the spot who are engaged in this work. . . . The constitution of the Society is catholic, and the objects before it simply the furtherance of Christ's cause and honor in China, without reference to any denominational views.[33]

31. *Quartalberichte der chinesischen Stiftung* 2 (1850): 50.

32. "The Report of the Chinese Society for Furthering the Promulgation of the Gospel in China, and the Adjacent Countries, by Means of Native Evangelists, 1851," *The Chinese Missionary Gleaner* 1.1 (June 1851): 1-2. For further detail on Ball's relationship with Gützlaff, see George Hood, "The Gützlaff Papers, Selly Oak Colleges, Birmingham, England" (paper presented at a meeting of the Yale-Edinburgh Group, Edinburgh, 1999).

33. "Report of the Chinese Society for Furthering the Promulgation of the Gospel in China," pp. 2-3.

This outlook was characteristic of most of Gützlaff's European supporters, except in the case of Holland, where Gützlaff was closely identified with the Dutch Missionary Society (Nederlandsch Zendeling Genootschap [NZG]) and the Dutch Reformed Church. In Holland he had the enthusiastic support of both the evangelicals and the sectarians.

Despite the hostility of established mission societies, especially the London Mission Society, Gützlaff had a considerable following in Great Britain. For example, in early 1848 Miss Chesney, of Ballincollig, Cork County, Ireland, marshaled a group of Chinese Union supporters and began, on behalf of this Irish group, sending contributions to the Chinese Union. [34] She sent the equivalent of 543 Spanish dollars. Richard Ball sent a contribution of 240 Spanish dollars in September 1849 and another contribution of 240 Spanish dollars in March 1850. Ball was doubtless collecting from the same people who later supported the Chinese Evangelization Society, and his contribution of March 1850 came from that society. Obviously Gützlaff had a number of contributing supporters in the British Isles well before he arrived there in person.

After completing his tour of Scotland in March 1850, Gützlaff crossed the English channel and went to Holland. There he suffered an attack of rheumatic fever and was consequently joined by an English supporter, Dora Gabriel, who acted as nurse and companion and who, in September, married Gützlaff.[35] In Holland Gützlaff was hailed as a native son because of the fact that he had lived and studied there and had functioned for several years as a Dutch missionary in the East Indies. Moreover, he was fluent in Dutch, addressed his audiences in their native language, and wrote letters and notes in Dutch to various persons and organizations. He had also held an honorary doctor's degree from the University of Gröningen for the last half-dozen years. Though Bernhard Ledeboer, the former inspector of the Dutch Missionary Society, and other important Dutch acquaintances of Gützlaff had passed from the scene, Ledeboer's son had succeeded his father as head of the Dutch Missionary Society, and Gützlaff had been carrying on a correspondence with him and other important Dutch personages for some years. Hence Gützlaff was very much a known personality when he arrived in Holland in 1850.

34. "Report of the Chinese Society for Furthering the Promulgation of the Gospel in China," p. 1. Also see "Übersicht der Einnahmen und Ausgaben des Chinesischen Vereins (Chinese Union) in Hongkong von September 1849 bis April 1850," *Quartalberichte der chinesischen Stiftung* 2 (June 1850): 93.

35. Gutzlaff to Hamberg, Rotterdam, 15 May 1850, Selly Oak Correspondence; Gutzlaff to Ball, Berlin, 4 June 1850, Selly Oak Correspondence; Gutzlaff to Ball, Alexandria, Egypt, 9 November 1850, Selly Oak Correspondence. Rheumatic fever was a generic term in the nineteenth century.

Rotterdam, the seat of the Dutch Missionary Society, was the first Dutch city in which Gützlaff held conferences and made speeches. From Rotterdam he went to Zeist, the main seat of the Moravians in Holland. When several Moravians expressed the wish to undertake a mission in the West Indies, Gützlaff gave them every encouragement.[36] From Zeist he went on to numerous Dutch cities and, in the process, founded support societies in many of them. Later, the support society in Amsterdam constituted itself as a kind of headquarters and succeeded in persuading many of the Dutch support societies to affiliate with it as the head association. During these travels in Holland, Gützlaff had an audience with the queen, who agreed to become honorary president of the many women's support societies he founded.

It is hard for us today to visualize the impact Karl Güzlaff had on the Europeans in 1850. If we were to pick a historical personality who could have had a similar impact on the Europeans of his era, we might follow A. J. Broomhall in selecting Lawrence of Arabia for comparison.[37] Both persons were surrounded with an aura of heroism and romance. Both had engaged in exciting and hazardous adventures, and both appeared in costume, Lawrence as an Arab and Gützlaff as a Chinese. Backed by his fame as a writer of and chief participant in missionary adventure stories, he could, with his dynamic personality, sweep large and small audiences off their feet.

In April Gützlaff made two side trips from Holland, one to Brussels and one to Paris, which were largely Roman Catholic but had significant Protestant minorities. The main event in both cities was a conference of Protestant pastors that drew church leaders from various areas of the two countries. In addition to speaking at these conferences, Gützlaff also spoke in other venues, including Roman Catholic ones. Gützlaff succeeded in founding support societies in both Brussels and Paris. The text of a speech which Gützlaff made in Brussels on 11 April 1850 was printed in the Belgium mission magazine *Glenau Missionaire,* and was later translated into German and published in the *Quartalsberichte der Chinesische Stiftung.* In that speech Gützlaff commented on the geographical and cultural isolation of China, on the arrogant attitude of Chinese toward all other peoples, whom they classified as "barbarians," and on the history of Christianity in China from ancient times up through his own missionary activities in China. The latter he capped with an ardent appeal for funds. He included, however, a rare acknowledgment of

36. Karl Gützlaff, *Bericht seiner Reise von China nach England und durch die verschiedenen Länder Europa's im Interesse der Chinesischen Mission* (Cassel: Chinesische Stiftung, 1851), p. 14.

37. Broomhall, *Hudson Taylor and China's Open Century,* 1:323.

his secular responsibilities: "I myself am not a missionary in the usual sense of the word but am under contract as a translator and secretary in the service of the English government. My responsibilities center on negotiations with the Chinese officials. However, in fact all my powers and means are devoted to the evangelization of the large empire to which God Himself has directed my steps." This admission appears not to have discouraged the Belgians, for they established a support society in Brussels to contribute funds to the Chinese Union via Richard Ball and the Chinese Evangelization Society.[38]

In May Gützlaff started his tour of cities in the German Confederation, beginning with Electoral Hesse. His first stop was in Treysa, where he was joined by Friedrich Wilhelm Krummacher, pastor of the Holy Trinity [Dreifaltigkeits] Church in Berlin.[39] Krummacher then accompanied Gützlaff on his tour through Electoral Hesse. Gützlaff's most important stop was in Cassel, the location of the Chinese Union's oldest support society, the *Chinesische Stiftung*, founded by the leaders of the Evangelical Mission Society of Electoral Hesse. In its yearbook for 1849, the Cassel Mission Society anticipated Gützlaff's forthcoming tour. They stated that one of the most important events of 1850 would be seeing Gützlaff face to face and receiving verbal communications regarding China's evangelization from one who had for twenty years shown himself to be "the chosen vessel of God."[40]

The Cassel society's anticipation of Gützlaff's visit was related to the interests and activities of its dominant officer, C. F. Elvers, chief justice of Electoral Hesse's Supreme Court of Appeals. Elvers had been following Gützlaff's career for several years, and he hoped to advance the fortunes of the Cassel Mission Society by associating that organization's development with the progress of Gützlaff's Chinese Union. He was simultaneously interested in promoting his own personal career. One of his steps had been the founding in December 1846 of an alter ego of the Cassel society, with an identical governing committee, which he would head. Initially called the *Deutsch-Chinesische Stiftung*, Elvers soon changed its name to *Chinesische Stiftung* in hopes of finding support among Protestants not only in Germany but in other European countries as well. The *Chinesische Stiftung* was dedicated to the support of Gützlaff's Chinese Union but was also interested in sending a missionary of its own to China to assist Gützlaff. Elvers soon found a suitable candidate in Karl Vogel, and the *Stiftung* sponsored Vogel's education at Marburg University. There he studied

38. See the correspondence directed by W. P. Tiddy, secretary of the Brussels support society, to Richard Ball, 3 May 1850 [A 23:1] and 8 November 1850 [A 23:2] in Richard Ball, "China Correspondence," in the collection of Selly Oak Colleges, Birmingham, England.

39. Gützlaff, *Bericht seiner Reise*, p. 19.

40. *Quartalbericht des evangelischen Mission-Vereins in Kurhessen*, 31 March 1850, pp. 3-4.

mathematics, astronomy, and theology in the pattern of the Jesuit missionaries of the seventeenth and eighteenth centuries. He sailed for China in August 1849 and arrived in the spring of 1850 while Gützlaff was still on his European tour.

Thus, when Gützlaff arrived in Cassel on 27 May 1850, the *Chinesische Stiftung* already had a missionary in China. Elvers and his colleagues welcomed Gützlaff joyously, and the latter spent two days delivering lectures and meeting mission supporters in Cassel. In a speech he gave on 27 May, he made the usual appeal for funds and missionaries. However, he gave special attention to the need for women missionaries supported by women's mission societies, referring to the unfortunate plight of the female sector of the Chinese population.[41] On 28 May, Gützlaff presided over the founding of Electoral Hesse's *Frauenverein für China*. On 29 May, the day after Gützlaff left Cassel, the *Chinesische Stiftung* published a general appeal, calling for the establishment of women's mission societies to send female workers to China.[42] The appeal was couched in language employed by Gützlaff throughout his Europe trip. Without the conversion of Chinese women to Christianity, China would remain heathen. Women were the key to the conversion of China, and the survival of Christianity in China hinged on Christian families. The article acknowledges that Chinese women who became Christian would be ridiculed and reviled, but contends that if their faith were strong, they would survive these social persecutions. Reiterating Gützlaff's argument, it insists that women missionaries are essential for establishing contact with Chinese women because Chinese women are shielded from contact with men.

The *Chinesische Stiftung*'s *Quartalsberichte* circulated widely among European missions and mission supporters and doubtless helped gain acceptance of women mission workers. Gützlaff left a growing succession of women's support groups wherever he went. Beginning with the British Isles, he inspired a number of women to volunteer for mission work in China, and a few of them actually did go there to work among the Chinese women and children.

On 29 May, Gützlaff bade farewell to the Hessians and went by train directly to Berlin, accompanied by the Rev. Friedrich Krummacher. Of all of Gützlaff's stops on the continent, the one in Berlin was the most fruitful, for it yielded two supporting mission societies, the *Berliner Missionsverein für China* and the *Berliner Frauenmissionsverein für China*, both of which survived for many years, and both of which sent mission workers to China. There was already an older mission society in Berlin, the *Berliner Missions-*

---

41. "Dr. Gützlaff's Vorträge über China und die Chinesische Mission, am 27 und 28 Mai d. J. in Cassel gehalten," *Quartalberichte der chinesischen Stiftung* 2 (30 June 1850): 62.
42. "Dr. Gützlaff's Vorträge über China," pp. 66-70.

gesellschaft, but its principal field of activity was southern Africa. During his Berlin stay, Gützlaff delivered a total of seven lectures. In his first lecture, Gützlaff took advantage of a mission convention being sponsored by the *Berliner Missionsgesellschaft.* On that occasion, the church was filled with pastors and other mission delegates from many parts of Germany, and since the convention lasted for several days, Gützlaff's seven lectures were well attended, not only by Berliners but by many of the convention delegates as well.

The most important of these lectures was the last one, presented on 3 June in Elizabeth Church, for it was immediately following that lecture that the two Berlin support societies were established.[43] Gützlaff himself appointed Friedrich Krummacher to the post of presiding officer of the men's mission society. The men's China mission organization immediately founded a monthly, *Evangelischer Reichsbote,* to publicize the China mission field. It also asked the *Berliner Missionsgesellschaft* for a missionary candidate from among the students in its mission school, and the older mission organization selected Robert Neumann, age twenty-seven, from among its graduating students. As soon as the women's mission organization learned of this choice, it selected a woman who would represent it in China and who would simultaneously become Robert Neumann's spouse.[44] Robert and Hermina Neumann left from London in October and arrived in Hong Kong in the spring of 1850, their passage to China made possible by a generous grant from Richard Ball's mission organization in England.[45]

As it turned out, the only European support societies which survived to play an important role in the China mission were those in London, Berlin, Cassel, and Pomerania. Each of these had a network of smaller local mission groups associated with it. Thus the influence of these four societies extended well beyond their city boundaries. The Stettin society, for example, called itself the *Pommerscher Hauptverein für Evangelischen Missionen in China,* and it served as the headquarters for local groups scattered throughout the Prussian province of Pomerania. Since the Pomerania organization was one of the four surviving ones, it will be highlighted here, particularly because Pomerania was Gützlaff's native province. Gützlaff arrived there in July following a tour of many cities. He was thrilled to be back in Stettin, where he had spent several years during his adolescence. He had occasionally attended the *Jakobiner-*

---

43. Berliner Missionsverein für China, "Bericht über die Entstehung und bisherige Wirksamkeit unseres Vereins," in *Evangelischer Reichsbote* 1.1 (January 1851): 2-5. The by-laws of the male organization, as well as the membership of the executive committee, can be found on p. 8.

44. "Bericht über die Entstehung und bisherige Wirksamkeit unseres Vereins," p. 4.

45. "Bericht über die Entstehung und bisherige Wirksamkeit unseres Vereins," p. 5.

kirche, and now he had the satisfaction of speaking as a celebrity to a very large audience in that church. During his stay in Cassel in late May he had befriended Pastor Bernsee, who would play a leading role in the founding and development of the Pomeranian *Hauptverein.* In Stettin, with Bernsee's assistance, Gützlaff convened a gathering of mission supporters in Pomerania and assigned to them the Chinese province of Shansi as their field of operation. The actual founding of the Pommeranian *Hauptverein,* however, took place four months after Gützlaff had left Stettin, with Bernsee as its chair.[46]

The visit to Pomerania gave Gützlaff the opportunity to return to his home city of Pyritz. This time he entered Pyritz as a national hero. Gützlaff chose as the locus for his major address a historic site, the Otto Fountain at the center of the city. It was there, allegedly, that the first Pomeranian Christians were baptized. "It was thrilling," he wrote, "to share the word of grace with such a large crowd of listeners, to bring to them a message which had once inspired their fathers."[47]

Gützlaff returned to Cassel in mid-October to attend a conference that had been planned by C. F. Elvers, leader of the *Chinesische Stiftung.* Elvers's goal was to found a parent organization under the aegis of the *Stiftung* to organize and control the burgeoning number of mission societies. Local loyalties and interests, however, made the such an overall coordinating organization impossible. Representatives of Basel, Barmen, and the Berlin missions were conspicuous by their absence, and representatives of only four mission organizations, plus Gützlaff and seven delegates from the Cassel society, were present.[48] Gützlaff was obviously disappointed, for he stayed for only the first day's session.

Negative Reactions against Gützlaff and the Chinese Union

The schedule Gützlaff followed in pursuing his eleven-month blitz of Europe was, as we have pointed out, a killing one. Indeed, it may have shortened his life, for he died nine months after leaving Europe, in August 1851. The Swedish historian Herman Schlyter paraphrases an account written by Professor

46. "Bericht über die am 6. November zu Stettin gehaltene Versammlung der Deputirten der Pomerschen Vereine für Evangelische Mission in China," p. 1, and the By-laws of the Pomeranian Hauptverein, pp. 2-7; these documents were appendices to the Pomeranian Hauptverein's *Geschichte der Missionen in China von den ältesten Zeiten bis auf Gützlaff* (Stettin: R. Grassmann, 1850).

47. Gützlaff, *Bericht seiner Reise,* pp. 22-23.

48. "Protokoll der ersten allgemeinen chinesischen Missionsconferenz, abgehalten zu Cassel am 17. und 18. Oktober 1850," *Quartalberichte der chinesischen Stiftung,* 31 October 1850, pp. 97-113.

Hofstede de Groot of Gröningen that presents a vivid description of the self-destructive schedule pursued by Gützlaff:

> Gützlaff arrived around 10:00 A.M. after traveling all night. His appearance was Chinese in every respect. He spoke of the Chinese as his people. Around 11:00 A.M. he addressed the students of theology. Around noon, he held a lecture on Chinese history in the town's Concert House, in the course of which he said that the Chinese Union needed 60 European missionaries. Around 4:00 P.M., he spoke in St. Martin's Church about the China mission and missions in neighboring lands before an audience of between 3000 and 4000. His call for help and financial support made a strong impression. Around 7:00 P.M., he participated in a session with the members of the support society of the Dutch Mission and Bible Society. Around 11:00, he departed for another destination.[49]

Not only did this schedule help to undermine Gützlaff's already fragile health; it brought other problems as well. His apparent founding of support societies throughout Europe was deceptive. Most of these were hurriedly founded in the course of a few hours, and were assigned Chinese provinces or smaller areas with utter disregard for the historical circumstances prevailing in those Chinese areas. The possibility of these societies sponsoring missionary activity in the areas assigned to them at that point in time was virtually nonexistent. As for the newly founded societies, many of them existed only on paper. They were established in such haste that they could not endure. In Herman Schlyter's opinion, "speed and superficiality, rather than concentration and thoroughness, characterized [Gützlaff's] mission oriented work in Europe."[50] This judgment is, of course, a matter of hindsight. In the beginning, Gützlaff's phenomenal accomplishments were accepted as authentic by both his supporters and his rivals.

In most of the cities and towns, the support societies Gützlaff founded were independent of the established mission societies, and this threw a scare into the older mission societies. Gützlaff appeared to be rapidly constructing a huge mission empire that was independent of them and which threatened to absorb the bulk of the financial support being directed at missions. By the time he left Europe, in November 1850, he had co-founded at least one hundred organizations.[51] All these new organizations had been established to support the work of one independent missionary in China.

49. Schlyter, *Karl Gützlaff*, pp. 228-29.
50. Schlyter, *Karl Gützlaff*, p. 226.
51. Schlyter, *Karl Gützlaff*, p. 226.

Not only was Gützlaff an independent missionary; he was also a full-time officer of the British government in Hong Kong. His missionary activities were carried on outside his regular working hours. The established missions were well aware of this limitation, but the general Christian public Gützlaff was courting was, for the most part, ignorant of it, for he rarely alluded it. Instead he played the role of a famous China missionary, which indeed he was, among other things.

Furthermore, his insistence that only Chinese evangelists could effectively communicate with Chinese was a backhanded critique of Western missionaries, who had been working for years in China and could claim less than two hundred baptized converts. In Gützlaff's presentations, the only viable role Western missionaries should be playing in China was instruction and supervision of Chinese evangelists and colporteurs. Thus Gützlaff's prescription for the effective evangelization of China was hardly reassuring to the Western missions that had for years been engaged in missionary activity in China.

Another feature of Gützlaff's activities that was disconcerting for many Christians was his pronounced bias in favor of the Moravians.[52] In Holland he often resided with the Moravians in Zeist, and almost everywhere he went, if there were a Moravian center nearby, he made it his headquarters. These Moravians were avid neo-pietists and a chief wellspring of the evangelical movement throughout Europe. If Gützlaff did not stay with Moravians, he usually associated with other staunch evangelicals. In Berlin, for example, he resided in the parsonage of Pastor Knak, head of Berlin's Bohemian-Lutheran community, and in Uppsala he stayed at the home of a former mayor who was head of Uppsala's neo-pietist community.

Though neo-pietism was in its heyday in the early decades of the nineteenth century, denominationalism began to challenge it vigorously by the middle of the century. The neo-pietists and staunch evangelicals, in reaction, had established an international association, the Evangelical Alliance, which was nonsectarian. In Uppsala, Sweden, the Lutheran majority had passed ordinances banning public prayer meetings, with the intention of crippling neo-pietism. The former mayor immediately defied the ordinance by holding open prayer meetings, and in response, the Lutherans had surrounded his house and threatened him with violence. Though he was unharmed, he was subjected to a fine.

Gützlaff unwittingly stepped into this situation and made himself an object of popular scorn by residing at the home of the former mayor. When Gützlaff and his supporters marched from the church to the ex-mayor's

---

52. See Gützlaff's comment to this effect in his *Bericht seiner Reise*, p. 29.

home, they were harassed en route and the clergy in their midst were pelted with stones. After the marchers had reached the home, it was surrounded by a mob which raised a clamor that lasted till late in the evening.[53] Such antagonism was one of several developments which helped to undermine Gützlaff's efforts.

Gützlaff was yet more grievously undermined by the arrival in Europe of information damaging to the reputation of Gützlaff's Chinese Union. Until mid-century most European Protestants received the information regarding the Chinese Union from Gützlaff himself, especially via his frequent reports published in Christian Barth's *Calwer Missionsblatt* and reprinted in other mission periodicals. Gützlaff had believed the information furnished him by his Chinese evangelists and had passed this information on to mission supporters in reports published under the subtitle *Chinesische Berichten*. But trouble was looming.

The two Basel missionaries, Hamberg and Lechler, who were sent to assist Gützlaff's work with the Chinese Union quickly become disenchanted. In September 1847, the two drew up a joint report critical of Gützlaff and of the Chinese Union and sent it to Inspector Hoffman in Basel.[54] In it they declared their independence from Gützlaff. They viewed Gützlaff's mission plans as overly ambitious and unrealistic. They added that the members of the union presented certain problems. It was almost impossible to get these union members to acknowledge that they, personally, had sinned; they rejected the idea of accepting the status of a sinner as a consequence of their own misdeeds. On the other hand, they accepted the idea that Adam was a sinner and that through his sin mankind was tainted with original sin and must, therefore, be saved through Jesus Christ. The problem was to get them, as individuals, to acknowledge that they had committed sins. This entailed a further and consequent difficulty: since they did not see the confession of sins as a necessary prerequisite to conversion, they did not require this from the persons they converted. To these two missionaries, this meant they had no genuine idea of what is involved in conversion; indeed, they did not really understand Christianity. They memorized whole passages of the Bible, and their preaching was largely a repetition of what they had memorized. If they discussed these memorized teachings with potential converts, they interpreted them from the standpoints of Chinese folk religion and Confucianism.

53. The circumstances and events were described by Gützlaff in *Bericht seiner Reise*, p. 34.

54. Theodor Hamberg and Rudolf Lechler to Inspector Hoffman, Hong Kong, 21 September 1847, BMG, A1.1 (1B), no. 14.

Hamberg and Lechler went on to reveal how useless it was to describe the shortcomings of the union evangelists to Gützlaff. He was so captivated by his goal of converting China to Protestant Christianity that he did not see the world as it was. Rather, he saw it through rose-colored glasses. He did not perceive that it was not concern for the salvation of their souls that brought Chinese Union candidates to Hong Kong, but rather the desire for means of livelihood. By the following spring Ferdinand Genähr, of the Barmen mission, had embraced this point of view. The other Barmen missionary, Heinrich Köster, had been murdered shortly after arrival.

Hamberg and Lechler's report of 21 September 1847 was a prelude to more negative revelations in 1850. Christian Barth, who was publishing Gützlaff's *"Chinesische Berichten,"* had close ties with Basel, and he read the report by Hamberg and Lechler. Thus began his disillusionment with Gützlaff and the Chinese Union. Other leading mission supporters were also appraised of the content of the report. The Basel Mission, which had received this report and earlier critical correspondence, rapidly lost its enthusiasm for Gützlaff. Hamberg and Lechler's joint report was reinforced by information supplied by LMS missionary James Legge, who had been on leave in England during 1846-1848. Yet despite Barth's disillusionment with Gützlaff and the Chinese Union, he continued to collect funds for the Chinese Union and to forward them to Hong Kong into the spring of 1850.[55] In April 1850, for example, the Chinese Union received the equivalent of 133 Spanish dollars from Barth. Later that year, in an article he published on 2 October in *Evangelische Kirchen-Zeitung,* he said that he continued to believe in the idea of converting Chinese with Chinese evangelists and that he thought that properly converted colporteurs could play a useful role in distributing Bibles.

James Legge returned to Hong Kong from England in the summer of 1849, and on 27 September he wrote a letter to LMS Secretary Arthur Tidman.[56] The letter is paraphrased, in part, by Tidman in his response dated 24 December 1849: "I received, in due course, your letter of 27 September in reference to the anticipated visit of Dr. Gützlaff. With respect to your convictions as to the exaggerated and utterly unfounded representations of Dr. G. relating to the Christian Union, I think you have pursued the course of Christian duty in giving us the result of your own personal observations. . . . I think it would in many quarters add weight to your testimony if, say, Mr. Dean, Mr. Stanton,

55. See "Übersicht der Einnahmen und Ausgaben des Chineisichen Verein," *Quartalbericht der chinesischen Stiftung* 2 (June 1850): 93.

56. Tidman to Legge, 24 December 1849, LMS, East China, Outgoing, 1849. For Legge's earlier letter to Tidman, see Legge to Tidman, Hong Kong, 27 September 1849, LMS, S. China, Incoming Correspondence, Box 5.

and Mr. Byrne — in fact the entire mission fraternity within reach can unite with you in any further representations that may be made as the real facts in the case."

Tidman's letter must have arrived in Hong Kong in early February 1850. On the basis of Tidman's letter, Legge planned and convened a meeting of Hong Kong missionaries, which held its first meeting on 20 February 1850. The resultant printed protocol cites Tidman's letter of 24 December 1849 as the basis for the meeting.

The sessions lasted till 26 February 1850. On the first day there were twelve missionaries present. One of these, Mr. Elgquist of the Lund Mission Society, dropped out after the first day. Of the remaining eleven, six were members of the London Missionary Society. In addition to the LMS missionaries, there two representatives of the English Presbyterian Church, one of the American Baptist Missionary Union, plus Hamberg and a teacher from the Anglo-Chinese School in Hong Kong. The six members of the LMS had a controlling majority after the first day. Thus, on the final day, when William Burns proposed that the protocol be made public without any additional comments, he was voted down in favor of a proposal made by James Legge that the one hundred printed protocols be divided among the committee members with the proviso that each member could append his own comments. The majority of the committee deemed the findings damaging, if not alarming. They expressed dissatisfaction with the Chinese preachers' understanding of Christian teachings. They were even more critical of the requirements for baptism set by Gützlaff and the preachers. Testimony indicated that a significant minority of the Chinese Union members were opium smokers, that some of the preachers had never left the Hong Kong area, and that some of the colporteurs had sold their tracts to book suppliers to be repurchased by Gützlaff.

By April 1850, copies of the *Protokoll* had reached Europe.[57] Gützlaff's protestations covered a wide range: the committee was biased; the findings were more inconclusive than indicated in comments by Legge and Hamberg; most of the committee members had little or no previous contact with Chinese Union workers and had never been in the field with them; the investigation was conducted after he left China, making it difficult for him and the Chinese to offer a defense; all missionaries had experienced instances of lapse by their converts, but publicizing such evidence did not help the cause of missions.[58]

---

57. *Protokoll eine Conferenze von Missionaren verochiedenen Gesellschaften* (Hong Kong, 1850). Basler Missionsgesellschaft Archives, China A-1.1 (1B), no. 1.

58. Gützlaff to Gillespie, Rotterdam, 8 May 1850, and Gützlaff to Hamberg, Rotterdam, 15 May 1850, Selly Oak, Chinese Correspondence; Gützlaff, "Ein Schreiben Gützlaff's an das Comite des Pommerschen Hauptvereins für Evangelische Mission in China, Posen, 8

Yet whatever the merit of Gützlaff's defense, the damage was great. Some societies, because of their commitment to the project, suspended judgment. Others expressed the hope that Gützlaff and new recruits from Europe could initiate reforms. Gützlaff's methods, they said, remained sound and offered the best hope for Christianization of China. If adequate instruction and controls were instituted, the goal of indigenous Chinese congregations could be realized.[59] Detrimental information mounted, however, while the controversy between Gützlaff and his critics grew ever more acrimonious. Maintaining faith in the rosy picture painted by Gützlaff before and during his tour became more and more difficult.

The revelations regarding the Chinese Union prompted Ernst Hengstenberg to challenge Christian Barth, Basel Inspector Josenhans, and Barmen Inspector Wallmann to reply to Karl Gützlaff in his journal *Evangelische Kirchen-Zeitung.* Hengstenberg reminded the readers that in 1834 the theologian Otto von Gerlach had in this periodical raised serious doubts about the character of Gützlaff's mission enterprise, most notably the dangers and susceptibilities associated with its status as an autonomous one-man mission. Barth was the only one of the three to accept Hengstenberg's challenge. Barth's response appeared in the 2 October 1850 issue of the *Evangelische Kirchen-Zeitung:*

> It is not a happy task to be obliged to move against a friend whom one has known personally for twenty-six years and with whom one has maintained a steady correspondence for the last fifteen years. . . . I am the one who introduced the Chinese Union of Hong Kong to German mission supporters, and I am the one who promoted its cause in Germany and England. . . .
>
> And now to answer the questions that have been put to me. The allegation that Gützlaff is prevented by his honest zeal from seeing things as they are is unfortunately true. Even his best friends admit that in his judgments and hopes he is far too sanguine. . . . It cannot be denied that Gützlaff is prevented by his political office from devoting his full powers to the mission activities. . . . He works indeed with giant power, sleeps only a little, is at work early in the day and late in the evening.

Oktober 1850," *Evangelische Kirchen-Zeitung, Beilage,* 26 October 1850, cols. 867-68, in Archives of Basel Missions Gesellschaft (BMG), A-1.1 (1B), no. 4.

59. Published by the Pomeranian *Hauptverein* and reprinted in the *Beilage* of the *Evangelische Kirchen-Zeitung,* 26 October 1850, section *Nachrichten,* cols. 867-72.

Barth added that, considering his full-time civil service position and the numerous obligations that his mission work entailed, it was not surprising that he handled the latter superficially. As Gützlaff began to expand the membership of the union rapidly, the quality of preparation and supervision was bound to suffer and improprieties intruded themselves. "There was no one there in the hinterland," Barth stated, "to control the preachers who had been sent out. Fabricated diaries and letters by alleged converts were written while the writer sat peacefully at home where he spent his insufficient travel money." Gützlaff must have known about the irregularities, but he was so intent on the realization of his plans that he was willing to overlook the shortcomings and to forgive. Even the colporteurs were dishonest.

"In England," Barth wrote, "the personal appearance of Gützlaff had everywhere aroused lively support for the mission in China. . . . This led to the creation of a society for the support of the Chinese Union. . . . However, news from Hong Kong concerning the findings of the investigating committee has had a sobering effect on them, raising complaints that Gützlaff could not answer because he had departed from England [for the continent]." Barth said that during his stay in London in May, he found the members of the support society sobered and more cautious but quite willing to offer further powerful support to the Chinese Union. He added that what he had said in relation to Gützlaff's English supporters applied as well to his German supporters.

> The Chinese Union in Hong Kong must be completely rebuilt if its activity is to have a favorable result and if it will awaken trust. Especially it is necessary that the administration should no longer be in the hands of one man who, as we say in Swabia, is a fatigued [*übernächtig*] person. A committee consisting of Europeans in Hong Kong should be established. Above all, it should take over the financial administration. . . .
>
> This much is virtually certain, namely that Gützlaff has pursued the right path when he seeks to convert China through Chinese. . . . Gützlaff knows as well as we do that the Chinese who are supposed to convert China must first themselves be converted, but he has not adhered to this principle strictly enough.

The same principle, he added, should apply to those Chinese who distributed Bibles; the colporteurs also needed to be Christian converts. But beyond this, the system would not work without a corps of Western missionaries who, according to the Gützlaff plan, were not only to convert the Chinese who served as evangelists and colporteurs, but also were supposed to supervise and control the native workers.

Having made his criticisms and suggestions, Barth now turned to Gützlaff's achievements.

Despite the fact that defects in the work of the Chinese Union have come to light, the enterprise is not without fruit and blessing. The Word of God has been widely spread, and the name of Christ has been made known in many areas which are not open to European missionaries. . . . Gützlaff's writings and letters have promoted an interest in and greater acquaintance with China. In any event, he has rendered an unquestionable service through the best and most colloquial translation of the Holy Scriptures. . . . In the light of what I have said I can do nothing other than recommend, under the above-mentioned restrictions, the further powerful support for the China mission.

Gützlaff did not reply directly to Barth's article. Instead, six days later, on 8 October, he sent a lengthy letter to the executive committee of the Pomeranian *Hauptverein* ostensibly responding to questions addressed to him by the committee.[60] It is clear from the contents of Gützlaff's letter, however, that he was aiming it principally at Barth. Gützlaff wrote, "An unknown writer moved against me . . . in the *Kirchen-Zeitung* and my dear friend [Barth] responded to his proposal in order to throw an apple of discord and to light a fire that threatens the whole mission enterprise. . . ."

Gützlaff insisted that Barth had made allegations that were unfounded. "What I have reported in the [*Calwer Missionsblatt's*] *'Chinesische Berichten'* is not something I have imagined but something I know to be true. As for the allegation respecting the financing of the Union, it was all above board. The uses made of the contributions were stipulated in detail to the donors. The greatest economy was observed, greater than that of any other institute in China. I, myself, have personally spent thousands on the Chinese Union." In his account, Gützlaff gave an idealized picture of the Chinese Union. His critics were trying to excuse their failure to carry out their assignments. Hamberg was the one who was duped by the union members, and he doled out Gützlaff's money to the union members until it was exhausted. He was outraged by this misuse of his funds. Whenever Gützlaff felt backed into a corner, he responded that he was doing God's work, and that therefore it was beyond criticism: "At the same time, I remark that I am doing the work of the Lord, not my own, and those

---

60. Carl Vogel, Gegenwartigen Sekretar des Vereins, ed., "Bemerkungen den Glieder des Chinesischen Vereins hinsichtlich Hamberg's Betragen," Hong Kong, 21 January 1851, BMG, A-1.1 (1B), no. 11.

who seek to cast reflections on this work or to distort it, their business is with Him and not with me, a miserable deplorable man."

Gützlaff left Europe in November 1850 determined to vindicate himself and the Chinese Union; he would reconstruct this great instrument for the conversion of China. Immediately upon arrival in Hong Kong in January 1851, Gützlaff launched into a flurry of activities. He called together his preachers and secured counter-confessions; some members stated that they had been coerced into signing false statements by threats of withdrawal of support.[61] He met with dozens of preachers for instruction and Bible reading in the morning before office hours and itinerated with them in the evening and on weekends. Letters of accusation and defense flowed back and forth between Gützlaff and Hamberg, Gützlaff and Barth, and Gützlaff and R. Ball, while both Gützlaff and Hamberg printed circulars justifying their actions.[62] At one point, Gützlaff tried to organize an executive committee of Chinese Union members, Hong Kong missionaries, and businessmen with the idea of formally dissociating himself from the union. He failed to gain the cooperation of the missionary community and, moreover, he could not really let go of what had become his alter ego. The will and desire of the man drove him on. He planned a reissue of his New Testament, drafted a history of China under the Dao Guan emperor (published after his death), and he continued to sketch plans for an expedition into Central Asia.

Gützlaff was, however, a sick man. His European tour had been interrupted for several weeks by an attack of rheumatic fever, and Gützlaff mentioned a little indisposition again in November 1850.[63] Shortly after Gützlaff arrived in Hong Kong in January 1851, Genähr wrote that Gützlaff seemed disquieted and unsteady; he complained of bodily aches and spoke of dying.[64] For someone who had earlier delighted in physical challenges and hardships, such comments were most uncharacteristic. Gützlaff continued to preach to the people of Hong Kong, to the boat people, and to Hakka villagers on nearby islands, but he sometimes had to crawl up hills because edema pre-

61. Carl Vogel, gegenwärtiger Sekretät des Vereins, ed., "Bemerkungen der Glieder des chinesischen Verein hinsichtlich Hamberg's Betragen," Hong Kong, 21 January 1851, BMG, A-1.1 (1B), no. 11.

62. Gützlaff, untitled circular, Hong Kong, January 1851, BMG, A-1.1 (1B), no. 12; Hamberg, *Report regarding the Chinese Union in Hong Kong.*

63. Gützlaff to Hamberg, Rotterdam, 15 May 1850; Gützlaff to Ball, Berlin, 4 June 1850; Gützlaff to Ball, Alexandria, Egypt, 9 November 1850, Selly Oak, OMFA, Chinese Correspondence.

64. Genähr to Barth, 28 January 1851, BMG, A-1.1 (1B), no. 2 (Abschnitten von Briefen an Dr. Barth, 1851).

vented him from walking.[65] Gützlaff died on 9 August 1851, seven months after returning to China.[66]

The Complexities of the Chinese Union Crisis

Despite efforts by Gützlaff's widow, the Chinese Union survived Gützlaff's death only briefly. Gützlaff's major and most loyal supporter, R. Ball of the Chinese Association, had already held up funds pending clarification of charges leveled against the Chinese Union. Robert Neumann of the *Berliner Missionsverein für China* arrived in the early spring of 1851. He itinerated with Gützlaff and took control of the Chinese Union following Gützlaff's death in August 1851, but he eventually became disillusioned with it. Because of illness, he and his wife remained in China only until the autumn of 1854. In the face of damaging evidence after high hopes, many European support societies disintegrated, and interest in China missions temporarily declined. It appeared that the Chinese Union was so much the creature of the independent missionary that it ceased to have life when the umbilical cord was cut.

Many factors contributed to the rise and fall of the Chinese Union. A high proportion of the Chinese assistants were undoubtedly motivated by the desire for employment, and a significant number failed to carry out their assignments. Many were minimally educated tutors or petty tradesmen hoping to improve their economic status. With the rapid expansion of membership and word spreading that enrollment meant easy income, increasing numbers apparently came from undesirable elements in the Hong Kong–Canton environs. The aftermath of the Opium War brought an increase in piracy, robbery, clashes between villages and clans, and warfare between ethnic groups such as the Hakka and the *bendi* (Punti). The volatile social environment of Hong Kong–Canton defied Chinese and British attempts to police the Chinese populace. Opium compounded the problem. Some of the preachers had turned to Christianity hoping to cure their addiction; more, perhaps, were

---

65. Robert Neumann, "Tagebuch, 24 April–21 May 1851," *Evangelischer Reichsbote* 1.9 (September 1851): 8; F. W. Krummacher, "Bericht am ersten Jahresfest," *Evangelischer Reichsbote* 1.12 (December 1851): 2.

66. Most obituaries stressed Gützlaff's devotion to the cause of Christianizing China, his faith in the power of the Holy Spirit to accomplish this conversion, and his unceasing efforts to bring the gospel to the Chinese. Rev. E. T. R. Moncrieff in his eulogy stated: "The details of his system may admit of debate, BUT THE GENERAL PRINCIPLE CANNOT [sic]." *Overland Friend of China and Hongkong Gazette,* August 1851, clipping in BMG A-1.1 (1B), no. 16.

simply desperate for money to supply their habit. Whatever the motive, a cure
was not easy, and lapse was common.

The "rice Christians" and the charlatans in the Chinese Union were highly
visible because of their numbers and because of the contrast between Gützlaff's
sanguine reports and the later exposé. Such instances of opportunism and
apostasy were, much to the sorrow of all missionaries, far from unique. Both
Gützlaff's assistants and the assistants of other missionaries included the faithful as well as the opportunistic; it would be impossible to estimate the proportions in either camp. William Dean, an American Baptist missionary who had
worked for several years to build a congregation in Hong Kong, reported on returning from home leave in 1849 that he found many disappointments and the
falling away of Chinese who had been left alone.[67] Chalmers and Legge regretfully dismissed a prime convert whom they were training as an assistant. He had
proved "unworthy." Chalmers concluded: "With this must end for the present at
least the scheme of training up young men for ministry to [the] Chinese and
supporting them while in training."[68] Such examples could be multiplied.

Those Chinese who associated with the missionary and his religion risked
ostracism and identification with the "foreign devils." Moreover, re-entry into
Chinese society was not a simple matter — a fact missionaries did not fully appreciate. Christian taboos against homage to the ancestors, concubinage, gambling, religious festivities, and theatricals, plus the required observance of the
Sabbath made life difficult for the convert. Few support mechanisms were provided by Chinese society. Despite the toleration edicts, converts met hostility
and discrimination. On 2 February 1855 the Basel missionary Philip Winnes reported on his visit to a Hakka village near Canton; the wife of a convert provided lodging and a place for religious services.[69] Her welcome, though
friendly, was accompanied by unease, for her husband, as a Christian, had been
forced to flee the village. Though ten villagers had been baptized, only three remained to attend the service. The rest had been driven out a year earlier.

Winnes traveled to a nearby village, where he encountered two more
Christians, one who had also been forced to flee his home town and one who
had worked for Gützlaff. Despite reporting that the latter's knowledge of
Christian doctrines was deplorably deficient, Winnes learned that this former

67. William Dean to Samuel Peck, Hong Kong, 23 January 1849, American Baptist Historical Archives Center, Dean Correspondence.

68. Chalmers to Tidman, Hong Kong, 26 January 1854, CWM, LMS, S. China, Incoming Correspondence, Box 5. See also "Journal of David Abeel," *The Missionary Herald* 38
(1842): 469.

69. Winnes, "Report to the Basel Committee on 'a little mission trip,'" February 1855,
BMG, A-1.3, 1855, no. 33.

Chinese Union member was so widely respected for his honesty and unselfishness that he was often requested to mediate local disputes. He housed Winnes and opened up his home to visitors desiring to converse with Winnes. Whether or not Winnes accepted him as a Christian, he himself retained his identity with Christianity as he understood it. The cost might be high, but there were those who chose to pay the cost.

Accentuating the divide between converts and other Chinese was the concept of a permanent patron-client relationship and of the responsibility of each to the other. Some of the assistants apparently reasoned that once they had become identified with the Christian missionary, they should comply with the foreigner's wishes, but that at the same time the foreigner had assumed responsibility for their welfare. Even after Hamberg dismissed Chinese Union members, some returned repeatedly to demand money; they were poverty-stricken and unable to return to former jobs, they said. One preacher argued that since Gützlaff had hired him, Hamberg lacked the authority to fire him. Yet another Chinese Christian, recalling his conversion by Gützlaff and Chinese Union members, said that he had resisted baptism for many months.[70] Though he found merit in Christian teachings, he was reluctant to abandon the gods and ancestors whom he had previously honored. One Gützlaff assistant had tried to reassure him: when one was in Hong Kong, he said, one did as the foreigner did; when one returned home, one observed the traditional customs. This Chinese Christian, however, expressed sorrow that Chinese Union assistants engaged in "squeeze" in relations with the foreign missionary without any apparent sense of guilt. He admired Gützlaff's affection for the Chinese people and commented that it was a shame that "dear Herr Gutzlaff" was so easily deceived. Gützlaff, however, was not alone among the foreigners to be deceived, according to this informant.

Hamberg, Lechler, and Genähr accused Gützlaff of failure to follow through on monitoring his preachers, especially those in the field. Gützlaff replied that if one treated Chinese Christians as children, they would respond as children, taking no responsibility; if one treated them as adults and gave them responsibility, they would respond accordingly and accept the duty of evangelism as their own.[71] Lapses were disturbing, though not necessarily cause for excommunication; rather, one should love and trust the sinner and bring him to renewed repentance.

70. Wang Guangliu (?), "Report by Wong kong lau on Gützlaff and His People," trans. by Lechler and appended to Lechler to Inspector, 22 March 1853, BMG, A-1.2, 1853, no. 27.

71. *Cassel Jahresbericht*, 1846, pp. 53-56, quoting a letter by Gützlaff, 10 April 1846; Hamberg to Inspector, Tungfo, 9 July 1848, BMG, A-1.1, 1848, no. 7; Gützlaff, "Ein Schreiben Gützlaff's."

True to his pen name, Gaihan, Gützlaff never abandoned his love for the Chinese people nor his goal of conversion of China in his lifetime. To do so would have been to acknowledge that his life had been a failure. Reactions by Hamberg and many missionaries to disillusioning and frustrating experiences contrasted with the hopefulness of Gützlaff.

Hamberg, who had spent much of his youth in the comfortable household of the British consul in Stockholm, participated in the musical culture of that city, and enjoyed an active social life before his conversion to evangelical Christianity, seems to have found it particularly difficult to adjust to the rigors of living in China.[72] During his first years of residency in China, he became disillusioned and generally critical of the Chinese. It was the hard heart of the Chinese that obstructed true conversion, he said. Many missionaries agreed, concluding that training of Chinese Christians by Western missionaries would be lengthy. The hope of Chinese leadership receded into the future.

Evangelicalism versus confessionalism was a source of conflict among the missionaries. Gützlaff, William C. Burns of the English Presbyterians, Issacher Roberts, an independent Baptist, and Hudson Taylor of the China Inland Mission (now the Overseas Missionary Fellowship) differed with church mission representatives over the definition of a Christian and the qualifications of an evangelist. During the interrogations in early 1850 examiners repeatedly questioned Chinese about the length of their training for evangelism, and they contrasted their own experience with the average of three to six months' instruction for the Chinese. The Chinese preachers could repeat in some detail stories of the Bible, but the committee members complained that the preachers recited as if by rote and provided stereotypical interpretations. One evangelist, when asked whether those whom he baptized were already converted, replied that if the man believed and was sincere and upright, then he baptized and continued instruction. He expected only a partial change of heart before baptism; change would be completed after baptism. Such a procedure accorded with Gützlaff's methodology, but was hardly satisfactory to the mainstream missionaries. Hamberg told the committee, "I must confess . . . a strong doubt in my mind as to the members of the Chinese Union in general being truly converted Christians, and particularly so as respects their fitness for being employed as preachers and ministers of the Church of God."[73]

Gützlaff, to the contrary, did not find the information derived from the

---

72. Herman Schlyter in *Theodor Hamberg den förste svenske Kinamissionären* (Lund: C. W. K. Gleerup, 1952); pp. 1-49 discuss Hamberg's youth in Sweden.

73. Hamberg, *Report regarding the Chinese Union in Hong Kong*, p. 1.

Chinese about their understanding of Christianity or their methods damaging.[74] The evangelists could repeat the Word of God and employ it to stress the need for repentance and salvation through Christ and the Holy Spirit. He pointed out that when the report of a Chinese differed from that of a Westerner, the latter was assumed to be true. He accused the committee members of putting a bad light on their findings. Burns, a committee member, did make several largely unsuccessful attempts to place the information in a different perspective. When one missionary asked, "Does any one in this meeting know of any member of the 'Christian Union' whom he considers to be a Christian?" Burns replied that he had worked with several members and found them honest. He could not attest to a "positive conviction of the spiritual regeneration" of these men, but he found their knowledge of the Christian viewpoint considerable and their prayers suitable and apparently sincere. He was not willing to criticize Gützlaff for not expecting a recently converted Chinese in a non-Christian environment to replicate Western evangelists.[75]

In view of the risks for China missions in general, why had Hamberg, Legge, and other missionaries insisted on an investigation and then given it such extensive and negative publicity? According to them, they saw it as their Christian duty to expose fraudulent claims and fraudulent Christianity.[76] From their standpoint, Gützlaff's flawed methodology was doing great harm to the cause of legitimate missions. But other motives, whether conscious or subconscious, entered in, for some of the language was extreme and emotional.

Legge wrote to London, "My own impression is that the so-called Christian Union is more a sink of iniquity ten-fold than our report will make it appear and my opinion is that the opium traffic is not so injurious to the cause of Christianity in China as that so-called Christian Union."[77] If Gützlaff would not alter his appeals to the European public, he concluded, "it is because the man is so shameless that nothing but absolute force would put him down." Though Walter Medhurst had earlier collaborated with Gützlaff in translating the Bible, his letters regarding Gützlaff and the Chinese Union were laced with sarcasm. If, he wrote, one deducted for native duplicity and

74. Gützlaff to [Barth?], September 1850; Gützlaff to Ball, Rotterdam, 8 May 1850, Selly Oak, OMFA, Chinese Correspondence.

75. Hamberg, *Report regarding the Chinese Union in Hong Kong*, pp. 3-4 (Hong Kong: *Hong Kong Register*, 1851), BMG, A-1.1 (1B), no. 18.

76. Legge to Tidman, Hong Kong, 27 September 1849, CWM, LMS, S. China, Incoming Correspondence, Box 5; Hamberg to Inspector, Hong Kong, 15 September 1849, BMG, A-1.1, 1849, no. 13.

77. Legge to Tidman, Hong Kong, 28 March 1850, CWM, LMS, S. China, Incoming Correspondence, Box 5.

Gützlaff's credulity, little would be left. Why, if there had been such an effusion of the Holy Spirit throughout the provinces of China, were no other Protestant missionaries aware of it?[78]

Gützlaff had generated great enthusiasm and high expectations for the Christianization of China. He had reported hundreds of baptisms and dozens of evangelists in the far interior of China. He was preparing to print tens of thousands of inexpensive New Testaments. All this while he was a full-time employee of the British administration. What were the full-time missionaries reporting? A few tens of converts, with counsels of patience and understanding. A few boys in parochial schools, but a high dropout rate. A new translation of the Bible, but irreconcilable disagreements over Chinese terminology for God, the Holy Ghost, and baptism. Slow progress in mastering a fearfully difficult language. Medhurst remarked that Gützlaff almost made the full-time missionaries seem unnecessary. As early as 1848, the head of the British tract society had written Legge that strong appeals for the Chinese Union were being made in England and many were surprised at the society's apparent neglect of the openings noticed by Gützlaff.[79] The secretary of the LMS also wrote Legge that he was being asked what his society was doing to support the Chinese Union; perhaps some of the best members of the Chinese Union could be employed as colporteurs by the society's missionaries.[80] Mainstream denominational missionaries felt that they were being unfavorably contrasted with Gützlaff and that it was essential that they set the record straight. Many English missionaries were unhappy that the British tract society and the British and Foreign Bible Society were funding the printing and distribution of Gützlaff's Bible and tracts to the neglect of works by their own countrymen.

Enmity between Legge and Gützlaff had a long and bitter history. In many respects, the two were polar opposites. A retiring scholar who took the pulpit regularly in the local church but rarely went on preaching tours, Legge believed in intensive evangelization. He spent much of his time on study of the written language, supervision of a small school, and translation of Chinese literature and philosophy. According to one report, he never mastered the local dialect sufficiently to be an effective preacher to the masses.[81] His experi-

78. Medhurst to Tidman, Shanghai, 17 September 1849, CWM, LMS, Central China, Incoming Correspondence, Box 1.

79. Extract of letters of Rev. Dr. Legge, 6 December 1848; 24 February 1849, CWM, LMS, S. China, Incoming Correspondence, Box 5.

80. Tidman to Legge, London, 24 December 1849; 23 February 1850, CWM, LMS, Outgoing Correspondence, Box 4.

81. B. Kay to Tidman, Hong Kong, 25 May 1849, CWM, LMS, S. China, Incoming Correspondence, Box 5.

ences with the Malacca Anglo-Chinese College and Hong Kong theological school had been frustrating, for most graduates preferred business to the ministry. Legge was typical of the church missionary in setting Western mainstream standards for baptism and ordination. Upon Gützlaff's departure for Europe in the fall of 1849, Legge had warned the London secretary not to be taken in by Gützlaff's eloquence. Gützlaff, he said, was a full-time government employee. He asked if it was reasonable to believe that Gützlaff was able to find time to organize and carry on a great spiritual movement among a people so sunk in apathy, sensuality, covetousness, and deceit as the Chinese. Where was the necessary organization of infant communities, the oversight of them, and discipline? "Gützlaff was one of the greatest deceivers in the world," and the Chinese Union was "one of the vilest impositions ever palmed off on the Public."[82]

The free-wheeling and flamboyant Gützlaff was, in contrast, highly adept at picking up dialects, and his goal was spreading the Word, not building denominational congregations. His relations with his Chinese helpers might have been that of patron to client, but they seem to have been cordial, and Gützlaff consistently defended the sincerity of his evangelists. One thing Gützlaff and Legge had in common: neither was easy to live with. Legge was frequently at odds with members of his own mission, and the correspondence files of his mission contain more than one letter complaining of Legge's intolerance toward those differing with him.[83] Gützlaff could be quite captivating on short acquaintance, but his egotism, self-righteous obsession with his cause, and inability to accept criticism from colleagues alienated long-term associates.

By the late 1840s Gützlaff and Legge had ceased to be on speaking terms. The two had recently engaged in a public quarrel, during which Legge had accused Gützlaff of mistranslating a Chinese phrase in a government document, and Gützlaff had in turn intimated that a parliamentary inquiry into Legge's conduct was called for.[84] One reason Legge gave for the formal inter-

82. Legge to Tidman, Hong Kong, 27 September 1849, CWM, LMS, S. China, Incoming Correspondence, Box 5; also, Legge to Tidman, 23 June 1849, CWM, LMS, S. China, Incoming Correspondence, Box 5.

83. See, for example, B. Kay to Tidman, Hong Kong, 25 May 1849, CWM, LMS, S. China, Incoming Correspondence, Box 5; John Evans to Directors of LMS, 5 November 1840, CWM, LMS, China General, Box 3, quoted in Wong Man Kong, *James Legge: A Pioneer at Crossroads of East and West* (Hong Kong: Hong Kong Educational Publishing Co., 1996), p. 22. Also, William Tarrant to Gützlaff, 25 February 1850, Selly Oak, OMFA, Chinese Correspondence.

84. Legge to Tidman, Hong Kong, 29 November 1848, CWM, LMS, S. China, Incoming Correspondence, Box 5; Original Correspondence, CO 129/33-35, Colonial Office, Hong Kong. For detail, see chapter 6.

rogation of Chinese Union members was that it was impossible for him to ask Gützlaff in person for information. Legge would, of course, go on to win fame as the incomparable translator of the Chinese classics. Gützlaff's empire went down in disgrace upon his death. How much this has affected the historiography of Gützlaff and the Chinese Union is difficult to say.

A rigid, sometimes melancholic individual, Hamberg reacted negatively to the Chinese in a way that was self-defeating. On one of his early visits to the home of an assistant, he found pictures of gods and ancestors on the wall and immediately tore them down.[85] The father of the Chinese preacher was enraged. The son might be a convert, he said, but the house belonged to the family, not to the son. If the family desired to do homage to their ancestors and deities, they had a right to do so. Less than four months after arrival, Hamberg was excusing his infrequent and restricted itinerations by detailing to Basel the dangers and hardships, including the likelihood of illness. Again in 1848 Hamberg explained that he was in Hong Kong because that was an excellent place to study the language, so necessary to effective preaching. He pleaded with Basel to be patient in expecting results. In the summer of 1848, Hamberg did move to a market town on the mainland coast north of Hong Kong. He wrote that he was obeying the will of the Lord and the "dear committee," though he had a sense of isolation and unease in the midst of Chinese society.[86]

By the end of 1848 Hamberg had dismissed all of his Chinese Union preachers assigned to posts in the deeper interior, retaining only three or four trusted helpers, whom he worked with on a day-to-day basis. In May 1849 he returned unexpectedly to his station to find two of his assistants smoking opium; they were so inebriated, he remarked, that they just grinned and replied flippantly to his exclamations.[87] Such depression settled upon Hamberg that he went into seclusion and was unable to conduct any missionary activities for days. Hamberg decided on 15 June 1849 to abandon his station because of piracy and local feuding. He departed hurriedly in the middle of the night just ahead of the pirates. His assistants, temporarily left behind, absconded with his clock, tub, and other items. Hamberg's reaction was that all goes well

---

85. Hamberg to Barth, Hong Kong, 28 November 1847, BMG, Hamberg Correspondence File.

86. Hamberg to Barth, Hong Kong, 28 November 1847, BMG, Hamberg Correspondence File; Hamberg to Inspector, Hong Kong, 30 March 1848, BMG, A-1.1, no. 3. Hamberg did eventually become an expert in the Hakka dialect, and he drafted a Hakka dictionary that was later revised by Lechler. Regrettably, Hamberg died in 1854 not long after he had attained language competence, had married, and had acquired greater appreciation of Chinese people and culture.

87. Hamberg to Inspector, 21 May 1849, BMG, A-1.1, no. 7.

as long as one was giving the Chinese money, but if anything happens to stop the flow, they begin immediately to show their bad side.[88] As a result, Hamberg, who had once criticized most foreign missionaries for living in the "English manner," now associated increasingly with the English missionary community, even lodging in their homes. He came to appreciate their emphasis on intensive rather than extensive evangelization. He also had become secretly engaged to Anna Louise Motander before leaving Sweden. Despite Basel's rule that a missionary must work in the field for five years before marrying, Hamberg repeatedly urged Basel to send his fiancée to China, arguing that female missionaries were required for building Christian families.[89]

By July 1849 Hamberg was expressing sorrow about the break in good relations with the Basel committee: "What the Committee asked of us, we could not deliver; what we wanted, the Committee was not inclined to endorse." Hamberg, unlike Gützlaff, was not an independent missionary, and he had in the final analysis to account to his society and justify his actions. After contemplating the founding of a separate Swedish mission, he chose to remain associated with the Basel society.[90] He had all the more reason, therefore, to justify to the Basel board his stance vis-à-vis Gützlaff.

That Hamberg's relations with the Chinese Union members would be uneasy comes as no surprise, and it is interesting to examine the tactics the Chinese assistants employed. When he sought to incorporate some Chinese assistants in administration, they declined, saying that the selection of head men would be difficult and they feared that those elected would be inadequate. They requested Hamberg to continue in the Gützlaff manner — that is, take full responsibility. In a subtle defensive move, the Hong Kong assistants sent Hamberg a letter on 1 October 1849. They insisted that irregular conduct was impermissible and that those who remained in Hong Kong after being commissioned to a tour should be expelled. But they also requested that when slanderous reports came to the "teacher's" attention, he would hold an open hearing, for "a biased ear will leave him in the dark." Above all, they desired that Hamberg continue Gützlaff's practices without change, sending out elder disciples to preach and instructing younger disciples. Hamberg acceded to the request of the Chinese that he retain sole responsibility [91] though he did not resume sending preachers to the interior.

88. Hamberg to Inspector, Hong Kong, 23 September 1849, BMG, A-1.1, no. 13.

89. See, for example, Hamberg to Inspector, 9 July 1848. On one occasion the Basel inspector sharply reprimanded Hamberg for spending time thinking of marriage instead of itinerating.

90. Schlyter, *Theodor Hamberg*, pp. 98-100.

91. Hamberg, *Report regarding the Chinese Union in Hong Kong*, p. 4.

Dissatisfaction on both sides mounted. Like many Westerners, Hamberg failed to appreciate Chinese social mores designed to avoid direct confrontation and prevent loss of face. Truth was truth, according to the Westerners, and Hamberg came to join those who viewed the Chinese as a nation of liars. In the confessions secured by Hamberg during May and June 1850, several members readily admitted that it was their father or grandfather who came from a distant province, not themselves. For Hamberg, this was an example of deliberate falsification; for a Chinese who often identified himself with his ancestral home, the admission might have seemed less serious. Other confessions were more damaging, some admitting that they had not always gone to their stated destination, though they offered inadequate travel allowances as an excuse. Hamberg interpreted the evidence as a "general confession on the part of the members, as to their former deceitful conduct." His criticisms had been vindicated.

By late spring 1850, those studying in Hong Kong had been reduced to about forty out of the several hundred Hamberg had started with, but the remnant membership was split into two factions: a small group of seven to eight who considered themselves clients of their patron Hamberg, and approximately thirty who looked to Gützlaff. Under these circumstances, discovering the reality behind accusations, confessions, and counter-confessions becomes impossible. Many of those who had in June signed a request to Hamberg to continue as administrator sent criticisms of Hamberg to Gützlaff in the fall. They contrasted Gützlaff's regular morning and evening instruction and his willingness to go out to preach in all kinds of weather with Hamberg's conduct. The latter, they wrote, remained quietly at home, looking out upon the sea but not venturing out on it to preach. He had also ceased to send out Chinese preachers or to provide support. Though he was supposed to give lessons at nine o'clock, he often played the piano instead. He did not observe the separation of men and women, but talked intimately with his assistant's wife, "even caressing her." He and his assistants used economic threats to extract confessions and persuade members to defame one another. Other letters and journals sent to Gützlaff included protestations of faithful performance and a lamentation over the difficulty that a Chinese and a Westerner (i.e., Hamberg) had in understanding what was in the heart of the other.[92] Many of these criticisms would be repeated in the counter-confessions obtained by Gützlaff in January 1851.

Hamberg's group, meanwhile, complied with his suggestion that they make "a clear and brief report as to the real state of the union."[93] Though they

---

92. Journals and letters of Chinese Union Members, Selly Oak, OMFA.
93. Hamberg, *Report regarding the Chinese Union in Hong Kong*, pp. 11-12.

confessed that there had been deceit after the rapid expansion of the union, the tone of the statement was equivocal. They insisted that the initial members had conscientiously fulfilled their duties and explained that later members were in such financial plight because of debts and the low pay scale that they were unable to complete their assignments. Gützlaff had, upon the whole, exerted himself very much for a good object. A conflict of loyalties pervaded the document and made it a vindication neither of Hamberg nor of Gützlaff.

Relations between Hamberg and Gützlaff were going from bad to worse, as personal egos and even careers and empires became involved. Gützlaff's reactions to criticisms undoubtedly contributed to the polarization. Gützlaff was so totally committed to his plan for conversion of China via national evangelists that he could acknowledge no alternatives. Like many radicals and revolutionaries, he yearned to see the accomplishment of his goals during his lifetime. Illness, age, obstacles, and criticisms only persuaded him to push ever faster and harder, ignoring mistakes and deterrents. Isolated from the Hong Kong missionary community, he had run the Chinese Union as his personal operation without checks by his colleagues; as a loner, he had become less and less capable of assimilating negative information. He resorted to purism. Those who opposed his methods defied Jesus' commission to his apostles and to all disciples to carry the gospel to every heathen. Those who questioned the efficacy of preaching the Word and distributing the scriptures lacked faith in the Holy Spirit.[94] He never backed away from his insistence that conversion was the work of God, not man: "If God therefore has aroused men from the sleep of sin and drawn them to the Son of his eternal love, they may be safely received in baptism." In lands of darkness, relapses could be expected, for converts were subject to the allurements of their pagan countrymen and continued to be influenced by earlier training. The correct response of the missionary was forgiveness, kindness, and further instruction, not malice. Gützlaff berated Hamberg for harshness toward the Chinese, for not loving and trusting them, for alienating them instead of helping them return to the right path.[95]

94. C. G. Barth, "Der Chinesische Verein in Hong Kong," *Evangelische Kirchen-Zeitung,* 20 November 1850, cols. 943-44; Gützlaff to Hamberg, Berlin, 30 September 1850; Gützlaff to Ball, Hong Kong, 26 February 1851; Gützlaff to Hamberg, n.d., n.p. (probably April 1851), Selly Oak, OMFA, Chinese Correspondence.

95. Gützlaff to Hamberg, Rotterdam, 15 May 1850 (printed formal reply); Gützlaff to Hamberg, Gottenberg, 3 August 1850, Selly Oak, OMFA, Chinese Correspondence; Gützlaff to Directors of the Basel Missionary Society, Bern, 29 October 1850, BMG, A-1.1 (1B), no. 6; Gützlaff to Inspector, Rome, 9 November 1850, BMG, A-1.1 (1B), no. 9.

An Outsider among Missionaries

As the son of a German artisan, Gützlaff had found an avenue of social mobility in the ministry. As a venturesome romantic, he had found in the China mission an outlet for his ambition. Few other means of mobility existed in early nineteenth-century Germany, and few challenges were as great as the China mission. But Gützlaff, like many who had risen via this route, remained an outsider.[96] With his piety and total commitment to his cause, he could sweep people off their feet on initial contact, but he had difficulty in sustaining workable relationships with equals.

In British-dominated Hong Kong, Gützlaff's sense of being an outsider was accentuated. He was considered an "enthusiast" lacking in moderation and decorum. Gützlaff found more in common with other free-spirited evangelicals such as William Burns and Issachar Roberts than with mainstream missionaries. His most cordial relations were with those who posed no social challenge: those Chinese who were under his tutelage or in his employ. These he felt he could trust. Toward these poor souls, he could show compassion and understanding. They would return his favors in kind. The barrage of criticism from the missionary community, on the other hand, he found unacceptable and malevolent. By the time Gützlaff returned to China in early 1851, he was more isolated than ever, unable to enlist the cooperation of most missionaries and dependent on his Chinese assistants for contact and information. His defense had no audience.

The major reason for the decline in support on the home front was, of course, the contrast between Gützlaff's claims and what seemed to be reality. Christians in the West had even less of a context in which to place the failings of the Chinese converts than missionaries. Their sense of letdown, of having being deceived, was unmitigated by experience in the field. With the founding of dozens of support organizations, existent mission and Bible societies had become uneasy about competition for funds and personnel. Legge and other missionaries believed that attention and monies were being shunted away from legitimate missions. Many opposed the fostering of a nondenominational Christianity. Gützlaff's death and the demise of most support societies occurred before transformation of the Chinese Union or revision of Gutzlaff's methods could be implemented. Throughout the re-

---

96. See the thesis set forth by Anthony J. La Vopa, *Grace, Talent, and Merit: Poor Students, Clerical Careers, and Professional Ideology in Eighteenth Century Germany* (Cambridge: Cambridge University Press, 1988), esp. part I, pp. 19-133. Also see Jon Miller, *The Social Control of Religious Zeal: A Study of Organizational Contradictions* (New Brunswick, NJ: Rutgers University Press, 1994), pp. 50-53.

mainder of the nineteenth century, denominational organizations represented the mainstream of China missions.

Most mission histories have concluded their discussions of Karl Gützlaff
on this dismal note. Yet, as noted above, a small but significant number of
former Chinese Union members became dedicated church members and effective evangelists. Their conversion was a process that continued as they un-
derwent further instruction and guidance from their Western mentors. They
internalized their Christianity as they proselytized in the countryside. The
Hakka Christian church remembers Gützlaff, Hamberg, and former Chinese
Union members Zhang Fuxing and Jiang Jiaoren as its founders. Gützlaff
never achieved his lofty goals, but his work was not in vain.

CHAPTER 9

Karl Gützlaff, Chinese Christians, and the Chinese Heterodox Communities

Mid-nineteenth century China was characterized by the growing popularity of heterodox sects, some primarily religious, others political in orientation, and still others protective or predatory. Some combined two of more of these functions. Though the Taipings and the Triads in various forms were the most prominent societies, the majority were local and regional associations appealing to a combination of needs. Christian converts, to a considerable extent, came from the same strata of the population, and quite a few members of Karl Gützlaff's Chinese Union moved from Christianity to the Taipings or the Triads, while former Taipings proved amenable to the Christian message, especially after the defeat of the Taipings. How does one account for the appeal of non-orthodox groups and teachings and the readiness of individuals to cross boundaries during this era?

Perhaps the schema elaborated by Mark R. Mullins in his study of Japanese indigenous Christian sects can order our discussion of Chinese heterodox communities during the mid-nineteenth century. In explaining the formation of new Christian movements in Japan during the second quarter of the twentieth century, Mullins employs three categories: (1) precipitating factors, particularly the rise of nationalistic anti-Westernism in late Meiji and Taisho, and the premise of Christian missionaries that Christianity and Japanese culture were oppositional; (2) enabling factors such as the reservoir of Japanese religious beliefs and practices, plus the insights and revelations of Japanese Christians who interpreted the Bible unmediated by Western church tradition; and (3) personal-innovative factors, or "minor founders" as Mullins calls them.[1] In

1. Mark R. Mullins, *Christianity Made in Japan: A Study of Indigenous Movements* (Honolulu: University of Hawaii Press, 1998), pp. 23-47.

China, precipitating factors were internal decline while the Western missionary, or more broadly the Western presence, acted as both precipitating and enabling factors. Like Protestant missionaries to Japan, most China missionaries assumed that Christian theology would displace the "erroneous" doctrines and practices of Buddhism, Daoism, and folk religion; the Confucian heritage would have to give way to Christian truth.

Precipitating Factors: Internal Decline

"Exhaustion of state," "twilight of values," "community closure," and "atomized relations" are some of the phrases scholars have employed to describe the society of south China during the mid-nineteenth century. The ability of existing institutions to cope with China's current difficulties, especially population pressures, appeared questionable.[2] Though the degree of alienation among gentry should not be exaggerated, it should also not be underestimated. Instances of scholars refusing to sit for examinations after an official rejected their request that he petition Beijing for tax relief, of examination candidates throwing their writing utensils at examination officials, of scholars and village elders joining to smash the sedan chair of a corrupt magistrate and drive him out of town — all these were not unknown. The rumblings of anti-Manchu sentiment reverberated among the disaffected. For protection and sometimes also for purposes of extortion, landlord-gentry formed extra-governmental militia *(tuan)*, often by recruiting marginal youths. And, as is well known, leadership of heterodox organizations such as the Taipings, secret societies, and religious sects frequently came from the ranks of failed degree candidates. Even so, most bureaucrats and scholar-gentry continued to accept imperial rule and Confucian society as the norm; they pinned their hopes on reform and restoration rather than revolution or modernization. The cultural preparation for innovative change was still in its initial stages.

Among the masses, however, pauperization, civil breakdown, natural disaster exacerbated by corruption, and overpopulation in relation to arable land had led many to take the "dangerous path." Piracy, social banditry, and heterodox societies multiplied. The demobilization of troops and militia at the end of the Opium War in 1842 had left guns and munitions in the hands of thousands of unemployed ex-soldiers, and many had turned to banditry

2. Albert Feuerwerker, *Rebellion in Nineteenth Century China* (Ann Arbor: Center for Chinese Studies, University of Michigan, 1975), pp. 50-51.

and blackmail to earn a living. Upon the opening of treaty ports north of Canton in 1842, trade routes shifted, throwing out of work tens of thousands of porters, trackers, boatmen, proprietors of inns and tea houses, money changers, pawn brokers, and others involved in the transport of goods to and from Canton. Growth of internal and external trade, along with the shifting of trade routes, stimulated internal migration and thereby created masses of people for whom social ties had been weakened or severed. Many joined the ranks of the floating population, ready recruits for landlord militia and bandit societies as well as lineages needing braves in their feuds.

Pirate chiefs assembled well-organized fleets of as many as 150 or more ships and preyed upon coastal shipping. So rampant did piracy in the Hong Kong region become that ships dared not make even the short journey from Hong Kong to Canton unless armed. In one instance, pirates captured the official in charge of the *Bogue,* cut off his ears, and absconded with his seals, demanding $60,000 ransom for return of the seals.[3] Attempts by the Hong Kong government to police the waters in the immediate vicinity of Hong Kong made them somewhat safer, but its ability to rid the Hong Kong shipping lanes of pirates was limited.[4] Even when pirate and Triad leaders were apprehended, the Hong Kong government faced a dilemma regarding their punishment. The jails were full. Furthermore, imprisonment failed to act as a deterrent. Deportation to the mainland was no solution, for it meant either execution by the Chinese government or escape to a continued life of robbery and blackmail.[5]

Subsequently, more forceful British campaigns against pirate fleets had greater success in clearing coastal waters, but many pirates succeeded in fleeing to the North, West, and Gui rivers of Guangdong and Guangxi, where they flourished, immune to British authority. Chinese government drives against bandits and pirates on the southeast coast likewise drove them into interior waters. At transshipment points the pirate gangs levied fees on goods moving along these new trade routes, and they largely controlled the opium and salt smuggling.[6] Indicative of the diminished authority of the govern-

3. Arthur Cunynghame, *The Opium War: Being Recollections of Service in China* (1845; Wilmington, DE: Scholarly Resources Inc., 1972), pp. 211-12.

4. Colonial Office, Public Records, Hong Kong, Original Correspondence, CO 129/10, 23 March 1844; 129/11, 4 March 1845.

5. Colonial Office, Public Records, Hong Kong, Original Correspondence, CO 129/11, 21 January 1845; 28 June 1845; CO 129/12, 3 May 1845.

6. Grace Fox, *British Admirals and Chinese Pirates* (London: Kegan Paul & Co., 1940), pp. 95-105; Laai Yi-faai, "The Part Played by the Pirates of Kwangtung in the Taiping Insurrection" (Ph.D. diss., University of California, 1950), pp. 62-68, 107-51.

ment is the fact that some of the bandit chiefs appropriated the title of *Da wang* (Great king) and presumed to ride in sedan chairs, a prerogative of the literati.[7] A high proportion of these pirates were Hakka, and most of them belonged to the Triad Society.[8]

Poverty, in addition to raising the death rate from disease and malnutrition, entailed an increase in female infanticide and in the number of "bare sticks," young men who had no chance of marrying and establishing a stable family life. The spreading opium scourge with its attendant smuggling trade only compounded the troubles. Especially among disadvantaged groups like the Hakka and Miao, alienation from the mainstream became prevalent. In Miao regions of Guangxi, for example, vulgar and immoral demon gods gained such popularity that they could terrorize villages. Competition and feuding characterized relations between these ethnic communities and the *bendi*, and also between lineages and villages. When in 1850 Hakka in Guangxi were driven off the land during a war with *bendi* and aboriginal peoples, thousands fled to the ranks of the God Worshippers for protection and sustenance.[9] Sect groups in trouble with Chinese officials sometimes turned to Christianity in order to benefit from the extraterritorial rights. By the 1840s many Guangxi counties and less accessible regions of western Guangdong had drifted out of imperial control; here, civil officials had largely abdicated responsibility for maintaining law and order.

Within the void, the Taipings, bandits, Triads, and other unorthodox societies thrived. Their membership could reach into the thousands or even tens of thousands before the government was forced to take notice and gear up for action against them. Religious sects and, for a few Chinese, Christian congregations offered community and social support amidst the volatile environment. All found a certain free space in which to function, whether it was the consequence of foreign protection or government impotence. As the traditional social and ethical fabric frayed, an ecology favorable to unconventional doctrines and organizations took shape.

7. *China Mail*, 2 January 1851.

8. Laai Yi-faai, "The Part Played by the Pirates of Kwangtung," p. 11; Dian Murray and Qin Baoqi, *The Origins of the Tiandihui: The Chinese Triads in Legend and History* (Stanford: Stanford University Press, 1994), p. 70.

9. Laai Yi-faai, "The Part Played by the Pirates of Kwangtung," pp. 111, 174-75.

Enabling Factors: Chinese Heterodox Societies and Chinese Christians

Southeast China, and more especially Guangdong, has been called China's cradle of revolution.[10] The area developed late and long resisted Qing rule; minorities were more widespread here than in the north. Also contributing to the region's unruliness were outside influences such as overseas trading and Western presence. During the nineteenth century, relations among the proliferating heterodox groups, Taipings, Christians, Triads, and religious sects were surprisingly permeable, even distressingly so in the view of the missionaries. Tracing the influence of individuals belonging to one group upon members of other societies is interesting and useful; in many cases, however, it is difficult to establish influence with any certainty. A study of individual crossovers, nevertheless, illustrates the widespread appeal of heterodox societies in the emerging subculture of south China, the continuing search of some individuals for moral certainty and protection, and the opportunism of others in these troublesome times. It helps to elucidate the Chinese rather than the missionary perception of these societies, and Chinese motivations for joining them. Though the Triads and the social bandit organizations differed in many ways from the religious societies, there were intersecting points as well as numerous transfers.

Data is available on a number of individuals who were associated with Karl Gützlaff and the Basel mission and who transferred to Chinese heterodox societies, so that Gützlaff, his European missionary recruits, and his union of Chinese evangelists can serve as a focus in studying this heterodox culture and relations within it. Upon Gützlaff's death in 1852 and the demise of the Chinese Union, numerous Chinese converts were left without employment. Even earlier, during Gützlaff's European tour in 1849-1850, Theodor Hamberg had fired many Chinese Union members whom he considered unreliable. These individuals, having been associated with foreigners and a foreign religion, found re-entry into Chinese society difficult. Some tried to find a home among the Triads; others turned to the Taipings. Wang Fengqing, for example, had been a member of the Chinese Union and had been sent to Guizhou to work among the Miao, but he lost his position in 1851. He thereupon joined the Taiping army, where he met several former Chinese Union members, some of them in official positions. He was even ushered into the presence of the southern king, Feng Yunshan, who welcomed him as an old

---

10. Jen Yuwen (Jian Youwen), *The Taiping Revolutionary Movement* (New Haven: Yale University Press, 1973), p. 1.

acquaintance. After participating in the Taiping Nanjing campaign, Wang returned to Hong Kong only to leave to join the Triad rebels holding Shanghai. He soon became disillusioned with conditions in the Triad camp and in the early 1860s renewed his interest in Christianity, attending Joseph Edkins's Protestant chapel in Shanghai.[11]

Not all who were attracted to heterodoxy were as opportunistic or inconstant as Wang, but many demonstrated a readiness to switch affiliations. Loyalty to China, religious conviction, or the need for protection could be the motivation. Li Bengshen, an assistant collector of grain revenue in Shanghai during the 1850s, became convinced of the merit of Christianity after reading *Village Sermons* by William Milne and the *Ten Commandments of God.* He opted for Taiping Christianity rather than Protestant Christianity and left Shanghai to join the Taipings in Nanjing. When Edkins met him in Suzhou in 1860, he impressed the LMS missionary as sincere in both faith and practice.[12]

The Taipings and Protestant Missionaries

Moving in a reverse direction from Taiping Christianity to Protestantism were relatives of the Taiping leaders Hong Xiuquan and Feng Yunshan in Huaxian. Forced to flee when imperial troops began destroying their ancestral graves, extorting money, and arresting kinsmen in 1851, many sought refuge in Hakka villages such as Lilang and Xinan. There some were proselytized by Gützlaff's Basel recruits and were converted to Christianity. Others moved in and out of Hong Kong.[13]

The prime example of Christian missionaries as an enabling factor in the rise of new religious movements in nineteenth-century China is, of course, the Taiping Rebellion. Even here, however, lacunae and differences in interpretation of the role and influence of Protestant missionaries exist. Reliance by historians on the biography of Taiping leader Hong Xiuquan as related by Hong's cousin Hong Rengan to Theodor Hamberg yields the following familiar narra-

---

11. Joseph Edkins, *Religion in China, Containing a Brief Account of the Three Religions of the Chinese,* 2nd ed. (London: Trübner & Co., 1878), pp. 195-96; Theodor Hamberg, *Report Regarding the Chinese Union at Hong Kong* (Hong Kong: Hong Kong Register, 1851), pp. 8, 14; *Jahresbericht des evangelischen Missionsvereins in Kurhessen,* 31 March 1850; *Hong Kong Register* 26.39 (27 September 1853): 154.

12. Edkins to Tidman, Shanghai, 12 April 1861, Church Missionary Society (hereafter CMS), Central China, Incoming Correspondence, 1855-1861, Box 2, Folder 3, Jacket 10.

13. Carl T. Smith, *Chinese Christians, Élites, Middlemen, and the Church in Hong Kong* (Hong Kong: Oxford University Press, 1985), p. 77.

tive.[14] On the occasion of Hong's second attempt to pass the *xiucai* examinations in 1836, he had listened to preaching by the ABCFM missionary Edwin Stevens[15] through a Chinese interpreter in Canton; he had also acquired *Good Words to Admonish an Age* by Liang Fa, an early convert of Robert Morrison and William Milne, but he only glanced at the pamphlet before putting it away. In 1837 Hong failed for the third time to pass the examination and thereupon suffered a nervous breakdown. During his illness, Hong had visions of going to heaven, where he was cleansed and then called into the presence of an august old man and his son. The old man recognized Hong as his second son and commanded him to return to earth to rid China of demons.

Six years later, Li Jingfang, a maternal relative, borrowed *Good Words*, and after reading it commended it to Hong, who found that the tract authenticated his earlier vision. He proceeded to interpret and elaborate upon Liang Fa's presentation of Christianity, drawing on both Chinese and Christian sources. The old man was God (Shangdi) and the son was Christ, who had been sent to earth earlier to sacrifice his life for the salvation of humankind. Hong, in accordance with his mission to usher in the new millennium, began proselytizing among his kinsmen, several of whom converted to Hong's new teaching. They destroyed images of deities, and Hong even removed the tablet of Confucius from his schoolroom. Later, Hong would study briefly with the Baptist missionary Issachar Roberts; this is doubtless the source of the Gützlaff Bible, the Doxology, and the Ten Commandments adopted by the Taipings. All three works would be repeatedly reprinted by the Taipings.[16] While in Canton with Roberts, Hong also participated in Christian rituals, including congregational hymn singing, which would be carried over into Taiping forms of worship.

In the Mullins scheme the missionaries and their converts served as an enabling factor in Hong's turn to heterodoxy. The significance of Gützlaff's role is also confirmed, for Gützlaff had been mentor to Hamberg, Roberts, and Stevens; they inherited his Chinese assistants and they utilized his scriptural translations and religious tracts. Impressed by Gützlaff's boldness in estab-

14. Theodor Hamberg, *The Visions of Hung-siu-tsuen and Origin of the Kwangsi Insurrection* (1854; New York: Praeger, 1968).

15. Stevens had been sent to China in 1832 as chaplain of the Seaman's Friend Society, but he became affiliated with the American Board of Commissioners for Foreign Missions (hereafter ABCFM) in 1836. He died of malarial fever the following year.

16. Thousands of copies of Gützlaff's Bible with Hong Xiuquan's emendations were printed in Nanjing during the 1850s. *Tiantiao shu* [Book of Heavenly Articles], the Taiping version of the Ten Commandments, was circulated through the whole Taiping army. Jen Yuwen, *The Taiping Revolutionary Movement*, p. 161.

lishing contact with villagers in the interior and desiring to ascertain for himself their friendliness, Stevens had accepted Gützlaff's invitation to accompany him on a trip up the Min River in 1835. In 1836 Issachar Roberts set sail for China, inspired by Gützlaff's depiction of the challenges and opportunities presented by China's vast population of heathens.[17] Gützlaff welcomed Roberts upon his arrival in Macao in May 1837 and lodged him in the Gützlaff home for eight months. He invited Roberts to accompany him on his itinerations, instructed him in Chinese, including Hakka, and supported and housed him in Hong Kong when Baptist mission funds were cut off. When Roberts decided to adopt Chinese dress and life style and to locate in Canton despite dangerous anti-Western sentiment, Gützlaff provided Roberts with evangelists from the Chinese Union. Thus in 1844 Roberts, accompanied by his first Hong Kong convert and several Chinese Union assistants, began his preaching mission in Canton. Since the Baptist society did not sanction Roberts's transfer to Canton, Gützlaff continued to send Roberts financial aid.[18]

According to Mullins's model, Hong Xiuquan was the personal-innovative factor or the "minor founder" of the Taipings. It was through Zhou Daoxing, a Chinese Union assistant provided by Gützlaff, that Roberts came into contact with Hong Xiuquan and Hong Rengan, who would be appointed prime minister in the Taiping government at Nanjing in 1859. Zhou visited Hua county in 1846 and urged Hong Xiuquan to come to Canton, where there was a foreigner preaching doctrines similar to Hong's. Having been informed of Hong's activities, Roberts then sent Zhou with a written invitation to Hong to visit him in 1847.[19] Hong Xiuquan and his cousin Hong Rengan arrived in Canton in March, though Rengan soon returned to his teaching position. Xiuquan, however, spent several months with Roberts attending worship services, reading the Gützlaff translation of the Bible, and studying religious tracts, some of them by Roberts himself. With Roberts delaying baptism and funds running low, Hong obtained travel money from Zhou Daoxing and left in July 1847 to join Feng Yunshan at Thistle Mountain in Guangxi.

17. For biographies of Roberts, see Margaret M. Coughlin, "Strangers in the House: J. Lewis Shuck and Issachar Roberts, First American Baptist Missionaries in China" (Ph.D. diss., University of Virginia, 1972), and George B. Pruden, "Issachar Jacox Roberts and American Diplomacy in China during the Taiping Rebellion" (Ph.D. diss., American University, 1977).

18. Gützlaff to Ledeboer, Nanjing, August 1842, Nederlandsh Zendeling Genootschap (hereafter NZG) Archives; Gützlaff to Ledeboer, Hong Kong, 24 May 1845, NZG Archives; I. J. Roberts, "Early Life of Charles Gutzlaff," *China Mission Advocate* 1 (January 1839): 31-32; Roberts, "The China Mission," *China Mission Advocate* 1 (November 1839): 321-24.

19. "Native Reporter's News," *Friend of China* 16.54 (11 July 1857), p. 219.

Were these the only contacts that Hong Xiuquan had with Christianity and Christian missionaries? Nagging questions remain, but thus far no firm evidence of additional interchange during this early period has come to light. Gützlaff and other missionaries had distributed thousands of religious tracts and scriptures among Chinese traders in Southeast Asia and in villages along the coast of southern China. Did any of these materials reach Hong before his study with Roberts in 1847? Roberts noted that Hong had greater Christian knowledge than he could account for simply on the basis of Liang's pamphlet.[20] Hong supposedly had merely glanced at *Good Words* before his vision of a visit to heaven. Yet when Hong went to teach in Li Jingfang's household, he brought *Good Words* with him. Why, if he considered the tract of little significance?

Feng Yunshan, one of Hong's initial converts, was actually responsible for the first major expansion of the God Worshippers in Guangxi during 1846-1847 and for the establishment of their base at Thistle Mountain. Partly because Feng died in 1852 from a wound incurred during the early stages of the Taiping northern campaign, much less is known about him than about other Taiping leaders. Some authors have suggested that Feng Yunshan was a member of Gützlaff's Chinese Union, or at least was instructed by Gützlaff. Except for the report of Wang Fengqing, cited above, most of the documentation is either vague or based on secondhand reports. The journal of the Chinese secretary of the Chinese Union for 23 June 1851, for instance, stated that he had heard from several mandarins that the Tian De emperor, Hong, had ordered the worship of God (Shangdi) and the observance of the Sabbath. The emperor's adviser was a certain Feng, "who had earlier been instructed in the Gospel."[21] As already noted, a former Chinese Union member who joined the Taiping army was greeted by Feng as an old friend. It is also worth noting that when Feng was arrested in 1847 for promotion of a secret organization, he was well enough acquainted with recent Sino-Western relations to argue for dismissal on grounds that the emperor had recently granted religious freedom, including the right of Chinese to convert to Christianity; in addition, he had maintained that the worship of God (Shangdi) was an indigenous Chinese teaching.[22] Feng's younger son and nephew were acquainted with Roberts

20. "The Chinese Struggle," quoting letter of I. Roberts, Canton, 6 October 1852, *The Chinese Gleaner* 2.9 (February 1853): 68-70.

21. "Tagebuch des Chinesischen Verein," Hong Kong, 23 June 1851, *Neuste Nachrichten aus China* 7 (1 October 1851): 97-103. E. G. Fishbourne also states that Feng had been instructed by Gützlaff. Fishbourne, *Impressions of China and the Present Revolution: Its Progress and Prospects* (London: Seeley, Jackson, & Halliday, 1855), p. 259.

22. Jen Yuwen, *The Taiping Revolutionary Movement*, p. 39.

and in 1853 traveled north with Roberts in an attempt to reach the Taiping capital, Nanjing.

Certainly there were continuing contacts among the Feng and Hong families, Chinese Christians, mission employees, and Basel and LMS missionaries. These ties merit examination, since they also illustrate a shared heterodox Chinese community and sometimes a shared membership. Chinese frequently viewed the societies and their teachings in much less exclusivist terms than the Westerners. By spelling out these relationships in detail, one gains a better understanding of the heterodox subculture that was sprouting in southeast China.

Li Zhenggao, the son or possibly the nephew of Li Jingfang, was an early convert of Hong. Even though he subsequently became a Basel evangelist, he remained in communication with Taiping leaders and their families throughout the 1850s and into the 1860s.[23] As a youth, Li Zhenggao was said to have been deeply concerned about his personal morality and also the general political and moral decline of his era. Thus when Hong Xiuquan visited the Li home, described his visions, proclaimed the power of God and his own commission to overthrow the demons and false gods, Li Zhenggao was convinced that Hong was God's chosen instrument to return China to truth and morality. He became a baptized convert of Hong. On Hong and Feng Yunshan's first trip to Guangxi in the spring of 1844, they stopped in the stronghold of the Li lineage, Qingyuan, where they converted many other Li kinsmen. Xiuquan's cousin Hong Rengan then came to Qingyuan to teach and continue the proselytism; he recruited over fifty Taiping followers. After the defeat of the Taipings, some of the Li clansmen would turn to Christianity.

In what appears to be the first foreign reference to God Worshippers in Guangxi, Gützlaff reported in 1845 that "a gifted man who settled there began to make heard the word of the Saviour," and in 1846 he wrote that there had been "established [in Guangxi] a Christian Union without our aid."[24] During the late 1840s, Gützlaff claimed to have sent a half-dozen or more Chinese Union evangelists to Guangxi; some undoubtedly did not reach their destination, but in one instance in 1845, an inquirer journeyed to Hong Kong saying that he already had some acquaintance with the gospel and requesting litera-

23. For a biography of Li Zhenggao, see "The Life of the Departed Deacon Li Zhenggao," in *Hakka Chinese Confront Protestant Christianity, 1850-1900*, ed. Jessie G. Lutz and R. R. Lutz (Armonk, NY: M. E. Sharpe, 1998), pp. 121-44.

24. Gützlaff to Ledeboer, Hong Kong, 29 December 1845, NZG Archives; Gützlaff's letter of 27 June 1846, quoted in Pommersche Hauptverein, *Geschichte der Missionen in China von den ältesten Zeiten bis auf Gützlaff* (Stettin: R. Grassmann, 1850), p. 31.

ture and preachers.[25] Responding quickly, Gützlaff began to make arrangements to dispatch Ho Ba and several other Chinese Union evangelists to Guangxi. Ho Ba operated principally in Gueilin, but Wang Shizhang and coworkers reportedly distributed literature and preached in Gueiping near Thistle Mountain, the headquarters of Feng and the God Worshippers. Evangelists were also dispatched to Wuzhou, Nanning, and other cities in Guangxi. Wang Fengqing, mentioned above, was also supposed to have preached in Guangxi.[26] By 1848 Gützlaff claimed the founding of five Chinese Union stations in Guangxi and the printing of the New Testament in Guilin.[27] When Gützlaff departed for Europe in September 1849 he carried with him as publicity two letters purportedly written and signed by Chinese Union members: fourteen individuals signed the letter from Guangxi and eleven signed the one from Jiangxi. The Chinese evangelists sent greetings to German Christians and stated that in ancient China God (Shangdi) had also been worshipped, but that during the Han dynasty false gods and idols had become popular because the people no longer understood the holy teachings. They were grateful for the coming of Pastor Guo (Gützlaff) so that they could be converted through the Holy Ghost.[28]

In Gützlaff's writing it is difficult to separate his exaggerated hopes from reality, but in this instance Gützlaff's report of God Worshippers in Guangxi had a factual basis. Also, Ho Ba and Wang were early recruits to the Chinese Union; thus they had undergone a lengthy period of apprenticeship and were more likely than later recruits to carry out their assignments. Even if the letters came from the hand of Gützlaff with minimal input by the Chinese Union members, it is interesting that Gützlaff employed a theme that came to be associated with Hong Xiuquan, namely, that the ancient Chinese had worshipped Shangdi, had fallen away from the truth, but should now return to their original, true faith. Hong Xiuquan declared that Shangdi was a universal God, not a Western deity brought to China by foreigners.[29]

How much overlap there was between the God Worshippers and those evangelized by the Chinese Union is, unfortunately, another of the un-

---

25. Gützlaff to NZG, Hong Kong, 26 December 1848.

26. Gützlaff to NZG, Hong Kong, 23 April 1846; 26 March 1847; 26 December 1848; *Jahresbericht der Pommerschen Hauptverein für Evangelisirung China*, 1:31, 51.

27. Gützlaff to NZG, Hong Kong, 26 December 1848.

28. "Schreiben der Chinesischen Brüder an die Christen des Abendlandes," *Neueste Nachrichten aus China* 1.5 (1 August 1851): 72-75.

29. Hong expressed this theme in *Tiantiao shu* [Book of Heavenly Commandments], published in 1852 but probably written several years earlier. Medhurst published an English translation of *Tiantiao shu* in the *North China Herald*, 14 May 1853.

knowns. In any case, it seems safe to say that religious tracts and scriptures were available in Guangxi by the late 1840s. Hong Xiuquan used Gützlaff's translation of the Bible, and when the Taipings began a massive reprinting of the Bible, they copied Gützlaff's version almost character for character.[30] Proclamations and other Taiping documents also employ Gützlaff's terms: *Huang Shangdi* (Supreme emperor God), *shen* for gods other than the Almighty, and *Jiuyizhao shengshu* for the Old Testament. Later, Westerners visiting the Taiping capital of Nanjing reported that Gützlaff's name was well known there.[31]

In 1850 Hong Xiuquan sent an emissary to guide the Hong and Feng family members to the Thistle Mountain base in Guangxi. Though many from the Hong lineage successfully joined the God Worshippers there, Feng Yunshan's eldest son was captured by imperial forces and imprisoned in Canton. Here he would remain over a decade and would be visited by the Christian evangelist Li Zhenggao, who brought moral support and Protestant tracts. Li reported that the son still retained his Christian faith, praying to Jesus morning and night. In 1851 Hong Rengan and members of the Li lineage tried unsuccessfully to make contact with the Taiping army; Li's father and elder brother were seized and put in prison, where they apparently died. Hong Rengan and Li Zhenggao escaped and went underground, posing as geomancers. Hong found refuge with a Hakka Christian in Dongguan, Zhang Jaixiu, who engaged him to teach in his home for a year.[32] Hong Rengan, making his way to Hong Kong, contacted Theodor Hamberg. Since Hamberg had by this time become quite competent in the Hakka dialect and concentrated on pros-

30. Eugene Boardman, *Christian Influence upon the Ideology of the Taiping Rebellion, 1851-1864* (Madison: University of Wisconsin Press, 1952); Spence, *God's Chinese Son: The Taiping Heavenly Kingdom of Hong Xiuquan* (New York: W. W. Norton & Co., 1996), pp. 177-79. For the New Testament, the Taipings employed the 1835 version produced jointly by Walter Medhurst and Gützlaff. Medhurst to Tidman, Shanghai, 29 December 1853, Church World Mission Society (hereafter CWM), Central China, Incoming, no. 1.

31. Prescot Clarke has presented considerable data on Gützlaff and the origins of the Taipings; see Clarke, "The Coming of God to Kwangsi," *Papers on Far Eastern History* (Australian National University) 7 (March 1973). For contemporary reports, see A. Wylie's letter to the London Missionary Society (hereafter LMS), 3 March 1859, quoted in *The Missionary Magazine and Chronicle* 23 (July 1859): 179-81; William Milne to Tidman, Shanghai, 6 May 1853, CWM, LMS Archives, Central China, Incoming Letters, Box 1, Folder 4A; and Fishbourne, *Impressions of China*, pp. 121-22.

32. Zhang would later join Rengan in Nanjing. Jen Yuwen, *The Taiping Revolutionary Movement*, p. 354. The grandson of Zhang, a Christian minister, provided this information to Jen Yuwen. For a translation of a poem that Hong Rengan presented to Zhang, see Franz Michael and Chung-li Chang, *The Taiping Rebellion: History and Documents*, 3 vols. (Seattle: University of Washington Press, 1966-1971), 3:531-32.

elytizing among the Hakka, it was natural for Hong Rengan and other Hakka seeking refuge or knowledge about Christianity to contact Hamberg or other Basel missionaries.

Taiping Visitors

In March 1853 the Taipings conquered Nanjing and made it their capital, the New Jerusalem. Almost immediately both Chinese and Westerners sought to visit the Taiping headquarters: Chinese who were hopeful that the Taipings would usher in a new era of strength and prosperity, and Westerners who desired to discover more about Taiping Christianity and to persuade the Taipings to tailor their Christianity after the Western Protestant model. Among the early aspirants was Issachar Roberts. Feng Yunshan's son and nephew, also hoping to reach Nanjing and lacking funds, posed as Robert's servants in order to accompany Roberts to Shanghai in 1853. The three, however, were unable to secure passage from Shanghai to Nanjing.[33] The nephew was baptized by Roberts in Shanghai and returned south to serve briefly as language tutor to an American Baptist missionary. Ill, he visited Lechler in Buji in hopes of recovery, but died in August 1855. Lechler reported, "Since he was a Christian, we gave him a Christian burial and many members of our community accompanied the coffin to the grave."[34] One individual who apparently did reach Nanjing in 1853 was named Liu, a member of the Chinese Union who had worked with Hamberg and was engaged by Lechler as a schoolteacher. He received an invitation from friends who were then with the Taipings in Nanjing and who informed him that there were three or four former Chinese Union members there. Since Liu was determined to go, Lechler gave him a supply of Christian works and wished him well.[35]

In May 1854 Li Zhenggao, Hong Rengan, and a relative also attempted to reach Nanjing via Shanghai. Rengan had been introduced to Hamberg by a relative from the Basel station of Lilang and had brought other kinsmen and friends to Hamberg for instruction before his own baptism on 20 September

---

33. The son apparently did reach Nanjing at a later date, for Jen Yuwen lists the son among those fleeing from Nanjing upon its occupation by Zeng Guoquan's troops in July 1864, *The Taiping Revolutionary Movement*, p. 534. See also Margaret E. F. Crawford, "Journals and Diaries, 1846-1881," 3 July 1853, Duke University Archives, China, 2G.

34. Rudolf Lechler, *Acht Vorträge über China gehalten an verschiedenen Orten Deutschlands und der Schweiz* (Basel: Verlag des Missionshauses, 1861), p. 153.

35. Lechler to Inspector, Tungfo, 22 October 1853, Archives of Basel Missions Gesellschaft (hereafter BMG), A-1.2, no. 41.

1853 in Buji.[36] It was during this period that Rengan provided Hamberg with materials for the *Visions of Hung-siu-tshuen*. Li, who had been in touch with Rengan about the proposed journey to Nanjing, made his way to Hong Kong, where he was welcomed by Hamberg and Lechler. Following instruction by the two, Li acknowledged that his baptism by Hong Xiuquan had been improper, and he and a relative from his home village were re-baptized on 28 February 1854.[37] Hamberg encouraged Li and Rengan to go to Nanjing so that they could bring "the truth of Christianity" to the Taipings. Not only did Hamberg provide them with financial aid; he also sent with them the Old Testament, the New Testament in three translations, Christian Barth's *Biblical History* translated by Gützlaff, Ferdinand Genähr's *Catechism,* a calendar, and other writings. In addition, he furnished maps in Chinese of the world, China, and Palestine; a model of a steel punch, copper matrices, and printing types in order to show how Chinese characters could be printed in the European manner, plus various miscellanies such as a telescope, compass, thermometer, and knives.[38]

In Shanghai they contacted LMS missionary Walter Medhurst, who temporarily provided them with food and lodging. Stymied in Shanghai, they were soon in desperate straits. Li reminisced: "At this time, I was really in distress, for I no longer had a friend in the world, and I lacked money for a return trip to Hong Kong. That was precisely the turning point at which I began to undergo a spiritual transformation. For the first time I began to pray in earnest from the heart: Lord pardon this sinner and do not damn him in judgment."[39] After an emotional conversionary experience of repentance and rebirth, "he was convinced that the Lord had an important assignment for him."[40] With Medhurst's aid, he made his way back to Hong Kong, and Lechler, who took him in, supported and instructed him for more than a year. He would become Lechler's principal evangelist, serving for almost thirty years.

Hong Rengan remained in Shanghai, where he studied astronomy, mathematics, and Christianity with Medhurst and Joseph Edkins for several months. He also met Wang Tao, who was Medhurst's principal assistant and would later collaborate with James Legge in translating the Chinese classics.

36. Hamberg, "Halbjähriger Bericht von Juli 1853 bis Jan 1854, Station Pukak," 1853, BMG, A-1.2, no. 47.

37. Li Chengen, "Das leben des Seligheimgegangenen Diakon Li Tschin-kau," Hong Kong, 1885, BMG, A-1.19, no. 38.

38. Hamberg to Inspector, Hong Kong, 4 May 1854, BMG, A-1.3, no. 10. Hamberg died on 13 May 1854, nine days after writing this letter.

39. Quoted in Li Chengen, "Das Leben des Seligheimgegangenen Diakon Li Tschin-kau."

40. Li Chengen, "Das Leben des Seligheimgegangenen Diakon Li Tschin-kau."

Returning to Hong Kong in 1855, Rengan worked with LMS missionaries James Legge and John Chalmers, as well as with William Burns and other Protestant missionaries. He became friends with Rong Hong (Yung Wing), who knew Roberts and had studied briefly at Mary Gützlaff's school before attending the Morrison Education Society School and Yale University. Rengan and Rong Hong shared a desire to strengthen China through adoption of Western technology and administrative procedures. Bonds like these are evidence of the genesis of a Chinese reform community energized by missionaries and foreign infringements on China. In 1858, when Lechler went on home leave, Rengan and Li Zhenggao served Lechler's Hakka congregation, which met in Legge's church. Rengan also assisted at the opening of one of the first Protestant chapels within the Canton city walls in 1858.

Loyalty to his kinsman, Hong Xiuquan, and a patriotic hope for a new China continued to beckon Rengan to Nanjing, and in the summer of 1858 he left on a long and perilous inland journey to the Taiping capital, finally arriving on 22 April 1859. Rengan found a regime in disarray. Suspicion reigned among the leadership and feuding had reached murderous proportions. Hong Xiuquan had retreated to the task of refining his "True Religion." Delighted to welcome a kinsman whom he could trust, Hong Xiuquan bestowed on Rengan numerous positions and titles: Gan Wang (Shield king), generalissimo, prime minister, and later, minister of foreign affairs. Multiple problems, however, severely limited Rengan's scope for restoring Taiping fortunes and bringing stability and reform to their government.

Hong Rengan, nevertheless, cultivated his connections with his former colleagues and friends in the hope of obtaining aid and of promoting understanding of the Taiping position. Only a year after arriving in Nanjing, Rengan wrote Li Zhenggao, instructing him to come to Suzhou and to bring Rengan's family with him.[41] After some hesitation and consultation with the Basel missionaries, Li declined, in the belief that Protestant Christianity, not Taiping Christianity, possessed the truth. Nevertheless, he retained an interest in the fate of the families of the Taiping leaders. In 1861, fourteen relatives of Hong Xiuquan and Hong Rengan finally did succeed in reaching Nanjing, with the assistance of LMS missionaries Griffith John and James Legge, the Dutch missionary H. Z. Klockers, and an official of the Olyphant trading company. Most of the group were Christians, and one was a catechist who carried a letter of introduction from Legge.[42] The number of Western Chris-

41. Philipp Winnes to Inspector, Hong Kong, 14 January 1861, BMG, 1860, A-1.4, no. 14.
42. R. G. Tiedemann, "Missionary Views on the Taiping Rebellion" (paper presented at Huitième Colloque International de Sinologie de Chantilly, September 1995).

tians who assisted in the transfer is itself an indication of the many links among the Chinese and Western Christian communities.

The attraction of the Taipings for Chinese desirous of strengthening China is illustrated by the visits of Rong Hong and Wang Tao, both of whom were participants in the Sino-Western communities of the treaty ports and Hong Kong. Rong Hong met with Taiping leaders in Suzhou during the fall of 1859 and presented a number of reform proposals. Though the Taiping officials were willing to offer Rong Hong government rank, they gave no assurance of implementing his recommendations. Rong Hong declined a Taiping title and left.[43] Wang Tao accompanied Joseph Edkins on journeys to meet with Taiping leaders in Nanjing during the summer of 1860 and again in the spring of 1861. On both occasions Wang assisted Edkins in explaining Western Christian theology to the Taiping Christians. Then in February 1862 Wang Tao addressed a letter to military commandant Liu Zhaojun suggesting that the pride and military strength of the British made it wise to avoid an immediate direct confrontation with them in Shanghai; rather, he proposed a strategy for the future wherein fifth columnists would rise up in the city while Taiping troops attacked from without.[44] Again the advice was not carried out.

On several occasions Rengan acted as intermediary in relations with Western visitors. He recalled fondly his foreign friends in Shanghai and Canton–Hong Kong, especially Lechler, Hamberg, Chalmers, Medhurst, Roberts, and Gützlaff. A delegation of English Baptist and LMS missionaries received a courteous welcome in the summer of 1860. Joseph Edkins, Griffith John, Hong Rengan, and Li Xiucheng all expressed a desire for good relations between the Taipings and the Western powers; Edkins and John presented a statement on Protestant theology composed by Wang Tao, and all joined in prayers and the singing of a Medhurst hymn. At the invitation of Hong Rengan, Edkins returned a second time to discuss with Rengan Protestant and Taiping teachings on the Trinity and the divinity of Christ and the Holy Spirit, a discussion that ended in a stalemate, since Hong Xiuquan and Hong Rengan believed that God alone was divine.[45] On more than one occasion

43. Yung Wing (Rong Hong), *My Life in China and America* (New York: Henry Holt & Co., 1909), pp. 107-10.

44. For a detailed discussion of this facet of Wang Tao's life and the historiography on the subject, see Paul Cohen, *Between Tradition and Modernity: Wang Táo and Reform in Late Ch'ing China* (Cambridge, MA: Harvard University Press, 1974), pp. 44-55. When Wang Tao's contacts with the Taipings became known to the imperial government and his life was endangered, he fled to Hong Kong, where he joined Legge in his massive translation of the Confucian classics.

45. Jane Edkins, *Chinese Scenes and People, with Notices of Christian Missions and Mis-*

Rengan indicated to Western visitors that the Chinese themselves could evangelize China; the Taiping leaders were in direct communication with God and did not need foreigners to explain the gospel to the Chinese.[46] As it turned out, the missionaries had as little influence on British and American policy as on Hong Xiuquan's theology, a fact that was dramatically illustrated a few days later. Taiping troops, approaching Shanghai, sent word promising protection to foreigners and churches, but to their dismay, British soldiers opened fire on them as they pursued imperial forces toward the West Gate.

Renewal of contact with Roberts likewise ended on a note of disillusionment. In 1860 Hong Rengan sent a former Triad member to Canton to invite Roberts to Nanjing. Upon Roberts's arrival, Rengan gave Roberts lodging in his own palace complex and made him vice-minister of foreign affairs. Roberts immediately assumed the task of explaining Taiping goals and views to the West through numerous articles and letters. To Roberts's dismay and astonishment, he soon discovered that Hong Xiuquan believed that God had given him a new dispensation, and that he, Hong, should be teacher, not pupil, to Roberts. Relations with Rengan likewise deteriorated. After fifteen months at the capital, Roberts left Nanjing in January 1862, an embittered man now eager to publicize the eccentricities of Hong Xiuquan and the heresies of Taiping Christianity.[47]

Continued intrigues within Taiping ranks and Hong Xiuquan's retreat from reality into his own esoteric theology undercut the attempts of both Rengan and the military commanders to implement a viable defense strategy. When Nanjing fell in 1864, Rengan fled with the heir apparent, only to be captured, interrogated, and executed on 23 November 1864. But he never abandoned his faith in the truth of Taiping Christianity.

Taiping and Triad Relations

Relations between the Taipings and the Triads (or Tiandihui, Heaven and Earth Society) are not the focus of this chapter, but they do point to the influence of the Western presence in the growth of heterodoxy, disorder, and rebellion. Among Chinese residing in the treaty ports, new perceptions of the world order, of the exercise of political and military power, and of economic

---

sion *Life* (London: James Nisbet & Co., 1863), pp. 266-70; see also Cohen, *Between Tradition and Modernity*, pp. 53-55.

46. Letter of W. Muirhead to LMS, *The Missionary Magazine and Chronicle* 25 (1861): 202.

47. Pruden, "Issachar Jacox Roberts," pp. 291-94.

possibilities were being introduced. Perhaps the most famous Triad to join the Taipings was Luo Dagang, a former pirate chieftain who had been driven into the interior by the campaigns against pirates mentioned above. During the early stage of the Taiping military campaign, when the God Worshippers needed aid, they welcomed alliances with bandit chiefs and Triad leaders if they accepted Taiping doctrines and discipline.[48] Two female chieftains, each with two thousand followers, and eight bands of river pirates joined the Taipings in 1850. Of these, only one of the two women and Luo Dagang proved willing to abide by Taiping strictures. Though there are few specifics on Luo's early life, he appears to have been employed on an opium-receiving ship at Lintin in 1837; he then saw military service during the Opium War, but according to Laai Yi-faai (Lai Yifei), it is not clear whether he served the British or the Chinese.[49] At any rate, Luo had conducted business with foreigners, spoke some English, and had some familiarity with Christian doctrines, having assisted Hong Kong administrators in establishing a church in Canton. He became a prominent Triad leader and river pirate in the Canton region, but he was forced to flee to Guangxi in 1850. To the Taipings he brought knowledge of Western ships and naval strategy, and he led many of the Taiping naval operations, especially during the drive to Nanjing.[50] He often served as spokesman in relations with foreign visitors, impressing them with his sincerity, enthusiasm for the Taiping cause, and supreme confidence in eventual Taiping victory. With his death in 1855 from battle wounds, the Taipings lost one of their most competent military strategists.

The leaders of the Triad offshoot, the Small Sword Society (*xiaodaohui*), who captured Shanghai in 1853, also give evidence of the continuing interaction of Westerners and Chinese dissidents. Most of the leaders were from Canton or Fuzhou, and the master of each branch had considerable experience in working with foreigners. Both were anti-Manchu, flying the Triad banner of Ming restoration. Liu Lichuan came from the Xiangshan district near Macao, had been a sugar broker in Canton, and in 1849 had transferred to Shanghai, where he earned a living as interpreter for a Western firm, sugar broker, and medical practitioner. Thus he had considerable appreciation of Western military and economic power and was acquainted with Western business practices. The other leader, Chen Alin, had been a groom for an En-

48. Elizabeth J. Perry, "Taipings and Triads: The Role of Religion in Inter-rebel Relations," in *Religion and Rural Revolt*, ed. János M. Bak and Gerhard Benecke (Manchester: Manchester University Press, 1984), pp. 344-51.

49. Laai, "The Part Played by the Pirates of Kwangtung," pp. 209-20; also Jen Yuwen, *The Taiping Revolutionary Movement*, p. 68.

50. Laai, "The Part Played by the Pirates of Kwangtung," pp. 291-316.

glishman in Fujian.[51] Immediately upon assuming control of the Chinese walled city of Shanghai, the two had assured foreigners that neither they nor their trade would be molested.

In the spring of 1853 Liu Lichuan had written Luo Dagang, suggesting that the Taipings send troops eastward to coordinate with a simultaneous Small Sword uprising in Shanghai. Receiving no direct offer of support from Taiping headquarters, Liu and Chen had delayed action until September. Once they had taken the Chinese section in the fall, they issued proclamations using both Ming and Taiping dating and minted coins in the name of both the Ming and the Taiping dynasties.[52] They sent a letter to Hong Xiuquan, addressing him as emperor and requesting that he send officials to help coordinate their two administrations. Yet they made no profession of Christianity and no attempt to adopt the anti-opium, anti-tobacco, and anti-gambling regulations of the Taipings. Only nine months later, when soliciting military aid, did they censure the worship of Buddhist and Daoist idols and acknowledge Shangdi. Liu and Chen even began attending Protestant Sunday services held by missionaries.[53] The Taiping leader Luo Dagang, having formerly been a Triad leader in Canton, appears to have been willing to give assistance, but was prevented from doing so by the presence of strong Qing forces between Nanjing and Shanghai and also by Hong Xiuquan's summons to return to Nanjing to protect the capital.[54] The Shanghai Triads went down in defeat as a consequence of dissension and decline in morale and of British and French cooperation with imperialist forces.

How does one interpret the attempts of the Small Sword leaders at cooperation with the Taipings? Were Liu and Chen simply opportunists, or did they believe that the common political goal of overthrowing the Manchus provided sufficient grounds for cooperation? Certainly, religious and ethical issues were of secondary importance for Liu and Chen, whereas for Hong the ousting of the Manchus from power had become a religious crusade, so that he refused cooperation. For Luo Dagang, military and tactical considerations were more persuasive, but even these were secondary to loyalty to Hong. There is no question, however, that the Taiping rebellion acted as a

51. John Scarth, *Twelve Years in China: The People, the Rebels, and the Mandarins, by a British Resident* (Edinburgh: T. Constable, 1860; repr. Wilmington, DE: Scholarly Resources, 1972), p. 196.

52. Maureen F. Dillon, "The Triads in Shanghai: The Small Sword Society Uprising, 1853-1855," *Papers on China* (Harvard East Asian Research Center) 23 (1970): 67-86.

53. Medhurst to Tidman, Shanghai, 11 October 1854, CWM, Central China, Incoming, no. 1.

54. Perry, "Taipings and Triads," pp. 350-51.

stimulus to other heterodox societies, for Triad uprisings occurred in Xiamen, Fuzhou, Wuhua, and Canton as well as Shanghai. Several of the rebel groups sought contact with Nanjing and several used the slogan "Feng Shangdi ming" (in obedience to the commands of Shangdi). They reveal the pervasiveness and the power of dissident groups in south China at mid-century and, in some instances, the growth of proto-nationalist sentiment based on anti-Manchuism. The Western presence in south China, combined with an increasing readiness to blame the Manchus for China's weakness and humiliations, meant that south China began to develop a national self-image earlier than other regions of China. Sun Yat-sen, nourished in his youth on stories of Hong Xiuquan's exploits, would take note of the emotional potency of anti-Manchu propaganda and incorporate it into his nationalist appeals for revolution.

Chinese Christians and Triads

Unlikely as it may seem, Chinese Christians joined Triad uprisings on several occasions. One interesting case involved a Dr. Chen and his relatives the Jiangs, the latter being one of the most important Christian lineages associated with the Basel mission in Lilang. Jiang Jiaoren, a Chinese union member, was the first Jiang convert. Working through kinship ties, he had brought numerous members from branch Jiang families to Hamberg and Lechler for instruction and baptism. Among these were Jiang Qimin and Jiang Shengyun. By August 1854 bitter factionalism had arisen among the Chinese evangelists, and the Basel missionaries held a conference with their assistants to try to resolve the conflicts. The problems ranged from personality conflicts to style of evangelism to financial complaints by relatives of Dr. Chen. In addition, the relatives claimed that another evangelist had opened a letter containing money addressed to Dr. Chen. Dr. Chen, a Chinese Union member, had previously converted some thirty fellow lineage members, thereby incurring the wrath of other Chen relatives, who plundered the converts' property and threatened bodily harm. Dr. Chen had escaped to Canton, where he now associated himself with the Triads.[55] At the conference, harsh words and inflammatory accusations ensued; as a consequence, Jiang Qimin and Jiang Shengyun were publicly criticized by the Western missionaries.

55. Hamberg to Inspector, Hong Kong, 4 May 1854, BMG, A-1.3, no. 10; Lechler to Inspector, 29 September 1854, BMG, A-1.3, no. 24; Philipp Winnes to Josenhaus, 21 August 1854, BMG, A-1.3, no. 23.

Meanwhile, rebel groups loosely associated with the Triads had taken control of Kowloon and other villages to the north, and Triad forces were besieging Canton. Dr. Chen and one of Hong Xiuquan's kinsmen, having preached Christianity among the Triads, sent word that a number were ready to embrace the worship of Shangdi and that Lechler should send two evangelists to instruct them. The messenger was also to bring back five hundred muskets. Though Lechler forbade any Christians to have anything to do with Dr. Chen or the rebels, Jiang Qimin enthusiastically led several baptized Lilangers to Canton and even became a captain among the rebels. Jiang Shengyun was also tempted, but it is not clear whether he actually joined the Triads. With the defeat of the rebels, Dr. Chen and his eldest son were killed. Lechler helped Jiang Qimin escape to Hong Kong but dismissed him as an evangelist and excommunicated him; Shengyun lost his job as catechist but was not excommunicated.[56]

The saga did not end here, however. Both Qimin and Shengyun fled to Australia, where they evangelized among Hakka communities. In 1858 Qimin returned to China and worked for a while as an assistant to the Berlin missionary, August Hanspach, then was reinstated by Basel.[57] By 1864 he was reported to have "reverted to heathenism," having taken a second wife and begun to practice geomancy. Yet after confessing his sins, he was reinstated two years later. Placed in charge of the Berlin station at Langkou, he regularly preached to a congregation of 100 to 150. He was still alive in 1901, an elder in the Lilang church.[58] Shengyun, a much less enterprising man than Qimin, returned to Lilang to live quietly as a Christian.

What was their motivation for joining the Triads? Was it pique at having been publicly reprimanded, a sincere hope of converting the rebels to Christianity, loyalty to Dr. Chen, or a combination of all three? Whatever their reasons, they continued throughout to identify themselves as Christians. Even Dr. Chen was not without a legacy for the Hakka Christian church. Upon his death, Mrs. Chen placed their three younger sons in the Basel parochial school. Chen Minxiu so impressed his instructors that after his graduation he was sent to Basel for theological training. In 1869 he became Basel's first ordained Chinese minister. Not only did he see distinguished service as an evangelist and church administrator in Guangdong, he fre-

56. Lechler to Inspector, 29 September 1854; Winnes to Josenhaus, 21 August 1854; Lechler to Inspector, 24 November 1854, BMG, A-1.3, no. 27.

57. Winnes to Inspector, Hong Kong, 12 October 1858, BMG, A-1.4, no. 8; Charles Piton, Lilong, 31 March 1880, BMG, A-1.14, no. 30.

58. Lechler to Inspector, Hong Kong, 5 October 1866, A-1.5, no. 21; G. Ziegler, Lilong, 8 January 1901, "Jahresbericht der Gemeinde Lilong pro 1900," A-1.35, no. 137.

quently represented the interests of Chinese Christians directly to the Basel home board.[59]

The sharp dichotomy that Western Christians saw between Taiping and Protestant Christianity or between Christianity and other heterodox sects obviously was blurred in the minds of many Chinese. The Chinese preference for inclusivism rather than exclusivism is part of the explanation for the differing Chinese and Western approaches. In the popular view, Buddhism, Daoism, Confucianism and folk religious practices were complementary: Buddhism for funerals and matters connected with death, Confucianism for ethics, and Daoism and folk religion for more mundane concerns, including illness, good fortune, and evil forces. To be sure, Hong Xiuquan adopted the exclusivism of Christianity, and even some of the religious sects had exclusory membership, but the same was not necessarily true of their followers. Chinese had been nurtured in a society where group loyalty, not individualism, was an overriding virtue. The demands of kinship and friendship were unending and almost unlimited. Thus Li Zhenggao's concern for the members of the Hong and Feng families lasted long after Li and the Taiping leaders had gone their separate ways, and even after the deaths of Hong Xiuquan and Feng Yunshan. Hong Xiuquan's sense of obligation to Roberts endured even though he believed that his new dispensation superseded that of Western Protestantism. Jiang Qimin did not necessarily see a conflict between being a Christian believer and joining the Triads, especially if it presented a chance of offering Christian instruction. Triad leaders and even the former Triad chieftain, Luo Dagang, were more favorably disposed toward Triad-Taiping cooperation than was the purist Hong Xiuquan.

Attitudes toward the Chinese religious heritage could be viewed as a continuum. Though a few religious sects were exclusivist, most were additive; members continued to participate in celebrations for the village deity, worship of the ancestors, and traditional rituals at weddings and funerals. Both the Taiping and Protestant leaders were rigorously iconoclastic toward Buddhist, Daoist, and folk deities, but Taiping leaders, having originally condemned Confucius as misguided, gradually became more favorably inclined toward Confucian teachings and ethics, even including them on their civil service examinations. With few notable exceptions, mid-nineteenth-century Protestant missionaries considered Confucianism imperfect at best and a serious deterrent to Christian conversion; converts were required to abandon rituals for the ancestors and remove ancestral tablets. Though long residence in China led many missionaries to a greater appreciation of Confucian ethics and greater

59. For information on Chen Minxiu, see Lutz and Lutz, *Hakka Chinese*, pp. 247-48.

tolerance of practices not deemed religious, differences of interpretation continued, and many Chinese resented what they considered the rigidity and ethnocentrism of the Westerners. Many Chinese converts did not place Confucianism in the same category with Buddhism, Daoism, and folk religion. The values associated with Confucian teachings and practices associated with familism seemed intrinsic to their Chinese identity and heritage; not only were they reluctant to abandon them, but they were frequently ostracized upon doing so. They were more apt to seek compatibility between Confucianism and Christianity and to consider Christianity the fulfillment of Confucianism.

Gützlaff had sent Rudolf Lechler to the Chaozhou region of Guangdong as his first assignment, and Lin Qi was one of Lechler's few converts there. The story of Lin Qi illustrates some of the complexities and ambiguities. Lin met with strenuous family opposition to his conversion; his wife was so fearful that disasters would be levied upon the family that she tried to commit suicide. Upon her death some months later, Lin was caught between family pressures to hold a traditional funeral and Lechler's insistence that there be no "superstitious rituals." Acceding to his family's wishes, Lin returned all his Christian literature to Lechler and ceased all public association with Christianity. Soon thereafter Lechler was ousted from the Shantou area, and he transferred from work among the Hoklo to work among the Hakka. Yet a decade later, when the English Presbyterians began mission work in Chaozhou, Lin requested that one of their missionaries come to his village to instruct them. Lin had remarried by this time, and he not only brought his whole family into the church, but he became a church elder and a mainstay of his congregation. One wonders if Lin continued throughout to consider himself a believer despite his temporary abandonment of a public profession of Christianity. One of Lin's sons would serve as minister in the Presbyterian church, while another assisted in the Presbyterian hospital.[60]

John Fitzgerald, in his work on the nationalist revolution, *Awakening China,* employs the concept of progressive awakening, beginning with the Opium War.[61] Unlike Japan, China developed a sense of self, a sense of nationalism, in fits and starts, two steps forward and one step back. A half-century of intellectual and political ferment preceded the 1911 revolution, and

60. William Gauld, "History of the Swatow Mission" (M.A. thesis, unfinished and unpublished, University of London, School of Oriental and African Studies, London, England), pp. 15-16; George A. Hood, *Mission Accomplished? The English Presbyterian Mission in Lingtung, South China* (Frankfurt am Main: Verlag Peter Lang, 1986), pp. 28, 71; Joseph Tse-hei Lee, *The Bible and the Gun,* pp. 33-34.

61. John Fitzgerald, *Awakening China: Politics, Culture, and Class in the Nationalist Revolution* (Stanford: Stanford University Press, 1996), pp. 6-7, 24-25.

even then Chinese nationalism remained inchoate and was confined to a minority of the population. But the number of disaffected was large and growing. Christians and Triad adherents at mid-century were far from revolutionaries, and the Taiping theocracy became more conservative as the years
passed. Chinese nationalism would, nevertheless, build on anti-Manchu and
anti-imperialist sentiments, both of which were strong among the Taipings
and the Triad rebels. Many Chinese Christians, having already accepted heterodox teachings, proved ready to follow Sun Yat-sen on his revolutionary
path by the close of the nineteenth century. Seeds of nationalism and revolution, sown at mid-century and nourished by internal and external humiliations, would come into blossom during the 1920s.

Gützlaff, the Chinese Union, and Heterodox Societies

Having traced the contacts of Chinese Union members and Basel converts
with Taiping and Triad followers, one must attempt to explain why relations
among these appear to have been more common than was the case with the
converts of denominational missionaries. Enabling factors as well as precipitating factors as defined by Mullins are relevant. Both Chinese Christian
evangelists and Taiping leaders incorporated elements from their own religious heritage into their presentation of Christianity. Sometimes, notably in
the case of Hong Xiuquan, they evolved a distinctive interpretation based on
their own reading of the Bible and their own revelations.

It is significant that Gützlaff's methodology and theology allowed considerable leeway to Chinese evangelists working in the interior. As Gützlaff indicated in his brief for the Chinese Union, he believed that Chinese converts,
with their facility in local dialects and sensitivity to Chinese mores, were
more effective evangelists among their fellows than any foreign missionary
could be. Their understanding of Christianity might lack depth, but even so,
they could successfully convey the essentials of Christianity. Guidance by
Western missionaries was desirable, but so long as millions of Chinese lacked
access to the message of salvation, Gützlaff was unwilling to wait for the
opening of China to foreigners and the arrival of the thousands of Western
evangelists needed. He would trust the Chinese preachers and the workings
of the Holy Spirit even as he acknowledged the possibility of lapses by some
Chinese Union members. His optimism and his compulsion to convert
China's 350 millions propelled him forward.[62]

62. For detail, see chapter 8.

Gützlaff, as a product of the Moravian, pietist tradition, preached a minimalist Christianity with the goal of spreading the gospel message as widely and rapidly as possible rather than founding denominational churches.[63] Rudolf Lechler, Theodor Hamberg, and other Basel missionaries, who built upon Gützlaff's work, did require more extensive instruction and a demonstration of reform before baptism. Even so, restrictions on foreign residence in the interior meant that their ability to oversee assistants during the 1850s and 1860s was limited. Chinese might minister to their congregations in the interior for months and occasionally a year or more with little contact with their supervisors. Though Hamberg, Lechler, and most of the Basel missionaries came out of a Lutheran background, and pietist Lutherans from Würtemberg dominated the Basel society leadership, the Basel society considered itself "überconfessional," that is, committed to neither the Augsburg Lutheran confession nor the Reformed confession.[64] Thus, they were less hampered than many Protestant missionaries by the denominationalism that Chinese found so perplexing.

As in the Moravian tradition, religion for Gützlaff was primarily experiential rather than doctrinal. A personal conviction of sin, a revival experience, and love and faith in Jesus were emphasized instead of dogma or denominational practices. God through the Holy Spirit is ever available to the faithful and will guide believers in this world. God is approachable, a Father to be loved, trusted, and obeyed. Not church tradition but the Bible is the standard by which to formulate and test creeds, ethics, and institutions. The great commission laid by Christ upon believers means first and foremost making the Sacred Book and its teachings available to all peoples. For Chinese Christians operating in a non-Christian environment, such theology and methodology could be liberating, though it could also lead to abuses and even heresies.

Hong Xiuquan devised his own interpretation of Christianity, which was influenced by the Chinese religious heritage; he was also minimalist. He annotated his edition of Gützlaff's translation of the New Testament, commenting profusely on certain passages and sometimes even altering the wording or omitting phrases.[65] His monotheism was so strict that he believed that God

---

63. For a discussion of Gützlaff and the Chinese Union, see chapter 8; see also Jessie G. and R. Ray Lutz, "Karl Gützlaff's Approach to Indigenization: The Chinese Union," in *Christianity in China*, ed. Daniel H. Bays (Stanford: Stanford University Press, 1996), pp. 269-91.

64. Thoralf Klein, *Die Basler Mission in Guangdong (Südchina), 1859-1931* (München: Iudicium Verlag, 2002), p. 109.

65. Spence, *God's Chinese Son*, pp. 291-97.

alone was divine; only God could bear the title Shangdi, ruler of all. Jesus as God's first son and Hong as God's second son, being lesser than God, were to be addressed as *zhu* or lord. Beyond acceptance of a belief in the one true God, Jesus as savior, and Hong as the new messiah, qualification for Taiping membership consisted primarily of observing certain rituals: saying grace before meals, repeating the doxology, praying regularly, and obeying certain rules of conduct: keeping the Sabbath holy and abstaining from opium, alcohol, and gambling. Neither a sacerdotal clergy nor an institutionalized church characterized Taiping Christianity. As with joining the Chinese Union, the break with the Chinese cultural heritage was less complete than if one joined a denominational church under Western leadership. The result was often a conversion that was less deeply rooted, so that reversion to former beliefs and practices was common. Nevertheless, examples of truly dedicated followers were present in both camps.

Though Western evangelists ordinarily recruited individual Chinese, proselytism by Chinese frequently followed kinship lines. Hong Xiuquan's first converts to his new faith were his cousin Hong Rengan and his maternal relatives Li Jingfang and Feng Yunshan; subsequently, he persuaded most of the members of his immediate family to join him. Even his first contacts upon traveling to Guangxi in 1844 were relatives named Wang.[66] The heavy reliance of Gützlaff and Basel missionaries on Chinese assistants contributed greatly to their expanding Christian communities, because the Chinese had access to the interior and to kinsmen. The Moravian concept of the Christian community also allowed room for the kinship ties so important in Chinese society, while their stress on Christian brotherhood encouraged the evolution of Christian communities into support societies. A majority of the first Hakka Christian congregation in Lilang, Guangdong, belonged to the Jiang clan and had been converted by Chinese Union member Jiang Jiaoren and other relatives. Similarly, the early Hakka church of Meixian, founded by Chinese Union member Zhang Fuxing and his first convert in Meixian, Xu Fugang, drew heavily from their powerful Zhang and Xu lineages. As both the Taiping founders and Chinese evangelists knew, kinship provided the support necessary for an individual embracing heterodoxy in China's communal culture.

The fact that a high proportion of the Basel converts, the early Taipings, and the southern Triads were Hakka enhanced their sense of community. Sharing a distinctive dialect also facilitated cohesion and communication.

66. Two members of the Wang family had visited Hong the previous year and had been baptized.

As an ethnic group subject to discrimination, they were often more receptive to heterodoxy than many other Han Chinese; Li Zhenggao, for example, reported that Hakka who had been expelled from the Foshan region by the *bendi* in 1863-1864 had pretty well lost faith in the gods and ancestors. "The people say, 'Our gods and ancestors have not protected us. We will now serve whoever can give us protection.'"[67] Simultaneously, this openness facilitated crossing boundaries from Christianity to Taiping and vice versa. Hong Xiuquan and all of his original converts were Hakka, and the Guangxi region where the God Worshipper Society first took root was heavily populated by Hakka, Miao, and Yao. Most of the pirates and many of the bandits were Triads as well as Hakka. Gützlaff habitually itinerated among the Hakka laborers in the Hong Kong–Canton nexus, and many of his Chinese Union members were drawn from this community.[68] Because his Basel missionary recruits had their first success among the Hakka of the Pearl delta and later the Meizhou region, the Basel mission decided to concentrate its Guangdong work among the Hakka. Thus the identity of the Basel mission with the Hakka and the fact that Gützlaff, Hamberg, and Lechler all became fluent in the Hakka dialect facilitated contacts between them and the Taiping converts.

Especially among fringe groups like the Hakka or Miao, membership in a religious community could convey a new sense of self-worth as well as protection. The convert had acquired a new identity; he had entered a select community wherein all members were brothers. Even women, though still subordinate to men, found new roles in the churches, the religious sects, and the Taiping army. A Singapore Chinese, in commenting on Gützlaff's converts, stated, "Such of his converts as I have known were only half converted to religion, but they had all of them notions of political emancipation."[69] For Taiping Hakka, the new faith elevated their struggles to a battle of the saved versus the minions of the devil; as Philip Kuhn noted, they could challenge Qing culture on the basis of an all-embracing cosmology.[70] Whether Protes-

---

67. Li Tschin-kau, "Fortsetzung des Bericht über die Arbeit des Reisepredigers Li Tschin-kau, 1870," trans. and ed. Lechler, BMG, A-1.7, no. 11.

68. Hamberg to Inspector, Hong Kong, 26 October 1849, BMG, A-1.1, no. 5.

69. Quoted in Charles MacFarlane, *The Chinese Revolution with Details of the Habits, Manners, and Customs of China and the Chinese* (1853; Wilmington, DE: Scholarly Resources Reprint, 1972), p. 159.

70. Kuhn, "The Taiping Rebellion," in *Cambridge History of China*, ed. J. K. Fairbank (Cambridge: Cambridge University Press, 1978), 10.1:280. For insightful discussions of this thesis, see also Nicole Constable, *Christian Souls and Chinese Spirits: A Hakka Community in Hong Kong* (Berkeley: University of California Press, 1994); Nicole Constable, ed., *Guest*

tant Christians or Taiping Christians, they had acquired a higher truth: they belonged among the saved and were vastly superior to the damned.

In numerous instances, the initial convert was someone who had a reputation as a "doctrine lover" — that is, he was troubled either by his own personal inadequacies or by what he perceived as the ethical breakdown of Chinese society, or by both. He was already searching for moral guidance or a deus ex machina. Both Liang Fa and Li Zhenggao, for example, had experimented with Buddhist disciplines before turning to Christianity, Li accepting first Taiping Christianity and then Protestant Christianity. Assurances of the protection of a more powerful god or promises of a better life either in the Taiping New Jerusalem or in the hereafter were attractive. Chinese Christians, in their proselytism, often appealed to the desire for a guardian and benefactor during these troublous times and tried to demonstrate that their Christian God was more effective than the local deities. To prove the reality and power of the Christian God, Zhang Fuxing and Hong Xiuquan blasphemed the local god in the presence of villagers, daring the deity to punish them if he weren't a false idol.

Pietists like Gützlaff, the Taiping leaders Hong Xiuquan and Feng Yunshan, as well as certain religious sects preached a millennialist religion that energized a utopian strain among the populace. Millennialism became especially attractive during times when moral certainties were in question and life was often short and brutal. Its promise was that the arrival of a new era would bring rewards to the faithful — and woe betide the non-believers.

Healing, closely associated with religious power and exorcism of evil spirits in China, was practiced by Protestant missionaries, who doled out quinine for malaria, eye wash for eye infections, ointment for sores, and so forth. Evangelism accompanied their medicines. Gützlaff, furthermore, often preached that recovery from illness was ultimately the work of God. Chinese evangelists likewise presented a Christian God with healing powers. More than one Chinese converted after prayer to the Christian God was followed by recovery from illness. When vaccinating for smallpox, the medical practitioner and Christian evangelist Zhang Zhongmu forbade his patients to pray to the Buddhist deity Guan Yin for protection; rather, they should look to the true God.[71] Yang Xiuqing, Taiping East King, assumed the title "Wind of the

---

People: Hakka Identity in China and Abroad (Seattle: University of Washington Press, 1998); and Robert P. Weller, *Resistance, Chaos, and Control in China: Taiping Rebels, Taiwanese Ghosts, and Tiananmen* (Seattle: University of Washington Press, 1994), p. 79.

71. Li Tschin-kau, "Bericht über die Reise des Gehilfe Tschong Hin nach Tschong Lok vom August bis Dezember 1855," trans. R. Lechler, BMG, A-1.3, no. 57.

Holy Spirit, Comforter Capable of Healing the Sick." He claimed he could cure the illnesses of all true believers by absorbing their sickness into his own body.

The God of both the Taipings and the Protestants was a personal God who was active in history. The range of interpretation was, however, wide. Among evangelical Protestants in the mid-nineteenth century, Gützlaff was not unique in his conviction that God determined his fate and that God even gave him direct guidance in decisions. But few so often explained and justified actions with this argument as Gützlaff. He, as noted above, construed several of his illnesses as a signal from God to change his course of action: training for mission work rather than continuing his education at the University of Berlin, or abandoning Southeast Asia for China. Gützlaff's conviction that he had been called by God as apostle to the Chinese sustained him throughout his career, and this was the phrase engraved on his tombstone in Hong Kong. God, Basel evangelists assured their audience, looked after the faithful who called on Him. Lai Xinglian, another Hakka evangelist, attributed the escape of his son from bandits to God's protection of the faithful and contrasted his son's good fortune with that of his executed heathen companion.

Even if the concept of an all-powerful personal God was lacking among most sect religions, they had their spirit writing and spirit possession. Sect masters often claimed privy information regarding the coming of the new millennium. Rituals in which gods transmitted messages through a medium who moved a stick across a surface of sand or flour were common; deities took possession of the bodies of spirit mediums to deliver healing prescriptions, advice on how to deal with problems, or predictions of individual fate.

Taiping Christianity carried the concept of a God active in this world much further. The Book had been reopened and a new dispensation made available. Drawing both on the Chinese tradition of shamans and mediums and on the Old Testament depiction of a God who talked with Adam and Eve, dictated the Ten Commandments to Moses, directed Abraham and Isaiah, and generally communed with His people on this earth, Hong accepted and elaborated on his fantasy of ascending to heaven. Before the throne of God, he had received a mandate that was simultaneously political and religious: destroy the agents of Satan — the Manchus — and establish a Taiping theocracy of God's chosen people. Both Yang Xiuqing, Taiping East King, and Xiao Chaogui, West King, spoke in tongues; Yang, being possessed by God, and Xiao, in communication with Jesus, conveyed directly God's will. Even when God, speaking through Yang, criticized Hong and called for his punishment, Hong accepted the possession as legitimate. The Taiping belief that they were implementing God's will, though it would in time become a fatal flaw, was initially a source of strength and an inspiration to bravery. Westerners, generally assured of their superiority and rectitude, remarked repeatedly on the confidence of the Taiping leaders that God had brought them their successes and would lead them to victory over the Manchus.[72] Whether or not Hong Rengan had read any of Gützlaff's secular works is uncertain, but he employed arguments that closely paralleled those of Gützlaff. China's troubles could be traced to China's having abandoned Shangdi; the power and prosperity of England is proof that God takes care of the faithful. China must return to the true faith if she is to be whole again.[73]

All of the heterodox societies drew heavily on marginal individuals for converts. In the case of the Protestants, the coastal Triads, and even the original Taiping converts, this meant not so much peasants as petty traders and artisans, geomancers and medical practitioners, and laborers along with a sprinkling of teachers who had been unable to pass the examinations leading to civil service. Worthy of note is the fact that many had been exposed to Westerners and their lifestyle; they had encountered new complexes of ideas concerning social mores, religious doctrines, and/or business techniques. This was true not only for Christian converts and Taiping leaders like Hong Xiuquan, Hong Rengan, and Feng Yunshan; several of the Canton leaders of the Triad uprising in Shanghai in September 1853 had associated with Western merchants and had obtained some knowledge of Christianity, Western technology, and the English language.

Many very real differences among the Taipings, the Triads, the Protestants, and the sect religions existed, of course, and a few should be noted. The Triads were restorationist, whereas Taiping ideology was revolutionary even if many of its ideals of land redistribution, communal wealth, and sexual equality were rarely implemented except among the first God Worshipper societies and Taiping armies. The Triads looked for a return of the Ming dynasty to the throne, and their utopianism was based on a golden past. They remained deeply embedded in Chinese tradition. Religious loyalties, insofar as they existed, were in the service of politics. Both the Taipings and the Protestants adopted a linear history; converts must work for a millennium in the future. Individual salvation and national reform were interdependent. The Taiping revolutionaries, however, linked politics and religion in ways that were foreign to China and unacceptable to Western missionaries. Protestant mission-

72. Report on Sir George Bonham's visit to Nanjing, *North China Herald* 145 (7 May 1853): 158; letter of E. C. Bridgman, 4 July 1854, *North China Herald*, 22 July 1854.

73. Rudolf G. Wagner, *Reenacting the Heavenly Vision: The Role of Religion in the Taiping Rebellion* (Berkeley: Institute of East Asian Studies, University of California, 1982), p. 53.

aries were often accused of serving the interest of their national governments, but most evangelicals believed in the principle of separation of church and state. Their Christianity was identified with Western culture rather than a Western polity, even if they occasionally assumed political roles.

Differences in range and degree of organization also set the Triads and sect religions apart from the Taipings and the Christians. The former were localistic, with Triad lodges functioning autonomously. They were rooted in the rural countryside in ways never achieved by the Taipings, but they rarely transcended parochial and kinship ties. Organization was loose, and for security purposes individual members might be acquainted with only a handful of fellow members. Membership could expand or contract rapidly according to the charisma of the master or the opportunities presented by government weakness or local grievances. Taiping Christianity and Protestant Christianity, on the other hand, claimed universality. Both were proselytizing faiths, the Taipings like the Protestants even employing a massive publication program to supplement personal evangelism.

Individual Chinese might move back and forth among the societies, but amalgamation was not possible. After the desertion of one of the female bandit chiefs and the seven pirate leaders, Hong Xiuquan became much less willing to accept Triad members or cooperate with the Triads in action against the Qing dynasty:

> [A]fter the lapse of two hundred years, we may still speak of subverting the Tsing (Qing), but we cannot properly speak of restoring the Ming.... How could we at present arouse the energies of men by speaking of restoring the Ming dynasty? There are several evil practices connected with the Triad Society, which I detest; if any new member enter the society, he must worship the devil, and utter thirty-six oaths; a sword is placed upon his neck, and he is forced to contribute money for the use of the society. Their real object has now turned very mean and unworthy.[74]

Both Hong Xiuquan and Gützlaff had a certain charisma. One Chinese remarked regarding reactions to Gützlaff: "I have myself seen his [Gützlaff's] books and tracts in the hands of thousands of Chinese; I have heard men, women, and children mention his name with reverence and awe, as though it was that of an inspired being endowed with supernatural powers."[75] But

74. Hamberg, *The Visions of Hung-siu-tsuen,* pp. 55-56.
75. Quoted in MacFarlane, *The Chinese Revolution,* p. 159.

Gützlaff could hardly qualify as a "minor founder" in Mullins's terms; Hong comes much closer.

In the long run, however, the Taiping empire and the Chinese Union disappeared from the Chinese scene. Neither Hong nor Gützlaff possessed the administrative skills and balanced judgment to establish and maintain an effective organization. The premature death of Feng Yunshan, who had established and expanded the God Worshippers in Guangxi, deprived the Taipings of a leader with much-needed political talent. Gützlaff's inability to delegate authority to colleagues seriously weakened the Chinese Union. Hong and Gützlaff each had a presence that could command attention and inspire loyalty, though Hong was by far the more compelling and persuasive seer. He was accepted by his associates as a new messiah, and even as he pursued policies that could only lead to disaster, Rengan and other military commanders continued to believe in the Taiping cause and remained loyal to Hong Xiuquan. Chinese who were formerly associated with Gützlaff but were no longer practicing Christians proved willing to aid Gützlaff's missionary colleagues because of memories of Gützlaff's friendship. Some Chinese Union evangelists expressed remorse that certain of their members took advantage of the naiveté of such a totally dedicated and devoted missionary as Gützlaff.

Legacies

The dissolution of the Chinese Union upon Gützlaff's death and the Tongzhi Restoration that followed the defeat of the Taipings has led to ambiguities concerning the legacy of both the Union and the Taipings. In discussions of the Chinese Union, the tendency has been to highlight the charlatans.[76] The Taiping religion, it has been said, never became part of Chinese folk culture, and so disappeared.[77] Undoubtedly, Christianity became closely associated with disloyalty and rebellion in the minds of many Chinese, especially government officials. Anti-Christian sentiment was strengthened. John Scarth, for instance, related the story of a Christian who journeyed to the Jiangxi border to visit relatives in the late 1850s. Because he carried a Bible, he was seized as having books similar to those of the Taiping rebels and thrown into prison.[78] During the late 1860s, when Li Zhenggao and Basel missionaries entered certain areas formerly controlled by the Taipings, they were met with hostility. Mem-

---

76. On the legacy of Gützlaff and the Chinese Union, see chapter 8.
77. Kuhn, "The Taiping Rebellion," p. 316.
78. Scarth, *Twelve Years in China*, p. 328.

ories of destructive warfare and heavy requisition of grain and labor service by the Taipings were still keen among the local populace. Yet there is evidence that some followers and kinsmen of the Taiping leaders never returned to their traditional beliefs; the evidence is available because of continuing contacts between Chinese Christians and former Taiping Christians.

Because Li Zhenggao had connections in the Qingyuan district and was acquainted with relatives and friends of Hong Xiuquan and Feng Yunshan in the Hua district, the Basel mission relied on him for work in these regions. Following an exploratory trip by Li to Qingyuan, Marie and Rudolf Lechler, escorted by Li, journeyed there in March 1866.[79] Prior contacts were essential, for strangers entered the area at considerable risk. Even Li had secured a letter of introduction from a member of the large Zeng lineage before venturing into the territory, and it was Li's previous associates and relatives who helped the evangelists gain a hearing. Because of government persecution of known Taipings, almost all were fearful of worshipping Shangdi publicly. Despite these dangers, former Taipings welcomed the Christians into their homes, entertained them, and provided them with the town watchman, also a former rebel, as protection. The latter, Lechler reported, no longer worshipped idols and was quite adroit at countering arguments of non-Christians.[80]

The evangelists actually found a variety of religious practices among the former God Worshippers. Some had reverted to their previous beliefs and practices. Door gods guarded their entrances, ancestral tablets were in the usual places, and the various deities had been repaired and returned to their traditional locations in the hall, kitchen, and elsewhere. Lechler reported, "I spoke to the people in wonderment over the fact that they had painstakingly restored all those things that their own fellow countrymen had discarded as false and worthless. . . . They replied: 'We don't know anything better. Come and stay with us and teach us the way of God; we will follow you.'"[81] On the other hand, when they visited members of the Chan lineage who had been baptized by Hong Xiuquan, they found no idols, but also no evidences of Christianity, according to Lechler.[82] Yet others worshipped Shangdi secretly in their homes. Several members of the powerful Zhan lineage considered themselves Christians and had been in contact with Basel headquarters in

79. Lechler to Committee, Hong Kong, 31 March 1866, BMG, A-1.5, no. 7.

80. Lechler to Inspector, Hong Kong, 16 July 1869, BMG, A-1.6, no. 18; Li Tschin-kau, "Übersetzung des Berichts von dem Reiseprediger Tschin Kau vom 8ten bis zum 10ten Monat," trans. Lechler, 17 February 1869, BMG, A-1.6, no. 3.

81. Lechler to Committee, Hong Kong, 31 March 1866, BMG, A-1.5, no. 7; Lechler to Inspector, 16 July 1869, BMG, A-1.6, no. 18.

82. Lechler to Committee, 31 March 1866.

Hong Kong. In the house of Chen Linpiao was the inscription, "Hall of the Heavenly Father, God in Fragrant Heaven."[83] Subsequent visits by Li and the Lechlers led to the baptism of a small congregation and the establishment of a substation at Qingyuan, with a Chinese evangelist in residence.[84] August Hanspach and Friedrich Hubrig of the Berlin society also proselytized among former Taipings and relatives in Hong Xiuquan's home district, Huaxiang. The Basel society sent evangelists to work among Taiping Hakkas who had fled to north Borneo.[85] On some occasions, however, the visits of outsiders and the baptisms provoked attacks on the converts by their kinsmen.

Contacts with relatives of the Taiping leaders also occurred through other avenues, including Marie Lechler's Hong Kong school for girls. The daughter of the former rebel Chen Ayi and one or more of Hong Rengan's daughters attended the school. Chen Ayi was Li Zhenggao's "old friend" and "comrade from Hong Xiuquan days" with whom Li had corresponded frequently.[86] Chen's daughter would graduate to become a teacher in the school. Another Hong relative also became a teacher in a Basel parochial school. The eldest son of Hong Rengan, Hong Guiyuan, sought employment with Basel and was initially assigned to a parochial school on the mainland, but for safety reasons was transferred to Marie Lechler's school in Hong Kong. He married one of Mrs. Lechler's girls and in 1878 emigrated, along with many members of the Basel church in Hong Kong, to Guyana (formerly British Guiana). There he served as pastor of their Georgetown church.[87]

Further research would doubtless reveal other legacies. Jean Chesneaux, for example, has argued that many survivors of the Taiping movement or their sons were active in secret societies during the late nineteenth century. These societies, in turn, were important in the development of revolutionism, for they provided a "withdrawal structure" for political and social forces opposed to the dynasty and imperial system.[88] Growing numbers of Chinese in the southeast were becoming acquainted with new perceptions of military and political power, new concepts of evolutionary history and economic progress, and a new perspective on international relations. In comparison

83. Li Tschin-kau, 17 February 1869, BMG, A-1.6, no. 3.

84. Lechler to Committee, Hong Kong, 30 January 1871, BMG, A-1.7, no. 91.

85. Tiedemann, "Missionary Views on the Taiping Rebellion," paper presented at Huitieme Colloque de Sinologie de Chantilly, 3 September 1995.

86. Smith, *Chinese Christians*, p. 85; Lechler to Committee, 30 January 1871; Lechler to Committee, Hong Kong, 1 February 1872, BMG, A-1.8, no. 2.

87. Lechler to Committee, 1 February 1872; Smith, *Chinese Christians*, pp. 84-85.

88. Jean Chesneaux, ed., *Popular Movements and Secret Societies in China, 1840-1950* (Stanford: Stanford University Press, 1972), pp. 6-11.

with China's total population, they were a tiny fraction, but as illustrated above, they formed a community, which gave them visibility. The cultural foundations for change and modernization were being laid.

At the present stage of knowledge, however, it does not seem possible to trace direct lines of influence from Taiping Christianity to the independent Chinese Protestant churches of the twentieth century. Nevertheless, Taiping Christianity, the Chinese Union, and religious sects of the nineteenth century foreshadowed many of the characteristics of today's house churches or meeting points and of independent churches such as the True Jesus Church (Zhen Yesu jiaohiu), the Little Flock or Assembly Hall (Jidutuhui), and the Jesus family (Yesu jiating).[89] They also incorporated many traits that distinguished the Japanese indigenous churches. Many Chinese, like many Japanese, were attracted to a powerful yet personal God who offered solace as well as aid and protection. Generally prominent were charismatic leaders who preached salvation and promised a new millennium. Their worship services often included healing and speaking in tongues. Both direct communication with God and their own independent interpretation of the Bible gave them authority to transform missionary Christianity and link it with their Chinese heritage.

89. For further information on the indigenous churches, see Daniel H. Bays, "Indigenous Protestant Churches in China, 1900-1937: A Pentecostal Case Study," in *Indigenous Responses to Western Christianity*, ed. Stephen Kaplan (New York: New York University, 1994), pp. 124-43; and Xi Lian, "No Earthly Salvation: Wang Mingdao, John Sung, Watchman Nee and the Rise of Indigenous Christianity in China" (paper delivered at the annual meeting of the Association for Asian Studies, Boston, March 1999).

CHAPTER 10

Karl Gützlaff:
"Parson and Pirate, Charlatan and Genius"?[1]

Few China missionaries have been more controversial than Karl Friedrich August Gützlaff. Extravagantly praised for his dedication to bringing the gospel to all China, he was censured with equal immoderation as his attempt to convert the whole nation through Chinese evangelists proved a fiasco. For a hundred years after his death in 1851, negative images of Gützlaff prevailed, but as Christianity has gained recognition as a world religion and the role of missionaries has changed, scholars have begun to reassess Gützlaff's life and work.[2]

Understanding this conflicted, multi-faceted individual is not easy. At one moment he gloried in his exploits, braving an ice storm or out-bluffing a mandarin in order to make known the Christian message; in the next, he referred to himself as the insignificant instrument of God. He chafed under the strictures of his Dutch missionary society and quickly became an independent missionary, beholden to none but God and responsible for his own support. For two years he acted as interpreter on opium smugglers so that he could make illegal forays to China coastal villages to distribute Bibles and religious tracts. Though he continued to consider himself primarily an evangelist, he held a full-time position with the British administration for almost fif-

---

1. Quoted in Arthur Waley, *The Opium War through Chinese Eyes* (New York: Macmillan, 1958), p. 233. See also G. Tiedemann, "Missionarischer Einzelgänger oder Visionär? Die Missionsmethoden Gützlaffs," in *Karl F. A. Gützlaff (1803-1851) und das Christentum in Ostasien. Ein Missionar zwischen den Kulturen,* ed. Thoralf Klein and Reinhard Zöllner (Nettetal: Steyler Verlag, 2005), pp. 193-232.

2. See the works of Thoralf Kein, Herman Schlyter, A. J. Broomhall, and Jessie and Ray Lutz listed in the bibliography.

teen years. Like many missionaries of his era, he operated on the premise that a higher law justified defying manmade restrictions on Christian evangelism.

Many of the questions that are the subject of debate among Christians today were raised during the controversies swirling around Gützlaff during the late 1840s and 1850s. Queries as to what it means to be a Christian and what the function of the foreign missionary is, frequently discussed today, were central to the investigations of the Chinese Union. True, the current world setting is vastly different from that of Gützlaff's day. Not only has Christianity become a global religion, but the majority of Christians are now located outside Western Europe and North America.[3] Africans, who compose the most rapidly expanding Christian communities, do not necessarily consider Christianity a Western religion; moreover, they are exercising their right to define Christianity within the context of their own cultures. In most countries today, Christianity is a minority religion in a pluralist society.

Other questions remain. What are the challenges for a Christian living in a non-Christian society? Who should set the standards of Christian conduct and faith? As nationals assume the major responsibility for evangelism, is there still a role for the foreign missionary and if so, what is it? How far can one go in contextualizing Christianity and still have it retain its distinctiveness? Is the canon closed? Definitive answers are not forthcoming, and Christians in different cultures continue to work out their own interpretations and approaches. The responses sometimes approach those of Karl Gützlaff more closely than they do those of the society missionaries in mid-nineteenth-century China. A few direct lines of succession from Gützlaff to the present are evident, though modifications of Gützlaff's methodology certainly occurred. In other instances, perhaps all that can be said is that Gützlaff represented views that have gained a new prominence, though some aspects of Gützlaff's career remain the object of criticism. Finally, research has unearthed additional facets of Gützlaff's legacy, some related to Gützlaff's civil career more than to religion and evangelism.

Origins of German Protestant Missions in China

Gützlaff was not only the first German Protestant missionary to China, but he was instrumental in persuading the Basel and Rhenish mission societies to expand their work to China. By the 1840s a German translation of Gützlaff's

---

3. "Annual Statistical Table on Global Mission, 2004," *International Bulletin* 28.1 (January 2004): 24-25.

Journal of Three Voyages plus his other publicity depicting the great opportunities for Christian missions in China had stimulated interest among German congregations. It was, however, Gützlaff's plan for evangelizing all China using Chinese under the supervision of Westerners that persuaded the Basel and Rhenish societies to send missionaries to China. In 1847 four German missionaries, Theodore Hamberg and Rudolf Lechler of Basel and Ferdinand Genähr and Heinrich Köster of the Rhenish society, were appointed specifically to work with Gützlaff and the Chinese Union. Except for a quarter-century hiatus following the establishment of the People's Republic of China, both societies have continued to maintain a presence in China until today.

Berlin's commitment to China came later as a consequence of the founding of the *Berliner Missionsverein* during Gützlaff's visit to Europe in 1850. The first Berlin representatives were Hermine and Robert Neumann, but their careers in China were cut short in 1854 by ill health. Next came August Hanspach and Dr. H. Göcking, arriving shortly before the Neumanns' departure for Germany. Hanspach was in some ways a replica of Gützlaff: restless, ambitious, hyperactive, flamboyant, and adventurous. In the company of Chinese assistants, he journeyed throughout Guangdong and southern Fujian preaching and distributing Christian literature. With contributions from the mercantile community of Hong Kong and Canton, he provided partial support to some 140 Chinese tutors on the condition that they add to the traditional Confucian curriculum the memorization of the Christian versions of the *Sanzi jing* (Three character classic) and the *Sizi Jing* (Four character classic). The effectiveness of such a strategy might be questioned, though Hanspach did return regularly to examine the pupils on their knowledge of Christian doctrines and to supplement their instruction. Later missionaries reported having occasionally met individuals who had become acquainted with Christianity through Hanspach's activities. In Canton he organized one of the first work-study industrial schools for boys too poor to study full time. He also established a normal school to train teachers for parochial schools.[4]

Of the one hundred or more Chinese Union support societies founded in Germany and the Netherlands during Gützlaff's 1850 visit, most collapsed upon the disintegration of the Chinese Union. Germany's interest was once more directed toward Africa, while the Dutch missions concentrated on their colonies, particularly Indonesia (Dutch East Indies). The Cassel society sur-

---

4. "Abscheidswort des Missionsprediger Hanspach," *Evangelischer Reishsbote* (hereafter *ER*) 4.12 (December 1854): 89-91; A. Hanspach, "Schools in Kwangtung Province," *Chinese Repository* (hereafter *CRep*) 2 (August 1869): 79; J. Weise, "The Early History and Development of Berlin Missionary Work in South China," *CRep* 56.6 (June 1925): 376-85.

vived for a few years and managed to appoint one missionary, Carl Vogel, before declining interest and financial support persuaded it to abandon the China mission. Eventually the *Berliner Missionsverein* became a subsidiary of the older *Berliner Missionsgesellschaft*.[5] In 1884 this *Gesellschaft* maintained eight Chinese stations whose Christian communities totaled roughly 2700 members, but southern Africa, not China, was the main focus of the society.

One other German society established amidst the enthusiasm of Gützlaff's visit survived: the *Berliner Frauen Missionsverein für China*. Gützlaff had made a special effort to cultivate women's mission groups and had called for women to volunteer for service.[6] Gützlaff was not alone in insisting that conversion of Chinese women was necessary to establish Christian families. Because women socialized young children in the home and taught them the family religious rituals and only women could gain access to women and children, female missionaries were essential. Initially, most societies were reluctant to appoint single women, even though the majority of missionary wives soon found much of their time devoted to rearing their children and maintaining a household. The death rate among the early missionary wives, furthermore, was appallingly high. Gützlaff asserted that both single and married women would be able to work in China without great difficulty, and he persuaded several women to volunteer. In actuality, the record of the first recruits was discouraging. They either died, married men belonging to other societies, or left the field because of hardship or ill health. The *Frauenverein* and the China Inland Mission gradually began to appoint single women, and eventually the majority of societies followed suit, so that by the twentieth century the number of missionary women in the China field surpassed that of men. Women often concentrated on educational and social service activities; they also served as role models for their pupils.

The *Frauenverein* assumed responsibility for a home for abandoned girls originally founded by Hermina Neumann in 1851, and finally in 1857 Mr. and Mrs. Laderdorf and their daughter Bertha Ladendorf were able to place the *Findelhaus Bethesda* in Hong Kong on a permanent footing. Enrollment grew slowly and attrition was high, but by 1904 there were 104 pupils. The following year the society reported twenty-three baptisms and three residents who had become Christian workers or assistants.[7] Since the primary goal was to

5. The Cassel and Berlin societies were singularly unfortunate in the loss of missionaries through death, ill health, disillusionment, etc. This experience may also have contributed to their decline.

6. "Berliner Frauen-Missionsverein für China," *ER* 1.3 (March 1851): 2-3. The Frauenverein provided support for Hermine Neumann.

7. "Berliner Frauen-Missionsverein für China," pp. 2-3; "The Berlin Foundling House,"

train Christian wives for fellow Christians, the educational standards were low: literacy in Chinese, perhaps a little arithmetic, housekeeping, and hygiene were to be emphasized. Both the Foundling Home and Marie Lechler's school for girls arranged the marriages of many of their students to assure that the girls married fellow Christians and thereby establish the Christian families vital to continuing Christian communities.

Data from the *Findelhaus* illustrates the significance of mission education in offering an opportunity for self-development and a means of social mobility for women. Most of the children who came to the home were either infants saved from infanticide, beggars, or girls slated for sale as servants or prostitutes. The *Findelhaus's* report for 1910 listed 94 former pupils who had married. Almost all had married teachers, doctors, pastors, or Chinese assistants. Less than 15 percent had married farmers, workers, or artisans. The *Findelhaus*, like many of the girls' schools, had expanded its curriculum by adding other academic subjects, so that a number of its graduates were teachers, Bible workers, mission assistants, and even doctors.[8] At the turn of the century, school alumnae, administrators, and teachers joined in campaigns against footbinding, abandonment of girls, and the adoption of "slave girls" *(niu zai)*. *Findelhaus Bethesda* in Hong Kong survived until World War I, when it was closed by the British; the *Frauenverein* then transferred its work to Africa.

Gützlaff insisted that his German recruits reside in the interior, not Hong Kong or port cities. Despite numerous difficulties and failed attempts, the Rhenish and Basel evangelists were actually among the first Protestant missionaries to settle on the mainland beyond the treaty ports. A decade later the Berlin missionary Hanspach was itinerating throughout Guangdong. All three missions would concentrate much of their work in the rural interior. Here they found villagers and minority peoples who were receptive to heterodox teachings.

During the early 1850s a few hundred individuals had been converted and small Christian communities and congregations had gradually developed. Henceforth, these could provide a supportive environment and monitoring services helpful to converts and missionaries. As the Westerners and Chinese evangelists ventured farther inland, they encountered individuals who had received copies of the Bible and Christian tracts, from Gützlaff himself, Chi-

---

Chinese Recorder 2 (April 1869); Findelhaus Bethesda auf Hongkong, *Jahresbericht*, 1921. See also Kenneth Latourette, *History of Christian Missions in China* (London: Society for Promoting Christian Knowledge, 1929), p. 576.

8. Findelhaus Bethesda auf Hongkong, *Jahresbericht*, 1910, pp. 32-37.

nese seamen, and Chinese Union, or Bible Society colporteurs.[9] Sometimes these local people became inquirers or offered guidance and protection in an environment that was hostile to outsiders. The evangelists came across villages with several Christian households, many in Hakka territory. A fragile infrastructure that the missionaries and *Gehilfen* could expand and strengthen had been established.

In contrast to Hamberg's disillusioning experiences with robbers, unfaithful assistants, and local hostility, Philipp Winnes met with considerable support on an itineration in Hakka territory during 1855.[10] Twice he was tipped off that robbers were lying in wait, which enabled him to change his route. He had little trouble finding housing because converts opened their doors despite the risks; they also provided him with an entrée to other villages by contacting relatives there. On his tour in Huizhou, Winnes met a Gützlaff convert holding a low-level examination degree; Winnes and Lechler took the man into their employ as their Hakka-language teacher while giving him further instruction in Christian doctrine. With the aid of their teacher, Christian congregations in this area expanded, and Basel was able to raise one of the towns, Zhangkengjing (Tschong hang kang), to the level of a main station some twenty-five years later.

The Basel, Berlin, and Rhenish missions continued to incorporate Chinese in their work and to rely heavily on them as evangelists. The missionaries did generally insist on a longer period of instruction and closer supervision of the *Gehilfen* than had been Gützlaff's practice, especially during the period of the Chinese Union's rapid expansion. They also emphasized the establishing of Christian communities and the building of churches and congregations. While the Westerners generally resided at one of the central stations and devoted much of their time to administration and education, Chinese did much of the proselytizing and managed the substations. This rural base continues to be one of the strengths of the Chinese Christian church. The rapid growth of "house churches" or meeting points, despite all the attendant problems, indicates that rural China and minority groups such as the Miao and Lisu continue to be fertile territory for Christian evangelists. The envi-

---

9. "Tagebuch von R. Lechler in Tiotschio, 20 Juni bis 8 Juli 1849," Archives of Basel Missions Gesellschaft (hereafter BMG), A-1.1, no. 10; Philipp Winnes, "Report to the Basel Committee on 'a little mission trip,'" Pukak, February 1855, BMG, A-1.3, no. 33; Lechler to Inspector, Hong Kong, 12 May 1866, BMG, A-1.5, no. 15; Lechler, "Dritter Quartalbericht to Inspector," 5 October 1866, BMG, A-1.5, no. 21; Legge and Chalmers to Tidman, Hong Kong, 9 July 1854, Church World Mission Society (hereafter CWM), London Missionary Society (hereafter LMS), S. China, Incoming Correspondence, Box 5.

10. Winnes, "Report to the Basel Committee," Pukak, 1855.

ronment may be different from that of nineteenth-century dynastic China, but most converts are still individuals living in poverty and hardship and searching for relief and hope either in this life or the next.

The Hakka Church and Indigenization

In some ways, progress toward indigenization of the Protestant church in China was retarded by the Chinese Union affair. During the first half of the nineteenth century the common wisdom of mission societies and pioneer missionaries had been that the era of missions would be brief. Christians from abroad would bring the glad message of salvation to a welcoming audience, and local converts would quickly take over the responsibility of spreading the word and establishing national churches. The devolution of missions would occur swiftly and easily. As late as mid-century such prominent leaders as Rufus Anderson of the ABCFM and Henry Venn of the CMS advanced this strategy, which was not unlike that of Gützlaff. Missionaries in China, however, encountered indifference or hostility more often than not; Christian converts were few and far between, while the rate of apostasy and dismissal was distressingly high. Many Western evangelists, lacking the resilience and unfailing optimism of Gützlaff, came to question the advisability of transferring the task of converting China to the Chinese within the foreseeable future. The Chinese Union fiasco appeared to confirm their growing conviction that Chinese evangelists would require a long period of tutelage before they would be ready for positions of authority. One missionary wrote in 1867, "this notion of employing a native ministry to supply the lack of foreign missionaries is not worth consideration. . . . An educated, vigorous, self-reliant ministry, worthy to stand side by side with the foreign missionary band, it will take time to raise. The most sanguine amongst us will count that time by generations rather than by years."[11] Rapid liquidation of missionary work in China became even less likely in the late nineteenth century, as Christianity and culture were conflated and institutions such as schools, hospitals, and social service centers were incorporated into the mission effort.[12]

Yet in certain instances the work of Chinese Union members contributed

11. Anonymous, "On Native Agency," *Chinese Recorder* 1.6 (June 1867): 33-34.

12. Daniel H. Bays, "Rise of Indigenous Christianity," in *Christianity in China, from the Eighteenth Century to the Present*, ed. Daniel H. Bays (Stanford: Stanford University Press, 1996), pp. 266-67; Philip L. Wickeri, *Seeking the Common Ground: Protestant Christianity, the Three-Self Movement, and China's United Front* (Maryknoll, NY: Orbis Books, 1989), pp. 36-38.

Baptism in a Hakka church in Wuhua   (Source: Basel Mission Archive)

to indigenization of Christianity in China. The Hakka Protestant church today considers as its founders Karl Gützlaff, his Basel recruits Theodor Hamberg and Rudolf Lechler, and their first Hakka converts. A volume commemorating the 140th anniversary of the Hong Kong Chong Zhen church begins its history in 1847, the year of Hamberg's and Lechler's arrival in China.[13] Because the Hakka appeared more receptive to the Christian message than most other Han Chinese, Gützlaff, Hamberg, and Lechler had concentrated their proselytism among these poor migrants in coastal Guangdong, and the Basel mission subsequently made the Hakka the focus of its work in Guangdong.

A major difference between the nineteenth century and the present has been the growing consciousness of Hakka ethnicity. It was only in 1898 that Wen Zhonghe, chief compiler of a Meixian gazetteer, published a scholarly history of the Hakka and the origins of their dialect. Through the efforts of

13. *Xianggang Chong Zhen hui lihui yi si ling zhounian jinian tekan, 1847-1987* [Special memorial publication on the anniversary of the establishment of the Hong Kong Chong Zhen Church, 1847-1987] (Hong Kong: Jidujiao Xianggang ChongZhen hui bianyin, 1987); also, *Shenxianhui zai Hua chuanjiao shi, 1847-1947* [The history of the propagation of the Lutheran Church in China, 1847-1947] (Hong Kong: Hong Kong Lutheran Church, 1968).

Chinese scholars, Western missionaries like Hamberg, Lechler, and Charles Piton, along with Chinese converts, a character syllabary for Hakka was created.[14] A Hakka written literature began to gain recognition. For some Hakka, the sense of Hakka identity served to consolidate the sense of Christian community; contrariwise, being set apart as Christians fostered a consciousness of Hakka ethnicity. To quote Nicole Constable: "European missionaries also lent support to ideas of Hakka 'high status' origins and provided the organizational structures — education facilities and occupational opportunities — that facilitated the formation of a Hakka community. Women who had been raised in mission orphanages or educated in mission schools were married to educated Christian men, thus establishing a stronghold of Hakka Christian leadership, households, communities, and future generations of Hakka Christians. From the mission-educated Hakka emerged a Christian Hakka elite of educators and politicians."[15] The strength and survivability of the Hakka church are partially dependent on this relationship.

Hakka Christians in the Meizhou and Huizhou regions of Guangdong survived the ravages of the Cultural Revolution. For many Hakka today, Christianity is part of their family heritage. The principal threat comes not from conflict between being Chinese and being Christian, but from consumerism, secularism, and migration to Canton, Shan Zhen, and other rapidly industrializing sectors. Nevertheless, numerous inquirers, frequent baptisms, and overflowing congregations continue to be reported. In the early 1990s representatives of the Chong Zhen Church in Hong Kong and of the Basel Mission made several visits to some fifty-seven congregations in the Meizhou, Huiyang, and Huizhou regions, where they received a warm welcome.[16] The Hakka Christians, while expressing a sense of kinship with international Christianity, are secure in their identity as Christian Chinese with their own independent church. At the same time, they have indicated a readi-

14. Charles Piton, "Correspondence: A New Method of Transcribing Hakka Colloquial," *Chinese Recorder* 13.6 (June 1882): 233; S. T. Leong, "The Hakka Chinese of Lingnan," in *Ideal and Reality: Social and Political Change in Modern China*, ed. David Pong and Edmund S. K. Feng (Lanham, MD: University Press of America, 1985), pp. 302-7; David C. E. Liao, *The Unresponsive: Resistant or Neglected? The Homogeneous Unit Principle Illustrated by the Hakka Chinese in Taiwan* (Pasadena, CA: Wm. Carey Library, 1972), pp. 31-32.

15. Nicole Constable, *Christian Souls and Chinese Spirits: A Hakka Community in Hong Kong* (Berkeley: University of California Press, 1994), p. 139.

16. Cheng Zhen Church in Hong Kong, "Fangwen Dong Mei Zhu san jiang Kejia jiaohui jianbao" [Brief report on an investigation of the Hakka churches of the three rivers, East, Mei, and Pearl], 4 January 1991, mimeo copy, Tsung Tsin Mission, Kowloon, Hong Kong.

ness to accept aid toward reconstruction of churches and the training of much-needed ministers; they hope for continuing contacts. During the nineteenth century, numerous Hakka Christians of the Basel and Rhenish mission emigrated to Indonesia, Australia, Southeast Asia, and Hawaii, where they established Christian communities. Today Basel and Barmen representatives maintain relations with Hakka Christians in Indonesia, Guyana, Hawaii, Surinam, and Sabah, as well as China.

Chinese Assistants and Indigenization

The history of Christian missions in China and the evolution of the Chinese Christian church is the story of a Sino-Western enterprise. Especially during the pioneering era, the work of the Chinese evangelists was crucial. The Westerners, of course, made the initial converts, and they retained responsibility for doctrinal instruction of inquirers and administering the rite of baptism. Their first converts, however, then became the primary agents in attracting the next generation of converts. Ordinarily, they concentrated on their kinsmen, both because access was easier and because they needed social support in a non-Christian society. A significant number of the Basel and Rhenish assistants were former Chinese Union members.[17] Both major centers of the Hakka church in Guangdong originated with Chinese Union members. The same was true for the Rhenish stations in Dongguan among the Cantonese along the east bank of the Pearl River. The careers of the founders, Jiang Jiaoren (Kong Jin), Zhang Fuxing (Tschong Hin), and Wang Yuanshen (Wong Jun), illustrate their contributions. Not only did they establish Christian communities, but their families furnished generations of church leaders, and many of their descendants became prominent in education, medicine, and other professions.

Jiang, originator of the Lilang congregation, belonged to an influential lineage in the Huizhou region.[18] For over three years he successfully proselytized among kinsmen in the vicinity of Lilang and reported regularly to Hamberg in Hong Kong. Upon Jiang's death in 1853, Hamberg wrote: "Be-

17. For further detail, see Jessie G. Lutz, "A Profile of Chinese Protestant Evangelists in the Mid-nineteenth Century," in *Authentic Chinese Christianity: Preludes to Its Development (Nineteenth and Twentieth Centuries)*, ed. Ku Wei-ying and Koen De Ridder (Leuven: Leuven University Press, 2001), pp. 67-86.

18. See the biographies of Jiang Jiaoren, Zhang Fuxing, and Wang Yuanshen in Jessie G. Lutz and R. R. Lutz, *Hakka Chinese Confront Protestant Christianity, 1850-1900* (Armonk, NY: M. E. Sharpe, 1998), pp. 13-54.

cause it is linked so intrinsically to the story of Jiang, I must tell you that last Sunday I had the honor of baptizing forty-one persons here. Most of them are Lilangers of the Jiang lineage. . . . Such baptism in the interior of China is a rarity. . . . Rather than praise myself, I shall gladly credit Jiang Jiaoren with these forty-one as the fruit of his labor."[19] After Jiang's death, his wife, Ye Huangsha, worked among the women and children of Lilang; she assisted in the girls' school and was instrumental in persuading the Basel mission and Lilang congregation to subsidize the rearing of abandoned female infants in Christian homes. When Marie Lechler toured the region, Ye provided her with entrée to the homes of villagers; the example of both these dedicated and independent women encouraged other women to become inquirers. Basel made Lilang a central station with Westerners in residence, a boys' school, a girls' school, and a seminary. In the region were a dozen or more churches. In 1901, at the age of 81, Ye joined in celebrating the fiftieth jubilee of the Lilang church. All three of Jiang's sons were educated in Basel schools, and one, Jiang Falin (Jiang Ayun), after receiving seminary training at Basel, became the second ordained Chinese minister of the Basel mission. He was a highly successful evangelist in northwest Guangdong and often acted as spokesman in conveying the views of Hakka Christians to Basel. Opposing the heavy reliance on Romanization in Basel schools, for example, he urged greater attention to Chinese characters and literature. He worked for the upgrading of outstations to central station status, with their own parochial schools, and he translated eight books of the New Testament into Hakka.

Zhang Fuxing, the acknowledged founder of the Hakka church in Meizhou, first studied and itinerated with Gützlaff, but then he and his wife were instructed by Hamberg, and they worked for a time with Hamberg in the vicinity of Hong Kong and Lilang.[20] In 1852 the couple transferred to Zhang's home region of Wuhua, Meizhou, where Zhang belonged to a large and powerful lineage. Here, he converted numerous relatives, some of whom joined him in proselytizing and distributing religious literature. Though Zhang and other lay workers journeyed to Hong Kong to report to Basel headquarters and obtain funds and books, they essentially operated on their own for ten years. By the time a Basel missionary first visited the area in 1862, there were about 170 believers located in some twenty hamlets. With this foundation, Basel began in 1864 to station Westerners in the Wuhua region, and by the late nineteenth century, Meizhou, the Hakka heartland, had also become the heartland of the Hakka church. Today, more than ninety congre-

19. Hamberg to Inspector, Pukak, 14 May 1853, BMG, A-1.2, no. 31.
20. Lutz and Lutz, *Hakka Chinese*, pp. 32-54.

gations are located there. Zhang's descendants intermarried with those of one of his early converts, Xu Fuguang (Tshi Fuk-kong), and subsequent generations included church, business, and professional leaders in Canada, Indonesia, and Sabah, as well as China.

Wang Yuanshen (Wong Jun), a Cantonese member of the Chinese Union, also became progenitor of a family of distinguished Christian pastors, educators, and government officials.[21] Having itinerated with Gützlaff in the Hong Kong region, Wang was assigned to Ferdinand Genähr of the Rhenish mission. He worked for over a decade in Fuyong, a fishing village near the mouth of the Pearl River that was a haven for pirates and did not welcome Christian evangelists. A visit by Lobscheid, who gave medical treatment to several inhabitants, helped overcome opposition, so that Wang was gradually able to found a small Christian community. Though Wang was often characterized as a man with a large body and limited mind, he was faithful despite persecution and he appreciated the need for mutual support among the converts. He encouraged them to reside in adjacent houses and held daily evening services in his home; during the Chinese New Year's holiday, he organized alternate festivities for the community. He enrolled both of his sons in the Lilang parochial school. Wang served the Rhenish mission in various Guangdong localities until his death in 1914 at the age of 97.

Though Wang Yuanshen himself refused ordination, he delighted in the ordination of both his sons, Wang Qianru, the second Chinese ordained by Rhenish, and Wang Yuchu, who became an influential minister associated with the LMS. Because Yuchu suffered from tuberculosis, he spent much of his career in Hong Kong, where he could receive medical treatment. Here, he engaged in campaigns against opium and against the abandonment of female infants; he managed the *Berliner Frauenverein's Findelhaus,* and he supported their efforts to educate blind girls, many of whom were brought by missionaries from the interior. In 1897 a separate school was organized for the growing numbers of blind pupils and was placed under the auspices of the Hildesheim Mission for Blind Girls in China. Remarkably, a visitor to Shaoguan church in northern Guangdong attended their Christmas service, 1988, which featured music by a women's choir with a dozen blind women. All

21. See Zha Shijie (James Shih-chieh Cha), *Zhongguo Jidujiao renwu xiaozhuan* [Concise biographies of important Chinese Christians] (Taipei: China Evangelical Seminary Press, 1982), pp. 5-8; Alfred Bonn, *Ein Jahrhundert Rheinische Mission* (Barmen: Verlag des Missionshauses in Barmen, 1928), pp. 262-69; "Zwei chinesische Christe Gemeinden," *ER* 1.10 (October 1851): 8; 1.12 (December 1851): 5-7; 2.2 (February 1852): 1-3; 2.5 (May 1852): 2-6; 2.6 (June 1852): 2-4; Genähr to Committee, Taiping, 1 September 1848, Vereinte Evanglische Mission, Archives of Rheinische Missionsgesellschaft (hereafter VEM), 2.181 (B/h2).

were graduates of the German school for blind girls located in Hong Kong.[22] As an outspoken advocate of an independent Chinese church, Wang Yuchu asserted that Chinese Christians could not attain autonomy until congregations supported and selected their own pastor. Accordingly, he was elected in 1884 as the fully supported minister of the Chinese Union Church of Hong Kong.[23] Sun Yat-sen frequently attended Yuchu's services at the Foundling Home.[24] Among the Wang descendants were Wang Chongyi, the first professor of pathology at the University of Hong Kong, and Wang Chonghui, who was associated with Sun Yat-sen's cause. Wang Chonghui held several ministerial posts with the republican and Guomindang governments, and eventually served as a judge with the International Court of Justice at the Hague.

Gützlaff furnished Chinese language teachers and assistants to numerous missionaries upon their arrival in China: Issachar Roberts, August Hanspach of the Berlin mission, the Presbyterian William Burns, Wilhelm Lobscheid of the Rhenish mission, and George Smith of the CMS. Even if many of the tutors were soon dismissed for moral lapses, lack of Christian dedication, or incompetence, a number of them proved to be valuable aides. Burns testified at the Chinese Union investigation of February 1850 that he had employed one Chinese Union member as a teacher and two others as preachers and assistants on his itinerations. They demonstrated considerable knowledge of Christian teachings, and they were honest.[25] Bishop Smith retained some ten or twelve Chinese Union men and reported that "the good work done with these men gives evidence that all Dr. Gutzlaff's labours have not been in vain."[26] Zhou Daoxing (Tschow Taohsing) worked as Roberts's senior assistant in Canton in 1844 despite the opposition and intense hostility of the Cantonese at the time. He is best known as the intermediary who brought the future Taiping leader,

22. "Kurze Geschichte der deutschen Blindenmission in China," Yale Divinity School Special Collection, Mission pamphlets, Rmn H54; D. MacGillivray, ed., *A Century of Protestant Missions in China, 1807-1907. Being the Centenary Conference Volume* (Shanghai: American Presbyterian Press, 1907), pp. 490-91; "Churches in Northern Guangdong," *Bridge* 33 (January-February 1989): 9-10. The 1988 service also included a Christmas tree and Santa Claus.

23. The name of the church changed several times: Independent Chinese Church of Hong Kong, To Tsai, or Hop Yat Church.

24. Zha Shijie, *Zhongguo Jidujiao renwu*, pp. 39-43; Bonn, *Ein Jahrhundert Rheinische Mission*, pp. 262-69; Lo Xianglin, "Zhongguo supu suoji Jidujiao zhi chuanbo yu xindai Zhongguo zhi guanxi," *Journal of Oriental Studies* 7 (1969): 1-22.

25. Hamberg, *Report regarding the Chinese Union in Hong Kong* (Hong Kong: Hong Kong Register, 1851), p. 4.

26. A. J. Broomhall, *Hudson Taylor and China's Open Century*, vols. 1-3 (London: Hodder and Stoughton, 1981-1982), 1:345.

Hong Xiuquan, in contact with Roberts in 1847, and he apparently joined Roberts in instructing Hong. Although Zhou had a reputation as an effective preacher and loyal assistant, he was, unfortunately, never able to overcome completely his addiction to opium. Later, Zhou was employed by Lobscheid as preacher and teacher in the girls' school, but was then dismissed for opium addiction. Opium seems eventually to have destroyed him.[27]

Though Jiang, Zhang, and Wang rank among the most prominent Chinese Union members, they are in some ways typical of that minority of union workers who became loyal Christians.[28] Most of them received additional instruction from the missionaries to whom Gützlaff assigned them, and these missionaries tried, not always successfully, to maintain close supervision. Christianity and more particularly parochial schools were for these converts and their offspring a source of mobility. Graduation often led to education abroad at a time when a foreign degree opened doors to careers in government and the professions. Despite their acceptance of what was then considered a Western religion, they identified themselves as Chinese working to reform and strengthen their country.

Legacies of the Chinese Union

Gützlaff went further than most mid-nineteenth Protestants in what might be labeled a minimalist approach. True, he came out of a pietist background in which the specific emotional conversion was considered the norm, but he did not expect a sudden personality transformation. The Holy Spirit was, for Gützlaff, the only true source of enlightenment, and it would continue to guide and inspire. Gützlaff was an activist, not greatly interested in complex theology; nor was he concerned with denominational doctrines and rituals. The Bible, especially the book of Genesis with its creation story and the Gospels narrating the life of Christ, were his texts. A favorite theme, repeated over

27. Gützlaff to Nederlandsh Zendeling Genootschap (hereafter NZG), Hong Kong, 24 May 1845, NZG Archives, Kast. 19, No. 1, Doss. G, no. 30; Gaihan [Gützlaff], *Chinesesiche Berichte von der Mitte des Jahres 1841 bis zum Schluss des Jahres 1846* (Cassel: Vorstand der Chinesischen Stiftung, 1850), 21 December 1854, pp. 50-53; *Friend of China and Hong Kong Gazette*, 11 July 1857, p. 219.

28. In Lutz, "A Profile of Chinese Protestant Evangelists," pp. 67-86, I analyzed sixty-seven Chinese evangelists who worked between 1830 and 1870 and for whom I could obtain enough information to make some generalizations. Of these sixty-seven, who may not be entirely typical of the earliest Chinese Protestant evangelists, at least twelve were former Chinese Union members.

and over in his tracts, was the sacrifice of Jesus for the love of humankind; Jesus would help those in need and forgive those in error.

Gützlaff did acknowledge the need for follow-up instruction and guidance after baptism; this was the task of Western missionaries. He expected, however, that the Chinese would form their own Christian communities. He had not come to China to establish branches of European churches, but to make known the gospel message to all Chinese. He was quite ready to accept expressions of repentance by those who had fallen, and he was reluctant to dismiss or excommunicate Chinese Union preachers. In what may be interpreted either as an expression of European ethnocentrism or as a recognition of the difficulties converts encountered in a non-Christian environment, Gützlaff expected less of the Chinese.

As revelations of duplicity by Chinese Union members were publicized, the Basel and Rhenish societies came to agree with Otto von Gerlach's contention in his 1834 article that charismatic individuals like Gützlaff required institutional checks on their strategy and ideology. Basel, however, continued through much of the nineteenth century to maintain an interdenominational stance. Neither Basel nor the Rhenish society abandoned the idea that the evangelization of China would be accomplished primarily by Chinese and that rural China would be the most fruitful field. Their modification of Gützlaff's methods represented a compromise between the evangelical and confessional strategies. It produced such loyal and effective *Gehilfen* as Zhang Fuxing, Wang Yuanshen, Jiang Jiaoren, and numerous successors.

Because the doctrinal freight was minimal with the interdenominational approach, the possibilities for Sinifying Christianity were greater. Chinese evangelists put their own stamp on the Christian message. Like Gützlaff, they preached an essentialist theology; denominational differences arising out of the Western experience were of no interest to them. Their teachings, designed to appeal to their Chinese audience, included resonances of Chinese folk religion and religious sects.

Resemblances with Taiping Christianity are notable. God the Creator was more powerful than the false deities to whom the villagers sacrificed. God was active in history and offered special protection to his people. Those who prayed to God in times of trial would escape disaster; a compassionate Father, He would aid them through the Holy Spirit. Endemic social disorder, lineage feuds, disease, and poverty made for a precarious existence, so Chinese found the concept of a loving and forgiving Jesus attractive; in some ways Jesus became a substitute for Guan Yin, the Goddess of Mercy.[29] Not original sin but

29. It is worth noting that the feminine Guan Yin had evolved out of the Indian male

salvation through Christ was emphasized. To loyal believers, Jesus promised a cure for illnesses, assistance in overcoming drug addition, and a better lot in life. Xu Fuguang, a coworker with Zhang Fuxing, explained to an inquirer,

> All who desire good fortune must venerate God and must believe in Jesus Christ as the only salvation. All idols are nonentities; all spirits are manifestations of the devil. Veneration of ancestors and grave sites is a deception. Not only can one not achieve good fortune through these, but one can bring accursedness and ruin upon one self. One must trust only in Jesus, who died for us on the cross that we might receive God's forgiveness and grace. Only in this manner can need and suffering be converted into good fortune and well being.[30]

Their Christianity was an experiential faith. The Bible was their primary source of information and inspiration; and it, along with the Catechism, the Creed, the Lord's Prayer, and the Ten Commandments, was sufficient basis for their Christianity. Most accepted the Bible as the inspired word of God, and they delighted in narratives from the Old and New Testaments. The most popular format for their sermons was a quotation or narrative from the Bible followed by an explication that linked the story with the current concerns of the audience. Chinese evangelists employed metaphors that were meaningful within Chinese culture. In one sermon, Jiang Jiaoren preached on the theme: Just as all food must be prepared with fire, so the human heart must be prepared through the Holy Ghost and through the suffering and resurrection of the Savior.[31] Worship led by these lay leaders could be quite informal, the congregation actively participating in the services and socializing at the conclusion of the meeting.

Essential to new converts was a separable congregation functioning as a support group for Christians in a non-Christian society. Christian communities adopted many of the characteristics of Chinese communal societies. The family, more than the individual, was the organizational unit. The church served as a social center as well as a hall of worship. Generally close by the chapel were the parochial school and a cemetery providing burial space for

---

deity, Avalokitesvara, as the Chinese Sinified Buddhism. In Roman Catholicism, the Virgin Mary came to bear striking resemblances to Guan Yin, particularly the Pai-i Kuan Yin or white-robed Guan Yin. See the work by Chun-fang Yü, *Kuan Yin: The Chinese Transformation of Avalokitésvara* (New York: Columbia University Press, 2000).

30. "Biography of Zhang Yunfa," trans. Heinrich Bender, Tschongtschun, 5 October 1868, BMG, A-1.6, no. 34.

31. Hamberg to Inspector, Hong Kong, 26 February 1851, BMG, A-1.1, no. 6.

members. Members attended weddings and funerals of fellow Christians. Like lineages, congregations established poor and festival funds, often investing in land, so that they could aid those in need and could hold impressive joint festivals on special occasions such as Christmas and Easter, incorporating "non-superstitious" aspects of the traditional New Year's and *qing-ming* (clear and bright) celebrations.

Christians differed in the degree to which they set themselves apart and formed separable communities. Insofar as possible, they arranged to have Christians marry Christians, but in southeast China, where lineages were strong, Christians paid a high price if they cut themselves off from kinfolk. In more than one instance, tension arose between a Western supervisor and a local Chinese Christian leader. Zhang Fuxiang, founder of the Christian community in Wuhua, did not gladly yield authority to the Basel missionary stationed there after he had presided over the congregation for a decade.[32] Nor was all sweetness and light within Christian communities, as the story of the Lilang Jiangs and the Triads indicated.

Divergent Strains of Christianity: Confessional, Denominational Missions and Evangelical, Nondenominational Missions

During the second half of the nineteenth century, denominational missions came to the fore. Increasing emphasis on parochial education, medical care, and social services fostered the institutionalization of China missions. As transportation and communications became easier and quicker, home mission boards could maintain closer touch with their representatives abroad. No longer were missionaries sent out with only vague instructions, and no longer were they so free to innovate because of the board's lack of information about the field and inability to provide them with timely instructions. With the number of missionaries in a single locale increasing, ecumenism declined, and the tendency was to socialize along denominational lines. Denominational institutions, furthermore, proved to be the most effective channel for raising and distributing funds, and this financial power made possible tighter control over field activities. The greater number of missionaries and their right to reside in treaty ports and inland cities meant that Chinese evangelists were less likely to work on their own. Thus the autonomy of the assistants, along with the autonomy of the missionary, declined. The image of the church mission, the denominational missionary, and the mission compound

32. Lutz and Lutz, *Hakka Chinese*, pp. 46-51.

situated in a treaty port prevailed in Protestant literature and even academic studies. The confessional tradition with its reliance on training, catechisms, and hierarchical control was perceived as the norm.

The pietist, evangelical tradition never disappeared entirely from the China field, however. Independent missionaries of this persuasion came out to China on their own or with the backing of one or two congregations. In 1852 the Chinese Evangelistic Society, founded as an English support organization for the Chinese Union, sent out Wilhelm Lobscheid, who had transferred from the Rhenish society; the following year, it dispatched Dr. Arthur Taylor and J. Hudson Taylor, who became founder of the China Inland Mission. The Taylor household had subscribed to the Chinese Evangelization Society's publication, *The Gleaner*, which depicted hundreds of millions of heathens in China on the brink of damnation, and Hudson was also influenced also by Gützlaff's earlier image of the Chinese masses awaiting the glorious gospel story in his decision to go to China.[33] At the beginning, Hudson also accepted Gützlaff's strategy of relying on Chinese evangelists under the guidance of Western missionaries as the best hope for Christianizing all China. For Taylor as for Gützlaff, faith in salvation through Christ and trust in the Holy Spirit were the essentials.

Taylor did not lose his sense of mission or abandon his goal of spreading the gospel of salvation throughout China when the Chinese Union collapsed. The China Inland Mission (CIM) under Taylor's personal leadership was, for all practical purposes, the successor to the Chinese Evangelization Society. The emphasis on evangelizing in interior China, the rejection of denominationalism, and the reliance on God's direct guidance and support carried over to the China Inland Mission (CIM). CIM missionaries, accompanied by Chinese assistants, were instructed to travel the length and breadth of China. Once the Westerners had attracted a number of inquirers, they were to move on, leaving the converts under the care of Chinese. As with Gützlaff, this simplistic strategy had its weaknesses. Inquirers faded away; Chinese catechists sometimes proved unequal to the responsibilities accorded them; Western missionaries did not put down roots and establish viable congregations. The strategy had to be modified, and the result was a more prominent role for the foreign missionary and hierarchical leadership under Taylor. Still, the evangelical emphasis, nonsectarianism, and experiential definition of Christianity remained.

By the end of the nineteenth century, the CIM had become the largest sin-

---

33. For data regarding Gützlaff's influence on Taylor, see Broomhall, *Hudson Taylor and China's Open Century*, pp. 282, 291-92, 324-25, 344-45, 349-50, 360-61.

gle sending mission in China. Early in the twentieth century it would be joined by other evangelical societies: the Christian and Missionary Alliance and the Seventh-Day Adventists, for example. The number of independent or "faith" missionaries, many from Pentecostal or charismatic movements, greatly increased. The China mission was becoming more diverse.

An important development of the early twentieth century was the founding and growth of independent Chinese churches. Best documented was the Church of Christ in China, established in 1922 under the leadership of Chinese espousing a liberal theology. Their Christianity, though Christocentric, emphasized the humanity rather than the divinity of Jesus. It shared with many denominational missions a Social Gospel approach, even if it was ecumenical; urban, educated Chinese were heavily represented in its membership. Numerous missionaries of liberal persuasion supported and worked with the Church of Christ in China, but their role was being redefined. In the Chinese view, the missionaries should supplement the work of the Chinese rather than lead. Like Gützlaff, the Chinese believed that evangelism and ministering to Christian congregations could best be conducted by Chinese Christians. Westerners, with their theological training, remained valuable for instructing seminary students and Christian candidates. Until the 1950s, however, the Church of Christ in China remained dependent on Western financial support, which meant that crucial decisions were often made in the West and Westerners were generally subject to the home board, not Chinese administrators. The Church of Christ in China would not attain its goal of self-propagation, self-administration, and self-support until the ousting of most Westerners after the establishment of the People's Republic of China in 1949.

The other independent Chinese churches, including the Jesus Family, the True Jesus Church, the Assembly Hall, and the Chinese Christian Independent Church Federation, may well have equaled 20 to 25 percent of the total Protestant membership by the 1940s, according to Daniel Bays.[34] They varied as to whether they were sectarian or non-sectarian, antiforeign or friendly toward the mission churches, loosely organized into congregations or a structured church group. Pentecostalism and millenarianism were popular among many of the independent churches. They were often rural-based and were deeply influenced by Chinese sect religions; lay leadership was characteristic. Their theology centered on God the protector, Jesus the healer and miracle worker, and the Holy Spirit as personal guide and voice of God. Even without

---

34. Bays, "The Growth of Independent Christianity in China," in Bays, ed., *Christianity in China*, pp. 307-17.

direct connections with Gützlaff, the Chinese assistants of the nineteenth century, or the Taipings, many independent churches shared a strain of Chinese religiosity still alive today in house churches.

Gützlaff's Civil Career and the Imperialism Question

Despite the fact that the term *diguozhuyi* was coined only in the late nineteenth century, imperialism and Christian missions have been linked in the minds of both Chinese and Westerners ever since the beginning of Protestant missions.[35] Karl Gützlaff, moreover, has often been cited as a prime illustration of the intertwining of Western religious, political, and economic expansion. Certainly the growth of nineteenth-century evangelism in Africa, the Middle East, and East Asia coincided with the global expansion of Western trade, international diplomacy, and political and military power. During the seventeenth century, the power at the disposal of the state and the level of technology and agricultural efficiency had probably favored China rather than the West. The Jesuit missionaries arrived unaccompanied by military force or economic interests. Though the Roman Catholic missionaries never doubted the superiority and universal truth of the Christian religion, their proselytism stressed the complementarity of Confucianism and Christianity. Veneration of the ancestors was defined as a secular ceremony and therefore permissible for converts. The Westerners' information regarding astronomy and geometry could be accommodated and even integrated into the Chinese corpus of knowledge. Only with the arrival of the Franciscans and Dominicans and the acrimony of the rites controversy did Christian missions come to be viewed as a serious threat to China's cultural integrity.

The situation was quite different by the time the Protestant missionaries arrived in the nineteenth century. The international power balance had shifted. Whereas Western national governments had become a focus of political, economic, and technological strength, Qing rule had entered upon a period of decline. Among Europeans and Americans, confidence in the superiority of Western Christendom had grown. The Christian religion, considered a source of Western progress, was viewed as inseparable from the West's wealth and strength. Missionaries and merchants alike operated on the assumption that China stood to benefit from opening her doors to trade, inter-

---

35. James A. Field Jr., "Near East Notes and Far East Queries," in *The Missionary Enterprise in China and America,* ed. John K. Fairbank (Cambridge, MA: Harvard University Press, 1974), pp. 23-55.

national intercourse, and Christianity, and no one was more avid in advocating the opening of China to all three than Karl Gützlaff. Even Elijah Bridgman in 1836 came close to advocating the use of force to open China:

> Nothing less than the permanent establishment of free and friendly intercourse between China and the western nations will satisfy the demands of this age. The present state in international relations, in some particulars, at least, is "utterly intolerable." . . . While we deprecate "a too precipitate" attempt to improve our intercourse with the people of this empire, we cannot recommend waiting . . . it must be the *moral powers* of Christendom (whose governments are or ought to be the repositories of such power) to attempt the amelioration of the condition of China. . . .[36]

Missionaries like Gützlaff and Bridgman did not look upon their hope of incorporating China into Christendom as a grab for Western power or a possible source of injury to China. Their goal was to serve the Chinese people, who would achieve a better life upon China's adoption of the Western model.[37]

To posit imperialism as a principal motivation for missions is to oversimplify a complex phenomenon. James A. Field Jr. has argued that the deployment of missionaries was more a matter of happenstance than a direct consequence of economic interests.[38] How else, he asks, can one account for the fact that both the Middle East and India were more important as American mission fields than China until the end of the nineteenth century? Why did a rapid increase in the number of British missionaries dispatched to China in the early twentieth century coincide with the decline in Britain's tea and opium trade? Trade between France and China was insubstantial, but France took on the role of protector of Roman Catholic missions. Karl Gützlaff, a Prussian, could hardly be considered a tool of German economic or political ambitions in China, for the loose confederation that was Germany was in no position to pursue imperial ambitions. At mid-century, its East Asian trade was minimal and its industrial base rudimentary. Capitalist incentives alone are insufficient explanations for the growth and locale of missions; other reasons must be added.

36. Bridgman, "Free Intercourse between China and Christendom," *CRep* 5.6 (October 1836): 241-42. Quotation marks and italics in the original.

37. There were, of course, certain nineteenth-century missionaries who considered spreading the gospel of salvation as their sole task and disclaimed any desire to alter Chinese civilization.

38. Field, "Near East Notes and Far East Queries."

The union of state and ideology, furthermore, was the norm in China, and Chinese often assumed as a matter of course that the missionaries were in the employ of their government and would look after the interests of their people. They had difficulty with the idea that Westerners would come to China solely for religious purposes. As far as the Chinese were concerned, a missionary who served as interpreter or even a government emissary was not necessarily exceeding his mandate. In the West, the ideal of separation of church and state was frequently honored in the breach, while Western missionaries in China accepted civil responsibilities. Robert Morrison and Peter Parker, both of whom held secular office, could hardly criticize Gützlaff for accepting office as Chinese secretary for the Hong Kong administration. With the shortage of individuals able to speak Chinese, even Walter Medhurst, David Abeel, E. C. Bridgman, and S. Wells Williams were pressed into service as interpreters and negotiators for government representatives.

Central to Chinese resentment of Western intrusion was the fact that opium dominated the Western trade with China and that it eventually led to military humiliation of China. Nineteenth-century missionaries, furthermore, denigrated Confucian teachings. Like Chinese sect societies, they undercut China's cultural synthesis. These issues, rather than the union of evangelist and civil activities per se, aroused enmity. Gützlaff was particularly vulnerable on all counts. He was, for a time at least, intimately associated with opium smuggling, and though he served on Jardine-Matheson opium clippers for only a little over two years, he was later, as Chinese interpreter for the British administration, frequently involved in cases arising from conflicts between Chinese and the crews or owners of opium smugs. During the British invasion of the China coast in 1840-42, Gützlaff accompanied the English commanders and soldiers as guide and interpreter. His network of Chinese spies kept British leaders informed of Chinese troop movements and strength, intercepted communications between the imperial court and the Chinese generals, and provided other information valuable for campaign strategy. Gützlaff also acted as magistrate of occupied territory.

The economic consequences of imperialism might be mixed, as some scholars have argued, but national disgrace and cultural discredit cut deeper emotionally than economic injury and were more unforgivable. Perhaps this helps explain why imperialism remains a flashpoint even though China today is sovereign and independent. In a recent survey of Chinese attitudes toward America, Chinese were asked to give the first words that came to mind at mention of the United States. Focusing on internal America, 34 percent answered "modernization," "affluence," or "high-tech," while 11.6 percent mentioned "democracy" or "freedom." Focusing on the United States in the international arena, 20 percent responded "overbearing," "hegemonic," "arrogant," or "the world's policeman."[39]

Perhaps association with national disgrace and cultural discredit is also one reason why missions came to be so closely associated with imperialism, why they became the prime target of opponents of cultural aggression during the 1920s and 1950s. In negotiating the treaties at the end of the two opium wars, China had few qualms about granting extraterritoriality to Western residents or most favored nation status to Western powers. Both policies accorded with China's traditional practice of allowing foreigners to police their own and of its expectation that it could play one enemy off against another. The combination of the two in an unequal power relationship became, however, a serious infringement on Chinese sovereignty. Christian missionaries, their institutions, and even their converts claimed immunity from Chinese law and administration, and frequently if not invariably they were supported by their national representatives. A rising national consciousness would foster the view that Christian missions were both a threat to national unity and a source of national humiliation.

How, then, does one assess Gützlaff's role? Should he be singled out as the prime example of the symbiotic relationship of merchant and missionary? In some ways, the answer is yes. Gützlaff's *Lord Amherst* voyage demonstrated the possibility of conducting illegal trade along the China coast beyond the confines of Canton. His journals and other communications insisted on the friendliness of the Chinese people and their desire for trade and communication. Western merchants, especially dealers in opium, took note, and coastal trading expanded until a significant proportion of Western goods entering China did so surreptitiously. China was thereby deprived of customs revenue on all such goods. Gützlaff aided the expansion not only by serving as interpreter on Jardine-Matheson's opium clippers, but also by gathering information on harbor facilities, possible way stations, and navigational hazards. Military commanders during the Opium War, along with captains of opium clippers, benefited from Gützlaff's findings. Gützlaff, as scout for British troops, aide to British officers, and magistrate of Dinghai and Ningbo, personified Britain's humiliation of China. All the pioneer Protestant missionaries, of necessity, depended on Jardine-Matheson and its opium clippers for transportation, delivery of mail, banking, and cashing of salary checks. They gladly accepted the financial assistance of the Canton business community for their publications and charities. Yet no other missionary became so blatantly involved in the opium trade as Gützlaff during

39. Wang Jisi, "Beauty and Beast," *The Woodrow Wilson Quarterly,* Spring 2001, p. 61.

his two-year stint with Jardine-Matheson. Few mission publications equaled Gützlaff's *China Opened, A Sketch of Chinese History,* "Mouyi," or *Shifei lüelun* as briefs for the triad of free trade, open international relations, and freedom of religion.

Criticism of Gützlaff by other missionaries, however, was not so much that he engaged in secular activities, but rather that he accepted full-time civil employment while continuing to present himself as a missionary accomplishing great things. His exaggerated claims of conversions contrasted with their meager number of converts; the great expectations which he aroused among home supporters inevitably resulted in a sense of letdown and disillusionment when they were not fulfilled. This kind of publicity, numerous missionaries thought, was a disservice to the mission cause. Many missionaries were not happy with Gützlaff's direct involvement in the opium trade, but their criticisms on this issue were more muted and apt to be in-house, for even they could not completely distance themselves from the trade. Only in the late nineteenth century, when Western attitudes turned strongly against the opium trade, did Gützlaff's association with opium become a major factor in his negative image. Ethnocentric the missionaries were, but they were children of their age; one may criticize their narrow vision, but to blame them for sharing a common Western perspective would be ahistorical. Their sincerity was not open to question. The mission of the Christian church has been conducted within human history. It cannot be divorced from the personnel involved, both missionary and convert; nor is it separable from the culture and environment of both parties at a specific time in history.

Dual and even contradictory attitudes characterized Gützlaff. Even if he did not consider the Chinese his equal, he assumed the role of patron and acquired a reputation as spokesman for the Chinese. During the Opium War he had sometimes accompanied British advance troops in order to assure Chinese that they would not be harmed if they offered no opposition, but his success had been limited, particularly among Manchu officials, who preferred suicide to disgrace. He tried, as magistrate of Dinghai, to restore law and order for the benefit of both the British soldiers and Chinese citizens. According to reports, it was at Gützlaff's insistence that the Nanjing treaty included a clause guaranteeing that Chinese who had been employed by British forces would not be punished. Especially in his role as Chinese secretary at Hong Kong did he serve as advocate of Chinese interests. Hong Kong's dual system of education and justice, though later subject to criticism, was initially proposed by Gützlaff to improve the lot of Chinese inhabitants of the island. He sent repeated requests to British administrators to induce them to allot funds for educating Chinese children, and he did finally secure at least minimal aid. He argued that the British legal code was so foreign to the Chinese that it often worked to their disadvantage; at least in the case of misdemeanors, Chinese should be allowed to police their own.

The extent to which Gützlaff's publicity and his communications with British officials influenced British foreign policy in East Asia is impossible to assay. Probably it was minimal. Except where events in China forced the hand of the British prime minister, Britain's foreign policy was determined at 10 Downing St., not in East Asia. Gützlaff, for example, strongly recommended that Zhoushan, not Hong Kong, be transferred to England as an administrative and trading base, but Hong Kong was chosen. He even recommended, to no avail, that England cease to support opium growing in India. On the other hand, Gützlaff's *Journals* and other English-language publications do seem to have contributed to the general impression that Chinese officials responded only to force and that China's military establishment was in such disrepair that a brief application of force would suffice to persuade China to grant free trade and intercourse. Lord Palmerston in 1839 did not anticipate a lengthy and expensive military campaign, and a significant flotilla of warships was not even dispatched to the China seas until 1840. The hardening of the imperial government's attitude toward Christian evangelism as a consequence of the intrusions of Gützlaff and Medhurst, the widespread dispersion of Christian materials, and Lord Napier's blunders made compromise more difficult on the eve of the Opium War. Gützlaff's contention that the Chinese populace was eager to trade nourished the myth of 350 million customers, a myth that still persists. Coincidental or not, the first five treaty ports opened at the conclusion of the Opium War were the ports that Gützlaff and Lindsay had presented as having good harbor facilities and the greatest commercial potential.

Also worth noting is the fact that Gützlaff tutored several future British diplomats in the Chinese language. Two were Harry Parkes, Shanghai consul (1855), minister to Japan (1865-1883), minister to China (1883-1885), and negotiator of the Britain's first trade treaties with Thailand and Korea; and Horatio N. Lay, who became first inspector general of customs in Shanghai.[40] Both of them became known for their command of spoken Chinese and their forceful policy in relations with China. Parkes's aggressive actions in Canton were background to the second Opium War, while the right to sta-

---

40. Parkes was a cousin of Gützlaff's wife, Mary Wanstall, and spent a year with the Gützlaff family in Zhoushan; he remarked on the rigorous standards Gützlaff set in language study. Lay is perhaps best remembered for the Lay-Osborn flotilla fiasco.

tion diplomatic representatives in Beijing was achieved through the insistence of Lay at the treaty negotiations concluding the war. Did they derive their emphasis on a forceful policy as well as their facility in Chinese from Gützlaff?

Gützlaff's Chinese-Language Writings: Durable Legacies?

The returns on the vast amounts of time and money absorbed in the writing and distribution of religious tracts by pioneer Protestant missionaries seem disproportionately small. Since Christian evangelism was illegal in China until the 1840s, these early evangelists believed that they had little choice but to use such "silent messengers"; they had, moreover, great faith in the persuasive power of the Word. Evidence that many Chinese were converted by tracts alone, however, is scanty, and even reports of Chinese becoming interested in Christianity solely as a consequence of reading tracts are relatively rare, though Hong Xiuquan is a notable exception. *Liangyou xianglun* (Two friends) by William Milne survived into the twentieth century, and Gützlaff's translation of the Lutheran catechism, the Anglican liturgy, and Barth's biblical history continued to be used for several decades. Most tracts, however, proved ephemeral, and relatively few of Gützlaff's many tracts went through a second edition. Even after China became open to Christian evangelism, tracts continued to be produced, but many were moralistic novels, usually about brave, pious children.

The composition of religious tracts did prove to be a useful means for newly arrived missionaries to learn Chinese syntax and vocabulary. Interest and support in the homeland for China missions was stimulated as funds were raised by British and American tract and Bible societies to print and distribute tens of thousands of pamphlets and booklets. The desire to print works in quantity, fed especially by Gützlaff's demand for a million pieces a year, encouraged the development of a metallic font for Chinese characters. This movable typeset was quickly adopted by Chinese for mundane works, newspapers and journals in particular. The use of punctuation, capitalization, and other aids, already employed to some extent in Chinese novels, received a boost and eventually became standard form.[41]

The early Protestant translations of the Bible by Robert Morrison, Medhurst, and Gützlaff served as a basis for the Delegates' version, which largely

---

41. Many Chinese still preferred the more aesthetic wood-block print for literary works and formal documents. Editions of the Chinese classics continued to be printed in the traditional style.

displaced them. These translations continued the process of evolving a Chinese vocabulary for Christian concepts and names, a task begun by the Jesuits centuries earlier. Even if unanimity in the case of a few crucial terms such as God, baptism, and Holy Spirit proved elusive, significant progress toward a Sinified Christian lexicon was made.

Missionary experiments with various styles in composing tracts and translating the Bible left a lasting legacy. Though Romanization never replaced characters, it has been widely employed in teaching reading during the first and second years of schooling. Romanized script also proved to be an easy way to introduce semi-literates to the Bible, for it could be learned quickly; in some instances, it was adopted for the creation of written versions of minority dialects. Using easy *wenli*, Gützlaff revised his translation of the New Testament ten times in an effort to make it more understandable while retaining formal correspondence with the original meaning. Other missionaries also produced easy *wenli* versions, though the Delegates' translation in classical Chinese became the version preferred by many Chinese until it was replaced by the Union Bible in the twentieth century. Even if the Delegates' Bible was less readily understood, it was thought to have the dignity and elegance appropriate to sacred scripture. Nevertheless, the Bible in simplified Chinese continued to be popular for daily use, and it helped to pave the way for *baihua*. Demand for the Bible in the vernacular rose with the campaign for adoption of *baihua* in the twentieth century. It, along with Chinese novels, could be used as a model.

To make the Bible more accessible to minorities without a written dialect, missionaries and their Chinese coworkers devised character syllabaries for the dialects. Gützlaff's missionary recruits and assistants Dai Wenguang, Hamberg, and Lechler contributed to the development of a Hakka lexicon in both character and transliteration. Oral histories and literature in Hakka could then be recorded and new literary works written. These in turn helped build a sense of identity and self-esteem among the Hakka and minority peoples.

As for Gützlaff's secular writings in Chinese, his essays on cultural geography doubtless reached a wider audience than other productions, though this was a consequence of having been incorporated anonymously into the geographies of Lin Xezu, Wei Yuan, and Xu Jiyu. To put the significance of Gützlaff's information on world geography in perspective, one must note that during the previous century, several Chinese geographies that included information on regions beyond the Middle Kingdom had already appeared. Along with information from Gützlaff, Bridgman, and other missionaries, these too were sources for Lin, Wei, and Xu. The audience for the mid-nineteenth-century geographies was confined to a small number of officials stationed in east China who witnessed Western power and wealth. But the expanding Western presence contributed to the desire to learn more about the enemy. Xu's work did gain considerable popularity in Japan during the 1850s, and it was reprinted in China as the reform movement gained momentum toward the end of the century.

It is true that China would eventually have come into contact with a new global cosmology without the mediation of missionaries, but the fact that much of the information actually came from geographies by missionaries made a difference on three counts. One is that the geographies were broadly conceived. They were actually introductions to the history, social customs, government institutions, religious practices, and economies of England, Europe, America, and the Middle East as well as to physical geography. They presented a world with several centers of civilization, each based on an ancient heritage. The Middle Kingdom no longer equated to civilization; rather the new global cosmology depicted modern European and Chinese civilizations as alternates, with the former far more advanced than the latter. Mission geographies depicted the competitive international scene in maps that were not Sinocentric and that illustrated the comparative size of the Chinese, Russian, Ottoman, and British empires. Wei and Xu concluded that it was urgent that China learn to offset Western pressures and that to do so, it must strengthen its political, military, and economic institutions. The Confucian view of agriculture as the primary producer must be altered to recognize the contributions of commerce and industry; the power and wealth of island England rested on the production of manufactures for worldwide trade and also the loyalty of its citizens. Such innovative concepts, frequently reiterated by Gützlaff, were not popular in conservative north China but found an audience in the southeast, where trade, handicraft, and commercial agriculture had long provided a livelihood for many. New information and perspectives, available in the new Chinese geographies, would eventually become a basis for reform as a favorable environment developed and powerful voices such as those of Liang Qichao, Zhang Zhidong, and Kang Youwei demanded changes.

Gützlaff's China Mission and the West

The significance of China missions for the home base has perhaps not received the attention it merits.[42] As the principal conduit for information regarding

42. Two useful works are Valentin H. Rabe, *The Home Base of American China Missions, 1880-1920* (Cambridge, MA: Harvard University Press, 1978), and Daniel Bays and

China during the nineteenth century, missionaries broadened horizons. Small-town congregations as well as communicants of large urban churches were learning about areas that they previously had scarcely been able to locate on a map. In many Christian households, a mission magazine was one of the few periodicals to which it subscribed. When in the mid-1830s these magazines excerpted long sections from Gützlaff's journals describing his exploits along the China coast, family members and friends enjoyed reading about his adventures among "wondrous strange" peoples in faraway places. Later, in America, local women's auxiliaries began to select one mission arena as their study topic for the year, and national denominational societies introduced study guides that provided basic data about the country. Even Sunday school leaflets occasionally featured a specific foreign mission for discussion. Based on mission appeals, the American Tract Society and the American Bible Society decided in the early 1830s to extend their work overseas.[43]

Exotica was frequently employed to enhance the appeal of foreign missions. G. Chinnery's sketch of Gützlaff in the dress of a Fujian sailor: turban, padded cape, loose trousers, and cloth shoes, with Chinese junks and a pagoda in the background, was enhanced and reproduced in mission magazines such as *Calwer Missionsblatt* (November 1836) and *Evangelical Magazine and Missionary Chronicle* (May 1846), and also in biographies of Gützlaff.[44] One enterprising company, seeking to profit from the exhibition of the portrait at the British Royal Academy, offered an engraving of the work for sale.[45]

Westerners during the nineteenth century perceived a sharp divide between Christian and non-Christian peoples. Both Harold Isaacs in *Scratches on Our Minds* and Edward Said in *Orientalism* demonstrated the distortions of Western images of "heathen" societies, whether African, Chinese, or Middle Eastern. Yet the images proved remarkably durable. Said contends with considerable truth that Western Christendom was the norm against which all other cultures were judged; heathen cultures were truly "other," almost the polar opposites of the West. They lacked the civilizing influence of Christianity. No matter what merit the missionaries might find in a non-Christian so-

Grant Wacker, eds., *The Foreign Missionary Enterprise at Home* (Tuscaloosa: University of Alabama Press, 2003). Both studies are confined to the American home base.

43. "Annual Report," *American Tract Magazine*, 1831, pp. 82-83; Henry O. Dwight, *The Centennial History of the American Bible Society* (New York: Macmillan Co., 1916), p. 112.

44. See H. Richter, *Lebens Geschichte von Bruder Gützlaff* (Barmen: Barmen and Schwelm, 1833).

45. See an advertising flyer in CWM, LMS, China Personal, Robert Morrison, Box 2. Gary Tiedemann very kindly pointed out that Chinnery's original work was a sketch, not a painting.

A well-known
depiction of
Karl F. A. Gützlaff
in the dress of a
Fujianese sailor

ciety, it was incomplete; it was not on a plane equal to that of the Christian West. The West, politically, economically, intellectually, and aesthetically superior, was the authority, teacher, and benefactor. Instead of "Orientals" speaking for themselves, missionaries from their hegemonic position *represented* the Orient to their audience — in fact, they created the Orient. This phenomenon Said calls Orientalism. Evangelists were not simply bringing God to the unbelieving Chinese; they were preaching *their* God and *their* culture. They resembled parents, hoping to guide their wards toward truth and moral righteousness.

Many missionaries, nevertheless, found it easier to romanticize their mission from afar than when in contact with real Chinese. They cringed before the poverty, disease, and filth they met in daily life. When their beneficiaries re-

Image of
Canton from
S. Wells Williams,
*The Middle
Kingdom,*
1883

jected them, they were hurt and angry. They explained their lack of success in
gaining converts by labeling the Chinese as hard-hearted and materialistic, interested only in matters of this world. Other distortions were based on misunderstandings arising from cultural differences. Nearly all missionaries, including Gützlaff, criticized the Chinese as devious and dishonest; at the same time,
they appreciated the courtesy and grace of Chinese social interactions. But
most missionaries failed to see the connection between the two. They didn't
understand that the emphasis on *li*, on giving and saving face, even to the ex-

tent of shading the truth, had its foundation in the attempt to maintain social harmony in a tightly-knit, densely populated, non-mobile society. Coming out of a puritanical background and associating primarily with the Chinese poor and lower-middle classes, they found Chinese males sensual, even lewd. Without realizing the economic foundation of infanticide and minor marriage, they concluded that Chinese parents were cruel and lacking in normal parental affection. They praised the respect accorded parents, but they condemned veneration of the ancestors as a source of stagnancy. S. Wells Williams wrote,

> With a general regard for outward decency, they are vile and polluted in a shocked degree; their conversation is full of filthy expressions and their lives of impure acts. . . . More ineradicable than the sins of the flesh is the falsity of the Chinese and its attendant sin of ingratitude. . . . There is nothing which tries one so much when living among them as their disregard of truth. . . . Their better traits diminish in the distance and patience is exhausted in its daily proximity and friction . . . all form a full unchecked torrent of human depravity and prove a kind and degree of moral degradation of which an excessive statement can hardly be made. . . . On the whole the Chinese present a singular mixture strangely blended.[46]

What clearer proof was required of the inadequacies of Confucianism and of China's need for Christianity, with its transcendent God and higher ethics?

Gützlaff in his popularization of China missions depicted all of the above defects, and he insisted that Confucianism, lacking a belief in the omnipotent God, was deficient. But Gützlaff was the eternal optimist, and furthermore, he had an abiding love for the Chinese. The Chinese, he asserted, were the most advanced of non-Christian peoples; upon the adoption of Christianity, they would join those in the highest ranks. Daily contact with individual Chinese he did not find a trial; instead, it fed his ego. Much to the distress of Hamberg and Lechler, he had great difficulty believing that "his Chinese" would deceive him. Gützlaff's call for volunteers, furthermore, was based on the thesis that the Chinese masses were friendly and would gladly welcome the gospel. It was the emperor and his officials who were hostile. Gützlaff therefore reserved his harshest criticisms for the upper echelons of society; venal, corrupt, arrogant, narrow-minded — these were the adjectives he ap-

---

46. S. Wells Williams, *The Middle Kingdom,* 2 vols. (New York: Charles Scribner's Sons, 1883), 1:834-36; also quoted in Harold Isaacs, *Scratches on Our Minds: American Images of China and India* (New York: John Day, 1958), pp. 136-37.

plied to the literati. Generally, he tried to depict the Chinese scene favorably; he described beautiful landscapes, verdant fields, industrious farmers, and cheerful, if poor, villagers. Though the distortions of Orientalism pervaded his writings, there were more highlights in his picture of China than in many missionary portraits. Shadows aplenty there were, but Gützlaff's goal was enticing Westerners to a China that had much need of salvation.

Long years of residency in China fostered greater tolerance on the part of many missionaries, and instances of individual friendships were not uncommon. A few of the early Protestant missionaries became deeply interested in China's cultural heritage, and a few, such as James Legge, Ernest Eitel, Joseph Edkins, John L. Nevius, and Ernest Faber, conducted scholarly research on China. They introduced Westerners to Daoism, Buddhism, Confucian philosophy, folk religion, and demon possession in China, and to the concept of *feng shui*. Even Gützlaff produced several academic works of merit, including articles in *Das Ausland, Journal of the Royal Asiatic Society,* and *Journal of the Royal Geographical Society.* Essays on the geography of Thailand, Cochin China, and Laos, on the Thai language, Chinese medical writings, and navigation routes along the coast of China were a source of useful data at the time, though they have been displaced by scholarly works with a stronger research base.[47] In addition, they provide insight into Western attitudes toward China at mid-century, and they can be useful as primary sources on contemporary conditions in southeastern China.

Gützlaff's pioneer translation of a Triad document giving the society's regulations and beliefs, describing initiation ceremonies, and detailing its organization continues to be consulted. Gützlaff's *Geschichte des chinesischen Reiches* and his *Life of Taou Kwang, Late Emperor of China* should also be mentioned. As a well-grounded history and balanced evaluation of the Dao Guang emperor, Gützlaff's biography has been cited by John K. Fairbank and Fang Chao-ying, among others.[48] The book's numerous translated edicts of the Dao Guang emperor vividly illustrate the extent to which the power of the theoretically absolute monarch was restricted by ritual, custom, and routine.

47. Among the authors who cited Gützlaff as a source are S. Wells Williams, W. A. P. Martin, George Staunton, Hosea Morse, and John F. Davis. Earl Pritchard described Gützlaff's *Sketch of Chinese History* as "one of the best early histories of China." See Pritchard, *Anglo-Chinese Relations during the Seventeenth and Eighteenth Centuries,* Studies in the Social Sciences, 17 (Urbana: University of Illinois Press, 1930), p. 233.

48. See Fairbank, "Chinese Diplomacy and the Treaty of Nanking, 1842," *Journal of Modern History* 12.1 (March 1940): 1-30; and Fang in *Eminent Chinese of the Ch'ing Dynasty,* 2 vols., ed. Arthur Hummel (Washington: U.S. Government Printing Office, 1943-1944), 1:574-75.

As some mission advocates recognized even in the early nineteenth century, missions revitalized congregations. Instead of depleting church funds, they often increased the total church budget. For example, the small, understaffed American Lutheran Church, when considering in 1837 whether to answer Gützlaff's call and undertake overseas missions, noted the intimate connection between efforts made for the conversion of the world and God's blessing upon the churches putting forth these efforts.[49] Friedrich W. Krummacher, president of the Berlin Missionary Association for China, credited Gützlaff with offering Christendom a chance to renew itself. In the midst of a dead and dying Christendom, he stated, a worthy servant of God had appeared. At stake in the decision to support Gützlaff and his Chinese evangelists was not simply China, but European Christianity itself.[50] Christian communities gained a new sense of purpose as they united in efforts to raise money for missions. Bake sales, mission teas, "mite boxes" to be filled by children during Lent and presented on Easter Sunday, special collections designated for missions, and a host of other activities brought greater cohesion to congregations. Donors identified with "their missionary" or "their hospital"; Marie Lechler and other missionaries encouraged Sunday school classes to adopt "their own orphan" for whom they collected clothes and monies. A two-way correspondence between the missionary on the field and the supporting congregation sustained interest. Missionaries on home leave visited churches, where they related their adventures, sacrifices, and achievements.[51] Women found new roles both as overseas workers and as organizers and supporters of mission support organizations. As both John Fairbank and Valentin Rabe have noted, missions were the first American institutions having global interests and ties.

Gützlaff, publicist par excellence, shared in all facets of the China missionary enterprise at home. Though all of the pioneer Protestant missionaries carried on an active correspondence with home mission societies and journals, few were as avid or as effective in publicizing the China field as Gützlaff. He cultivated people in high places, such as Frederick William III and Frederick William IV of Prussia, Christian Barth, a leader in the Wurtemberg neopietist movement and editor of *Calwer Missionsblatt,* and George Staunton, British MP and co-founder of the Royal Asiatic Society. He wrote directly to

49. "Our Foreign Missionary Operations," *Evangelical Review* 5 (July 1853): 106-9.

50. Missionsverein für China zu Berlin, "Aufruf zur Betheiligung an dem Missionwerke in China" (Berlin, July 1850), pamphlet included in BMG, A-1.1 (1B), no. 2.

51. For details about one congregation and "its hospital," see Lawrence D. Kessler, *The Jiangyin Mission Station: An American Missionary Community in China, 1895-1951* (Chapel Hill: University of North Carolina Press, 1996).

executives of the Bible and tract societies of Britain, America, and the Netherlands, and to officials of numerous mission societies. He corresponded with business leaders such as Richard Ball, who would become editor of *The Gleaner* and the principal advocate of the Chinese Union in Britain, and P. Perit, an American associated with the China trade, who contributed medical supplies and funds for tracts to be distributed by Gützlaff. Perit also provided outlets for Gützlaff's publicity in the *New York Observer* and elsewhere. Gützlaff wrote to relatively obscure donors, such as the father who named his son after Gützlaff or an anonymous donor who had contributed funds specifically to support Gützlaff's distribution of tracts. He even reported to Karl Marx on "socialistic" rebellions in China, whereupon Marx concluded that the rebellions would so damage British trade and profits as to usher in the revolution in England.[52] To many individuals as well as to mission periodicals, he also sent a copy of a Chinese tract, a Bible chapter, or a letter ostensibly written by a Chinese convert.

Gützlaff was astute in tailoring his correspondence for a specific audience. With little booklets about Mary Gützlaff's blind orphan girls, he appealed to Sunday school children. Americans, specially blessed by God, had a special responsibility to aid the less fortunate. England, as the world's dominant nation in trade, diplomacy, and technology, must also take the leadership in missions. Surely his fellow Germans were not going to ignore the example of other nations, but would fulfill their duty to the heathen. Even though he no longer had formal ties with the Netherlands mission society, he appealed to the Dutch as his brothers in mission, and they continued to provide financial aid.

Gützlaff's efforts to awaken Christian congregations to Christ's great commission inspired missionaries who worked in fields other than China. Guido H. F. Verbeck was so moved by Gützlaff's appeals that he volunteered for East Asia. Assigned to Japan, he had a distinguished career not only as Christian emissary, but also as tutor to Japan's future elite, legal consultant to the Japanese government, and administrator of the new imperial school that became Tokyo University. Touched by Gützlaff's visions, David Livingstone volunteered for China, though he later chose Africa as his venue. Like Gützlaff he became an independent and controversial missionary determined to introduce commerce, civilization, and Christianity to his people. Gützlaff's contacts with the Hernhutter community in 1850 led to the departure of three

---

52. Rudolf G. Wagner, *Reenacting the Heavenly Vision: The Role of Religion in the Taiping Rebellion* (Berkeley: Institute of East Asian Studies, University of California, 1982), pp. 2-3.

Moravians from Saxony for Mongolia. Though they failed to reach their destination, they established one of the first Protestant missions on the fringes of Tibet.

Gützlaff bears a special responsibility for the swing cycle of optimism and pessimism regarding China missions during the 1830s and 1840s. Always the optimist, Gützlaff in the 1830s insisted that "the fields are white unto harvest" and "a great and effectual door is opening in China." Three hundred fifty million Chinese awaited salvation; "I had ample reason to praise our Savior for opening so wide a door to the introduction of the holy Gospel. . . . My most sanguine expectations have been far surpassed. I marvel and adore in the dust."[53] Such glowing prospects were more successful in attracting volunteers than the more realistic and sober appeals of other missionaries.

The arrival of new recruits from Britain and America in the mid-1830s, however, coincided with a new imperial offensive against Christian evangelism and the printing and distribution of Christian literature. Subsequent to Gützlaff's overblown expectations came doubt and reassessments at home. Gützlaff buoyantly put a good face on events. Over fifty million Chinese remained accessible in Southeast Asia and along the coasts of China. The imperial edicts were only for show, not meant to be enforced; they "harm us as little as Papal bulls."[54] Nevertheless, the realities of an unhealthy climate and the hostility or indifference of most Chinese resulted in a sharp but temporary decline of interest and volunteers for China missions.

The opening of five ports to foreign residence in the Treaty of Nanjing and imperial edicts of tolerance soon raised new hopes at home and among China workers. Elijah Bridgman wrote, "The time has come when your missionary work in China must assume a more permanent character, and be conducted on a much broader scale than hitherto. In His own way, by the wrath of man, Jehovah has opened parts of the empire. . . . A large body of missionaries is needed for immediate action."[55] Peter Parker's assessment was less sanguine: "I painfully feel the difficulty of conveying a true impression of the state of China. That erroneous conceptions will be formed is almost certain. Surely this will be the case if any suppose that no obstacles now remain to the

53. "An Appeal in Behalf of China," *Missionary Herald* 30 (November 1834): 422-24. Also issued separately as a pamphlet.

54. Gützlaff, *China Opened or, a Display of the Topography, History, Customs, Manners, Arts, Manufactures, Commerce, Literature, Religion, Jurisprudence, etc. of the Chinese Empire*, 2 vols., rev. by Andrew Reed (London: Smith, Elder & Co., 1838), 2:79, 237; "Evangelization of China: Letter of Rev. Charles Gutzlaff," *Foreign Missionary Chronicle* 5 (October 1837): 147.

55. "Letter from Mr. Bridgman, 2 November 1842," *Missionary Herald* 10.6 (1843): 256.

spread of the gospel in this country."[56] Missionary boards, soliciting recruits and funds, were more apt to cite Gützlaff. Upon the signing of the Treaty of Nanjing in 1842, Gützlaff reported, "From this moment, the groundwork has been laid for the transformation of the greatest empire on earth. China is no longer sealed off; proud China has been humbled. China is now open to the Gospel and trade. . . . I shall bow down before the cross of our Savior."[57]

Home societies responded with enthusiasm. The *Foreign Missionary Chronicle* exulted, "We say, then, that viewed politically and commercially, the recent treaty with China is the most important event which has occurred since the discovery of America, and as respects the moral interests of our race, we must go back to the Reformation for an event of equal interest and importance."[58] The British and Foreign Bible Society quoted a correspondent: "We are all bending forward on the tiptoe of expectation. I can fancy that the angels are also stooping to look into the mighty empire. . . . Surely it is a time pregnant with the most important results to the cause of our Lord in the world."[59] Once again the figures for recruits and funds rebounded.

But Parker proved the more accurate prophet. China still was not open, and converts were not flocking to the cross. Disappointed expectations brought the inevitable decline, with high hopes not to be revived until news of the Taiping Christians reached the West. Gützlaff, meanwhile had adopted a new tactic: China would be Christianized by Chinese evangelists, free to travel throughout China and cognizant of Chinese mores and values. As denominational societies came to the fore, Gützlaff turned to individuals and groups on the fringes of mainstream churches in England and America. Increasingly, he looked to Germany and the Netherlands for support of his Chinese Union, as demonstrated by his European tour in 1849-1850.[60]

Conclusion

The cycle of high expectations followed by disappointment and depression would spill over into other aspects of Sino-Western relations. It resembled the love-hate syndrome that James Reed has delineated in Sino-American rela-

56. "Letter from Doct. Parker, 23 November 1842," *Missionary Herald* 10.6 (1843): 257.

57. Gützlaff to NZG, Nanjing, 30 August 1842, NZG Archives, Kast. 19, No. 1, Doss. Gützlaff, Correspondence, no. 23.

58. "China, Extent of the Missionary Field Now Accessible," *Foreign Missionary Chronicle* 11 (October 1843): 330-31.

59. British and Foreign Bible Society, Thirty-ninth Report, 1843, p. cviii.

60. For the story of the Chinese Union, see chapter 8.

tions.[61] Distorted information and misunderstandings based on ethno-centrism contributed to the cycle. But it also derived from the fact that West-erners viewed the expansion of contacts during the nineteenth century as a crusade. The intrusion of the more advanced West was considered necessary to propel China out of stagnancy. Gützlaff had realized that teaching those in error and giving to those in need are both ego-inflating; they build up the self-esteem of the benefactor. He had deliberately and successfully exhorted those favored by God to aid the less fortunate; those in possession of the truth had an obligation to bring enlightenment to those dwelling in darkness. The Chinese, of course, were not lacking in pride and self-assurance based on their own history and tradition; they had no desire to be the beneficiaries of the West's largesse. Yet their resistance and hostility created resentment among Westerners. Such was the general context of the Protestant missionary campaign during the nineteenth century. Gützlaff's grandiloquence had sim-ply added an extra note of unreality to the crusade. His very success in stimu-lating interest in China missions contributed to overreaction when images of conversions, trade, and a friendly reception proved to be mirages. Even today, whenever relations between China and the West are friendly, the myth of the open door quickly revives.

A protean individual, Gützlaff participated between 1831 and 1851 in all as-pects of Sino-Western relations: economic, diplomatic, military, religious, and information exchange. It cannot be argued that he altered their historical course, but he undoubtedly influenced perceptions and attitudes on three continents. Myths and biases, however inaccurate, are not unimportant in de-termining the actions of individuals and nations. The German mission to China owes its origin to Gützlaff's publicity, and the Hakka Christian church quite rightly considers Gützlaff one of its founders. Evangelical Christianity, of which Gützlaff was a prominent exponent, has maintained a presence in China ever since the arrival of the first Protestant missionaries. With modern communications and transportation, the incorporation of China into the world economy, the international order, and the global knowledge commu-nity was inevitable sooner or later. Western traders and pioneer missionaries had a role in the process. They left an ambivalent legacy, and in Gützlaff the contradictions seem magnified. A loner, he was not subject to the institu-tional restrictions and social interplay that often rein in extremes.

Two of Gützlaff's co-workers attempted an assessment of his complexi-ties. Ferdinand Genähr wrote in April 1848,

61. James Reed, *The Missionary Mind and American East Asian Policy, 1911-1915* (Cam-bridge, MA: Harvard University Press, 1983).

Concerning Gutzlaff himself, I am unable to render a judgment. He seems to have too many sides to his character. With respect to the Chinese, I can say it no better than this: he is beloved, with all the worthy and bad qualities that inhere in this description. He returns their love fully and is preoccupied with one idea, China's conversion. However, his attempt to bring this about is marred by an enthusiasm so excessive that it is unsuited to the history of the kingdom of God.[62]

Lechler wrote in a similar vein in 1861, but in an essay written on the centennial of Gützlaff's birth, 1903, he took a longer view:

Gützlaff's great zeal and burning love for the cause played a preparatory role. We can be thankful to him that the three mission societies of Berlin, Barmen, and Basel sent missionaries to China. We have all followed Gützlaff's plan and have penetrated into the interior. Above all, Hudson Taylor, the Englishman, later fulfilled what Gützlaff had been attempting, for he personally has led his own troop and has established posts in all provinces.[63]

Gützlaff's true character and personality may still remain a puzzlement, but his role in stimulating Western interest in China and China missions and his position at the center of Sino-Western relations during the second quarter of the nineteenth century are clear. It is hard to imagine the history of this time and place without him.

62. Genähr to Committee, Hong Kong, 20 April 1848, VEM, Genähr Korrespondenz und Tagebucher, 1846-1864.
63. Lechler, "Zur Würdigung Gützlaffs, des ersten deutschen Chinesenmissionars" (mimeo copy), BMG, Schachtel A-10.

Bibliography

Archival Sources

American Baptist Foreign Mission Society, Archives Center. Annual Report, 1843-1845; William Dean Correspondence, 1843-1851; Issachar Roberts Correspondence, 1842-1843. Valley Forge, PA.

American Bible Society (ABS), Archive of. Gützlaff correspondence with John C. Brigham, Corresponding Secretary, 1841-1850; Gützlaff to ABS, 1833-1834, 1836-1839, 1845; MS of Rebecca Bromly, "History of the American Bible Society." New York City, NY.

American Board of Commissioners for Foreign Missions (ABCFM). Papers: South China, ABCFM 16.3.8; vol. 1, 1831-1844; vol. 2, 1846-1860. Harvard University, Houghton Library. Cambridge, MA.

Basler Missionsgesellschaft (BMG), Archives of. China: Berichte und Korrespondenz, 1846-1900; Schachtel, Miscellaneous MSS; Hamberg Korrespondenz, 1847-1854; Lechler Fascicle; Winnes Fascicle; Alphabetisches Verzeichnis sämtlicher Haupt-und-Aussensstationes der Basler Mission in China; photographs. Basel, Switzerland.

Birmingham, University of. University Library. Missions of the East Asia Committee: China Missions, 1834-1860. Birmingham, England.

British and Foreign Bible Society (BFBS), Archive of. Correspondence: Home and Foreign, China. Incoming and Outgoing Series, 1832-1851; Monthly Extract, 1833; G. Tradescant Lay Papers. Cambridge University, Cambridge, England.

Colonial Office, Public Records, Hong Kong. Original Correspondence, 1841-1854; C.O. 129; Probate #258 of 1851 (Gützlaff's will).

Council for World Mission, Archives of Church Missionary Society (CMS). Committee of Correspondence, Karl Gützlaff; Female Education Society, 1834-1863. University of London, School of Oriental and African Studies. London, England.

Council for World Mission, Archives of London Missionary Society, China. Personal, James Legge; Robert Morrison; South China Incoming Correspondence, 1820-1869; Central China, Incoming, 1843-1854; East China, Outgoing, 1841-1854. University of London, School of Oriental and African Studies. London, England.

Council for World Mission, Archives of United Reformed Church (Presbyterian Church of England). Foreign Missions Committee, Boxes 41B, 42, 46, 48, 94.

Duke University. Collection of American Women's Diaries. Margaret E. F. Crawford, "Journals and Diaries, 1846-1851." Durham, NC.

Jardine-Matheson Papers. Reels 28, 31, 158, 462, 495, 571, 572, 577, 580, 585, 587; Gützlaff Correspondence, 2/6, 2/7, 2/18, 2/19. Cambridge University Library, MS Division, Microfilm, Cambridge, England.

National Archives, Public Record Office, Colonial Office. Hong Kong: Correspondence, 1841-1846. Kew, Richmond, Surrey, United Kingdom.

National Army Museum. Department of Records. Papers of Sir Hugh Gough, 8303-105-697 to 8303-105-856 (1840-1842). London, England.

Nederlandsch Zendeling Genootschap (NZG). Archives of the Board of Missions of the Netherlands Reformed Church. Gützlaffiana, Kast. 19, Doss. G; Copy Book; Extract-Acten, 1823-1851. Leiden, The Netherlands.

Presbyterian Church of the U.S.A. Board of Foreign Missions. China Letters: Canton-Macao, 1837-1844; A. P. Happer, Macao, 1846-1851; Ningpo Mission, 1848-1853. Philadelphia, PA.

Reformed Church of America. David Abeel Papers. New Brunswick Theological Seminary, NJ.

Selly Oak College. Archive of the Mission Library. China Correspondence, 1849-1851; Papers relating to Karl Gützlaff. Birmingham, England.

Vereinte Evangelische Mission (VEM). Archives of the Rheinische Missionsgesellschaft. *Monatsberichte der Rheinische Missionsgesellschaft*, 1847; Genähr Korrespondenz and Tagebücher, 1846-1864; Gützlaff Korrespondenz, 1827-1851; Lobscheid Korrespondenz, 1847-1851; Carl Vogel, Korrespondenz, 1847-1850; Tagebuch, 12 March–23 April 1850; Protocol Buch, 1845-1850. Wuppertal, Germany.

Yale Divinity School Library. Special Collections, China. China Mission Pamphlets; Berliner Frauen Missionsverein für China, 1910-1912; Evangelische Missionsgesellschaft in Basel, 1818-1864; Rheinische Missionsgesellschaft, 1869-1897; *Monatsberichte der Rheinische Missionsgesellschaft*, 1849-1852. New Haven, CT.

Selected Books, Pamphlets, Tracts, and Translations by Gützlaff

Initially, Gützlaff used "Ai hanzhe" (Lover of the Chinese) as his pen name for his Chinese publications; after 1836, he generally used "Shan de" (Admirer of virtue). Many of his articles in the *Chinese Repository* are signed Philosinensis. In his correspondence with Christian Barth about the Chinese Union during the 1840s, he signed himself "Gaihan." Even though some of Gützlaff's Chinese tracts do not provide publication data, most of them were printed either at the LMS Press in Malacca or at the ABCFM Press in Singapore.

Aan mijne mede-Christenen in Nederland Afschiedswoord, met eenige aanteekeningen door H. C. Millies. [To my fellow Christians in Holland; valedictory address by Dr. K. Gützlaff, with a foreword by H. C Millies.] Amsterdam: J. C. Loman, 1850.

Abschiedswort an alle Chinesischen Vereine Europas. [Farewell Address to All European Chinese Unions.] Pamphlet. Stargard, 1850.

Abschiedsworte gesprochen bei der Jahresfeier der Preuss. Haupt-Bibel-Gesellschaft am 9 Oct. 1850. [Farewell Address delivered at the Annual Meeting of the Prussian Head Bible Society on 9 October 1850.] Berlin: W. Schultze, 1850.

An Appeal in Behalf of China. American reprint, n.d., n.p., 12 pp. Originally published in *Chinese Repository,* 1833.

Baolo yanxing lu. [A record of the life of Paul.] Singapore: ABCFM, 1837.

Bericht seiner Reise von China nach England und durch die verschiedenen Länder Europa's im Interesse der Chinesischen Mission. Cassel: Verlag und Druck der Expedition der Chinesischen Stiftung, 1851. [Also translated into Dutch and published in Rotterdam, 1851.]

Bideluo yanxing quanzhuan. [Complete account of the life of Peter.] Singapore: ABCFM, 1838.

Brief van Dr. Gützlaff aan het Comite der Pommersche hoofel vereeniging voor de Evanlische Zending in China. [Letter of Dr. Gützlaff to the committee of the Pomeranian union for the evangelical mission in China.] 's-Gravenhage, 20 December 1850. 11 pp.

Changhuo zhi danzhuan. [Doctrine of eternal life.] 44 leaves. 1834.

Chengchong bai lei han. [Faithful letters.] 60 leaves. 1834.

China en Deszelfs Inwoners en de Geschiedenis van de kleine Mary Gutzlaff. [China and its inhabitants and the history of little Mary Gutzlaff.] Rotterdam: M. Wijt & Zonan, 1850.

China, mit besonderer Rücksicht auf die Verhältnisse der Europäer zu diesem Reich und auf den jetzigen Krieg mit England nach den neuesten Werken darüber, dargestelt von Th. Vockerode. Leipzig: C. F. Döffling, 1842.

China Opened, or, a Display of the Topography, History, Customs, Manners, Arts, Manufactures, Commerce, Literature, Religion, Jurisprudence, etc. of the Chinese Empire. 2 vols. Revised by Andrew Reed. London: Smith, Elder & Co., 1838.

"Chinese Grammar, Part 1. Ethnography and Etymology." Compiled by Gützlaff, revised and reproduced by W. Medhurst. Lithographed, 148 pp., unfinished. Batavia: Mission Press, 1842. [Held by New York Public Library.]

Chinesesiche Berichte von der Mitte des Jahres 1841 bis zum Schluss des Jahres 1846. Cassel: Vorstand der Chinesischen Stiftung, 1850. Published under the name Gaihan. Letters originally printed by Christian Barth in *Calwer Monatsblätter.*

Da Yingguo tongzhi. [Short account of England.] Malacca: LMS, 1834.

"Dagverhaal van Februari tot Augustus 1827." [Diary from February to August 1827.] NZG, Kast. 19, No. 1, Doss. G (typescript).

"Dagverhaal van verblijf of het eiland Bintan van 24 Augustus 1827 tot 9 Maart 1828," entry for 9 December 1827, NZG, Kast. 19, No. 1, Doss. G (typescript).

Danyeli yanxing quanzhuan. [History of Daniel.] Singapore: ABCFM, 1837.

Dong-Xi yangkao meiyue tongji zhuan [East-West monthly magazine]. Canton and Singapore, 1833-1835, 1837-1839.

Dreijähriger Aufenthalt im Königreich Siam nebst einer kurzen Bescheibung seiner drei Reisen in den Seeprovinzen Chinas in den Jahren 1831-1833. Basel: Verlag des Evangelischen Missionsinstituts, 1835. Translated from the English version.

Fuyin zhi jingui. [Gospel precepts.] Singapore: ABCFM, 1836.

Gaixie guiyi zhi wen. [Abandoning depravity and turning to righteousness.] N.d.

Geschichte des chinesischen Reiches von dem ältesten zeiten bis auf den Freiden von Nanking. Stuttgart, Tübingen: J. G. Cotta, 1847. Also, a Dutch edition, 1852.

Geschiedenis der uitbriding van Christus koningrijke op aarde Sedert de Dagen der Kerkhervorming tot op den tegenwoordigen Tijd inbezonderheid met betrekking tot de Zendelingen en Zendeling-Genootschappen. [History of the extension of Christ's kingdom on earth from the days of the founding of the church, to the present time, with special attention to the missionaries and missionary societies.] 2 vols. Rotterdam, 1928.

Guanxi zhongda lüeshuo. [Important consequences.] Singapore: ABCFM, 1837.

Gujin wanguo gangjian. [Ancient and modern history of the world.] Singapore: ABCFM, 1838.

Huangcheng xinshi. [Augsburg Confession of Faith.] No publication date, but after 1843.

Huimo xundao. [Persuasion and instruction.] Singapore: ABCFM, 1838.

Hui zui zhi daluo. [A treatise on repentance.] Undated, but before 1838.

Jiaotiao. [Systematic theology.] 1849.

Jinli zhangdao zhuan. [True religion.] N.d.

Jinyao wanda. [Catechism of essentials.] N.d.

Jiu yizhao shengshu. [Old Testament.] 1836-1840. [Gützlaff, Bridgman, Medhurst, and J. R. Morrison collaborated in the translation of the Old Testament through Joshua; Gützlaff completed the translation of the Old Testament largely alone. A revised edition by Gützlaff was published in 1855.]

Jiushi yesu shousi quanzhuan. [Narrative of the death of the Savior Jesus.] 1843.

Jiushizhu yanxing quanzhuan. [A complete biography of the Savior of the world.] N.d. Revised and reprinted in 1855 in the name of the Chinese Union.

Jiushizhu Yesu. [Jesus, Savior of the world.] N.d.

Jiushizhu Yesu xinyi jiaoshu. [New Testament.] Batavia, 1837. Modification of Medhurst's version. Ten subsequent revisions by Gützlaff.

Jiushizhu Yesu zhi shengxun. [Sacred instructions of the Savior, Jesus.] Singapore: ABCFM Press, 1836.

Jiushu heyi. [Theory of redemption.] N.d.

Journal of a Residence in Siam and a Voyage along the Coast of China to Mantchou Tartary. Canton, 1832. Also published in the *Chinese Repository,* 1932. Also a Dutch edition, 1833.

Journal of Three Voyages along the Coast of China in 1831, 1832, and 1833. Taipei: Ch'ng-wen Publishing Co., 1968. Reprint of London: Frederick Westley and A. H. Davis, 1834. Second ed., 1834; third ed., 1840. Originally published in installments in the *Chinese Repository,* 1832-1833. Also an American edition and editions in French, Dutch, German, and Swedish.

Journal of Two Voyages along the Coast of China in 1831 and 1832. New York: J. P. Haven, 1833. Also published in Dutch, 1835.

"Kurzgefaszte Lebensbeschreibung, Karl Friedrich August Gützlaff." NZG, Kast. 19, No. 1, Doss. G. Typewritten and dated 5 June 1823.

"Life of Kang-He, Emperor of China." Appended to Thomas Allom, *China in a Series of Views,* vol. 1. London: M. A. Fisher, 1843.

Life of Taou-kwang, late emperor of China, with memoirs of the court of Peking; including a sketch of the principal events in the history of the Chinese empire during the last 50 years. London: Smith, Elder & Co., 1852. Also a German edition.

Mijne reis van China naar Engeland en door de vershillende landen van Europa, in 1849 en 1850, in het belang der Evangelie-verkondiging in China. [My trip from China to England and various lands of Europe in 1849 and 1850 in the interest of proclaiming the gospel in China.) Rotterdam: W. Wenk, 1851.

Die Mission in China. Vorträge in Berlin gehalten. Berlin: Wohlgemuth's Buchhandlung, 1850.

Mouyi tongzhi. [Treatise on commerce.] 1840.

Moxi yanxing quanzhuan. [Complete account of the life of Moses.] Singapore: ABCFM, 1836.

"On the Present State of Buddhism in China." Pamphlet. London, 1851.

Predigt über Apostelgeschichte IV. 12, gehalten am Dec. 22, 1822 in Berlin. Berlin: Wohlgemuth's Buchhandlung, 1844.

Quanren juhuo. [The perfect man's model.] Singapore: ABCFM Press, 1836.

"Reisverhaal van Zendeling Gützlaff, 11 Sept 1826-12 Feb 1827." [Journey of missionary Gützlaff, 11 Sept 1826–12 Feb 1827.] NZG, Kast. 19, No. 1, Doss. G.

"Remarks on the Siamese Language." Printed separately as a pamphlet, 1833. Also published in *Transactions of the Royal Asiatic Society* 3 (1835).

"Riouw op Bintang: Uittreksel uit het Dagboek van Broeder Gutzlaff van 1 April tot 8 Juli 1828." *Maandberigt van het Nederlandsch-Zendeling Genootschap* [Monthly report of the Dutch Missionary Society] 8 (1828), NZG, I 63.

Shangdi ai ren. [God's love of mankind.] N.d.

Shangdi chuangzao. [God created.] N.d. First line of a tract in tetra metrical verse.

Shangdi wanwu zhi dazhu. [God, the great Lord of all creation.] Singapore: ABCFM, 1838(?).

Shangdi zhenjiao zhuan. [Theology or narrative of the true teaching of God.] 1834.

Shanshang xuan dao. [Sermon on the Mount, with commentary.] N.d.

Shenghui daozhi. [English church liturgy.] Selections. N.d.

Shenghui zhi shi. [History of the church.] N.d.

Shengjing zhi shi. [History of the Bible.] N.d. Translation of Christian G. Barth's church history. Revised and reprinted in the name of the Chinese Union in the 1850s.

Shengming wuxian wujiang. [Life without limits and without boundaries.] Singapore: ABCFM, 1838.

Shengshu liezhu quanshuan. [Complete account of illustrious biblical patriarchs.] Singapore: ABCFM, 1838.

Shengshu quanyan. [Scripture exhortations.] N.d.

Shengshu zhusu. [Explanation of the Scriptures.] Singapore: ABCFM, 1839.

Shifei lüelun. [Correction of erroneous impressions.] Malacca: LMS, 1835.

Shiren jiuzhu. [Savior of mankind.] Singapore: ABCFM, 1838.

Shuzui zhi daozhuan. [Doctrine of redemption.] Singapore: ABCFM, 1834. Condensed version, 1836.

A Sketch of Chinese History, Ancient and Modern: Comprising a Retrospect of the Foreign Intercourse and Trade with China. 2 vols. London: Smith, Elder, & Co., 1834. Reprinted, New York: John P. Haven, 1834.

Smeekschrift, ten behoeve der Heidenen en Mahomedanen, gerigt aan all Christenen van Nederland. [Plea on behalf of heathens and Muhammadans addressed to the Christians of Holland.] Amsterdam: H. Hoveker 1826. German edition published in 1833.

Songyan zanyu. [Eulogy and praise.] Singapore: ABCFM, 1838.

Tianjiao getiao wanda jieming. [Luther's small catechism.] N.d.

Translation of a comparative Vocabulary of the Chinese, Corean, and Japanese Languages: to which is added the Thousand Character Classic, in Chinese and Corean; the whole accompanied by copious indices of all the Chinese and English words occurring in the work. Batavia: Parapattan Press, 1835.

"Übersetzung eines Briefes von demselben an Herrn Prediger van den Ham in Rotterdam," 11 May 1832, VEM, Archives of Rheinische Missionsgesellschaft, Gützlaff Correspondence.

Wanguo dili quanji. [Universal geography.] N.d.

Wanguo shizhuan. [Universal history.] N.d.

Xiaoxin xiaofu. [Little faith, little happiness.] N.d.

Yesu biyü zhushuo. [Parables of Jesus.] Singapore: ABCFM, 1841.

Yesu fusheng. [Resurrection of Jesus.] N.d.

Yesu jiangshi zhi zhuan. [Birth of Jesus.] Singapore: ABCFM, 1836.

Yesu jilidu wo zhu jiuzhe. [Jesus Christ, our Lord and Savior.] N.d.

Yesu shenji zhuzhuan. [Miracles of Jesus.] Singapore: ABCFM, 1836.

Yesu shousi. [Death of Jesus.] N.d.

Yesu shui ye? [Who is Jesus?] N.d.

Yesu zhi baoxun. [Precious teachings of Jesus.] Singapore: ABCFM, 1836.

Yohan fuyin zhi zhuan. [Gospel of John.] Singapore. In Japanese, Kitagana characters.

Yohan shangzhongxia shu. [Epistles of John.] Singapore: ABCFM, 1837. In Japanese, Kitagana characters.

Yohan yanxing lu. [Life of John.] Singapore: ABCFM, 1837.

Yosefo yanxing lu. [Life of Joseph.] Singapore: ABCFM, 1838.

Youtaiguo shi. [History of Judea.] Singapore: ABCFM, 1839.

Zendelings Reizen in China met het doel om den Bijbel te Verspeiden. [Mission trips in China with the object of spreading the gospel.] Rotterdam: M. Wijt & Zonen, 1848.

Zhendao zhi cheng. [Proofs of truth.] Singapore: ABCFM, 1838.

Zhendao zhi lun. [Discourse upon truth.] 1836.

Zhengjiao anwei. [Consolations of true teachings.] Singapore: ABCFM, 1836.

Zheng xie bijiao. [Orthodoxy and heterodoxy compared.] Singapore: ABCFM, 1838.

Zhiguo zhi yang dalüe. [Outline of political economy.] 1839.

Zhihui boai. [Kindness and universal love.] Singapore: ABCFM, 1839.

Zhuanhuo wei fu zhi fa. [The way from misery to happiness.] Singapore: ABCFM, 1838.

With H. H. Lindsay. *Report of Proceedings on a Voyage to the Northern Ports of China in the Ship Lord Amherst.* London: B. Fellowes, 1833. Extracted from papers printed by order of the House of Commons.

With Jacob Tomlin. *Acht Maanden te Bankok Medegedeeld door de Herren Gützlaff en Tomlin uit het Engelsch.* [Eight months in Bankok related by Gützlaff and Tomlin, from the English edition.] Rotterdam: Wijt & Sonen, 1851.

Books, Periodicals, and Articles

ABCFM. *Report.* Boston: Crocker Brewster, 1830-1853.

Abeel, David. *Journal of a Residence in China and the Neighboring Countries.* 2nd ed. New York: J. Abeel Williamson, 1836.

Actuelle China Nachrichten. Hamberg: China InfoStelle, 2001-2004.

Allgemeine Kirchen-Zeitung. Darmstadt, 1832.

American Baptist Mission Union. *Thirty-eighth Annual Report.* Hong Kong, 1852.

American Bible Society. *Report.* New York, 1829-1848.

American Tract Magazine. New York. 1824-1842. (Superseded by *American Messenger.*)

American Tract Society. *Annual Report.* Boston, 1825-1853.

Amity News Service. Kowloon, Hong Kong: Amity Foundation, 2002-2004.

Anderson, Gerald H., ed. *Biographical Dictionary of Christian Missions.* Grand Rapids: Eerdmans, 1999.

Anthony, Robert J. "Peasants, Heroes, and Brigands: The Problems of Social Banditry in Early 19th Century South China." *Modern China* 15.2 (1989): 123-48.

Asiatic Journal and Monthly Register. Boston, 1827-1843.

The Athenaeum. London: Journal of English and Foreign Literature, Science and the Fine Arts, 1831-1852.

Bak, János, and Gerhard Beneché, eds. *Religion and Rural Revolt.* Manchester: Manchester University Press, 1984.

Baptist Banner and Western Pioneer. Louisvillle, KY, 1842-1848. (Later, *Western Recorder.*)

Baptist Missionary Magazine. Boston: Board of Managers of the Baptist General Convention, 1829-1848.

Barnett, Suzanne W. "American Missionaries and Chinese Officials in the Context of the Opium War." Paper presented at the Conference on the Impact of American Missionaries on U.S. Attitudes and Policies toward China, San Diego, CA, October 1987.

———. "Practical Evangelism: Protestant Missions and the Introduction of Western Civilization to China, 1820-1850." Ph.D. dissertation, Harvard University, 1973.

———. "From Route Books to International Order: The Early Protestant Missionary Press and Chinese Geographical Writings." History of Christianity in China Project, 1990.

———. "Wei Yuan and Westerners: Notes on the Sources of the *Hai-kuo T'u-chih.*" *Ch'ing-shih wen-tí* 2.4 (November 1970): 1-20.

———, and John K. Fairbank, eds. *Christianity in China: Early Protestant Missionary Writings.* Cambridge, MA: Harvard University Press, 1985.

Bays, Daniel H. "Indigenous Protestant Churches in China." In *Indigenous Responses to Western Christianity,* ed. Stephen Kaplan. New York: New York University Press, 1994.

———. "Missions and Christians in Modern China, 1850-1950." Paper delivered at the Symposium on American Missionaries and Social Change in China, Linfield College, McMinneville, OR, 14-17 July 1994.

———, ed. *Christianity in China, from the Eighteenth Century to the Present.* Stanford: Stanford University Press, 1996.

———, and Grant Wacker, eds. *The Foreign Missionary Enterprise at Home.* Tuscaloosa: University of Alabama Press, 2003.

Belcher, Edward. *Narrative of a Voyage Round the World Performed in HM Ship Sulphur, 1836-1842, including naval operations in China, 1840-1842.* 2 vols. London: Henry Colburn, 1843.

Berliner Missions-Berichte. Berlin: Gesellschaft der Missionen zu Berlin, 1834, 1847.

Bernard, William D. *The Nemesis in China, comprising the history of the late war in that country; with an account of the colony of Hong-Kong.* 3rd ed. New York: Praeger Publishers, 1969. Reprint of 1846 ed.

Bernhardt, Kathryn. *Rents, Taxes and Peasant Resistance: The Lower Yangzi Region, 1840-1950.* Stanford: Stanford University Press, 1992.

Bigler, Robert M. *The Politics of German Protestantism: The Rise of the Protestant Elite in Prussia, 1815-1848.* Berkeley: University of California Press, 1975.

Bingham, John E. *Narrative of the Expedition to China from the Commencement of the War to Its Termination in 1842.* 2 vols. 2nd ed. London: Henry Colburn, 1843.

Blaikie, William G. *The Personal Life of David Livingstone.* New York: Harper & Bros., 1881.

Blakiston, T. W. *Five Months on the Yang-Tse, with a narrative of the exploration of its upper waters and notices of the present rebellion in China.* London: John Murray, 1862.

Blatt, Marilyn. "Problems of a China Missionary — Justus Doolittle." *Papers on China* 12 (1958). Cambridge, MA: Center for East Asian Studies, Harvard University.

Blindenmission in China. *Kurze Geschichte der deutschen Blindenmission in China heraus gegeben vom Hildesheimer Evangelischer Lutheran Missiionsverein für China.* Darmstadt: C. S. Wintersche Buchdruckerei, 1914.

Boardman, Eugene P. *Christian Influence upon the Ideology of the Taiping Rebellion, 1851-1864.* Madison: University of Wisconsin Press, 1952.

————. "Millenary Aspects of the Taiping Rebellion (1851-1864)." In *Millenarian Dreams in Action,* ed. Sylvia L. Thrupp, pp. 70-79. Comparative Studies in Society and History. The Hague: The Netherlands, 1962.

Bohr, Paul Richard. "The Heavenly Kingdom in China: Religion and the Taiping Revolution, 1837-1853." *Fides et Historica* 17.2 (1985): 38-52.

————. "The Politics of Eschatology: Hung Hsiu-ch'üan and the Rise of the Taipings, 1837-1853." Ph.D. dissertation, University of California, 1978.

Bonham, Sir George. "Trip of Her Britannic Majesty's Plenipotentiary Sir George Bonham in the *Hermes* to Nanking, April 22, 1853." Extracted from the *North China Herald* of 7 May 1853 by W. Medhurst.

Bonn, Alfred. *Ein Jahrhundert Rheinische Mission.* Barmen: Verlag des Missionshauses in Barmen, 1928.

Bridgman, Elijah J. *Meilige heshengguo shilue.* [A short account of the united provinces of America.] Singapore: ABCFM, 1838.

Bridgman, Eliza. *Daughters of China or Sketches of Domestic Life in the Celestial Kingdom.* New York: Robert Carter and Bros., 1853.

————, ed. *The Life and Labors of Elijah Coleman Bridgman.* New York: Anson D. F. Randolph, 1864.

Brine, Lindsay. *The Taiping Rebellion in China: A Narrative of Its Rise and Progress, Based upon Original Documents and Information Obtained in China.* London: John Murray, 1862.

British and Foreign Bible Society. *Report.* London, 1828-1854.

Britton, Roswell S. *The Chinese Periodical Press, 1800-1912.* Shanghai: Kelly & Walsh, 1933.

Brook, Timothy, and Andre Schmid, eds. *Nation Work: Asian Elites and National Identities.* Ann Arbor: University of Michigan Press, 2000.

Brook, Timothy, and Bob Tadashi Wakabayashi, eds. *Opium Regimes: China, Britain, and Japan, 1839-1952.* Berkeley: University of California Press, 2000.

Broomhall, A. J. *Hudson Taylor and China's Open Century.* Vols. 1-3. London: Hodder and Stoughton, 1981-1982.

Burns, Islay. *Memoir of the Rev. William C. Burns, Missionary to China from the English Presbyterian Church.* New York: Robert Carter & Bros., 1870.

Cai Wo. "Tantan 'Dong-Xi yang kaomeiyue tongjizhuan': Zhongguo jingnian diyizhong xiandai Zhongwen qikan." [Comments on the "East-West Monthly Magazine," the first modern Chinese periodical published in China], *Guoli zhongyang tushuguan quankan* [National Central Library Bulletin], New Series, 2.4 (April 1969): 23-46.

Callery, Joseph M. *Journal des Opérations diplomatiques de la Légation Française en Chine.* Macao, 1845.

——, and Melchoir Yvan. *History of the Insurrection in China, with Notices of the Christianity, Creed, and Proclamations of the Insurgents.* Trans. John Oxenford. New York: Harper & Bros., 1853.

Calwer Missionsblatt. Cassel, 1847-1854. Edited by Christian G. Barth.

Canton, William. *A History of the British and Foreign Bible Society.* 2 vols. London: John Murray, 1904.

Carlson, Ellsworth C. *The Foochow Missionaries, 1847-1880.* Cambridge: Harvard University Press, 1974.

Cassel Jahresbericht des Evangelischen Missions-Verein in Kurhessen. Cassel, 1844-1850.

Cha shisu meiyue tongjizhuan. [A general monthly magazine examining the course of affairs.] Edited by William Milne and later by W. Medhurst. Malacca: LMS Press, 1815-1817, 1821.

Chang Hsin-pao. *Commissioner Lin and the Opium War.* Cambridge, MA: Harvard University Press, 1964.

Chao, Samuel H. *Practical Missiology: The Life and Mission Methods of John Livingston Nevius, 1829-1893.* New York: P. Lang, 1996.

Chen Qitian (Gideon Chen). *Lin Tse-hsü: Pioneer Promoter of the Adoption of Western Means of Maritime Defense in China.* New York: Paragon Book Gallery, 1961. Reprint of 1934 ed.

Ch'en Kuan-sheng (Kenneth Ch'en). "The Growth of Geographical Knowledge concerning the West in China during the Ch'ing Dynasty." M.A. thesis, Yenching University, 1934. (Located at Harvard-Yenching Institute.)

——. "Matteo Ricci's Contribution to and Influence on Geographical Knowledge in China." *Journal of the American Oriental Society* 59.3 (September 1939): 325-59.

Cheng Zhen Church in Hong Kong. "Fangwen Dong Mei Zhu san jiang Kejia jiaohui jianbao." [Brief report on an investigation of the Hakka churches of the three rivers, East, Mei, and Pearl.] 4 January 1991. Mimeo copy. Tsung Tsin Mission, Kowloon, Hong Kong.

Chesneaux, Jean, ed. *Popular Movements and Secret Societies in China, 1840-1950.* Stanford: Stanford University Press, 1972.

China Mail. Victoria, 1851-1853.

China Mission Advocate. Boston, 1839. Edited for one year by Issachar Roberts.

Chinese Missionary Gleaner. London: The Chinese Society for Furthering the Propagation of the Gospel in China, 1851-1855. (Until 1853, the title was *The Chinese and General Missionary Gleaner.*)

Chinese Recorder. Shanghai, 1868-1887.

Chinese Repository. Canton. Edited by E. C. Bridgman and S. Wells Williams. 1832-1851.

Chinese Social and Political Science Review. Beijing, 1928-1937.

Chinese Theological Review. Holland, MI: Foundation for Theological Education in Southeast Asia, 1994-1997.

Christensen, Torben, and William R. Hutchison, eds. *Missionary Ideologies in the Imperialist Era, 1880-1920.* Struer, Denmark: Christensens Bogtrykkeri, 1982.

Church Missionary Intelligencer. London: Church Missionary Society, 1849-1854.

"Churches in Northern Guangdong." *Bridge* 33 (January-February 1989).

Clarke, Prescot. "The Coming of God to Kwangsi." *Papers on Far Eastern History,* no. 7 (March 1973). Australian National University.

Coates, Austin. *Prelude to Hong Kong.* London: Routledge & Kegan Paul, 1966.

Cohen, Paul. *Between Tradition and Modernity: Wang T'ao and Reform in Late Ch'ing China.* Cambridge, MA: Harvard University Press, 1974.

Constable, Nicole. *Christian Souls and Chinese Spirits: A Hakka Community in Hong Kong.* Berkeley: University of California Press, 1994.

———, ed. *Guest People: Hakka Identity in China and Abroad.* Seattle: University of Washington Press, 1998.

Coughlin, Margaret M. "Strangers in the House: J. Lewis Shuck and Issachar Roberts, First American Baptist Missionaries in China." Ph.D. dissertation, University of Virginia, 1972.

Cunynghame, Arthur. *The Opium War: Being Recollections of Service in China.* Wilmington, DE: Scholarly Resources Inc., 1972. Reprint of 1845 ed.

Davis, John Francis. *China, during the War and since the Peace.* 2 vols. London: Longman, Brown, Green, & Longmans, 1852.

———. *Sketches of China.* 2nd ed. London: Charles Knight & Co., 1846.

Dillenberger, John, and Claude Welch. *Protestant Christianity Interpreted thru Its Development.* New York: Scribners, 1954.

Dillon, Maureen F. "The Triads in Shanghai: The Small Sword Society Uprising, 1853-1855." *Papers on China* 23 (1970). Cambridge, MA: Harvard East Asian Research Center.

Doezema, William. "Western Seeds of Eastern Heterodoxy: The Impact of Protestant Revivalism on the Christianity of the Taiping Rebel Leader, Hung Hsiu-ch'üan, 1836-1864." *Fides et Historia* 25 (Winter/Spring 1993): 73-98.

Downing, Charles Toogood. *The Stranger in China; or the Fan Qui's Visit to the Celestial Empire in 1836-1837.* 2 vols. Philadelphia: Lea & Blanchard, 1838.

Drake, Fred W. *China Charts the World: Hsü Chi-yu and His Geography of 1848.* Cambridge, MA: Harvard University Press, 1975.

————. "A Nineteenth-Century View of the United States from Hsü Chi-yu's *Ying-huan chih-lüeh.*" *Papers on China* 19 (1965): 130-54. Cambridge, MA: Harvard East Asian Research Center, 1965.

Dwight, Henry O. *The Centennial History of the American Bible Society.* New York: Macmillan Co., 1916.

Eames, James B. *The English in China, Being an Account of the Intercourse and Relations between England and China from the Year 1600 to the Year 1843.* London: Sir Isaac Pitman & Sons, 1909.

Eber, Irene, et al., eds. *Bible in Modern China: The Literary and Intellectual Impact.* Sankt Augustin: Institut Monumenta Sinica, 1999.

Edkins, Jane. *Chinese Scenes and People, with Notices of Christian Missions and Mission Life.* London: James Nisbet & Co., 1863.

Edkins, Joseph. *Religion in China, Containing a Brief Account of the Three Religions of the Chinese.* 2nd ed. London: Trübner & Co., 1878.

Eitel, E. J. *Europe in China: The History of Hongkong from the Beginning to the Year 1882.* Taipei: Ch'eng-wen Publishing Co., 1968. Reprint of 1895 ed.

Endacott, George B. *A History of Hong Kong.* Hong Kong: Oxford University Press, 1973.

Eppler, Paul. *Geschichte der Basler Mission, 1815-1899.* Basel: Verlag der Missionsbuchhandlung, 1900.

Erdbrink, G. R. *Gützlaff, De apostel der chinezen in zijn leven en zijne werkzaamheid geschetst.* [Gützlaff, the Apostle of the Chinese portrayed in his life and activities.] Rotterdam: M. Wijt & Zonen, 1850.

Evangelical Christendom. London: Evangelical Alliance, 1847-1848.

Evangelical Magazine and Missionary Chronicle. London: London Missionary Society, 1829-1840.

Evangelical Review. Gettysburg, PA: American Lutheran Church, 1845-1854.

Evangelische Heidenbote. Basel: Basler Missionsgesellschaft, 1837-1851, 1863.

Evangelische Kirchen-Zeitung. Edited by Ernst Hengstenberg. Berlin, 1850.

Evangelischer Reichsbote. Berlin: Berliner Missionsverein für China, 1851-1865.

Evangelisches Missions-Magazin. Basel: Evangelische Missionsgesellschaft in Basel, 1831-1863, 1895, 1903.

"Extract from the *Journal of a Residence in Siam and Voyage along the Coast of China.*" *Das Ausland,* 1834, pp. 1043-44, 1047-48.

Fairbank, John K. "Assignment for the '70s." *American Historical Review* 74.3 (December 1969): 480-511.

————. "Chinese Diplomacy and the Treaty of Nanking, 1842." *Journal of Modern History* 12.1 (March 1940): 1-30.

————. *The Great Chinese Revolution, 1800-1985.* New York: Harper & Row, 1986.

————. *Trade and Diplomacy on the China Coast: The Opening of the Treaty Ports, 1842-1854.* 2 vols. Cambridge, MA: Harvard University Press, 1953-1956.

————. *The United States and China.* 4th ed. Cambridge, MA: Harvard University Press, 1983.

————, ed. *The Missionary Enterprise in China and America*. Cambridge, MA: Harvard University Press, 1974.

Family Magazine or Weekly Abstract of General Knowledge. New York, 1833-1841.

Fay, Peter W. "The French Catholic Mission in China during the Opium War." *Modern Asian Studies* 4 (1970): 115-28.

————. *The Opium War, 1840-1842: Barbarians in the Celestial Empire in the Early Part of the Nineteenth Century and the War By Which They Forced Her Gates Ajar*. Chapel Hill: University of North Carolina Press, 1975.

————. "The Protestant Mission and the Opium War." *Pacific Historical Review* 40 (May 1971): 145-61.

Feuerwerker, Albert. *Rebellion in Nineteenth Century China*. Ann Arbor: Center for Chinese Studies, University of Michigan, 1975.

Fiedler, Klaus. *Christianity and African Culture: Conservative German Protestant Missionaries in Tanzania, 1900-1940*. Leiden: E. J. Brill, 1996.

Findelhaus Bethesda. *Jahresbericht*. Berlin: Selbstverlag des Berliner Frauen Missions-Verein für China, 1910, 1911, 1921.

Fishbourne, Edward G. *Impressions of China and the Present Revolution: Its Progress and Prospects*. London: Seeley, Jackson, & Halliday, 1855.

Fitzgerald, John. *Awakening China: Politics, Culture, and Class in the Nationalist Revolution*. Stanford: Stanford University Press, 1996.

Foreign Missionary Chronicle. Pittsburgh: Western Foreign Missionary Society, 1833-1849. (In 1842, it became *Missionary Chronicle*.)

Fortune, Robert. *Three Years' Wanderings in the Northern Provinces of China*. New York: Garland, 1979. Reprint of 1847 ed.

Foster, John. "The Christian Origins of the Taiping Rebellion." *International Review of Missions* 40 (April 1951): 156-67.

Fox, Grace. *British Admirals and Chinese Pirates*. London: Kegan Paul & Co., 1940.

Friend of China and Hong Kong Gazette. Hong Kong, 1845-1859. (*Overland Friend of China* was, for a time, published separately.)

Gauld, William. "History of the Swatow Mission." M.A. thesis, unfinished and unpublished. University of London, School of Oriental and African Studies. London, England.

Gerson, Jack J. *Horatio Nelson Lay and Sino-British Relations, 1854-1864*. Cambridge, MA: Harvard University Press, 1972.

Giquel, Prosper. *A Journal of the Chinese Civil War, 1864*. Honolulu, 1864.

Girardot, Norman J. *The Victorian Translation of China: James Legge's Oriental Pilgrimage*. Berkeley: University of California Press, 2002.

Goslinga, A. *Dr. Karl Gützlaff en het Nederlandsche Protestantisme in het midden der vorige eeuw*. [Dr. Karl Gützlaff and Dutch Protestantism in the middle of the previous century.] 's-Gravenhage: Boekencentrum N.V., 1941.

Greenberg, Michael. *British Trade and the Opening of China, 1800-1842*. Cambridge: Cambridge University Press, 1951.

Gregory, J. S. "British Missionary Reaction to the Taiping Movement in China." *Journal of Religious History* 3.3 (1963): 204-18.

Grundmann, Christoffer H. *Gesandt zu heilen! Aufkommen und Entwicklung der ärztlichen Mission im neunzehnten Jahrhundert.* Gutersloh: Gutersloher Verlagshaus, G. Mohn, 1992.

Gu Changsheng. "Guo Lishi (Charles Gutzlaff, 1803-1851)." In *Zong Malisu dao situ Leideng — Lai hua xinjiao chuanjiaoshi pingzhuan.* [From Morrison to Stuart — critical biographies of Protestant missionaries in China.] Shanghai: Shanghai renmin chubanshe, 1985.

Gulick, Edward. *Peter Parker and the Opening of China.* Cambridge, MA: Harvard University Press, 1973.

Gully, Robert. *Journals Kept by Mr. Gully and Capt. Denham during a Captivity in China in the Year 1842.* London: Chapman & Hall, 1844.

Haas, Waltraud, ed. *Mission History from the Women's Point of View.* Basel: Verlag der Basler Missionsbuchhandlung, 1989.

Hallemcreutz, C. F. "Theodor Hamberg and the Taiping Revolution: A Swedish Source on Taiping Religiosity." Upsala: Upsala University, 1977. (In Basel Archives.)

Halsberghe, Nicole, and Keizo Hashimoto. "Astronomy." In *Handbook of Christianity in China,* ed. Nicolas Standaert, vol. 1, pp. 711-37. Leiden: Brill, 2001.

Hamberg, Theodor. *Report Regarding the Chinese Union at Hong Kong.* Hong Kong: Hong Kong Register, 1851. Basler Missionsgesellschaft Archives, China. A-1.1 (1B), no. 18.

———. *The Visions of Hung-siu-tshuen and Origin of the Kwangsi Insurrection.* New York: Praeger, 1968. Reprint of 1854 ed.

Hanan, Patrick. "The Missionary Novels of Nineteenth-Century China." *Harvard Journal of Asiatic Studies* 60.2 (December 2000): 413-43.

Handelingen in de Buiten gewone vergadering der Directeuran van het NZG te Rotterdam. [Provincial meeting of the NZG at Rotterdam.] Rotterdam, 1826-1833.

Hannich, Gustav. *Treue bis ans Ende: Erlibnisse schwedischen Missionars Theodor Hamberg in China.* Basel: Basler Missionsbuchhandlung, 1941.

Hao Yen-p'in and Erh-min Wang. "Changing Chinese Views of Western Relations, 1840-1895." In *The Cambridge History of China,* ed. J. K. Fairbank and Kwang-ching Liu, 11.2:142-201. Cambridge: Cambridge University Press, 1980.

Hefner, Robert W., ed. *Conversion to Christianity: Historical and Anthropological Perspectives on a Great Transformation.* Berkeley: University of California Press, 1993.

Ho, Herbert Hoi-Iap. *Protestant Missionary Publications in Modern China, 1912-1949: A Study of Their Programs, Operation, and Trends.* Hong Kong: Chinese Church Research Centre, 1988.

Hoe, Susanna. *The Private Life of Old Hong Kong: Western Women in the British Colony, 1841-1941.* Hong Kong: Oxford University Press, 1991.

Holborn, Hajo. *A History of Modern Germany, 1648-1840.* New York: Knopf, 1964.

Hong Kong Register. Hong Kong, 1844-1859. Owned by Jardine-Matheson. (Formerly the *Canton Register.*)

Hood, George A. "The Gützlaff Papers, Selly Oak Colleges, Birmingham England." Paper presented at a meeting of the Yale-Edinburgh Group, Edinburgh, 1999.

———. *Mission Accomplished? The English Presbyterian Mission in Lingtung, South China.* Frankfurt am Main: Verlag Peter Lang, 1986.

Hsu, Immanuel C. Y. "The Secret Mission of the *Lord Amherst* on the China Coast in 1832." *Harvard Journal of Asiatic Studies* 17 (1954): 231-52.

Hummel, Arthur, ed. *Eminent Chinese of the Ch'ing Dynasty.* 2 vols. Washington: U.S. Government Printing Office, 1943-1944.

Hunter, Jane. *The Gospel of Gentility: American Women Missionaries in Turn-of-the-Century China.* New Haven: Yale University Press, 1984.

Hyatt, Irwin. *Our Ordered Lives Confess: Three Nineteenth-Century American Missionaries in East Shantung.* Cambridge, MA: Harvard University Press, 1976.

International Bulletin of Missionary Research. New Haven: Overseas Ministries Study Center, 1998-2004.

Isaacs, Harold R. *Images of Asia: American Views of China and India.* New York: John Day, 1958.

Jahresbericht der Pommerschen Hauptvereins für Evangelisirung China. Stettin, Germany, 1851.

Jahresberichte des evangelischen Missionsvereins in Kurhessen. Cassel, 1833-1850.

Jen Yuwen (Jian Youwen). *The Taiping Revolutionary Movement.* New Haven: Yale University Press, 1973.

Jenkins, Paul. *A Short History of the Basel Mission.* Basel: Basler Missions Buchhandlung, 1989.

Jocelyn, Robert. *Six Months with the Chinese Expedition, or Leaves from a Soldier's Notebook.* London: John Murray, 1841.

Journal of the Royal Asiatic Society, Hong Kong Branch. Hong Kong, 1835-1850.

Journal of the Royal Geographical Society. 1834, 1849-1851.

Kaplan, Stephen, ed. *Indigenous Responses to Western Christianity.* New York: New York University Press, 1994.

Karl, Rebecca. "Creating Asia in the World at the Beginning of the Twentieth Century." *American Historical Review,* October 1998, pp. 1096-1118.

Kessler, Lawrence D. *The Jiangyin Mission Station: An American Missionary Community in China, 1895-1951.* Chapel Hill: University of North Carolina Press, 1996.

Kesson, John. *The Cross and the Dragon, or the Fortunes of Christianity in China.* London: Smith, Elder & Co., 1854.

King, Charles W. *The Claims of Japan and Malaysia upon Christendom exhibited in notes of voyages made in 1837 from Canton in the ship Morrison and Brig. Himmaleh.* 2 vols. New York: E. French, 1839.

King, John. "Horatio Nelson Lay, C.B." *Journal of American Asiatic Association* 14.2 (March 1914): 48-54.

Klein, Thoralf. "Die Anfänge der deutschen protestantischen Mission in China, 1846-

1880: Kulturelle Missverständnisse und kulturelle Konflikte." M.A. thesis, Freiburg University, 1995.

———. *Die Basler Mission in Guangdong (Südchina), 1859-1931*. München: Iudicium Verlag, 2002.

——— und Reinhard Zöllner, eds. *Karl F. A. Gützlaff (1803-1851) und das Christentum in Ostasien. Ein Missionar zwischen den Kulturen*. Nettetal: Steyler Verlag, 2005.

Kruijf, E. F. *Geschiedenis van het Nederlandische Zendelinggenootschap en zijne Zendingsposten*. [The history of the Dutch Mission Society and its mission stations.] Groningen, 1994.

Krummacher, Friedrich W. *Gützlaff's Heimgang: Gedächtnis predigt*. 19 October 1851. Staatsbibliothek zu Berlin.

Ku Wei-ying and Koen De Ridder, eds. *Authentic Christianity: Preludes to Its Development*. Leuven: Leuven University Press, 2001.

Kuhn, Philip A. "Origins of the Taiping Vision: Cross Cultural Dimensions of a Chinese Rebellion." *Comparative Studies in Society and History* 19.3 (July 1977): 350-66.

———. "The Taiping Rebellion." In *Cambridge History of China*, ed. J. K. Fairbank, 10.1:264-317. Cambridge: Cambridge University Press, 1978.

Kuo Pin-chia. *A Critical Study of the First Anglo-Chinese War, with Documents*. Shanghai: Commercial Press, 1935.

Laai Yi-faai. "The Part Played by the Pirates of Kwangtung in the Taiping Insurrection." Ph.D. dissertation, University of California, 1950.

Lamb, Christopher, and M. Darrol Bryant, eds. *Religious Conversion: Contemporary Practices and Controversies*. London: Cassell, 1999.

Lane-Poole, Stanley. *The Life of Sir Harry Parkes*. 2 vols. London: Macmillan Co., 1894.

———. *Sir Harry Parkes in China*. Taipei: Ch'eng-wen Publishing Co., 1968. Reprint of 1902 ed.

Latourette, Kenneth. *A History of Christian Missions in China*. London: Society for Promoting Christian Knowledge, 1929.

La Vopa, Anthony J. *Grace, Talent, and Merit: Poor Students, Clerical Careers, and Professional Ideology in Eighteenth Century Germany*. Cambridge: Cambridge University Press, 1988.

Lay, George Tradescent. *The Chinese as They Are*. Albany: George Jones, 1843.

———. *The Claims of Japan and Malaysia upon Christendom exhibited in notes of voyages made in 1837 from Canton in the ship Morrison and brig Himmaleh*. 2 vols. New York: E. French, 1839.

Lazich, Michael C. *E. C. Bridgman (1801-1861), America's First Missionary to China*. Lewiston: The Edwin Mellen Press, 2000.

Lechler, Rudolf. *Acht Vorträge über China gehalten an verschiedenen Orten Deutschlands und der Schweiz*. Basel: Verlag des Missionshauses, 1861.

Ledderhose, Karl Friedrich. *Johann Jänicke der evangelisch-lutherische Prediger an der böhmischen- oder Bethlehems-kirche zu Berlin. Nach seinem Leben und Wirken dargestellt*. Berlin: G. Knak Selbstverlag, 1863.

Lee, Joseph Tse-Hei. *The Bible and the Gun: Christianity in South China, 1860-1900.* New York: Routledge, 2003.

———. "God's Villages: Christian Communities in Late-Nineteenth-Century South China." Paper presented at a meeting of the Yale-Edinburgh Group. New Haven, July 2003.

Legge, Helen E. *James Legge, Missionary and Scholar.* London: Religious Tract Society, 1905.

Legge, James. *The Notions of the Chinese concerning God and Spirits, with an examination of the defense of an essay, on the proper rendering of the words Elohim and Theos, into the Chinese language by William J. Boone.* Hong Kong: Hong Kong Register, 1852.

Lehmann, Hartmut. *Pietismus und weltliche Ordnung in Wurttemberg vom 17 bis zum 20 Jahrhundert.* Stuttgart: Kohlhammer, 1969.

Leonard, Jane K. "Chinese Overlordship and Western Penetration in Maritime Asia: A Late Ch'ing Reappraisal of Chinese Maritime Relations." *Modern Asian Studies* 6.2 (1972): 151-74.

———. "W. H. Medhurst: Rewriting the Missionary Message." In *Christianity in China,* ed. Suzanne W. Barnett and John E. Fairbank, pp. 48-55. Cambridge, MA: Council on East Asian Studies, Harvard University Press, 1985.

———. *Wei Yuan and China's Rediscovery of the Maritime World.* Cambridge, MA: Harvard University Press, 1984.

Leong, Sow-Theng. "The Hakka Chinese of Lingnan." In *Ideal and Reality: Social and Political Change in Modern China,* ed. David Pong and Edmund S. K. Feng, pp. 302-7. Lanham, MD: University Press of America, 1985.

Levenson, Joseph R. *Confucian China and Its Modern Fate.* 3 vols. Berkeley: University of California Press, 1964.

Lewis, Bernard, "I'm Right, You're Wrong, Go to Hell." *Atlantic Monthly,* May 2003, pp. 36-42.

Li Hongshan and Zhaohui Hong, eds. *Image, Perception, and the Making of US-China Relations.* Lanham, MD: University Press of America, 1998.

Li Zhigang. "Guanshi huijiaozongyixi guozhong yu shimu guo lishi." [The connection of the Chinese Lutheran Church and Pastor Gützlaff.] *Jidujiao zhoubao* [Church news], 27 December 1991.

Lian Xi. "No Earthly Salvation: Wang Mingdao, John Sung, Watchman Nee and the Rise of Indigenous Christianity in China." Paper presented at the annual meeting of the Association for Asian Studies, Boston, March 1999.

Liang Fa. *Chuanshi liangyou.* [Goods words to admonish an age]. In Mai Zhansi, *Liang Fa zhuan.* [Life of Liang Fa.] 2nd ed. Appendix. Hong Kong: Council on Christian Literature for Overseas Chinese, 1968.

Liao, David C. E. *The Unresponsive: Resistant or Neglected? The Homogeneous Unit Principle Illustrated by the Hakka Chinese in Taiwan.* Pasadena, CA: Wm. Carey Library, 1972.

Lin Zhiping, ed. *Jidujiao yu Zhongguo bense hua.* [Christianity and Chinese indigenization.] Taipei: Yuchouguang, 1990.

Lindsay, Hugh Hamilton. *Remarks on Occurrences in China since the Opium Seizure in March 1839, to the Latest Date.* London: Sherwood, Gilbert & Piper, 1840.

The Literary Gazette. London, 1829-1834, 1843.

Littell, John B. "Missionaries and Politics in China: The Taiping Rebellion." *Political Science Quarterly* 43 (1928): 566-99.

Lo Xianglin. "Zhongguo zupu suoji Jidujiao zhi chuanbo yu xindai Zhongguo zhi guanxi." [The spread of Christianity and its influence on modern China as seen through Chinese genealogical records.] *Journal of Oriental Studies* 7 (1969): 1-22.

Loch, Granville G. *The Closing Events of the Campaign in China: The Operations in the Yang-Tze-kiang and Treaty of Nanking.* London: J. Murray, 1843.

Lockhart, William. *The Medical Missionary in China: A Narrative of Twenty Years' Experience.* London: Hurst & Blackett, 1861.

Lodwick, Kathleen L. *Crusaders against Opium: Protestant Missions in China, 1874-1917.* Louisville: University Press of Kentucky, 1996.

Lörcher, Jakob. *Die Basler Mission in China.* Basel: Verlag der Missionsbuchhandlung, 1862.

Lovett, Richard. *The History of the London Missionary Society, 1795-1895.* 2 vols. London: Henry Frowde, 1899.

Lowrie, Walter M. *Memoirs of the Rev. Walter M. Lowrie, Missionary to China.* Ed. by his father. New York: R. Carter & Brothers, 1850.

Luther, Martin. *Three Treatises.* Philadelphia: Muhlenberg Press, 1947.

Lutz, Jessie G. *Chinese Politics and Christian Missions: The Anti-Christian Movements of 1920-1928.* Notre Dame, IN: Cross Cultural Publications, 1988.

————. "The Grand Illusion: Karl Gützlaff and Popularization of China Missions in the United States during the 1830s." In *United States Attitudes and Policies toward China: The Impact of American Missionaries,* ed. Patricia Neils, pp. 46-77. Armonk, NY: M. E. Sharpe, 1990.

————. "Karl Gützlaff and Changing Chinese Perceptions of the World during the 1840s." In *Jidujiao yu Zhongguo wenhua congkan* [Christianity and cultural communication], ed. Ma Min, pp. 354-392. Hubei: Hubei Jiaoyu chubanshe, 2003.

————. "Karl F. A. Gützlaff: Missionary Entrepreneur." In *Christianity in China,* ed. Suzanne W. Barnett and John E. Fairbank, pp. 61-85. Cambridge, MA: Council on East Asian Studies, Harvard University Press, 1985.

————. "The Missionary-Diplomat Karl Gützlaff and the Opium War." In *Zhongguo jindai zhengjiao guanxi guoji xueshu yantaohui lunwenji* [Proceedings of the first international symposium on church and state in China], ed. Li Chifang. Taipei: Danjiang daxue, 1987.

————. "A Profile of Chinese Protestant Evangelists in the Mid-Nineteenth Century." In *Authentic Chinese Christianity: Preludes to Its Development (Nineteenth and*

Twentieth Centuries), ed. Ku Wei-ying and Koen De Ridder, pp. 67-86. Leuven: Leuven University Press, 2001.

———. "Western Nationalism, Chinese Assistants, and Translations of the Chinese Bible." Paper delivered at Conference on "A Bridge between Cultures: Commemorating the 200th Anniversary of Robert Morrison's Arrival in China." University of Maryland, March 15-16, 2007.

———. "Japanese Castaways, China Missionaries, and Renga Kusha in the Opening of Japan" (forthcoming).

Lutz, Jessie G., and R. R. Lutz. *Hakka Chinese Confront Protestant Christianity, 1850-1900.* Armonk, NY: M. E. Sharpe, 1998.

———. "Karl Gützlaff's Approach to Indigenization: The Chinese Union." In *Christianity in China, from the Eighteenth Century to the Present,* ed. Daniel H. Bays, pp. 269-91. Stanford: Stanford University Press, 1996.

———. "The Invisible Missionaries: The Basel Mission Chinese Evangelists, 1844-1866." *Mission Studies* 12.2 (October 1995): 204-27.

———. "Zhang Fuxing and the Origins of Hakka Christianity in Northwest Guangdong." In *Guoli kejia xueyantaohui lunwenji* [The proceedings of the first international conference on hakkaology), ed. Zhang Shuangqing and John Lagewey. Hong Kong: Chinese University of Hong Kong, 1994.

Ma Min, ed. *Jidujiao yu Zhongguo wenhua congkan.* [Christianity and Chinese cultural communication.] Hubei: Hubei Jiaoyu chubanshe, 2003.

Maandberigt van het Nederlandsch-Zendeling Genootschap. [Monthly report of the Dutch Missionary Society.] Rotterdam, 1826-1829, 1844.

McFarland, George B., ed. *Historical Sketch of Protestant Missions in Siam, 1828-1928.* Bangkok: Bangkok Times Press, 1928.

MacFarlane, Charles. *The Chinese Revolution with Details of the Habits, Manners, and Customs of China and the Chinese.* Wilmington, DE: Scholarly Resources Reprint, 1972. Reprint of 1853 ed.

MacGillivray, D., ed. *A Century of Protestant Missions in China, 1807-1907. Being the Centenary Conference Volume.* Shanghai: American Presbyterian Press, 1907.

Mackenzie, Keith S. *Narrative of the Second Campaign in China.* London: Richard Bentley, 1842.

Madancy, Joyce A. *The Troublesome Legacy of Commissioner Lin: The Opium Trade and the Opium Suppression in Fujian Province, 1820s to 1920s.* Cambridge, MA: Harvard University Press, 2003.

Magazin für die neuste Geschichte der evangelischen Mission-und Bibelgesellschaften. 1835, pp. 3-176.

Magazine of the Reformed Dutch Church. New Brunswick, NJ, 1826-1830.

Malcolm, Elizabeth. "The *Chinese Repository* and Western Literature on China, 1800-1850." *Modern Asian Studies* 7.2 (1973): 165-78.

Martin, Robert M. *China: Political, Commercial, and Social; in an Official Report to Her Majesty's Government.* 2 vols. London: James Madden, 1847.

Martin, W. A. P. *A Cycle of Cathay.* 2nd ed. New York: Fleming H. Revell, 1897.

Medhurst, W. H. *China: Its State and Prospects, with especial reference to the spread of the Gospel.* Boston: Crocker & Brewster, 1838.

————. *Connection between Foreign Missionaries and the Kwangsi Insurrection.* Shanghai: North China Herald, 1853.

————. *A Dissertation on the Theology of the Chinese, with a view to the elucidation of the most appropriate term for expressing the Deity in the Chinese language.* Shanghai: Mission Press, 1847.

————, comp. *History of the Kwang-se Rebellion, Gathered from the Peking Gazette.* Shanghai: North China Herald, 1853.

Melancon, Glenn. *Britain's China Policy and the Opium Crisis: Balancing Drugs, Violence, and National Honour, 1833-1840.* Hampshire, England: Ashgate Publishing, 2003.

Menzel, Gustav. *Die Rheinische Mission aus 150 Jahren Missionsgeschichte.* Wuppertal: Verlag der Vereinigten Evangelischen Mission, 1978.

Michael, Franz H., and Chung-li Chang. *The Taiping Rebellion: History and Documents.* 3 vols. Seattle: University of Washington Press, 1966-1971.

Miller, Jon. *The Social Control of Religious Zeal: A Study of Organizational Contradictions.* New Brunswick, NJ: Rutgers University Press, 1994.

Milne, William. *Zhang Yuan liangyou xianglun.* [Conversations between two friends, Zhang and Yang.] Singapore: ABCFM, 1836.

Missiology. South Pasadena, CA, 8 (1980), 13 (1985).

Missionary Chronicle. London: LMS, 1829-1835.

Missionary Herald. Boston: ABCFM, 1829-1855.

Missionary Magazine and Chronicle. London: LMS, 1836-1868.

Missionary Record. Protestant Episcopal Church in the United States. 1833-1837.

Missionary Register. London: CMS, 1829-1844.

Missionary Reporter. Philadelphia: Presbyterian Church of the USA, 1829-1832.

Missions-Evangelischen Blatt. Barmen: Rheinische Missionsgesellschaft, 1851.

Missions-Tidning. Stockholm: Swedish Mission Society, 1847-1854.

Modern Asian Studies. Cambridge: Cambridge University, 1972-2004.

Modern China. Berkeley Hills, CA: Sage Publications, 1990-2004.

Morrison, Elizabeth A. *Memoirs of the Life and Labours of Robert Morrison, D.D.* 2 vols. London: Longman Orme, Brown, Green, & Longmans, 1839.

Morse, Hosea B. *The Chronicles of the East India Trading Co. Trading to China, 1635-1834.* 5 vols. Oxford: Clarendon Press, 1922.

————. *The International Relations of the Chinese Empire.* Vol. 1, *The Period of Conflict, 1834-1860.* London: Longmans Green, 1910.

————. *The Trade and Administration of the Chinese Empire.* Shanghai: Kelly & Walsh, Ltd., 1908.

Mullins, Mark R. *Christianity Made in Japan: A Study of Indigenous Movements.* Honolulu: University of Hawaii Press, 1998.

Mungello, David E. *The Forgotten Christians of Hangzhou.* Honolulu: University of Hawaii Press, 1994.

Murray, Dian H., and Qin Baoqi. *The Origins of the Tiandihui: The Chinese Triads in Legend and History.* Stanford: Stanford University Press, 1994.

Neuste Nachrichten aus China. Cassel: Chinesischen Stiftung, 1851.

Nevius, Helen S. C. *The Life of John Livingston Nevius, for Forty Years a Missionary in China.* New York: Fleming H. Revell, 1895.

———. *Our Life in China.* New York: R. Carter, 1869.

Nevius, John L. *China and the Chinese.* New York: Harper & Bros., 1868.

New York Observer. New York: Sidney E. Morse & Co., 1832-1844.

Newcomb, Harvey, ed. "China." In *A Cyclopedia of Missions.* Rev. ed. New York: Charles Scribner, 1856.

Nicolson, John. "The Rev. Charles Gutzlaff, the Opium War, and General Gough." *Missiology* 133 (1985): 353-61.

Niles' Weekly Register. Baltimore, 1833-1840.

North, Eric M., ed. *The Book of a Thousand Tongues.* New York: Harper & Bros., 1938.

North China Herald. Shanghai, 1850-1862.

Noyes, Harriet Newell. *A Light in the Land of Sinim and History of the South China Mission of the American Presbyterian Church, 1845-1920.* Shanghai: Presbyterian Mission Press, 1927.

Oehler, Wilhelm. *Die Taiping-Bewegung: Geschichte eines chinesischen-christlichen Gottesreichs.* Gütersloh: Bertelsmann, 1923.

Overmyer, Daniel L. "Alternatives: Popular Religious Sects in Chinese Society." *Modern China* 2 (1981): 153-90.

Ouchterlony, John. *The Chinese War: An Account of All the Operations of the British Forces from the Commencement to the Treaty of Nanking.* 2nd ed. London: Saunders and Otley, 1844.

Ownby, David. *Brotherhoods and Secret Societies in Early and Mid-Qing Society.* Stanford: Stanford University Press, 1996.

Parker, Edward H., trans. *Chinese Account of the Opium War.* Shanghai, 1888.

Pas, Julian F., ed. *The Turning of the Tide: Religion in China Today.* Hong Kong: Oxford University Press, 1989.

Perry, Elizabeth J. "Taipings and Triads: The Role of Religion in Inter-rebel Relations." In *Religion and Rural Revolt,* ed. János M. Bak and Gerhard Benecke. Manchester: Manchester University Press, 1984.

Perry, Matthew C. *The Japan Expedition, 1852-1854: The Personal Journal of Commodore Matthew C. Perry.* Ed. Roger Pineau. Washington: Smithsonian Institution Press, 1968.

Philip, Robert. *The Life and Opinions of the Rev. William Milne, D.D., Missionary to China.* London: John Snow, 1840.

Polachek, James M. *The Inner Opium War.* Cambridge, MA: Council on East Asian Studies, Harvard University Press, 1992.

Pommersche Hauptverein für Evangel-Missionen in China. *Geschichte der Missionen in China von den ältesten Zeiten bis auf Gützlaff.* Stettin: R. Grassmann, 1850.

———. *Jahresbericht.* Stettin: R. Grassmann, 1851-1858.

"Preussen, Unterrichts-Abteilung des Ministerium der Geistlichen Unterrichts-und-Medicinal Angelegenheiten, an Bernhard Ledeboer, Sekretär." NZG. Berlin, 6 September 1826, NZG, Kast. 19, No. 1, Doss. G.

Pritchard, Earl H. *Anglo-Chinese Relations during the Seventeenth and Eighteenth Centuries*. Studies in the Social Sciences, 17. Urbana: University of Illinois, 1930.

Protokoll eine Conferenze von Missionaren verschiedenen Gesellschaften. Hong Kong, 1850. Basler Missionsgesellschaft Archives, China. A-1.1 (1B), no. 1.

Pruden, George B., Jr. "Issachar Jacox Roberts and American Diplomacy in China during the Taiping Rebellion." Ph.D. dissertation, American University, 1977.

Quartalberichte der chinesischen Stiftung. Cassel, 1850-1853.

Quarterly Review. London: J. Murray, 1827, 1833-1841, 1854.

Rabe, Valentin H. *The Home Base of American China Missions, 1880-1920*. Cambridge, MA: Harvard University Press, 1978.

Rambo, Lewis R. *Understanding Religious Conversion*. New Haven: Yale University Press, 1993.

Records of the General Conference of Protestant Missionaries of China, Held in Shanghai, May 10-23, 1877. Shanghai: Mission Press, 1878.

Reed, James. *The Missionary Mind and American East Asian Policy, 1911-1915*. Cambridge, MA: Harvard University Press, 1983.

Reichardt, J. C. "Gützlaff's Eintritt in die Missionslaufbahn und seine Erweckung." *Evangelisches Missions-Magazin*, 1859, pp. 450-61.

Rheinische Missionsgesellschaft. *Monats-Berichte*. Barmen, 1847.

Richter, H. *Lebens Geschichte von Brüder Gützlaff*. Barmen: Barmen and Schwelm, 1833.

Richter, Julius. *Geschichte der Berliner Missionsgesellschaft, 1824-1924*. Berlin: Verlag der Buchhandlung der ev. Missionsgesellschaft, 1924.

Rubinstein, Murray. *The Origins of the Anglo-American Missionary Enterprise in China, 1807-1840*. Lanham, MD: Scarecrow Press, 1996.

Said, Edward W. *Orientalism*. New York: Vintage Books, 1979.

Sanneh, Lamin. *Translating the Message: The Missionary Impact on Culture*. Maryknoll, NY: Orbis Books, 1989.

———. *Whose Religion Is Christianity?* Grand Rapids: Eerdmans, 2003.

Sansom, George B. *The Western World and Japan*. 1949; New York: Vintage Books, 1973.

Scarth, John. *Twelve Years in China: The People, the Rebels, and the Mandarins, by a British Resident*. Edinburgh: T. Constable, 1860. Reprinted, Wilmington, DE: Scholarly Resources, 1972.

Schattschneider, David A. "William Cary, Modern Missions, and the Moravian Influence." *International Bulletin of Missionary Research* 22.1 (January 1998) 8-12.

Schlatter, Wilhelm. *Geschichte der Basler Mission, 1815-1915*. Vols. 1 and 2. Basel: Verlag der Basler Missionsbuchhandlung, 1916.

———. *Rudolf Lechler, Ein Lebensbild aus der Basler Mission in China*. Basel: Verlag der Basler Missionsbuchhandlung, 1911.

Bibliography

Schlyter, Herman. *Der China-Missionar Karl Gützlaff und seine Heimatbasis: Studien über das Interesse des Abendlands an der Mission des China.* Lund: C. W. K. Gleerup, 1976.

———. *Karl Gützlaff als Missionar in China.* Lund: C. W. K. Gleerup, 1946.

———. *Theodor Hamberg, den forste svenske Kinamissionaren.* Lund: C. W. K. Gleerup, 1952.

Shenxianhui zai Hua chuanjiao shi, 1847-1947. [The history of the propagation of the Lutheran Church in China, 1847-1947.] Hong Kong: Hong Kong Lutheran Church, 1968.

Shuck, Henrietta. *Scenes in China: or Sketches of the Country, Religion, and Customs of the Chinese.* Philadelphia: American Baptist Publication Society, 1852.

Sirr, Henry Charles. *China and the Chinese, Their Religion, Character, Customs, Manufactures: The Evils arising from the Opium Trade.* 2 vols. London: William S. Orr & Co., 1849.

Smissen, Sister Hellegonda van der. *The History of Our Missionary Societies.* Trans. J. Quiring. Women's Home and Foreign Missionary Association, General Conference, Mennonites of North America. Located in Yale Divinity School Library, Special Collection, Pamphlet Collection: China.

Smith, Carl T. *Chinese Christians, Élites, Middlemen, and the Church in Hong Kong.* Hong Kong: Oxford University Press, 1985.

———. "Notes on Friends and Relations of Taiping Leaders." *Ching Feng* 19.2 (1976): 105-19.

———. *A Sense of History: Studies in the Social and Urban History of Hong Kong.* Hong Kong: Hong Kong Educational Publishing Co., 1995.

Smith, George. *A Narrative of an Exploratory Visit to Each of the Consular Cities of China and to the Islands of Hong Kong and Chusan in Behalf of the Church Missionary Society in the Years, 1844, 1845, 1846.* New York: Harper & Bros., 1847.

Southern Baptist Missionary Journal. Richmond, VA, 1846-1851.

Spelman, Douglas G. "Christianity in Chinese: The Protestant Term Question." *Papers on China* 22A (1969): 25-52. Cambridge, MA: East Asian Research Center, Harvard University.

Spence, Jonathan. *Chinese Roundabout.* New York: W. W. Norton & Co., 1992.

———. *God's Chinese Son: The Taiping Heavenly Kingdom of Hong Xiuquan.* New York: W. W. Norton & Co., 1996.

———. *The Search for Modern China.* New York: W. W. Norton & Co., 1991.

Spirit of Missions. Burlington, NJ: Protestant Episcopal Church of USA, 1836-1852.

Standaert, Nicolas. "Christianity in Late Ming and Early Qing China as a Case of Cultural Transmission." In *China and Christianity: Burdened Past, Hopeful Future,* ed. Stephen Uhalley Jr. and Xiaoxin Wu. Armonk, NY: M. E. Sharpe, 2001.

Strandenaes, Thor. *Principles of Bible Translation.* Stockholm: Almqvist and Wikell, International, 1987.

Stanley, Brian. *The Bible and the Flag: Protestant Missions and British Imperialism in the Nineteenth and Twentieth Centuries.* Leicester, England: Apollos, 1990.

Sweeting, Anthony. *A Phoenix Transformed: The Reconstruction of Education in Post-War Hong Kong.* Hong Kong: Oxford University Press, 1993.

Teng Ssu-Yü. *Chang Hsi and the Treaty of Nanking, 1842.* Chicago: University of Chicago Press, 1944.

———, and John K. Fairbank, eds. *China's Response to the West: A Documentary Survey, 1839-1923.* Cambridge, MA: Harvard University Press, 1954.

Thrupp, Sylvia L., ed. *Millennial Dreams in Action: Essays in Comparative Study.* Comparative Studies in Society and History. The Hague, The Netherlands, 1962.

Tiedemann, R. Gary. "Christianity in a Violent Environment." In *Historiography of the Chinese Catholic Church: Nineteenth and Twentieth Centuries,* ed. Jeroom Heyndrickx, pp. 130-44. Leuven: Ferdinand Verbiest Foundation, K. U. Leuven, 1994.

———. "Conversion Patterns in North China: Sociological Profiles of Chinese Christians, 1860-1912." In *Authenic Chinese Christians,* ed. Ku Wei-ying and Koen De Ridder, pp. 107-33. Leuven: Leuven University Press, 2001.

———. "Missionary Views on the Taiping Rebellion (1850-65): A Tale of Progressive Disenchantment." Paper presented at Huitième Colloque de Sinologie de Chantilly, 3-6 September 1995.

Tomlin, Jacob. *Missionary Journals and Letters, Written during Eleven Years' Residence and Travels among the Chinese, Siamese, Javanese, Khassias, and Other Eastern Nations.* London: James Nisbet & Co., 1844.

Tsien Tsuen-hsuin. "Western Impact on China through Translation." *Far Eastern Quarterly* 13.3 (May 1954): 305-27.

Uhalley, Stephen, Jr., and Xiaoxin Wu, eds. *China and Christianity: Burdened Past, Hopeful Future.* Armonk, NY: M. E. Sharpe, 2001.

Wagner, Rudolf G. *Reenacting the Heavenly Vision: The Role of Religion in the Taiping Rebellion.* Berkeley: Institute of East Asian Studies, University of California, 1982.

Wakeman, Frederic. *Strangers at the Gate: Social Disorder in South China, 1839-1861.* Berkeley: University of California Press, 1966.

Waley, Arthur. *The Opium War through Chinese Eyes.* New York: Macmillan, 1958.

Walls, Andrew F. *The Missionary Movement in Christian History: Studies in the Transmission of Faith.* Maryknoll, NY: Orbis Books, 1996.

Walravens, Hartmut. "Bibliographie Karl Gützlaff." Typed MSS, courtesy of Walravens.

———. *Karl Friedrich Neumann (1793-1870) und Karl Friedrich August Gützlaff (1803-1851): Zwei deutsche Chinakundige im 19. Jahrhundert.* Wiesbaden: Harrassowitz Verlag, 2001.

Wang Jiajian. *Wei Yuan dui Xifang di renshi ji chi haifang suxiang.* [Wei Yuan's understanding of the West and his ideas of coastal defense.] Taipei: Taiwan University, 1964.

Ward, Kevin, and Brian Stanley, eds. *The Church Missionary Society and World Christianity, 1799-1999.* Grand Rapids: Eerdmans, 2000.

Watson, James L., and Evelyn S. Rawski, eds. *Death Ritual in Late Imperial and Modern China.* Berkeley: University of California Press, 1988.

Weller, Robert P. *Resistance, Chaos, and Control in China: Taiping Rebels, Taiwanese Ghosts, and Tiananmen.* Seattle: University of Washington Press, 1994.

Westminster Wesleyan Missionary Review. London: Wesleyan Methodist Missionary Society, 1832, 1834, 1840, 1853.

White, E. Aldersey. *A Woman Pioneer in China: The Life of Mary Ann Aldersey.* London: Livingston Press, 1932.

Wickeri, Philip L. "Christianity and the Taiping Rebellion: An Historical and Theological Study." M.D. thesis. Princeton Theological Seminary, 1974.

————. *Seeking the Common Ground: Protestant Christianity, the Three-Self Movement, and China's United Front.* Maryknoll, NY: Orbis Books, 1989.

Williams, S. Wells. *The Middle Kingdom.* 2 vols. rev. ed. New York: Charles Scribner's Sons, 1883.

Williamson, G. R. *Memoir of the Rev. David Abeel, DD, Late Missionary to China.* New York: R. Carter, 1848.

Witek, John. "Creating an Image of Nineteenth-Century China from Catholic Missionary Publications." Paper presented at Neuvième Colloque International de Sinologie de Chantilly, 7-9 September 1998.

Wong Man Kong. "The China Factor and Protestant Christianity in Hong Kong: Reflections from Historical Perspectives." *The Edinburgh Review of Theology and Religion* 8.1: 115-37.

————. *James Legge: A Pioneer at Crossroads of East and West.* Hong Kong: Hong Kong Educational Publishing Co., 1996.

————. "On the Limits of Biculturality in Hong Kong: Protestantism as a Case Study." *Fides et Historia* 35 (Winter/Spring 2003): 9-25.

Wright, Arthur, ed. *Studies in Chinese Thought.* Chicago: University of Chicago Press, 1953.

Wu Yixiong. "Xinjiao chuanjiaoshi yu yapin quan hou di xixue shuru." [Protestant missionaries and the importation of Western learning before the Opium War.] Paper presented at the Conference on Modern Science and Technology and Sino-Western Cultural Communication, Wuhan, 15-20 August 1999.

Wylie, Alexander. *Memorials of Protestant Missionaries to the Chinese: Giving a List of Their Publications, and Obituary Notices of the Deceased, with Copious Indexes.* Taipei: Ch'eng-wen Publishing Co., 1967. Reprint of 1867 ed.

Xianggang ChongZhen hui lihu yi si ling zhounian jinnian tekan, 1847-1987. [Special Memorial publication on the anniversary of the Hong Kong Chong Zhen Church, 1847-1987.] Hong Kong: Jidujiao Xianggang ChongZhen hui bianyin, 1987.

Yang Tianheng. *Jidujiao yu xindai Zhongguo.* [Christianity and Modern China. Subtitle: A study of the anti-Christian movement in China.] Chengdu: Sichuan Peoples Press, 1994.

Yip, Ka-che. *Religion, Nationalism and Chinese Students: The Anti-Christian Movement of 1922-1927.* Bellingham: Western Washington University, 1980.

Yü Chun-fang. *Kuan-yin: The Chinese Transformation of Avalokiteśvara.* New York: Columbia University Press, 2000.

Yung Wing (Rong Hong). *My Life in China and America.* New York: Henry Holt & Co., 1909.

Zetzsche, Jost. *The Bible in China: History of the Union Version; or: The Culmination of Protestant Missionary Bible Translation in China.* Monumenta Serica Monograph Series 45. Nettal: Monumenta Serica, 1999.

Zha Shijie (James Shih-chieh Cha). *Zhongguo Jidujiao renwu xiaozhuan.* [Concise biographies of important Chinese Christians.] Taipei: China Evangelical Seminary Press, 1982.

Zhang Kaiyuan, ed. *Shehui zhuanxing yu jiaohui daxue.* [Social change and Christian universities.] Wuhan: Huazhong shifan daxue, 1998.

Zhang Kaiyuan and Arthur Waldron, eds. *Zhong-Xi wenhua yu jiaohui daxue.* [Christian universities and Chinese-Western cultures.] Wuhan: Hubei jiaoyu chubanshe, 1991.

Zhang Mingjiu. "*Yinghuan zhilüe* yu *Haiguo tuzhi* bijiao yanjiu." [A comparative analysis of *Yinghuan zhilüe* and *Haiguo tuzhi.*] *Jindai shi yenjiu* 67 (January 1992): 68-81.

Zhao Qing. "Cong fan 'Kongjiao' yundong dao 'Fei zongjiao datongneng' yundong." [From the "Anti-Confucian" movement to the "Anti-Religious League Movement"]. In *Zhong-Xi wenhua yu jiaohui daxue* [Christian universities and Chinese-Western cultures], ed. Zhang Kaiyuan and Arthur Waldron, pp. 61-83. Wuhan: Hubei jiaoyu chubanshe, 1991.

Zhu Weizheng. *Coming Out of the Middle Ages: Comparative Reflections on China and the West.* Trans. Ruth Hayhoe. Armonk, NY: M. E. Sharpe, 1990.

Zöllner, Reinhard. "Gützlaff's Japanreise und das Bojutse yume mongatai." In *Karl F. A. Gützlaff (1803-1851) und das Christentum in Ostasien. Ein Missionar zwischen den Kulturen,* ed. Thoralf Klein und Reinhard Zöllner. Nettetal: Steyler Verlag, 2005.

Index